Legal Evolution and Hybridisation

The Law of Shares Transfer in England

Matteo Solinas

Legal Evolution and Hybridisation

The Law of Shares Transfer in England

intersentia

METRO

Ius Commune Europaeum

Matteo Solinas

Legal Evolution and Hybridisation
The Law of Shares Transfer in England

Intersentia Publishing Ltd
Trinity House | Cambridge Business Park | Cowley Road
Cambridge | CB4 0WZ | United Kingdom
Tel.: +44 1223 393 753 | Email: mail@intersentia.co.uk

ISBN 978-1-78068-207-5
D/2014/7849/16
NUR 820

Cover photograph © Jeff-Ho – Thinkstock

British Library Cataloguing in Publication Data. A catalogue record for this book is available from the British Library.

FOREWORD

The growth of financial intermediation in today's world presents challenges for sound regulation and has the potential, ultimately, to undermine the stability of markets. One of the challenges which has been prominent among those considered by supranational and national authorities alike is the increased legal uncertainty caused by a mismatch between the practice of holding interests in securities through intermediaries and the jurisprudence of ownership, which itself reflects concepts long since settled in every legal jurisdiction round the globe.

If we are to negotiate this minefield of legal uncertainty successfully, we will need to think broadly and deeply in order to gain a rich understanding of this relatively new practice of holding and circulating interests in securities through intermediaries. And if we are to do that, then we can do no better than to start with this hugely valuable and clever book.

Dr Matteo Solinas does not stop, however, at proposing a new cross-cultural understanding of the law on securities intermediation. He has a much higher purpose. He would like to give the world a new intellectual framework within which to understand legal change and its complexities. In this respect, as in others, we should regard his book as an exercise in thought leadership for the modern world. If the defining legal philosophical task of the twentieth century was to account for the legitimacy of law in a world of conflicting political and moral rights, that of the twenty-first century will undoubtedly be to explain and justify the law in a world of rapid social and industrial change.

I first met Matteo through the work of the Financial Markets Law Committee, which is greatly indebted to him for the painstaking research he undertook, informing several of its most important papers. Matteo's highly perceptive analyses revealed his intellectual tenacity, his incisive focus and his ability to draw on a broad array of themes from diverse legal cultures. It is these qualities which ensure that this study is not only important and relevant but also one which makes that most valuable of intellectual contributions: a whole new schema within which to reappraise our collective received wisdom.

This book is particularly welcome as dealing with a topic, namely the dematerialisation and intermediation of securities, which has been thrown into sharp relief by the post-2008 financial crisis. The audience to whom the book will be of interest is undoubtedly a large one. It will appeal to students, teachers and practitioners of both financial markets law and comparative law. It will also be a useful reference work for all those who would like to obtain a multijurisdictional overview of the law relating to the transfer of interests in intermediated securities. My hope is that the ideas which it presents will come to the attention of policy-makers who must devise the laws and regulations for the new financial world order. If they do, we can trust that the intellectual underpinnings of the new order will be all the more convincing than those of the old.

Joanna Perkins
Chief Executive, Financial Markets Law Committee

PREFACE

This is a book on comparative law and legal change. With a focus on corporate law and the law of personal property, it reviews the current state of the comparative debate on the evolution of law.

It takes as a starting point the similarities and differences between legal systems as a means to understand the factors that shape legal growth and tests the well-established thesis according to which law tends to develop as a consequence of the movement of legal rules from one country to another. The analysis carried out in the first part of the book finds this thesis perplexing, as, above all, it does not put forward a persuasive account of the mechanisms of legal reception. In attempting to fill that gap, this study contends that recent contributions on culture contact and culture change offer an interesting explanation for the circulation of juridical models across national boundaries.

In brief, this book suggests that the notion of 'hybridity', as originated in postcolonial theory, provides a valid conceptual means to examine the intricacies of legal evolution, to refine and to give content to the observation of the reception of law. The notion of hybridity overcomes the rigid dualist perception of culture in the colonial contexts that neatly distinguished between colonisers and colonised and promotes the view that cultural norms in colonial contexts are more than the result of the fusion of features of colonial and indigenous background. They are neither colonial, nor indigenous 'in disguise', but they occupy a 'third space' between colonial and indigenous cultures. In this light, hybridity is a powerful tool in explaining the pattern of cultural change in social sciences in general and in law in particular. Borrowing reflects a general trend of social life, a mechanism of culture diffusion. It applies to law too because law is itself a form of culture. As with colonial norms and standards, borrowed legal paradigms outside their original meanings become unsettled. They interact at different levels with local traditions, with certain indigenous perceptions, and do not survive in their original identities. A new legal tradition, a hybrid space that is peculiar to the specific contact situation is therefore created. Borrowed legal paradigms become almost the same as the original ones, but not quite.

The analysis of comparative jurisprudence put forward in this book does not rest exclusively on theoretical grounds, but it is explored and tested with reference to a specific case study. This is the legal mechanism by which shares in companies are transferred in England. The case is appealing for a number of reasons. First of all,

England is an interesting jurisdiction for investigating the theory of legal transplants against the controversial historical argument that the development of English law has consisted in an autochthonous national achievement, independent from continental law. Second, it deals with a distinguishing structural characteristic of modern company law, which apparently involves peculiar national legal implications, as the method of transfer of registered shares and share warrants to bearer is rooted in the history of the law of personal property. Finally, the chosen test case addresses the issues of legal uncertainty that have arisen from the evolution in financial practice and, in particular, the debate on post-trading law reform connected to the advent of the indirect system of holding securities. This scheme of legal evolution is particularly challenging for the purpose of this study, as, contrary to the pattern in the growth of state legislation either by independent creation or by mere borrowing, this one consists of a regulated mechanism of harmonisation set out by the contributions of delegates and national experts at international *fora* to be later implemented in the domestic legal framework.

The book endeavours to describe the state of the law at August 2013. Some later development and some further references were incorporated after the final submission of the manuscript.

ACKNOWLEDGEMENTS

This book is the revised and updated version of my doctoral dissertation. In writing it, I have incurred many debts and have many people to thank for comments and encouragement. In particular, at LSE I was fortunate enough to have as supervisors Eva Micheler, Joanna Benjamin and David Kershaw. They have helped me at various stages by providing valuable comments and sharing many penetrating insights into the project and advanced drafts of the manuscript. In mid-2011, Dan Prentice and Sir Ross Cranston examined the thesis and made the day of my viva a memorable experience for all the right reasons.

Outside LSE, my thanks go to Anthony Beaves, Marcus Smith, Mark Evans, David Nelken, Ross Anderson, Matteo Bascelli, Antonio Serra, Joshua Getzler and to my greatest friend Pedro Fernandes who have been unfailingly generous with their time and ideas. I am also very grateful to Joanna Perkins for having found time to write the Foreword. Notwithstanding the contributions, the usual disclaimer applies: I bear sole responsibility for the views presented and all remaining errors are my own.

I would also like to express my gratitude to Ann-Christin Maak and Rebecca Pound at Intersentia for their patience with a first-time author and assistance in bringing the book to publication.

Finally, and closer to home, I would like to apologise to Annamaria, Giacomo and Agata for spending so much time in writing this book when I should have been playing with the family. Their support and good humour have kept me in one piece during four eventful years in London and have maintained the relative importance of my work firmly in perspective. This book is dedicated in gratitude to them.

La Maddalena, 8 August 2013

CONTENTS

TABLE OF CASES

Alipour v UOC Corp [2002] 2 BCLC 770
AMG Global Nominees (Private) Ltd v SMM Holdings Ltd [2008] EWCA Civ 1278
Armitage v Nurse [1998] Ch 214
Ashby v Blackwell (1765) Amb 503; 27 ER 326
Ashworth v Munn (1880) 15 ChD 363 (CA)
Automatic Self-Cleansing Filter Syndicate Co. Ltd v Cuninghame [1906] 2 Ch 34
BA Peters plc (in administration), Re [2008] ER 392
Bahia and San Francisco Rly Co, Re (1868) LR 3 QB 584
Bailey v Barnes [1894] 1 Ch 25 (CA)
Baku Consolidated Oilfields Ltd, Re [1993] BCC 653
Balkis Consolidated Co Ltd v Tomkinson [1893] AC 396
Bank of Baroda Ltd v Punjab National Bank Ltd [1944] AC 176
Banks v Sutton (1732) 2 P Wms 700; 24 ER 922
Banner Homes Group Plc v Luff Developments Ltd and Another [2000] Ch 372
Barclays Bank Ltd v Quistclose Investment Pty Ltd [1970] AC 567 (HL)
Barclays Bank plc v O'Brien [1994] 1 AC 180 (HL)
Barlow Clowes International Ltd (in liquidation) v Vaughan [1992] 4 All ER 22
Barton v London and North Western Rly Co (1888) 38 ChD 144
Barton v London and North Western Rly Co (1889) 24 QBD 77 (CA)
Barton v North Staffordshire Ry Co (1888) 38 ChD 458
Baytur SA v Finagro Holdings SA [1992] QB 610 (CA)
BCCI v Akindele [2001] Ch 437
Bechuanaland Exploration Co v London Trading Bank Ltd (1898) 2 QB 658
Belvoir Finance Co Ltd v Stapleton [1971] 2 QB 210
Biddle v Bond (1865) 6 B&S 225
Bligh v Brent (1837) 2 Y&C Ex 268; 160 ER 397
Boardman v Phipps [1967] 2 AC 46 (HL)
Borland's Trustee v Steel Bros & Co. Ltd [1901] 1 Ch 279 (ChD)
Bradstock Trustee Services Ltd v Nabarro Nathason [1995] 1WLR 1405 (ChD)
Brandao v Barnett (1846) 3 CB 519
Brook v Hook (1871) LR 6 Exch 89
Brown v Westminster Bank Ltd [1964] 2 Lloyd's Rep 187
Buller v Crips (1703) 6 Mod 29

INTRODUCTION

This introductory chapter sketches the themes to be addressed in the book. It first sets out the context and highlights the aims and the structure of the theoretical inquiry on the relationship between comparative law and legal change, the underlying themes of the book. It then outlines how such inquiry operates in the specific analysis of the transfer of (directly and indirectly held) shares in England.

The idea of comparative law as a way of building bridges between legal systems and even cultures is fascinating and has stimulated interesting initiatives for the use of such methodology. One particular debate looks at the relevance of foreign law and foreign legal ideas as a means of shaping national law. The fundamental idea is that legal comparison is a powerful tool to unveil the interaction between different jurisdictions, and to uncover the circumstances and the mechanisms by which law develops. In the wake of the lively discussions on globalisation, convergence among legal systems and on the unification of private law, the exact significance of how legal paradigms are connected and circulate across national frontiers is, however, still largely uncertain. The comparative conundrum, in particular, rests on the appropriateness of describing the movement of law from one country to another by employing the metaphor of 'legal transplant'.

Broadly put, two approaches have emerged. These are, it would seem, irreconcilable. One school of thought, greatly relying on legal history, maintains that the evolution of law is primarily a function of rules being imported from other legal systems in accordance with the unpredictable directions imposed by domestic lawyers. It follows from this perspective that legal growth is largely autonomous from society. It operates in its own dimension, often detached from those of other social institutions. Postmodernist theorists, on the contrary, claim that legal transplants are an imaginative scholarly construction. Reasoning, language and judgement are at large determined by inescapable and incommensurable epistemic, linguistic, cultural and moral frameworks. The development of law mirrors, and is necessarily responsive to, a specific legal culture. It cannot take place through borrowing because rules are culturally situated phenomena and not simply bare prepositional statements. In Chapter 1, this study contends that both perspectives offer elements of truth, but that they also contain flaws in explaining the process of the diffusion of law and the pattern of legal change. The weakness of the first theory, in particular, concerns the explanation of the interaction between legal comparison and sociology of law. This is because law is not an empire of its own that develops autonomously in accordance to internal dynamics. Law cannot be reduced to a static entity composed of legal doctrine and intellectual history. Rather, it must be understood in relation the society in which it originates and operates. The postmodernist approach is also flawed in its orthodox version because it is equivocally over-conceptualised and neglects the significance of the historical evidence of borrowing. Moreover, it relies on certain simplistic assumptions about language and culture, suggesting that there can be easily defined and insulated from external relationships and stimuli. This is possibly misleading. Although language is bound to culture, it has an open and evolving character that allows for linguistic change and cross cultural communication. Culture is also not a static entity that can be easily confined within national boundaries.

In an attempt to overcome the criticisms just outlined, this book offers a corrective interpretation, *de facto* a gloss to the transplant theory. This is based on an overlooked circumstance relating to the circulation of legal models across national frontiers. The argument stems from acknowledging that historically the practice of borrowing has been one of the most fruitful and vital sources of legal change in the western world. It is not, however, a phenomenon peculiar to law. Borrowing reflects a general trend of social life, a mechanism of culture diffusion. It applies to law because law is itself a form of culture. What is missing in the literature on legal transplants is, above all, a convincing discussion on the rationale for transplantation and an explanation for the reception mechanisms. As already suggested, the rigid description of the pattern of transplants based on the postulate of the autonomy of law from society, on the assumption that law largely exists and operates independently from other social institutions, is not convincing. That scheme focuses on exceptional cases and it oversimplifies the significance of the law as a system of meanings by which human experience is shaped and represented. It does not give due attention to the interactions of the borrowed model with the social/economic settings of the country where the borrowing occurs. In other words, the mere acknowledgment of the occurrence of borrowing demonstrates nothing about cultural interaction and the assimilation process. It is not an independent explanatory principle *per se*, as it does not consider the contents of the process. In this setting, this study demonstrates that the movement of legal paradigms from one country to another rarely consists of a mere transplantation of rules, but generally involves a complex and gradual process of interaction between legal and social characters, between imported models and indigenous traditions. Running along these lines, Chapter 2 considers recent contributions on culture contact and culture change to determine whether they can provide an explanation for the process of borrowing and legal evolution. The ambition is to explore whether recent insights from the theoretical debates on acculturation, colonialism and contact situations in general can be used to explain the pattern of development of certain areas of law. The focus of the analysis is on the notion of 'hybridity', a fundamental theme in cultural and post colonialist studies. Hybridity is based on the understanding that cultural norms that arise in colonial contexts are necessarily original. They are neither colonial nor indigenous, but peculiar to each specific contact situation. They are the 'third space' between colonial and indigenous cultures, a (hybrid) culture in their own right.

This book suggests that the notion of hybridity is a powerful tool in understanding the pattern of cultural change in social sciences in general and in law in particular. It can provide a conceptual means to explain some of the complexities of the pattern of legal change, to refine and give content to the observation of the reception of law. As with colonial norms and standards, legal paradigms borrowed outside their original meanings become unsettled. They interact at different levels with local traditions and with certain indigenous perceptions, and do not survive in their original identities. When transplantation occurs, a third space that is peculiar to the specific contact situation is therefore created. Borrowed legal paradigms become almost the same as the original ones, but not quite. Chapter 3 concludes the inquiry into comparative jurisprudence by examining the idea beyond the boundaries of postcolonialist studies. In doing so, it presents a definition of contact situations outside the modern imperialistic perspective of colonialism ('pseudo-colonialism') and examines two well-known episodes of transplantation of the entire legal system under hegemonic and non-hegemonic contact situations.

Parts II and III implement and clarify the theoretical arguments of the book by offering a focus. They analyse the law regulating the circulation of shares in England both where shares are held directly by the owner (direct holding system) and where one or more persons stand in the chain of ownership (indirect holding system).

Part II consists of Chapters 4 and 5. It looks retrospectively at legal transplants as a possible source for explaining the development of law. It argues to begin with that the concept of transferable joint stock capital and the scheme of circulation of registered shares have not been an English invention, but rather the result of a complex evolution likely including medieval Genoese models of commercial association. These were employed in early English maritime partnerships in the sixteenth and seventeenth centuries following earlier intense commercial (non-hegemonic) contacts. Chapter 4 concludes that the reception of foreign models in England amounted to a process cultural integration and hybridisation of the original paradigm along the lines set out in Part I for postcolonial studies. A similar pattern for legal reception is also identified and explored for share warrants to bearer in Chapter 5. This scheme has strong roots in certain Italian notarial exchange contracts and the contract of *cambium* as effected under the machinery of the *tratta* (bill of exchange).

Part III, encompassing Chapters 6 and 7, discusses the new practice of holding and circulation of (interests in) shares through intermediaries and deals with the debate on law reform. This practice has been difficult to square with settled legal concepts. Concerns over legal uncertainty with potential systemic consequences for the financial markets have been raised, leading to a call for legislative intervention. Given the connection between national financial markets, the discussion has not been limited to domestic law, but it has rather focused on the formation of a harmonised regime for intermediated securities. It is argued in Part III that the pattern of legal change that emerges from the analysis of the normative proposals in the area supports the theoretical idea put forward in this book. The argument is that legal change in this context involves a process of negotiations consisting of a regulated mechanism of harmonisation and hybridisation set out by the contributions of delegates and national experts at international *fora* to be later implemented at national level. Chapter 6 deals with the economic and legal themes at the roots of the evolution of market practice, emphasising the English legal characterisation for indirectly held shares. It subsequently examines them against the pattern of negotiation underlying the formation of the most advanced normative instruments in the area and finds that this scheme consists of a process of cultural interaction not different from the one observed in the theoretical discussion developed in Part I.

Chapter 7 reflects on the general inquiry offered in Chapter 6 and focuses on the analysis of the methods of protection of the innocent purchaser of intermediated shares from adverse claims. It compares the position under English law with the one currently in force in Italy and with the model provided by Article 8 UCC before showing that the pattern of formation of the recent law reform proposals on the matter can also be described in terms of hybridisation.

Finally, the Conclusion looks back at the scheme set out in Part I and, by reviewing its fundamental arguments on legal change and hybridisation, draws together the findings reached in the analysis of the test case developed in Parts II and III.

PART I

THE IDEA OF HYBRIDITY IN COMPARATIVE LAW

Chapter 1

THE DEBATE ON THE DIFFUSION OF LAW

Understanding the pattern, meaning and significance of the circulation of legal paradigms and ideas across national frontiers is a central theme in comparative law.[1] Recently, this has attracted a great deal of academic interest especially under the impetus of studies on globalisation,[2] convergence among legal systems[3] and the unification of private law.[4]

1 See DA Westbrook 'Theorizing the Diffusion of Law: Conceptual Difficulties, Unstable Imaginations, and the Effort to Think Gracefully Nonetheless' (2006) 58 Harv Int'l LJ 493.

2 In general, see HM Watt 'Globalization and Comparative Law' in M Reinmann and R Zimmermann (eds) *The Oxford Handbook of Comparative Law* (OUP Oxford 2006) 578; MR Ferrarese *Le Istituzioni della Globalizzazione* (Il Mulino Bologna 2000); W Heydebrand 'From Globalization of Law to Law under Globalization' in D Nelken and J Fest (eds) *Adapting Legal Cultures* (Hart Oxford 2001) 117; L Friedman 'Borders on the Emerging Sociology of Transnational Law' (1996) 32 Stan J Int'l L 65; D Nelken 'Comparatists and Transferability' in P Legrand and R Munday (eds) *Comparative Legal Studies: Traditions and Transitions* (CUP Cambridge 2003) 437 at 460 and D Gerber *Global Competition: Law, Markets and Globalization* (OUP Oxford 2010) 79. Cranston has suggested that globalisation in areas of banking law (the legal techniques of modern international lending, for example) has its roots in nineteenth century banking practice: it is not a new phenomenon – R Cranston 'Globalization: Its Historical Context' in S Worthington (ed) *Commercial Law and Commercial Practice* (Hart Oxford 2003) 3.

3 In general, see the contributions in BS Markesinis (ed) *The Gradual Convergence: Foreign Ideas, Foreign Influences, and English Law on the Eve of the 21st Century* (OUP Oxford 1994) and B De Witte 'The Convergence Debate' (1996) 3 Maastr J Eur & Comp L 105. The scholarly debate is intense in the area of corporate law. Apart from the fundamental contribution of M Siems *Convergence in Shareholder Law* (CUP Cambridge 2007), see also RJ Gilson 'Globalizing Corporate Governance: Convergence of Form or Function' (2001) 43 Am J Comp L 329; LA Bebchuck and M Roe 'A Theory of Path Dependence in Corporate Ownership and Governance' (1999) 52 Stan L Rev 127; WM Bratton and JA McCahery 'Comparative Corporate Governance and the Theory of the Firm: The Case Against Global Cross Reference' (1999) 38 Colum J Transnat' L 213; and JC Coffee 'The Future as History: The Prospects for Global Convergence in Corporate Governance and its Significance' (1999) 93 Northwest U L Rev 641.

4 This is not entirely new. It has been one of the original tasks of comparative legal studies. Reference, inevitably, should be made to the initiatives carried out by UNIDROIT (International Institute for the Unification of Private Law) since the end of WWI and, more recently, from the 1960s, by UNCITRAL (United Nations Commission on International Trade Law). However, the projects for unification of private law have recently acquired a growing interest in shaping the agenda for the creation of EU. One of the most significant European initiatives in the area is the (Trento) Common Core of European Private Law Project. Established in 1993, it is designed to see how much common ground exists between the private laws of the Member States of the European Union (a map of private law). It mirrors the case methodology employed by Schlesinger at Cornell in 1968 in his work on the formation of contracts (see RB Schlesinger 'Introduction' in RB Schlesinger (ed) *Formation of Contracts: A Study of the Common Core of Legal Systems*, vol I (Oceana

Many themes and views have emerged, but, for the most part, the debate has centred on the appropriateness of describing and explaining the phenomenon in terms of legal transplants. There is concern both over this mode of innovation in law and over the conceptual framework suggested by the terminology.[5] It is said in particular that borrowing and imitation are not relevant in understanding the pattern of legal evolution[6] and that 'since a transplanted institution continues to live on its old habitat as well as having been moved to a new one, the choice of the word transplant is inappropriate'.[7]

New York 1968)). On the Trento project, see M Bussani 'Integrative Comparative Law Enterprises and the Inner Stratification of Legal Systems' (2000) 8 Euro Rev Priv L 85; M Bussani and U Mattei 'The Common Core Approach to European Private Law' (1977) 3 Colum J Eur L 339 and M Bussani and U Mattei (eds) *The Common Core of European Private Law* (Kluwer London 2002). Outside the realm of specific contributions in the setting out of the 'principles' in the areas of contract law (see *The Principles of Contract Law* begun on the initiative of Lando and published in three parts in 1995, 2000 and 2003 and the *Avant-project of a European Contract Code* published by Accademia dei Giusprivatisti Europei established in Pavia in 2000), tort law (see the *Principles of European Tort Law* published in 2004 by the Group on European Tort Law based at the European Centre of Tort and Insurance in Vienna), trust law (see the *Principles of European Trust Law* drafted by an international working group based in Nijmegen and published in 1999), insolvency law (see the *Principles of European Insolvency Law* drafted by an international working group based in Nijmegen and published in 2003), family law (see the *Principles of European Family Law regarding Divorce and Maintenance between Former Spouses* drafted by an International Commission on European Family Law in Utrecht and published in 2004), insurance law (see the works of the project group on *Restatement of Insurance Contract Law* established in 1999 in Innsbruck and Hamburg), commercial contracts (see *UNIDROIT Principles of International Commercial Contracts* published in 1994 and in 2004), civil procedure (see the *Principles of Transnational Civil Procedure* prepared by UNIDROIT and ALI and published in 2005) and the initiatives for the preparation of a European Civil Code (see the *Study Group on a European Civil Code* established in 1998 and directed by Christian von Bar), reference should be made to The *Draft Common Frame of Reference* (DCFR), a legislative toolbox for the Commission in order to achieve a more consistent and coherent European Union legislation, prepared by the Study Group on a European Civil Code and the Research Group on EC Private Law (Acquis Group). On this specific initiative, see the comments gathered at an international symposium held in 2007 at the Centre for European Private Law (CEP) at the University of Muster, Germany by R Schulze *Common Frame of Reference and Existing EC Contract Law* (Sellier Munich 2008); O Lando 'The Structure and Legal Values of the Common Frame of Reference (CFR)' (2007) 3 ERCL 245; H Beale 'The European Civil Code Movement and the European Union's Common Frame of Reference' (2006) Legal Information Management 11; Id 'The Future of the Common Frame of Reference' 3 (2007) ERCL 257; H Collins *The European Civil Code – The Way Forward* (CUP Cambridge 2008) 77; P Larouche and F de Chirico (eds) *Economic Analysis of the DCFR* (Sellier Munich 2010); and recently H Eidenmuller, F Faust, HC Grigoleit, N Jansen, G Wagner and R Zimmermann 'The Common Frame of Reference for European Private Law – Policy Choices and Codification Problems' (2008) 28 OJLS 659, and C von Bar and E Clive (eds) *Principles Definitions and Model Rules of European Private Law – Draft Common Frame of Reference* (OUP Oxford 2010) six volumes. Very sceptical comments on the scope of DCFR (and possible implementation in England) have been offered by S Whittaker in the paper entitled 'The Draft Common Frame of Reference – an assessment', commissioned by the Ministry of Justice (UK) and published in 2008.

5 G Teubner 'Legal Irritants: Good Faith in British Law or How Unifying Law Ends Up in New Divergences' (1998) 61 MLR 10.

6 In particular, see P Legrand 'The Impossibility of "Legal Transplants"' (1997) 4 Maast J Eur & Comp L 111; and Id 'What "Legal Transplants"?' in D Nelken and J Fest (eds) *Adapting Legal Cultures* (Hart Oxford 2001) 59.

7 E Orucu 'Law as Transposition' (2002) 51 Int & Comp L Q 205 at 206.

A critical overview of the theory of legal transplants and a discussion of its major criticisms are presented below.

1. The Terms of the Debate

1.1. Legal Transplants

1.1.1. Orthodoxy

The notion of 'legal transplant' as metaphor for the movement of law from one country to another belongs to Alan Watson's pioneering works on legal change.[8] It was later adopted by many[9] and today it represents the predominant terminology.[10]

Observing the historical and comparative pattern of the reception of Roman law in most countries of medieval, renaissance, and nineteenth century continental Europe,[11] Watson suggested that borrowing had been the most fertile source of legal growth. Legal evolution, he maintained with a variety of accents,[12] rarely stems from isolated national

8 A Watson *Legal Transplants: An Approach to Comparative Law* (Scottish Academic Press Edinburgh 1974); Id *Society and Legal Change* (Scottish Academic Press Edinburgh 1977); Id 'Legal Change: Sources of Law and Legal Culture' (1983) 131 U Pa L Rev 112; Id *Making of the Civil Law* (Harvard UP Cambridge MA 1981); Id *Law Out of Context* (University of Georgia Press Athens GA 2000); and Id *The Evolution of Western Private Law* (John Hopkins UP Baltimore 2001).

9 The literature on legal transplants is vast and fragmented in its scope. Generally, see N Foster 'Transmigration and Transferability of Commercial Law in a Globalized World' in AJ Hardin and E Orucu (eds) *Comparative Law in the 21st Century* (Kluwer Leiden 2002) 55, the academic contributions in JW Cairns and OF Robinson (eds) *Critical Studies in Ancient Law, Comparative Law and Legal History* (Hart Oxford 2001), and the attempt to systematise the subject put forward by M Cohn 'Legal Transplants Chronicles: The Evolution of Unreasonableness and Proportionality Review of the Administration in the United Kingdom' (2010) 58 Am J Comp L 583. With specific reference to some recent studies in area of comparative corporate law, see H Kanda and CJ Milhaupt 'Re-examining Legal Transplants: The Director's Fiduciary Duty in Japanese Corporate Law' (2003) Columbia Law School – The Centre for Law and Economic Studies, working paper no 219 available at <www.law.columbia.edu/center_program/law_economics/wp_listing_1/wp_listing/211-220#6990> (accessed 7 August 2013); J Gillespie 'Transplanted Company Law: an Ideological and Cultural Analysis of Market-Entry in Vietnam' (2002) Int & Comp L Q 641 and D Berkovitz, K Pistor and J Richard 'The Transplant Effect' (2003) 51 Am J Comp L 163. See also L Stout 'On the Export of US Style Corporate Fiduciary Duties to Other Cultures: Can a Transplant Take?' and K Pistor and C Xu 'Transplanting the Concept of "Fiduciary Duty": Evidence from Transition Economies' in CJ Milhaupt (ed) *Global Markets, Domestic Institutions: Corporate Law and Governance in a New Era of Cross-Border Deals* (Columbia UP New York 2003).

10 M Graziadei 'Transplants and Receptions' in M Reinmann and R Zimmermann (eds) *The Oxford Handbook of Comparative Law* (OUP Oxford 2006) 441; and Id 'Legal Transplants and the Frontiers of Legal Knowledge' (2009) 10 Theoretical Inq L 723.

11 'In Catholic, Calvinist and Lutheran territories, in agricultural nations, in trading cities ruled by a merchant oligarchy, in monarchies and republics alike' – A Watson 'Comparative Law and Legal Change' (1978) 37 CLJ 313 at 313.

12 As Ewald puts it in his attempt to systematise Watson's detailed historical arguments in theoretical terms, Watson has sometimes 'presented his theory in a somewhat loose and intuitive fashion' using different formulations. What is considered in his study discards Watson's extreme views and focuses on his conventional claims in comparative jurisprudence ('weak Watson' according to Ewald's

innovation (*creatio ex nihilo*),[13] but is rather the result of borrowing from other jurisdictions, or the 'moving of a rule [...] from one country to another, or from one people to another'.[14] More fundamentally, by contrast to one of the most established preconceptions of modern legal thought, according to which legal development is a rational response to existing social, economic and political circumstances,[15] Watson argued that the scale of the empirical evidence of legal transplants shows that law has a vitality of its own and does not necessarily progress in a rational way. In other words, he rejected the postulate that law is a mirror of society,[16] that there must be a close relationship between law and the society in which it operates. On this view, the frequency of borrowing proves the fallacy of seeking to correlate developments in law with the internal growth of the society. Two main arguments are put forward in support of this proposition.

(i) *The Highly Developed Autonomy and Specific Role of the Legal Profession.*[17] Law is the province of lawyers and legal rules are treated as ends in themselves, as existing in their own right. Because of their training and experience, lawyers, who have been historically entrusted to shape, preserve and interpret the law, have a very restricted perception of (and interest in) the social implications of law.[18] This is particularly evident in certain branches of law that develop with no input from society.[19] In most of the fields of law, 'and especially of private law, in most political and economic circumstances, political rulers have no interest in determining what the rules of law are or should be (provided always of course that revenues roll in and that the public peace is kept)'.[20]

(ii) *The Very Nature of the Legal Rules.* In addition to being part of the social structure, legal rules operate at the level of ideas. Law develops by transplanting, not because a

terminology). See W Ewald 'Comparative Jurisprudence (II): The Logic of Legal Transplants' (1995) 43 Am J Comp L 489 at 492. This interpretation has been criticised by R Cotterrell 'Is There a Logic of Legal Transplants?' in D Nelken and J Feest *Adapting Legal Cultures* (Hart Oxford 2001) 71.

13 Apart from limited exceptions. Roman law of the late Republic is for example seen as self-reliant. See A Watson *The Nature of Law* (Edinburgh UP Edinburgh 1977) 100.

14 A Watson *Legal Transplants: An Approach to Comparative Law* (University of Georgia Press Athens GA 1993) 21.

15 Montesquieu, for example, in asserting that the law is intimately connected with the society on which it operates, argued that law reflects the 'spirit of the people' – CS Montesquieu *De l'Esprit des Lois* (Gallimard Paris 1970), reprint JP Mayer and AP Kerr (eds), book 1, chapter 3. Friedrich Carl von Savigny also conceptualised that law reflects the spirit of the people (*Volksgeist*) (albeit this conventional interpretation is questioned by W Ewald 'Comparative Jurisprudence (I): What it was Like to Try a Rat?' (1995) 143 Penn L Rev 1189 at 2031 footnote 288). On the same issue, see P Stein *Legal Evolution: The Story of an Idea* (CUP Cambridge 1980) 56, and R Pound *Contemporary Juristic Theory* (Claremont College Claremont 1940) 79.

16 The term is contained in Ewald's analysis referred above (W Ewald 'Comparative Jurisprudence (II): The Logic of Legal Transplants' (1995) 43 Am J Comp L 489).

17 The 'legal elite' according to Watson's terminology. See, in particular, A Watson *The Evolution of Law* (John Hopkins UP Baltimore 1985).

18 A Watson *The Evolution of Law* (John Hopkins UP Baltimore 1985) 41–42.

19 e.g. conflict of laws.

20 A Watson *Roman Law and Comparative Law* (University of Georgia Press Athens GA 1991) 97.

given rule was the inevitable consequence of the social structure and would have emerged even without a model to copy, 'but because the foreign rule was known to those with control over law making and they observed the (apparent) benefits which could be derived from it'.[21]

The extent to which law is autonomous from changes in society appears to be particularly evident when noting that unsuitable legal rules have sometimes persisted for centuries in a country even if they were commonly perceived to be out of step with society. The case of the English system of land tenure and registration provides a good example of the divergence between law and society.[22] Here (by contrast to Scotland or South Africa, for example), a system of compulsory registration of title to land was introduced only in 1925.[23] Although the law of real property 'contained so many antiquated rules and useless technicalities that additional and unnecessary impediments had arisen to hinder the facile transfer of land',[24] it survived almost unchanged as a cumbersome, expensive and complex system of conveyances for more than six hundred years. The major cause of the slow introduction of registration in England is not attributable to the fact that the work involved in the simplification was enormous and expensive, but rather to the role of lawyers. Lawyers could not be expected to press for the reform. Conveyancing represented such a large proportion of their work 'that they could not greet with enthusiasm any plan which would make more difficult to justify their fees. Moreover, lawyers enjoy their own technicalities. In addition, such expensive reform as was needed could only come from legislation, and English lawyers traditionally have been suspicious of statute.'[25]

In short, according to Watson,[26] comparative legal history suggests that the evolution of law is primarily a function of rules being imported from another legal system following the impulse of the legal elites. This calls into question the plausibility of the assumption that there is an inevitable correlation between legal development and social change. Law is largely autonomous from society. It operates in its own dimension, separate from those of other social institutions. Social and economic circumstances are simply not an insurmountable obstacle for legal transplants.

21 A Watson A 'Comparative Law and Legal Change' (1978) 37 CLJ 313 at 315.

22 A Watson *Society and Legal Change* (Scottish Academic Press Edinburgh 1977) 47–59.

23 Land Registration Act 1925.

24 EH Burn and J Cartwright *Cheshire and Burn's Modern Law of Real Property* (OUP Oxford 2006) 6.

25 A Watson *Society and Legal Change* (Scottish Academic Press Edinburgh 1977) 58. By way of analogy see R Goode 'The Case for the Abolition of the Floating Charge' in J Getzler and J Payne (eds) *Company Charges (Spectrum and Beyond)* (OUP Oxford 2006) 11 at 21 in response to the Law Commission's inquiry *Company Security Interests* (Law Com No 296 August 2005), available at <www.lawcom.gov.uk/docs/lc296.pdf> (accessed 7 August 2013) at para 3.164. On the same issue, see H Beale 'Reform of the Law of Security – Another View' (2004) 4 JIBFL 117; M Bridge 'How Far Is Article 9 Exportable? The English Experience' (1996) 27 CBLJ 196; and Id 'The Law Commission's Proposals for the Reform of Corporate Security Interests' in J Getzler and J Payne (eds) *Company Charges (Spectrum and Beyond)* (OUP Oxford 2006) 267.

26 And his followers. See the contributions from the section entitled 'Transplants, Receptions and Comparisons' in JW Cairns and OF Robinson (eds) *Critical Studies in Ancient Law, Comparative Law and Legal History* (Hart Oxford 2001) 213.

1.1.2. A Doctrinal Refinement

A less radical explanation for the significance of legal borrowing[27] and for the relationship between changing in law and changing in society was offered by Otto Kahn-Freund[28] some thirty years ago. Kahn-Freund pointed out that that there are 'degrees of transferability' and that the viability of borrowing requires congruent donor and host country socio-political structures. In contrast to Watson's thesis,[29] Kahn-Freund reasoned that since most laws are deeply embedded in their social and institutional matrices, it cannot be assumed that all rules or institutions are transplantable.[30] Legal institutions are in fact ordered along a spectrum which ranges from the 'mechanical', where transfer is relatively easy, to the 'organic', where transfer is very difficult, if not impossible. Hence, as laws have been decoupled to some extent unevenly from their socio-political roots, some are more prone to being transplanted than others.[31]

Kahn-Freund supports a piecemeal practical approach to borrowing and reception.[32] Contrary to the thesis of a recent scholarship on the very specific issue of the role of legal doctrine,[33] he argued that it does not represent *per se* an insurmountable obstacle to the further development of legal transplants. Taught law, Kahn-Freund states, is tough law 'and what is taught are primarily the general doctrinal foundations to which in after life the lawyer will cling as he may cling to the religious beliefs he learned at his mother's knees. Practical details are negotiable. Fortunately, for the future of

27 This has been specifically formulated with reference to labour law.

28 O Kahn-Freund 'On Uses and Misuses of Comparative Law' (1974) 37 MLR 6. The same position has been *de facto* reiterated by G Teubner 'Legal Irritants: Good Faith in British Law or How Unifying Law Ends Up in New Divergences' (1998) 61 MLR 11 at 17.

29 Kahn-Freund's position originated in sharp contrast to the series of lectures delivered by Watson at Virginia University and published in A Watson *Legal Transplants: An Approach to Comparative Law* (Scottish Academic Press Edinburgh 1974). Following Kahn-Freund's article, Watson reiterated his original thesis in A Watson 'Legal Transplants and Law Reform' (1976) 92 LQR 79. An independent view of this debate is offered by E Stein 'Uses, Misuses – and Nonuses of Comparative Law' (1977) 72 NW U L Rev 198.

30 O Kahn-Freund 'On Uses and Misuses of Comparative Law' (1974) 37 MLR 6 at 7–11 and at 27. See also O Kahn-Freund 'Common Law and Civil Law-Imaginary and Real Obstacles to Assimilation' in M Cappelletti (ed) *New Perspectives for a Common Law Europe* (LeMonnier Firenze 1978) 160.

31 On this theme and on the terminology adopted, see also G Gillespie 'Transplanted Company Law: an Ideological and Cultural Analysis of Market-entry in Vietnam' (2002) ICLQ 645; P Nicholson *Borrowing Court Systems: The Socialist Experience of Vietnam* (Brill Academic Publishers Leiden 2007); and P Nicholson and J Gillespie 'Interpreting Legal Transfers: The Implications for Law and Development' in P Nicholson and J Gillespie (eds) *Law and Development and the Global Discourses of Legal Transfers* (CUP Cambridge 2012).

32 An interesting attempt to rationalise the subject is offered by R Peernboom 'Towards a Methodology for Successful Legal Transplants' (2013) The Chinese Journal of Comparative Law 4; and Id 'What Have We Learned About Law and Development? Describing, Predicting and Assessing Legal Reforms in China' (2006) 27 Mich J Int'l L 823.

33 Reference is to the thesis put forward by E Micheler 'English and German Securities Law: A Thesis in Doctrinal Path Dependence' (2007) LQR 251; and Id *Property in Securities. A Comparative Study* (CUP Cambridge 2007).

Europe what matters are the practical details, and the diverse doctrinal foundations can look after themselves'.[34]

1.2. Postmodernist Approach to Legal Borrowing

By contrast to the 'legal change as legal transplants' thesis, postmodern scholarship is sceptical about the role of history and comparative law as a tool to detect the pattern and the drivers of legal change. The postmodernist approach reflects a radical trend of recent critical international scholarship to comparative law.[35] It is based on the assumption that comparative law is a mere scholarly imaginative construction. Since there is no neutral (external) ground on which the comparativist can stand, comparative law is a futile attempt to compare the incomparable.[36] The postmodernist objection to traditional comparative law stems from the premise that 'reasoning, language and judgement are determined by inescapable and incommensurable epistemic, linguistic cultural and moral frameworks'.[37] It reflects on the need for legal comparison and claims that legal frameworks are incommensurable since they are not comparable across history and cultures.[38] The conclusion is that legal comparison fails when it does not follow 'a rigorous experience of distance and difference'.[39]

The idiosyncrasies of diverse legal cultures, according to the anthropologically informed culturalist perspective[40] of Pierre Legrand,[41] simply prevent the possibility of

34 O Kahn-Freund 'Common Law and Civil Law-Imaginary and Real Obstacles to Assimilation' in M Cappelletti (ed) *New Perspectives for a Common Law Europe* (LeMonnier Firenze 1978) 147.

35 See the general introduction on critical legal studies in U Mattei 'Comparative Law and Critical Legal Studies' in M Reinmann and R Zimmermann (eds) *The Oxford Handbook of Comparative Law* (OUP Oxford 2006) 815; and U Mattei and A Di Robilant 'The Art and Science of Critical Scholarship: Postmodernism and International Style in the Legal Architecture of Europe' (2001) 75 Tul L Rev 1054. The classification under the label of 'postmodernism' tends in part to oversimplify the peculiarities of the various critical approaches to traditional comparative law. The basic assumptions are, however, shared by JE Ainsworth 'Categories and Culture: On the "Rectification of Names in Comparative Law"' (1996) 82 Cornell L Rev 19, G Frankenberg 'Stranger than Paradise: Identity & Politics in Comparative Law' (1997) 2 Utah L Rev 259; D Kennedy 'New Approaches to Comparative Law: Comparativism and International Governance' (1997) 2 Utah L Rev 544; V Curran 'Cultural Immersion, Difference and Categories in US Comparative Law' (1998) 46 Am J Comp L 43; and J Hill 'Comparative Law, Law Reform and Legal Theory' (1989) 9 OJLS 101.

36 V Curran 'Cultural Immersion, Difference and Categories in US Comparative Law' (1998) 46 Am J Comp L 67. See also N Berman 'Aftershocks: Exoticization, Normalization, Normalization and the Hermeneutic Compulsion' (1997) 2 Utah L Rev 282.

37 A Peters and H Schwenke 'Comparative Law Beyond Postmodernism' (2000) 49 ICLQ 800 at 802.

38 See HP Glenn 'Are Legal Traditions Incommensurable?' (2001) 49 Am J Comp L 133; R Chang 'Comparison and Justification of Choice' (1998) 146 U Pa L Rev 1569; and C Rogers 'Gulliver's Troubled Travels, or the Conundrum of Comparative Law' (1998) 67 Geo Wash L Rev 149.

39 G Frankenberg 'Critical Comparisons: Re-thinking Comparative Law' (1985) 26 Harv Int'l LJ 411 at 453.

40 This definition belongs to G Teubner 'Legal Irritants: Good Faith in British Law or How Unifying Law Ends Up in New Divergences' (1998) 61 MLR 11 at 14.

41 P Legrand 'The Impossibility of "Legal Transplants"' (1997) 4 Maast J Eur & Comp L 111; Id 'European Legal Systems are not Converging' (1996) 45 ICLQ 52; Id 'Against a European Civil Code' (1997) 60

legal borrowing. He argues that law is a culturally situated phenomenon. Since it is not an autonomous entity unencumbered by historical, epistemological, linguistic or cultural baggage,[42] legal rules cannot travel (unchanged) across jurisdictions. More precisely, every language and culture produces an indigenous system of meanings. What can be imported is a rule with similar wording, a comparable prepositional statement but, inevitably, with a different meaning. This is because the ultimate meaning of the rule is 'a function of the interpreter's epistemological assumptions which are themselves historically and culturally conditioned'.[43] A rule is necessarily an incorporative cultural form. It does not have 'any empirical existence that can be significantly detached from the world of meanings that defines a legal culture'.[44] The borrowed rule is *ipso facto* a different rule. What can be displaced from one jurisdiction to another is a meaningless collection of words. The development of law reflects and is responsive to a specific legal culture. It does not take place through the transplantation of legal rules because rules are not simply bare prepositional statements.

In short, legal comparison is a pointless venture if the analysis does not depart from the assumption that law is a culturally-situated phenomenon and that 'law lives a profound way within a culture specific – and therefore contingent – discourse'.[45] Against this background, legal transplants are simply impossible.

2. Limits

The outline of the terms of the debate on the diffusion of law above has highlighted the nature and the complexities of the arguments put forward by the supporters of the 'legal change as legal transplants' thesis and the ones advanced by critical legal scholars. However, these views do not provide a satisfactory and conclusive explanation for the movement of law across national borders and for the pattern of legal change. They contain elements of truth, but they also present significant theoretical flaws. Two fundamental aspects will be considered in turn.

2.1. The (Marginalised) Sociological Aspect of Law

According to Watson's thesis, law is insulated from society. It is an empire of its own which develops in accordance with internal dynamics and is autonomous from external forces. Under Watson's thesis, law amounts largely to legal doctrine and intellectual history.[46]

MLR 44; and Id 'The same and the different' in P Legrand and R Munday (eds) *Comparative Legal Studies Traditons and Transitions* (CUP Cambridge 2003) 240. See also TV Lee 'Risky Business: Courts Culture, and the Market Place' (1993) 47 U Miami L Rev 1335.

42 P Legrand 'The Impossibility of "Legal Transplants"' (1997) 4 Maast J Eur & Comp L 111 at 115.

43 Ibid 111 at 114.

44 P Legrand 'What "Legal Transplants"?' in D Nelken and J Fest (eds) *Adapting Legal Cultures* (Hart Oxford 2001) 55 at 59.

45 P Legrand 'The Impossibility of "Legal Transplants"' (1997) 4 Maast J Eur & Comp L 111 at 124.

46 See, in particular, A Watson *Legal Origins and Legal Change* (Hambledon London 1991) 72.

Watson's perception is misleading. Rather, law must be understood in relation both to the society in which it originates and to the one in which it operates.[47] It has been argued convincingly[48] that without legal sociology, the theory of legal transplants explains very little. A sociological inquiry is essential to predict how and under what conditions legal elites shape the law in a given period.[49]

Moreover, the dysfunctional character of some legal rules together with empirical evidence of borrowing do not prove that legal developments always occur independently from other reasons to be found in society. Mirror theories are not wrong *per se*. As they do not explain every legal development, they merely need supplementing.[50] To overlook that is a fundamental fallacy in Watson's reasoning, the result of a formalistic approach to law. He does not succeed in proving an absolute negative, 'that no interests of any kind are served by the law? Or that there could be no social reason for it?'[51]

Finally, the idea that legal systems are formed of rules and principles that serve nobody's interests, but nevertheless persist over centuries because legal professional elite control the patterns of development of legal doctrine, greatly simplifies the significance of law as a social phenomenon.[52] Legal systems are not static entities, persistent and insulated from their contexts.[53]

In short, Watson's radical approach to borrowing offers an impoverished explanation for the pattern of legal change. In his attempt to argue that the frequency of legal transplants demonstrates the limits of the sociology of law, it overlooks cases where legal transfers occurred by imposition[54] or as a part of socio-legal changes.[55] Above all, placing 'law in context' is crucial for explaining the pattern of legal change. It greatly contributes to '[appreciating] the social and (even more) the political context in which law was shaped in order to avoid rejection of a legal transplant'.[56] What survives from the theory

47 See D Nelken 'Legal Transplants and Beyond: of Disciplines and Metaphors' in A Harding and E Orucu (eds) *Comparative Law in the 21st Century* (Kluwer London 2002) 21.

48 See R Cotterrell 'Is There a Logic of Legal Transplants?' in D Nelken and J Fest (eds) *Adapting Legal Cultures* (Hart Oxford 2001) 70. Watson's sociological conclusions are ludicrous according to Friedman. Attacking Watson on his interpretation of law as a social phenomenon is 'like shooting fish in a barrel' – L Friedman 'Some Comments on Cotterrell and Legal Transplants' in D Nelken and J Fest (eds) *Adapting Legal Cultures* (Hart Oxford 2001) 93.

49 R Cotterrell 'Comparative Law and Legal Culture' in M Reinmann and R Zimmermann (eds) *The Oxford Handbook of Comparative Law* (OUP Oxford 2006) 709 at 724.

50 See RL Abel 'Law as Lag: Inertia as a Social Theory of Law' (1982) 80 Mich L Rev 785 at 790.

51 R Cotterrell *Law, Culture and Society* (Ashgate London 2006) 113.

52 A different criticism of this same issue that considers legal rules as entities with 'a life of their own' in the hands of legal elites is put forward by G Teubner in *Law as a Autopoietic System* (Blackwell Oxford 1993) 40 where he states that 'professionalism is of minor importance compared with the structural phenomenon of self-reference in law. The fact that legal standards appear to have a life of their own can be explained by the relation between self-reference and formality'.

53 L Friedman 'Some Comments on Cotterrell and Legal Transplants' in D Nelken and J Fest (eds) *Adapting Legal Cultures* (Hart Oxford 2001) 95.

54 e.g. the case of the diffusion of the Napoleonic code. See below *sub* Chapter 2, section 1.3.

55 See D Nelken 'Comparatists and Transferability' in P Legrand and R Munday (eds) *Comparative Legal Studies: Traditions and Transitions* (CUP Cambridge 2003) 447.

56 D Nelken 'Legal Transplants and Beyond: of Disciplines and Metaphors' in A Harding and E Orucu (eds) *Comparative Law in the 21st Century* (Kluwer London 2002) 23.

of legal transplant is minimal: it is the emphasis on comparative legal history for explaining the significance of borrowing in the evolution of law.[57] This element alone, however, amounts to a mere description of the itineraries of legal culture. It does not help to explain the reasons for the pattern of legal change and the peculiar traits of the assimilation process.[58]

2.2. *The Opacity of the Postmodernist Perspective*

Like Watson's theory, the claim of postmodernists that law cannot move from one society to another without a change in content is also not entirely convincing. It rests on certain flawed assumptions of law as a product exclusively embedded in a set cultural and linguistic context. These assumptions are questionable. Language is certainly bound to culture, but it has an open and evolving character 'that allows for linguistic change and cross cultural communication'.[59] The idea of a complete and autarchic linguistic system is misleading.[60] Moreover, empirical evidence of legal systems that have adopted multilingual laws suggests that the same rules can be expressed in different languages and that, therefore, they can be transferred from one community to another.[61]

In addition to that, culture 'is too weak a concept to act as an epistemological model in itself'.[62] It is not an entity that can be confined within rigid boundaries as empirical evidence gathered from the studies of comparative legal history suggests. The assumption that there are closed cultural frameworks is simply flawed.[63] Culture is not a monolith, but rather an 'adaptive and porous multilayered compound where actors having different stakes in the game are at work'.[64] If, as Legrand argues, an Italian lawyer cannot think like an English one, 'why should it be assumed that a lawyer from Welsh-speaking North Wales can think like an English lawyer born and bred in London?'. Above all, 'what are

57 With slightly different accents, the same view is shared by R Sacco 'Legal Formants: a Dynamic Approach to Comparative Law' (Instalment II) (1991) 39 Am J Comp L 343 at 395 when he discusses about the circulation of 'legal formants'; and J Gordley 'Why Look Backward' (2002) 50 Am J Comp L 657.

58 This issue is also highlighted by M Chen-Wishart 'Legal Transplants and Undue Influence: Lost in Translation or a Working Misunderstanding?' (2013) 62 ICLQ 1.

59 M Graziadei 'Transplants and Receptions' in M Reinmann and R Zimmermann (eds) *The Oxford Handbook of Comparative Law* (OUP Oxford 2006) 441 at 468.

60 See B Großfeld 'Comparatists and languages' in P Legrand and R Munday (eds) *Comparative Legal Studies: Traditions and Transitions* (CUP Cambridge 2003) 181 and, in general terms, R Caterina 'Comparative Law and the Cognitive Revolution' (2004) 78 Tul L Rev 1501.

61 With specific reference to European legal integration, see W Twining 'Surface Law' in H Petersen, AL Kjaer, H Krunke and MR Madsen (eds) *Paradoxes of European Legal Integration* (Ashgate Aldeshot 2008) 157. *Contra*, see the critical comment of P Legrand 'Word/World (of Primordial Issues for Comparative Legal Studies)' in H Petersen, AL Kjaer, H Krunke and MR Madsen (eds) *Paradoxes of European Legal Integration* (Ashgate Aldeshot 2008) 185.

62 G Samuel *Epistemology and Method in Law* (Aldershot Ashgate 2003) 50.

63 A Peters and H Schwenke 'Comparative Law Beyond Postmodernism' (2000) 49 ICLQ 800 at 814.

64 M Graziadei 'The Functionalist Heritage' in P Legrand and R Munday (ed) *Comparative Legal Studies: Traditions and Transitions* (CUP Cambridge 2003) 126.

the important boundaries and essential elements of cultures for purposes of comparison?'[65]

Further, the postmodernists' argument is *per se* unhelpful. It is obvious that the practice of legal transplants is impossible in its narrow sense, if it is treated as the attempt to use laws and legal institutions to reproduce identical meanings in different cultures.[66] This refutation of the theory of legal transplants, however, greatly trivialises Watson's more general position and reduces the investigation to a meaningless rigid terminological dispute.[67] Above all, it is not clear why some '(even minor) change in meaning has to have the radical consequence that only a meaningless form of words remains, and that the process of influencing consequently is not worthwhile examining at all'.[68] The empirical evidence gathered especially from mixed jurisdictions points against the claim that cultures are mutually incompatible and transplants are inherently impossible.[69] What is still valuable in Legrand's approach is that it allows a more careful reflection on the complexities of the process of displacement and assimilation of the legal paradigms. These are not just mechanical transfers, but rather involve a process of cultural change that needs to be considered appropriately.

3. The Way Forward

This study attempts to remedy the shortcomings identified in the academic debate analysed above. The following analysis rests on an overlooked argument on the circulation of legal models across national frontiers, rarely raised in the debate on legal transplants. It stems from the acknowledgment that the practice of borrowing has been one of the most fruitful and vital sources of legal change in the western world. This is simply a truism[70] that cannot be defeated by any culturally oriented approach *à la* Legrand. It is not, however, a phenomenon peculiar to law. Instead, borrowing reflects a general trend of social life, a mechanism of cultural diffusion. It has been probably one of the most successful mechanisms and 'so common that in any socio-cultural system the overwhelming majority of traits has originated in other societies'.[71] It applies well to law because law is itself a form of culture.

65 R Cotterrell 'Comparative Law and Legal Culture' in M Reinmann and R Zimmermann (eds) *The Oxford Handbook of Comparative Law* (OUP Oxford 2006) 709 at 725.

66 D Nelken 'Comparatists and Transferability' in P Legrand and R Munday (eds) *Comparative Legal Studies: Traditions and Transitions* (CUP Cambridge 2003) 445.

67 D Nelken 'Beyond the Metaphor of Legal Transplants? Consequences of Autopoietic Theory for the Study of Cross-Cultural Legal Adaptation' in J Priban and D Nelken (eds) *Law's New Boundaries: The Consequences of Autopoiesis* (Aldershot Dartmouth 2001) 265.

68 J Du Plessis 'Comparative Law and the Study of Mixed Legal Systems' in M Reinmann and R Zimmermann (eds) *The Oxford Handbook of Comparative Law* (OUP Oxford 2006) 488.

69 D Visser 'Cultural Forces in the Making of Mixed Legal Systems' (2003) 41 Tul L Rev 44.

70 This is also the view taken by R Sacco 'Legal Formants: a Dynamic Approach to Comparative Law' (Instalment II) (1991) 39 Am J Comp L 343 at 395 and E Orucu 'Law as Transposition' (2002) 51 ICLQ 206.

71 M Harris *Culture, Man, and Nature. An Introduction to General Anthropology* (Crowell New York 1971) 152.

It has already been said that law is not an autonomous entity detached from society and that it is not merely the province of lawyers. It is a system of meanings by which human experience is shaped and represented. Law cuts across all social life and is so closely intertwined 'into the texture of society that no neat dichotomy is possible between legal and extra-legal or social reality'.[72] A special explanation for borrowing in law should therefore be given only when it is distinguished from other forms of cultural diffusion. It is generally suggested that it is not clear that it does so significantly. It follows that any investigation into the movement of legal paradigms across national frontiers is necessarily part of a broader discourse on cultural diffusion.[73]

3.1. *The Process of Reception*

Building upon this awareness, this study proposes an original perspective for considering the significance of legal borrowing and for explaining the pattern of legal change. What is found to be missing in the theory of legal transplants is a convincing explanation for the reception mechanism, for the mechanism of appropriation of foreign elements. Watson's rigid description of the pattern of borrowing based on the postulate of the autonomy of law from society, on the assumption that law largely exists and operates independently from other social institutions, is not convincing.

It has been shown above that the claim that law is an autonomous institution is based provocatively on certain exceptional cases of legal rules being 'out of step' with the needs and aspirations of society. This idea oversimplifies the significance of law as a system of meaning by which human experience is modelled and expressed. In particular, it does not give sufficient attention to (or at least greatly overlooks) the interactions of the borrowed model with the social/economic setting of the country where the borrowing occurs. It is unsatisfactory to treat episodes of legal borrowing merely 'as the internal history of legal doctrine enlarged to take account of foreign sources of inspiration'.[74] The mere acknowledgment of the occurrence of borrowing demonstrates nothing about cultural interaction and the assimilation process. It is not an independent explanatory principle *per se*, as it does not reflect on the contents of the process. Borrowing cannot be considered 'a causal principle for explaining sociocultural differences and similarities since to say that a trait diffused from A to B', among other things, 'leaves unanswered the question of how and why the trait was accepted in B'.[75] Briefly, it is simply impossible 'to explain variables by constants'.[76]

The main argument of this study is that the movement of legal paradigms from one country to another rarely consists of a mere transplantation of rules, but generally involves a complex and gradual process of interaction between legal and social

72 EM Wise 'The Transplant of Legal Patterns' (1990) 38 Am J Comp L 1 at 21.

73 This view is shared by BS Jackson 'Evolution and Foreign Influence in Ancient Law' (1968) 16 Am J Comp L 372 at 374.

74 EM Wise 'The Transplant of Legal Patterns' 38 1990) 38 Am J Comp L 1 at 18.

75 M Harris *Culture, Man, and Nature. An Introduction to General Anthropology* (Crowell New York 1971) 154.

76 Ibid 154.

consciousness, between imported models and indigenous traditions. In this respect, specific attention is given to recent studies on culture contact and culture change. It will be shown that these studies can provide an explanation for the process of borrowing and the pattern of the legal change. The underlying claim is that recent insights from the theoretical debates on acculturation, colonialism and contact situations in general can be used to explain the pattern of the development of certain areas of law. The focus is put on the notion of 'hybridity' as a fundamental theme in cultural and postcolonial studies.

3.2. *The Causes of Borrowing*

Before the concept of hybridity is investigated further, the dynamics and forces that lead to borrowing will be examined. In this respect, three factors can be broadly identified: domination, chance/prestige, and economic efficiency. Legal borrowing resulting from domination through military conquest or expansion[77] is a self-explanatory case and will not be considered any further in this study. Chance/prestige and economic efficiency will be discussed briefly below.

That said, no attempt will be made to analyse these factors in great detail in this study, as they are unhelpful in explaining the process of diffusion of law. The rationale is straightforward: there is no possible conclusive single explanation for the factors of borrowing. Any comprehensive investigation on the matter inevitably results in a descriptive and unsatisfactory intellectual exercise. The variety of cases and circumstances are impossible to be reduced at unity. In presenting below the essence of the two most recurring arguments on the matter, it is therefore argued that a piecemeal approach is the only viable solution for dealing with the matter.

3.2.1. Chance/Prestige

Watson advocates that the rationale for legal borrowing is arbitrary in nature.[78] Legal transplants have not usually been the outcome of a systematic search for the most suitable foreign model, but largely a matter of historical accident depending on accessibility and prestige.[79] This is because the process of law-making is essentially driven by lawyers who act independently from society both as legislators and interpreters. Exogenous factors are sometimes relevant, but they are generally filtered through the medium of consolidated national legal traditions.[80]

77 e.g. the imposition of the western models on colonised regions or the extension of German law to Austria after the Anschluss of 1938.

78 See A Watson *The Nature of Law* (Edinburgh UP Edinburgh 1977) 106.

79 See A Watson 'Comparative Law and Legal Change' (1978) CLJ 313; and Id *The Nature of Law* (Edinburgh UP Edinburgh) 91–113.

80 See A Watson *The Evolution of Law* (John Hopkins UP Baltimore 1985) 28. See also the thesis on doctrinal path dependence put forward by E Micheler 'English and German Securities Law: A Thesis in Doctrinal Path Dependence' (2007) LQR 251.

3.2.2. Economic Efficiency

Mattei[81] and Ogus,[82] on the contrary, claim that there is a close correlation between social, economic or political circumstances and the evolution of law. Legal change is often driven by the search for arrangements and processes which maximise economic welfare (i.e. efficiency)[83] under the force of economic[84] and normative competition.[85] Efficiency is given by the competitive advantage of the borrowed model over alternative schemes with higher transaction costs.[86] This is not necessarily true for all areas of law,[87] but it is often the case for commercial law, which is not devised in the abstract but as 'a response to the practice and legitimate needs of merchants. It is mercantile practice that fashions commercial law'.[88] Barriers to transplants may of course be in place for example when it is considered desirable to sacrifice some economic growth to attain greater fairness in society.

Both views have significant limits when reflecting on their possible general application.

The first view, highlighting the role of chance/prestige, is limited because it identifies a factor of change (i.e. prestige), which is 'largely an empty idea'.[89] Moreover, as already pointed out, it detaches the law from its social setting and considers the development of legal phenomena to be entirely explicable by reference to other legal phenomena. The context in which law is embedded is overlooked and so too are the intricacies in the historical relations between legal forms and social practices. As suggested above, it is unsatisfactory to consider cases of legal borrowing 'as the internal history of legal doctrine enlarged to take account of foreign sources of inspiration'.[90]

[81] U Mattei 'Efficiency in Legal Transplants: An Essay in Comparative Law and Economics' (1994) 14 International Review of Law and Economics 3; Id *Comparative Law and Economics* (University of Michigan Press Ann Arbor 1997); and Id and A Monti 'Comparative Law and Economics: Borrowing and Resistance' (2001) 2 Global Jurist Frontiers 5.

[82] A Ogus 'Competition between National Legal Systems: A Contribution of Economic Analysis to Comparative Law' (1999) 48 ICLQ 405. See also N Garoupa and A Ogus 'A Strategic Interpretation of Legal Transplants' (2003) CEPR Discussion Paper No 4123, available at <www.mle.economia.unibo.it/Papers%20MTM/Garoupa%20-%20Legal%20Transplants.pdf> (accessed 7 August 2013); and A Ogus 'The Economic Basis of Legal Culture: Networks and Monopolization' (2002) OJLS 419.

[83] A Ogus *Costs and Cautionary Tales: Economic Insights for the Law* (Hart Oxford 2006) 26.

[84] See S Woolcock 'Competition Among Rules in the Single European Market' in W Bratton, J McCahery, S Picciotto and C Scott (eds) *International Regulatory Competition and Coordination: Perspectives on Economic Regulation in Europe and the United States* (OUP Oxford 1996) chapter 10.

[85] A Ogus 'Competition between National Legal Systems: A Contribution of Economic Analysis to Comparative Law' (1999) 48 ICLQ 415, and Id 'The Economic Base of Legal Culture: Networks and Monopolization' (2002) 22 OJLS 419.

[86] See TJ Zywicki 'The Rise and Fall of Efficiency in the Common Law: A Supply-Side Analysis' (2003) 97 NW U L Rev 1551.

[87] Especially when the difference among jurisdictions reflects a divergence in social values (e.g. family law).

[88] R Goode, H Kronke and E McKendrick *Transnational Commercial Law* (OUP Oxford 2007) 6.

[89] U Mattei 'Efficiency in Legal Transplants: An Essay in Comparative Law and Economics' (1994) 14 International Review of Law and Economics 3.

[90] EM Wise 'The Transplant of Legal Patterns' (1990) 38 Am J Comp L 1 at 20.

The second view, highlighting the role of efficiency, is limited because it focuses on a rather rigid 'law and economics' model that does not consider carefully the dynamics of the transfer process. Moreover, it promotes a historically and socially flawed explanation for the process of legal change. The case of the reception of laws that formed the Turkish legal system in the years 1924–1930 described by Orucu may help to clarify this criticism. The choice there 'was driven in some cases by the perceived prestige of the model, in some by efficiency and in others by chance'.[91] In most of the cases the search for cultural legitimacy prevailed over efficiency. It is not the case that a universal model from a single jurisdiction was adopted. It was rather 'the civil law, the law of obligations and civil procedure from Switzerland, commercial law, maritime law and criminal procedure from Germany, criminal law from Italy and administrative law from France that were chosen, translated, adapted and adjusted to solve the social and legal problems of Turkey and to fit together'.[92]

It follows from the above analysis that while the influence of economic competition is an important factor in driving the evolution of law, it cannot be regarded as the only possible one. The pattern is much more complex. Other factors contribute to legal change, sometimes directed by arbitrary (chance), political (prestige) and military (domination) rationales. As already suggested, this scenario renders the analysis of the causes and circumstances for legal borrowing pointless, an exercise of little meaning for understanding the process of legal evolution.

91 E Orucu *Critical Comparative Law: Considering Paradoxes for Legal Systems in Transition* (Kluwer Deventer 1999) 81. See also Id 'A Synthetic and Hyphenated Legal System: The Turkish Experience' (2006) 1 J Comp L 27.

92 E Orucu *Critical Comparative Law: Considering Paradoxes for Legal Systems in Transition* (Kluwer Deventer 1999) 81. See also E Orucu 'Turkey: Change Under Pressure' in E Orucu, E Attwooll and S Coyle (eds) *Studies in Legal Systems: Mixed and Mixing* (Kluwer London 1996) 89; and Id 'The Impact of European Law on the Ottoman Empire and Turkey' in WJ Mommsen and A de Moor (eds) *European Expansion and Law: The Encounter of European and Indigenous Law in 19th and 20th Century Africa and Asia* (Berg Oxford 1992) 39.

Chapter 2

THE LEITMOTIF OF THE BOOK

Chapter 1 showed the boundaries of the current debate on the diffusion of law and explained the limits of the most influential works in the area. It also introduced the contribution of this study to the comparative discussion. The present chapter develops this. In particular, it addresses the theoretical grounds for explaining the process of legal change through the appropriation of foreign legal paradigms and ideas. In doing so, it focuses on the notion of 'hybridity' as shaped in postcolonial studies, and tests it against a number of possible applications, as well as in 'pseudo-colonial' situations outside the modern imperialist pattern. A clarification of the impact and relevance of this investigation within the specific debate on legal borrowing will be provided in the next chapter.

1. The Concept of Hybridity

1.1. Foundation

The term hybridity originated in the mid-nineteenth century in the context of biological and evolutionary debates to describe a cross between animal or plant species.[1] Although it has also been occasionally used as a metaphor to indicate a lack of racial purity,[2] the term today[3] defines a research theme in cultural and postcolonial studies involving 'processes of interaction that create new social spaces to which new meanings are given'.[4]

1 Darwin devotes a whole chapter (Chapter 8) in the *Origin of the Species by Means of Natural Selection* (J Murray London 1859) to 'Hybridism' where he argues that degrees of hybridity meant that species could no longer be regarded as absolutely distinct.

2 i.e. 'mixed' or 'intermediate' races. A general outline of the history of the term is provided by R Young *Colonial Desire. Hybridity in Theory, Culture and Race* (Routledge London 1995).

3 Generally. For examples, studies in 'linguistic hybridity' are not considered in this analysis. See MM Bakhtin *The Dialogic Imagination: Four Essays* (University of Texas Press Austin 1981).

4 R Young *Postcolonialism. A Very Short Introduction* (OUP Oxford 2003) 79. See also B Ashcroft, G Griffith and H Tiffin *Key Concepts in Post-Colonial Studies* (Routledge London 1998) 118 where hybridity is defined as 'the creation of new transcultural forms within the contact zone produced by colonialism'.

1.2. *The Theoretical Background*

The concept of cultural hybridity is usually associated with the pioneering works of Homi Bhabha who attempted to overcome the rigid dualist perception of culture in the colonial contexts that neatly distinguished between colonisers and colonised.[5] Bhabha, developing the 'orientalist' discourse initiated by Said,[6] essentially criticised the conventional way of binary thinking whereby the inhabitants of a colonised region are regarded as either colonial or indigenous.[7]

The claim for a hierarchical purity of cultures is untenable in colonial situations. So is the picture of a rigid process of acculturation where one group becomes more like another by borrowing discrete cultural traits.[8] Rather, there are areas of 'in-betweenness' of people and their actions, and it is the 'in-between' space that carries the burden and meaning of culture.[9]

1.3. *The Contents and the Effects*

Building on the above-mentioned findings, Bhabha suggested that the notion of cultural hybridity expresses the result of cross-cultural exchange or 'the effect of an ambivalence produced within the rules of recognition of dominating discourses as they articulate the signs of cultural difference'.[10] The ambivalent relationship between coloniser and colonised, in particular, qualifies as 'mimicry'[11] because the copying of the colonisers' culture and values is not a mere reproduction of the same traits. Rather, it creates a blurred copy of the original model, sometimes not far from mockery. The reproduced

5 H Bhabha *The Location of Culture* (Routledge London 1994). See also A Prabhu *Hybridity: Limits, Transformations, Prospects* (State University of New York Press Albany 2007).

6 In his celebrated book (EW Said *Orientalism* (Penguin London 1985) 98), Said maintained that the notion of the Orient is a western invention. Orientalism is a 'kind of western projection onto and will to govern over the Orient'. See also R Young *Colonial Desire. Hybridity in Theory, Culture and Race* (Routledge London 1995) 161.

7 H Bhabha 'Signs Taken for Wonders: Questions of Ambivalence and Authority Under a Tree Outside Dehli, May 1817' in H Bhabha (eds) *The Location of Culture* (Routledge London 1994) 145. The mixed character of colonial situations in the is also well presented in N Papastergiadis 'Tracing Hybridity in Theory' in P Werbner and T Modood (eds) *Debating Cultural Hybridity: Multi-cultural Identities and the Politics of Anti-racism* (Zed Books London 1997) 279.

8 R White *The Middle Ground: Indians, Empires, and Republics in the Great Lakes Region, 1650–1815* (CUP Cambridge 1991). See also S Jones *The Archaeology of Ethnicity. Constructing Identities in the Past and Present* (Routledge London 1997) 45.

9 B Ashcroft, G Griffith and H Tiffin *Key Concepts in Post-Colonial Studies* (Routledge London 1998) 119.

10 H Bhabha 'Signs Taken for Wonders: Questions of Ambivalence and Authority Under a Tree Outside Dehli, May 1817' in H Bhabha (eds) *The Location of Culture* (Routledge London 1994) 162.

11 From 'mimicking' the coloniser.

colonised subject 'is almost the same, but not quite'.[12] It is the effect of 'a flawed colonial mimesis in which to be Anglicised is emphatically not to be English'.[13]

The essence of the effect of mimicry is the creation of a 'third space' between colonial and indigenous cultures. In the words of White, who coined the term to describe the interactions between the Native Americans and Europeans in the Great Lakes Region of North America between 1650 and 1815, it is a 'Middle Ground', an area of mediation where the worlds of the natives and colonist melt at the edges.[14] This is where hybridity constitutes its meaning and where an alternative authority to the colonial one may potentially be set up.[15] Hybridity is therefore the moment where the discourse of colonial authority loses its univocal grip on meaning and finds itself open to the effects of the language of the other.[16] It is 'the name for the strategic reversal of the process of domination through disavowal (that is, the production of discriminatory identities that secure the 'pure' and original identity of authority)'.[17]

It follows that cultural norms in colonial contexts are neither colonial nor indigenous 'in disguise', but peculiar to each specific contact situation. Hybrid culture is more than the result of the fusion of features of colonial and indigenous backgrounds. It is a new creation in its own right[18] that, inevitably, locates 'a crack in the certainty of colonial dominance, [...] in its control of the behaviour of the colonized'.[19]

1.4. *The Limits of the Notion of Cultural Hybridity*

One of the fundamental criticisms of Bhabha's work has been that the notion of cultural hybridity is based on the presumption of the existence of once pure cultures and on the understanding that pre-colonial culture is an authentic, well-defined and autonomous entity.[20] As already seen when discussing Legrand's arguments, this criticism is devastating. Pure cultures do not exist. Hybrid cultures are no less authentic than the

12 H Bhabha 'Of Mimicry and Men' in H Bhabha (eds) *The Location of Culture* (Routledge London 1994) 123. In general, see also B Parry 'Problems in Current Discourse Theory' (1987) 9 Oxford Literary Review 27.

13 H Bhabha 'Of Mimicry and Men' in H Bhabha (eds) *The Location of Culture* (Routledge London 1994) 125. See also R Young *White Mythologies. Writing History and the West* (Routledge London 1990) 141–156.

14 R White *The Middle Ground: Indians, Empires, and Republics in the Great Lakes Region, 1650–1815* (CUP Cambridge 1991).

15 H Bhabha 'The Commitment to Theory' in H Bhabha (eds) *The Location of Culture* (Routledge London 1994) 28.

16 See R Young *Colonial Desire. Hybridity in Theory, Culture and Race* (Routledge London 1995) 22.

17 H Bhabha 'Signs Taken for Wonders: Questions of Ambivalence and Authority Under a Tree Outside Dehli, May 1817' in H Bhabha (eds) *The Location of Culture* (Routledge London 1994) 159.

18 J Neederveen Pieterse 'Hybrity, So What? The Anti-hybridity Backlash and the Riddles of Recognition' (2001) 18 Theory, Culture & Society 219.

19 B Ashcroft, G Griffith and H Tiffin *Key Concepts in Post-Colonial Studies* (Routledge London 1998) 139. See also H Bhabha 'The Commitment to Theory' in H Bhabha (eds) *The Location of Culture* (Routledge London 1994) 28.

20 See, for example, J Friedman 'Global Crises, the Struggle for Cultural Identity and Intellectual Porkbarrelling: Cosmopolitans Versus Locals, Ethnics and Nationals in an Era of Dehegemonisation' in P Werbner and T Modood (eds) *Debating Cultural Hybridity: Multi-cultural Identities and the Politics of Anti-racism* (Zed Books London 1997) 72.

pre-colonial ones. The various cultural traits are combined into a new and internally equally coherent culture.[21] This is because the relation between meaning and origin is not an intrinsic one and cultural 'forms become separated from existing practices and recombine with new forms in new practices'.[22]

1.5. A Terminological Alternative

The conceptual pitfall inherent in the notion of cultural hybridity referred to above can be overcome by redefining it with the term 'hybridisation'. This gives a fair representation of the process of interaction and negotiation between the social actors in the colonial situation. It also avoids any reference to a reified concept of culture and culturally predetermined identities. The inhabitants of a colonised region (both colonial and indigenous) are not simply the objects of culture change, of the interaction between two different cultures.[23] They are rather the protagonists of cultural encounters.

The term hybridisation therefore essentially captures the process underlying the 'culture mixture [which] is the effect of the practice of mixed origins'.[24] It is a sort of conceptual reorientation to observe the process of construction of local identities in the specific contact situation.[25]

2. The Scope of the Postcolonial Debate

The idea of hybridisation as the process of cultural mixture for colonial situations, originally developed in postcolonial studies, is not specifically modern or Western. It goes beyond particular temporal and spatial contexts.[26] The phenomenon of ambivalence can be observed in all colonial and 'pseudo-colonial' situations, not only in the modern ones.

A clarification of the above statement is proposed below. The analysis first considers the meaning of 'pseudo-colonialism' and then argues that the process of hybridisation is also applicable to 'pseudo-colonial' situations.

2.1. The Concept of 'Pseudo-Colonialism'

The term 'pseudo-colonialism' is formally unknown in the literature and has been coined exclusively to clarify the boundaries of this inquiry. It does not reflect an abstract concept,

21 See J Friedman 'The Hybridization of Roots and the Abhorrence of the Bush' in M Featherstone and S Lash (eds) *Spaces of Culture. City, Nation, World* (Sage London 1999) 230 at 245.

22 J Nederveen Pieterse 'Globalization as Hybridization' in M Featherstone, L Lash and R Robertson (eds) *Global Modernities* (Sage London 1995) 49.

23 See J Friedman 'The Hybridization of Roots and the Abhorrence of the Bush' in M Featherstone, L Lash and R Robertson (eds) *Spaces of Culture. City, Nation, World* (Sage London 1999) 230 at 234.

24 J Friedman 'Global System, Globalization and the Parameters of Modernization' in M Featherstone, L Lash and R Robertson (eds) *Global Modernities* (Sage London 1995) 69 at 84.

25 R Young *Postcolonialism. A Very Short Introduction* (OUP Oxford 2003) 6.

26 N Thomas *Colonialism's Culture: Anthropology, Travel and Government* (Polity Cambridge 1994) 33–65.

restricted to the dominance assumptions of European historical experience,[27] of a consequence of imperialism.[28] It does not coincide with the meaning and connotations of colonialism in modern times, which has often been associated with the idea of political, military and economic domination by intrusive foreign groups over indigenous people.[29] Nor does it imply violent occupation or exploitation of the region involved as the case of European cultural hegemony in science in the early political independence of United States and Australia demonstrates[30] or the influence of Anglo-Saxon corporate governance in shaping the evolution of corporate law in Europe in the twentieth century.[31]

'Pseudo-colonialism' refers to a much broader idea that applies to non-hegemonic contexts, as the contributions of Osborne[32] and De Angelis[33] on the history of Greek overseas settlements have pointed out. In this light, 'pseudo-colonialism' refers primarily to the 'absence from home and being in a foreign country',[34] a notion more akin to the Greek *apoikiai*[35] than to the Latin equivalent *colonia*.[36]

It follows that not only the Greek cities in southern Italy and Sicily from the eighth century BC qualify as 'pseudo-colonies',[37] so too do other situations of 'non-hegemonic contact' such as the Mesopotamian trade settlements in Syria and southeast Anatolia of

27 Even if *de facto* already implicitly included in some (arguably, over-stretched) definitions of colonialism. See R Horvath 'A definition of colonialism' (1972) 13 Current Anthropology 45. See also G Stein 'Colonies without Colonialism: A Trade Diaspora Model of Fourth Millennium B.C. Mesopotamian Enclaves in Anatolia' in CL Lyons and JK Papadopulos (eds) *The Archaeology of Colonialism* (Getty Research Institute Los Angeles 2002) 27.

28 EW Said *Culture and Imperialism* (Knopf New York 1994) 9.

29 See N Dirks 'Introduction: Colonialism and Culture' in N Dirks (eds) *Colonialism and Culture* (University of Michigan Press Ann Arbour 1992) 1–25.

30 N Reingold and M Rothenberg 'Introduction' in N Reingold and M Rothenberg (eds) *Scientific Colonialism: A Cross Cultural Comparison* (Smithsonian Institute Press Washington 1987) x. On the impact of imperial science on indigenous people rather than nation-states, see L Whitt Sciente *Colonialism and Indigenous People: the Cultural Policy of Law and Culture* (CUP Cambridge 2009).

31 A Thomas 'Cultural Hegemony: the Exportation of Anglo-Saxon Corporate Governance Ideologies to Germany' (1998) 73 Tul L Rev 69.

32 R Osborne 'Early Greek Colonization? The nature of Greek settlement in the West' in N Fisher and H van Wees (eds) *Archaic Greece: New Approaches and New Evidence* (Duckworth London 1998) 251.

33 F De Angelis 'Ancient Past, Imperial Present: the British Empire' in TJ Dunbabin's 'The Western Greeks' (1998) 72 Antiquity 539. See also G Shepherd 'The Pride of Most Colonials: Burial and Religion in the Sicilian Colonies' (1995) 6 Acta Hypeborea 51.

34 P van Dommelen 'Ambiguous Matters: Colonialism and Local Identities in Punic Sardinia' in CL Lyons and JK Papadopulos (eds) *The Archaeology of Colonialism* (Getty Research Institute Los Angeles 2002) 121.

35 See the definition provided by G Stein 'Colonies without Colonialism: A Trade Diaspora Model of Fourth Millennium B.C. Mesopotamian Enclaves in Anatolia' in CL Lyons and JK Papadopulos (eds) *The Archaeology of Colonialism* (Getty Research Institute Los Angeles 2002) 26 at 30.

36 See J Webster 'Roman Imperialism and the Post-Imperial Age' in J Webster and N Cooper (eds) *Roman Imperialism: Post-Colonial Perspectives* (University of Leicester Leicester 1996) 5.

37 See TJ Dunbabin *The Western Greeks* (OUP Press Oxford 1948).

the Uruk period[38] and the Greek establishments in southeast Spain.[39] The latter, in particular, were essentially no more than trading contacts without foreign occupation and without submission of the host community. In this respect, they were not dissimilar from the various Phoenician trade posts in central and western Mediterranean,[40] the Greek *emporia*[41] or, as will be seen in Part II, the Genoese economic networks in southern England.[42] The object of 'pseudo-colonisation' may therefore well be 'the web of connectivity itself rather than the productive terrain'.[43] There is a clear thread that links the cases of Miletos in the sixth century BC, the medieval 'aristocratic diasporas'[44] and the commercial expansion of Genoa outside the Mediterranean borders.

2.2. *Hybridisation and 'Pseudo-Colonialism'*

2.2.1. 'Pseudo-Colonialism' and Hegemony

Against this understanding of the concept of 'pseudo-colonialism', it is argued below that the process of hybridisation is a recurring feature not just in colonial situations, but also in 'pseudo-colonial situations', where the modern imperialistic connotations are not in place. By distinguishing between 'non-hegemonic' and 'hegemonic' contacts, the following inquiry will show how the pattern is not the same in both scenarios. The underlying theory[45] is based on the idea of hegemony as a manifestation of coloniser's supremacy, both in terms of 'intellectual and moral leadership'[46] and the 'domination'.[47]

38 3700 BC. See G Stein 'Colonies without Colonialism: A Trade Diaspora Model of Fourth Millennium B.C. Mesopotamian Enclaves in Anatolia' in CL Lyons and JK Papadopulos (eds) *The Archaeology of Colonialism* (Getty Research Institute Los Angeles 2002) 26 at 27.

39 Sixth century BC. AJ Dominguez 'Greeks in Iberia Colonialism without Colonization' in CL Lyons and JK Papadopulos (eds) *The Archaeology of Colonialism* (Getty Research Institute Los Angeles 2002) 65.

40 Until the fifth century BC. See ME Aubet *The Phoenicians and the West: Politics, Colonies, and Trade* (CUP Cambridge 1993) 183–276.

41 Broadly, trading stations. See JP Wilson 'The Nature of Greek Overseas Settlements in the Archaic Period: *Emporion* or *Apoikia*?' L Mitchell and PJ Rhodes (eds) *The Development of the Polis in Archaic Greece* (Routledge London 1997) 199.

42 See, by way of introduction, TH Lloyd *Alien Merchants in England in the High Middle Ages* (The Harvester Press Limited Brighton 1982).

43 N Purcell 'Colonization and Mediterranean History' in H Hurst and S Owen (eds) *Ancient Colonizations (Analogy, Similarity and Difference)* (Duckworth London 2005) 124.

44 R Bartlett 'Colonial Aristocracies of the High Middle Ages' in R Bartlett and A MacKay (eds) *Medieval Frontier Societies* (OUP Oxford 1989) 23.

45 See D Kurtz 'Hegemony and Anthropology. Gramsci, Exegeses, Reinterpretations' (1996) 16 Critique of Anthropology 103.

46 i.e. predominance based through consent of the subordinate people. See J Femia 'Hegemony and Consciousness in the Thought of Antonio Gramsci' (1975) 23 Political Studies 30. This is the classical definition provided by Gramsci where hegemony is the predominance obtained by consent rather than by force of one class or group over other classes. See A Gramsci *Opere di Antonio Gramsci. Il Risorgimento vol IV* (Einaudi Torino 1949) 70.

47 See L Gruppi 'Il Concetto di Egemonia' (1967) 3 Prassi Rivoluzionaria e Storicismo in Gramsci, Critica Marxista 78 where he maintains that 'for Gramsci the concept of hegemony normally includes those of "leadership" and "domination" together'.

2.2.2. An Archaeological Perspective

This search for the process of hybridisation in 'pseudo-colonial' situations focuses on pre-modern examples and relies primarily on archaeological studies. The recourse to archaeology follows the simple rationale that this discipline (arguably more than any other social science) provides for accurate, verifiable and reliable results. In considering material culture deriving from physical evidence, archaeology studies cultures and people who 'did not inscribe their own narratives in writing' and it 'gives voice to people marginally represented or excluded even in literate cultures'.[48] As in the often quoted Chippindale's example, 'to be a slave girl at the wrong end of town in Classical Athens was not to experience Plato's world'.[49]

2.2.2.1. General

The outcomes of a great number of archaeological studies on the settlements established by Phoenicians, Greeks, Carthaginians and Romans in the western Mediterranean have provided evidence that commercial contacts were intense from the Mycenaean period onwards and that people from across the Mediterranean Sea met and interacted, and no doubt shared many ideas and views alongside their trading goods.[50] Contacts rarely amounted to a claim to possession of new territories overseas or to the creation of settlements limited to citizens of the foreign community. At the root of *apoikia* there was a search for economic benefits, not only for the city of origin, but for other homeland cities and for non-Greek peoples too. From 'the point of view of state policy, its initial motivation seems to have been as much a negative as a positive one, to ease pressure on the land of the founding city and to rid it of restless elements'.[51] This is clearly in contrast with a traditional view of ancient overseas settlements based on assumptions taken from the modern age's imperialism,[52] with the practice of 'thrusting the desired modern standards on to the antiquity'.[53] There is archaeological evidence that in most cases commercial and cultural relationships between local inhabitants and foreigners were not antagonistic or a clash between isolated entities.[54] They rarely amounted to mechanistic

48 CL Lyons and JK Papadopulos 'Archaeology of Colonialism' in CL Lyons and JK Papadopulos (eds) *The Archaeology of Colonialism* (Getty Research Institute Los Angeles 2002) 1 at 11.

49 C Chippindale 'Theory in Archaeology: A World Perspective' (20 October 1995) Times Literary Supplement 1 at 9.

50 See S Antoniadou and A Pace *Mediterranean Crossroads* (Pierides Foundation Athens 2007).

51 A Snodgrass '"Lesser Breeds": The History of a False Analogy' in H Hurst and S Owen (eds) *Ancient Colonizations (analogy, similarity and difference)* (Duckworth London 2005) 50.

52 e.g. the case of the indigenous Sicilians converted into 'artificial Greeks' claimed by EA Freeman *A History of Sicily from the Earliest Times*, vol I (OUP Oxford 1891) 8, the argument of Greek superiority (the 'trade before the flag' argument) advanced by A Blakeway 'Prolegomena to the Study of Greek Commerce with Italy, Sicily and France in the Eight and Seventh Centuries BC' (1932) 33 ABSA 170 or the imperialistic character of English colonisation suggested by J Hasebroek *Trade and Politics in Ancient Greece* (Biblio and Tannen New York 1965) 110.

53 J Boardman *The Greeks Overseas: Their Early Colonies and Trades* (Thames & Hudson London 1999) 268.

54 See the references to the works cited above and the useful summary of the recent bibliography on the extent to which Etruscans adopted Greek institutions provided by M Torelli 'The Encounter with the

relationships of acculturation, of cultural 'colonisation' of the indigenous population.[55] Even in the rare cases of political domination, as in the case of the Roman colonies, the distinction between coloniser and colonised was not straightforward or stable.[56] Rather, a local 'middle ground' of cultural mediation and accommodation and areas of 'in-betweenness' of people and their actions emerged. New traditions peculiar to each contact situation were invented. This is, of course, in line with the findings of postcolonial theories and consistent with the notion of hybridisation as a process of culture change.

As suggested earlier, this inquiry distinguishes between 'non-hegemonic' and 'hegemonic' contacts. These will be of helpful reference when dealing with the process of reception of legal paradigms in Part II and Part III.

2.2.2.2. Non-Hegemonic Contacts

The perception of the cultural intricacies of 'pseudo-colonial' encounters and the process of development of new local cultural norms in their own right is straightforward in the absence of any direct hegemonic relationship. The 'pseudo-colonial' situation is less constrained by antagonistic interests. It is, therefore, usually open to novelty and change and conducive to the formation of a cultural middle ground where the process of hybridisation occurs. In this respect, the study of archaeological remains in Greek (Pithekoussai[57] and

Etruscans' in G Pugliese Caratelli (eds) *The Greek World: Art and Civilization in Magna Grecia and Sicily* (Rizzoli New York 1996) 567.

55 Consider the case of 'Hellenization' in the overviews presented by D Adamensteanu 'Greeks and Natives in Basilicata' and F D'Andria 'Greek Influence in the Adriatic: Fifty Years after Beaumont' in JP Descoeudres (eds) *Greek Colonist and Native Populations* (OUP Oxford 1990) 143 and 281.

56 M Millett *The Romanization of Britain: an Essay in Archaeological Interpretation* (CUP Cambridge 1990).

57 The remains of the Greek commercial *emporium* in the bay of Naples on the island of Pithekoussai evidence mutual contacts between colonisers and Etruscan and local Italic communities. Pithekoussai essentially represents a model of early Greek colonisation 'one of touching and tapping rather than grabbing and possessing' (I Malkin 'A Colonial Middle Ground: Greek, Etruscan, and Local Elites in the Bay of Naples' in CL Lyons and JK Papadopulos (eds) *The Archaeology of Colonialism* (Getty Research Institute Los Angeles 2002) 154). It was a very early form of the flexible model for the founding Greek institutions, constituting a new entity, independent from its mother city. Pithekoussai was a colonial middle ground of regular exchanges where nobody was an absolute other in terms of binary-oppositional model. Although it is generally agreed that the Greek presence provided the Etruscans with unprecedented social, cultural and political stimuli, it is also clear that this was not a unilateral affair. There is no sign that a direct domination of the Greek culture over the others took place. On the contrary, Etruscans formed a significant part of the Greek experience in the course of the eighth century. The contents of Greek tombs in Pithekoussai, for example, illustrate that personal ornaments used by Greek in the second half of the eight century were identical to those used in Etruria and in Latium (see G Buchner 'Early Orientalizing: Aspects of the Euboean Connection' in D Ridgway and F Ridgway (eds) *Italy before the Romans: The Iron Age, Orientalizing and Etruscan Periods* (Academic Press London 1979) 133. See also D Ridgway 'La Presenza Etrusca nella Campania Meridionale' in P Gastaldi and G Maetzke (eds) *La Presenza Etrusca nella Campania Meridionale: Atti delle Giornate di Studio, Salerno-Pontecagnano 16–28 novembre 1990* (Olschki Firenze 1994) 513). It is, of course, also true that during the second half of the eighth century the Etruscans adopted the Euboian alphabet, learning it from the Euboian settlers in Pithekoussai. This was, however, shaped according to the special needs of Etruscan phonetics. Moreover, the same Greek colonials contributed to the spread of

Morgantina)[58] and Phoenician (west Sardinia)[59] settlements has clarified that in the presence of 'pseudo-colonial', 'non-hegemonic' situations the pattern of cultural change does not amount to a unidirectional process of civilisation of the indigenous population. Rather it consists of a complex original phenomenon of social and cultural interaction (hybridisation) between new settlers and local indigenous population.

the motifs from Greek epics in Italy. They were, however, adapted in Etruscan pottery to suit the local taste (see FH Massa-Pairault *Iconologia e Politica nell'Italia Antica: Roma, Lazio ed Etruria dal VII al I secolo AC* (Longanesi Milano 1992) 19). In short, Pithekoussai expresses a frontier zone for both Greeks and Etruscans where a new colonial culture emerged, a normative process that fused 'mother-cities', settlers and natives alike. It was not exclusively Greek, nor Etruscan. It was a middle ground where Greeks and Etruscans mixed with local elites and where Greek elements and frameworks were being introduced, amended and appropriated.

58 The analysis of the burial customs in the Greek cemetery of the colony of Morgantina in Enna Province (Sicily) is also a good example illustrating hybridisation and the pattern of diffusion of material culture in a non-hegemonic context. The archaeological excavations carried out by five different American universities have provided evidence in particular that despite the site was culturally and politically Greek from at least the sixth century, a large percentage of the material recovered was not Greek, but indigenous (Sikel). The fact that Greek objects were often mixed with non-Greek ones, in particular, was contrary to orthodox Greek burial conventions. The combination clearly shows that Greek customs were integrated into the local traditions (see CL Lyons 'Sikel Burials at Morgantina: Defining Social and Ethnic Identities' in R Leighton (eds) *Early Societies in Sicily: New Developments in Archaeological Research* (Accordia Research Centre, University of London London 1996) 77) and that, therefore, in the specific colonial situation, the Greek objects *per se* do not denote as such any more an 'original' Greek culture. The meaning and significance of Greek objects must consequently be sought in the local web of meanings that developed around local and imported material culture in the specific indigenous setting. In short, Morgantina's material culture, especially in the Archaic and early Classical periods is neither wholly Greek, nor indigenous. It is the outcome of a specific colonial identity, the original consequence of the process of hybridisation (see C Antonaccio 'Hybridity and the cultures within Greek culture' in C Dougherty and L Kurke (eds) *The Cultures Within Greek Culture: Contact, Conflict, Collaboration* (CUP Cambridge 2003) 57).

59 This is the case of the unevenly distributed Punic colonies from the end of the fifth century BC in west-central Sardinia (in general, see F Barreca *La Civiltà Fenicio-punica in Sardegna* (Delfino Sassari 1986) 31–40). A coherent colonial settlement pattern is missing. While some colonial settlements were located in the Campidano and Marmilla and were closely associated with the abandoned *nuraghi*, the *emporia* in the costal areas do not show traces of previous occupation. Although they both qualify as 'colonial' settlements, they are very different. The identification of '*nuraghic*' features in the rituals of Marmilla, for example, 'suggests that colonial settlements somehow seems to have been 'less colonial' in the interior of the west central Sardinia than in the costal area' (P van Dommelen 'Ambiguous Matters: Colonialism and Local Identities in Punic Sardinia' in CL Lyons and JK Papadopulos (eds) *The Archaeology of Colonialism* (Getty Research Institute Los Angeles 2002) 133). The most reliable explanation for the distinction is that, contrary to the 'Romanisation' of the island that took place in the Imperial period, the Punic presence was only in part hegemonic. Certain settlements were less uniformly colonial simply because indigenous inhabitants were not fully assimilated to the colonial Punic culture. They were 'able to retain and express a distinct sense of identity, even if they had to do so by taking recourse to new – Punic – material culture' (P van Dommelen 'Ambiguous Matters: Colonialism and Local Identities in Punic Sardinia' in CL Lyons and JK Papadopulos (eds) *The Archaeology of Colonialism* (Getty Research Institute Los Angeles 2002) 137). The transformation of local culture in those colonial situations as evidenced in the study of the remains of locally produced pottery and amphorae was therefore not an imposition of colonial norms, but merely the result of a non-hegemonic process of cultural interaction.

2.2.2.3. Hegemonic Contacts

The notion of hybridity as elaborated in postcolonial studies applies equally well to the ancient colonial situations where a dominance relationship between colonisers and colonised is present. The modern hegemonic colonial scheme, however, does not overlap exactly with the ancient one. There are structural differences that make drawing a parallel between ancient and modern empires misleading, a result of *a priori* definitions. The analogy is in fact based on a flawed interpretation drawn from Western national historiography. The best example is probably the case of Roman expansion and colonialism. Since the beginning of the nineteenth century the Roman Empire has often been presented as the archetype for modern nationalism and imperialism. The idealisation of the Roman conquest inspired the adoption of Roman symbols to legitimise the colonial cultural mission of modern European nations.[60] In Italy, this process was taken to extremes during fascism with the use of the *fasces*.[61] In archaeological terms, it led to attention being given to certain data such as urban layout, public monuments and elite manifestations in general, which conformed well to the pictured pattern of nationalistic cultural diffusion.[62] This historical reconstruction is, however, flawed. The Roman military expansion and colonial organisation was hegemonic, but the ancient notion was very different from the modern Western examples. The modern political agenda has obscured the importance of non-Roman components in the formation of the Roman Empire. The role of the communities incorporated has generally been ignored.[63] Particularly in the largely urbanised Mediterranean basin, 'non-Roman aristocracies played an important role in negotiating the terms of the incorporation of their communities within the Roman Empire and in participating in the benefits of the Empire'.[64] Ethnic boundaries were easily crossed and new and strong political networks emerged from the interaction of Roman and non-Roman aristocratic families.[65] Evidence for this can be found when examining the career of leaders from colonies, as the case of Emperor Hadrian illustrates so well. This is of course very different from modern imperialism; it was difficult, for example, for an Indian Rajah to become a member of the House of Lords under the British Empire. With the development of postcolonial approaches, archaeological research on Roman colonialism[66] showed that settlements in

60 See R Hingley *Roman Officers and English Gentlemen: the Imperial Origins of Roman Archaeology* (Routledge London 2000).

61 M Munzi *L'Epica del Ritorno* (L'Erma di Bretshneider Roma 2001).

62 N Terrenato 'The Deceptive Archetype: Roman Colonialism in Italy and Postcolonial Thought' in H Hurst and S Owen (eds) *Ancient Colonizations (analogy, similarity and difference)* (Duckworth London 2005) 64.

63 SJ Keay and N Terrenato (eds) *Italy and the West. Comparative Issues in Romanization* (Oxbow Oxford 2001).

64 N Terrenato 'The Deceptive Archetype: Roman Colonialism in Italy and Postcolonial Thought' in H Hurst and S Owen (eds) *Ancient Colonizations (analogy, similarity and difference)* (Duckworth London 2005) 66.

65 See G Woolf 'Beyond Romans and Natives' (1997) 3 World Archaeology 339.

66 J Webster and NJ Cooper (eds) *Roman Imperialism: Postcolonial Perspectives* (University of Leicester Leicester 1996).

'native' lands were rarely areas of conflicting interests, but rather involved a close interaction and cultural exchange. What went on in most cases 'was mainly a political and territorial reorganization, largely involving non-Roman people already residing in the area, and carried out by the central power with the cooperation of native elites'.[67]

2.2.2.4. Conclusions

The analysis above has suggested that the process of hybridisation is a recurring feature of all colonial and 'pseudo-colonial' situations. This is even if 'pseudo-colonialism' does not necessarily form part of the twentieth century imperialistic agenda, as it refers to a much broader idea, which deals with relationships not based on dominance and hegemony,[68] on the overwhelming superiority of the colonisers' culture. The study of archaeological remains, in particular, has shown that 'pseudo-colonisation' often involves non-antagonistic cultural and commercial relationships where the role of the local population in the process of settlement is not ignored. Even when hegemonic contact situations are in place (e.g. Romanisation), cultural evolution never amounts to a one-way process. It never consists of a process of mere acculturation[69] where the use of the colonisers' styles indicates the adoption of their cultural identity by local populations. Rather, it involves a more complex phenomenon of interaction and negotiation between colonisers' and indigenous traditions which eventually lead to the formation of a middle ground, of an original hybrid culture. In other words, it involves a process of hybridisation in line with the one observed in postcolonialist studies.

67 N Terrenato 'The Deceptive Archetype: Roman Colonialism in Italy and Postcolonial Thought' in H Hurst and S Owen (eds) *Ancient Colonizations (analogy, similarity and difference)* (Duckworth London 2005) 66.

68 Sometimes it has been quite the opposite, as the case of the Greek colonies which had to pay tribute to local powers well suggests. See the case of the Odrysian Kingdom in Thrace described in ZH Archibald *The Odrysian Kingdom of Thrace: Orpheus Unmasked* (OUP Oxford 1998).

69 The paradigm of barbarian versus civilised society.

Chapter 3

HYBRIDISATION AND LEGAL RECEPTION

Chapter 2 has shown that the idea of hybridity originating in postcolonial theory is applicable outside the boundaries of modern colonialism. It is a powerful tool to understanding the pattern of cultural change both under hegemonic and non-hegemonic contact situations. It may be of great relevance for social sciences in general. This chapter, by way of analogy with postcolonial discourse, argues for its employment in law. The process of hybridisation, it claims, is a formidable conceptual means to explain some of the complexities of the pattern of legal change, to refine and provide contents to the observation of the reception of law.

1. Analogy

1.1. Introduction

As discussed above,[1] the significance of legal borrowing as one of the most fertile sources of the evolution of law in the western world is undeniable. Historical evidence leads to the conclusion that legal change often follows from the stimulus of foreign models. Borrowing, however, is not peculiar to law. It reflects a general phenomenon of any socio-cultural system. Merely observing the episodes of borrowing in itself explains little about the characteristics of the process of development of law. It is a superficial achievement. While it is 'an important corrective to provincialism in the writing of legal history which, like most other forms of history, has been primarily national history',[2] it does not provide, among other things, a satisfactory explanation for the phenomenon of assimilation and the interaction between legal cultures.

In this light, the rigid perception of legal change suggested by the theorisation of 'legal transplants' is not helpful. It tends to oversimplify the pattern of reception and the relationship between legal paradigms. Hybridisation instead recognises the complexities of cross-cultural exchange and gives meaning to the consequences of borrowing. The interaction between cultures proceeds with the illusion of transferable forms and transparent knowledge, 'but leads increasingly into resistant, opaque and dissonant

1 See above *sub* Chapter 1, section 1.1.

2 EM Wise 'The Transplant of Legal Patterns' (1990) 38 Am J Comp L 1 at 22.

exchanges. It is in this tension that a "third space" emerges which can affect forms of political change that go beyond antagonistic binarisms between rulers and ruled'.[3]

1.2. Colonialism and the Process of Legal Borrowing

Building on this general understanding of the process of culture contact, this study finds an interesting analogy between the dynamics at the basis of colonialism and the movement of law from one country to another. It suggests that similar arguments to the ones posed in the postcolonial debate, refined by the employment of a broader notion of 'pseudo-colonialism', can explain the reception mechanism, the process of interaction between imported legal models and indigenous legal traditions.

As with colonial norms and standards, borrowed legal paradigms outside their original meanings become unsettled. They interact at different levels with local traditions, with certain indigenous perceptions and do not survive in their original forms. In the colonial context, neither colonial norms nor indigenous traditions survive; both give way to an entirely new way of doing things and perceiving meanings which is peculiar to each colonial situation. A new legal tradition, a third space that is peculiar to the specific contact situation is therefore created. Borrowed legal paradigms become 'almost the same, but not quite' in similar ways as, 'to be Anglicised is emphatically not to be English'.[4] It follows that legal hybrid identities are not the mere sum of features of colonial and indigenous background, but new creations in their own right.

1.3. Patterns of Legal Reception: an Overview

The significance of the process of hybridisation in unveiling the mechanism of legal reception is immediate when reflecting upon the conventional understanding of certain classical cases of borrowing involving entire legal systems. These are generally labelled as legal transplants and very little attention is paid to explaining the reception process.

A preliminary discussion that examines two of these 'broad' episodes of reception is set out below. It intends to show the limits of the model of legal transplants as a guide for interpreting the process of legal evolution and the importance of considering the role of culture contact in that respect. It will be argued that the idea of pure transferable forms and transparent knowledge is largely an illusion. It is only by focusing on the nature of the process of hybridisation that a meaning can be given to legal borrowing and to the mechanism of reception. In line with the scheme outlined in Chapter 2, this inquiry distinguishes between non-hegemonic and hegemonic contact situations. The reception of Roman law in Germany and the diffusion of the *Code Napoleon* in continental Europe will be adopted as examples of non-hegemonic and hegemonic contact situations, respectively.

[3] N Papastergiadis 'Tracing Hybridity in Theory' in T Werbner and T Modood (eds) *Debating Cultural Hybridity: Multi-cultural Identities and the Politics of Anti-racism* (Zed Books London 1997) 257–258.

[4] H Bhabha 'Of Mimicry and Men' in Bhabha H (eds) *The Location of Culture* (Routledge London 1994) 125.

1.3.1. Non-Hegemonic Contacts

1.3.1.1. The Context

The non-hegemonic diffusion of Roman law in Germany following the work of the glossators in Bologna (1070 AD circa) who examined and adapted the *Digest*[5] from the perspective of the contemporary reality[6] offers a well-known example of diffusion of a legal model and reception of an entire legal system.

1.3.1.2. Legal Transfers

The consolidated Justinian scheme of the *Corpus Iuris* as reinterpreted by Irnerius and Accursius (1185–1263) in Bologna made its way across most of continental Europe on the back of its clarity and conceptualisations that were apt to be implemented in late medieval culture.[7] The glossators' program of study created a trend in legal scholarship, and a convergence of interest on Italy took place. Roman law, in particular, embodied legal ideas about property that were useful to an emerging commercial and manufacturing elite and 'at the same time its uniform methods for the protection and management of possessions appealed to a growing corps of technicians engaged in these tasks'.[8] Above all, in contrast with existing native laws, the *Corpus Iuris* represented a closed body of thought that suggested a strong sense of comprehensiveness and integration.

Roman law was intended to act as a common system of justice for all the countries that formed part of the Empire (*ius commune*).[9] As established in the form of the *mos italicus*[10] doctrine promoted by the commentators Bartolus (1314–1357) and Baldus (1327–1400), Roman law generally applied on a subsidiary basis when local laws were uncertain or gave no basis for judgment.[11]

5 i.e. one of the founding parts of the *Corpus Iuris Justiniani* (i.e. the codification of Roman law carried out by the Emperor Justinian in the early sixth century AD) that gathered in fifty books the opinion and commentaries of Roman juriconsults.

6 As the pandectist scholarship later evidenced. See R Zimmermann *Roman Law, Contemporary Law, European Law* (OUP Oxford 2000) 44.

7 See F Wieacker *A History of Private Law in Europe* (OUP Oxford 1995) 38 and M Bellomo *The Common Legal Past of Europe, 1000–1800* (Catholic University of America Press Washington 1995).

8 G Strauss *Law, Resistance and the State: The Opposition to Roman Law in Reformation Germany* (Princeton UP Princeton 1986) 60. In general, see P Stein *Roman Law in European History* (CUP Cambridge 1999).

9 *Ius commune* is generally defined as anything that has to do with university teaching of law 'be it Roman law or canon law, be it public law or private law, be it in England or on the Continent' – C Donahue Jr 'Ius Commune, Canon Law and Common Law in England' (1991) 66 Tul L Rev 1748.

10 i.e. the 'Italian' way of understanding Roman law.

11 See DP Kelly 'Civil Science in the Renaissance: Jurisprudence Italian Style' (1979) 22 The Historical Journal 777 and G Dahm 'On the Reception of Roman and Italian Law in Germany' in G Strauss (ed) *Pre-Reformation Germany* (Macmillian London 1972) 282 at 296.

1.3.1.3. Legal Reception in Germany

Although it has been suggested that the process of reception of Roman law in Germany has been the result of direct legal transplantation,[12] recent contributions in legal history have demonstrated that it was not a unilateral imposition from above, nor did it take place in unison. The process has been more complex. It began from the cultural movement driven by contingents of students (most of whom were clerics) who crossed the Alps to learn the *mos italicus* and who then exported it to the universities of Cologne, Erfurt, Rostock, Leipzig and Heidelberg from the early fifteenth century. These legal experts, who later operated in the government and in the judiciary, introduced Roman methods in German law. They succeeded 'over the course of a century or so in transforming native law and legal procedure by making it learned, scholarly, professional, scientific'[13] in a process known in German scholarship as *Verwissenschaftlichung*. The reception was not *en bloc* or automatic. It was a gradual process that accelerated after the collapse of royal power and the rise of local forces.[14] It involved a dramatic conflict between Roman law and native law as the tensions around the interpretation of the old territorial code in Saxony (the *Sachsenspiegel*) suggests.[15] The reform of the judiciary, where appointment to the high courts was restricted to 'learned' judges,[16] the circumstance that after the constitution of the Imperial Chamber Court in 1495 judges had to make and explain their decisions in compliance with the principles of Roman law and the development of the habit of recurring to academic lawyers for opinions on difficult points of law, caused the end of the conflict in favour of the reception of Roman law as subsidiary body of law.[17] The final picture is not one of a uniform model, but rather consists of a patchy 'Romanised German law', very different from one place to another. This emerges clearly at the time of the municipal and territorial 'reformations' when old rules were replaced by single codes in a search to end uncertainty for clarity and uniformity. The comparison of Wutteenburg and Frankfurt (reformation) laws of 1557 and 1578, where a few traces of old native customs remained, with the Saxon code published in 1572, which left intact all indigenous territorial laws that had been found to agree with each other, is emblematic of the situation.[18]

1.3.1.4. Conclusions

The above outline of the diffusion of *ius commune* in the Middle Ages in Germany shows the limits of the paradigm of legal transplants. This leaves unanswered the

12 P Anderson *Lineages of the Absolutist State* (NBL London 1974) 22.

13 G Strauss Law, Resistance and the State: The Opposition to Roman Law in Reformation Germany (Princeton UP Princeton 1986) 76.

14 F Wieacker *A History of Private Law in Europe* (OUP Oxford 1995) 80.

15 Ibid 110 and 178.

16 See the comments on the inadequacy of the previous regime in JP Dawson *A History of Lay Judges* (Harvard UP Cambridge 1960) 94.

17 F Wieacker *A History of Private Law in Europe* (OUP Oxford 1995) 132.

18 G Strauss Law, *Resistance and the State: The Opposition to Roman Law in Reformation Germany* (Princeton UP Princeton 1986) 87.

question of the origin of the transfer, whether it is driven by mere admiration (prestige), historical necessity or political opportunity driven by the idea of an uninterrupted Roman reign carried forward by German emperors.[19] Above all, the theory of legal transplants provides an unsatisfactory account of the phenomenon of borrowing and legal reception. Describing the advent of Roman law in Germany in terms of transplant does not take into account the peculiarities of the interaction with local customs, the force of local resistance, and the way the original Roman scheme has been amended to create new original cultural meanings. More than the simple observation of the circulation of the Roman model as such, it is the study of the process of hybridisation and the creation of the new hybrid Romanised local paradigm that gives significance to the process of cultural change, of the evolution of law. The essence of legal change was not the adoption of Roman law *per se*, but the result of a pattern of cultural contacts, 'the outcome of a combined political, social, and cultural process, namely the ongoing penetration from the thirteenth to the sixteenth centuries of the writings of the Italian (and French) jurists of the Middle Ages, of the lawyers they trained, and of the methods and precepts they inculcated'.[20] It follows that hybridisation is more than just a way of describing the phenomenon of legal reception as an alternative to transplantation. Hybridisation offers more sophisticated way of understanding the complexities involved in the process of legal evolution as it gives meaning to the pattern of cultural interaction and makes it possible to identify the peculiarity of the resulting model as a new paradigm in its own right.

1.3.2. Hegemonic Contacts

1.3.2.1. General

The case of the introduction of the French Civil Code in Europe under the influence of the Napoleonic army provides a good example of imposition of foreign legal models.[21] This is not far from the typical pattern of legal domination generally imposed by colonial rulers.[22]

1.3.2.2. The Mechanism of Reception

The *Code Napoleon* enacted in 1804 entered into force in the countries that were annexed to France or brought under its rule as the result of military expansion. Although it is often reported as a classical example of legal transplant,[23] a closer look shows that the

19 The so-called 'imperial connection'. Quite significantly, Roman law was later designated by German emperors as 'Imperial law' (*Kaiserrecht*).

20 F Wieacker *A History of Private Law in Europe* (OUP Oxford 1995) 95.

21 In general, see K Zweigert and H Kotz *Introduction to Comparative Law* (OUP Oxford 1998) 100.

22 See U Baxi 'The Colonialist Heritage' in P Legrand and R Munday (ed) *Comparative Legal Studies: Traditions and Transitions* (CUP Cambridge 2003) 46 and L Benton *Law and Colonial Cultures* (CUP Cambridge 2002).

23 M Graziadei 'Transplants and Receptions' in M Reinmann and R Zimmermann (eds) *The Oxford Handbook of Comparative Law* (OUP Oxford 2006) 444 and 447.

pattern of enactment and reception has not been uniform. Sometimes the original scheme was imposed in the original form (Belgium), sometimes in a slightly altered way to accommodate national legal practices (Netherlands, Baden) and, occasionally, it was not even translated, but enacted in French (Poland). Although the *Code* was imposed by force, the ideas contained in it were not generally abolished following Napoleon's fall. In Germany, the *Code* was repealed *in toto* in 1814 where it had only been introduced shortly before.[24] This was not the case in some regions of the left bank of the Rhine (Rhineland and Palatinate), nor the case of Baden where the German version of the *Code* (the *Badisches Landrecht* of 1809)[25] remained in force until 1890. Not to mention, of course, the case of Alsace and Lorraine where the *Code* not only remained in force until 1900, but was reinstated after the re-annexation in 1919.[26] In Italy, the *Codice civile* of 1865 was in its essential elements a translation from the French code.[27]

The reasons for the various patterns of reception at the time of enactment and during the age of restoration cannot be understood by referring to the paradigm of legal transplants. An explanation can be found only in the history of the mechanism of culture contact.[28] The different patterns of reception testify to the existence of a process of hybridisation for the formation of new legal identities and meanings. For example, where reception was most successful and the interaction of the local legal traditions with the scheme of the *Code* proved not conflicting, it was because the scheme of the *Code* was not entirely novel. It rested in fact to a great extent on the foundation of a common background given by the *ius commune* tradition and answered to the shared needs and interests of the nineteenth-century bourgeoisie. Even in those circumstances, the acceptance of the model did not necessarily mean abandoning local legal culture for entirely new elements. The text in fact proved flexible and it was often accompanied by a great work of mediation, by 'reforms that excluded parts of it, such as the articles on marriage or divorce. Other parts that were considered defective from a technical point of view were also often rejected by importing countries (e.g. the regulation of mortgages)'.[29]

24 e.g. the Hanse cities and Lippe (1812).

25 Done by Bräun taking German conditions properly into account. See F Wieacker *A History of Private Law in Europe* (OUP Oxford 1995) 274.

26 F Wieacker *A History of Private Law in Europe* (OUP Oxford 1995) 272. On the pattern of reception of the Code Napoleon in Germany, see the qualitative comparative analysis carried out by EE Arvind and L Stirton 'Explaining the Reception of the Code Napoleon in Germany: a Fuzzy-set Qualitative Comparative Analysis' (2010) 30 Legal Studies 1.

27 S Solimano *Il Letto di Procuste': Diritto e Politica nella Formazione del Codice Civile Unitario. I Progetti Cassinis (1860–1861)* (Giuffrè Milano 2003). See also the comments in K Zweigert and H Kotz *Introduction to Comparative Law* (OUP Oxford 1998) 104. It has, however, authoritatively been held that the Italian Codice civile enacted in 1865 (and the following code in 1942) was interpreted in accordance to the historical method of German Pandectism. Thus, the 'private law of Italy is linked to the French legal family by shared Latin attitudes and awareness of the French Revolution (which was also the first Italian one) and it is connected with the German legal family through the Pandectism of the nineteenth century, whose influence there is still quite strong'. F Wieacker *A History of Private Law in Europe* (OUP Oxford 1995) 275.

28 See J Gordley 'Myths of the French Civil Code' (1994) 42 Am J Comp L 459.

29 M Graziadei 'Transplants and Receptions' in M Reinmann and R Zimmermann (eds) *The Oxford Handbook of Comparative Law* (OUP Oxford 2006) 450.

1.3.2.3. The Significance of the Reception of the Civil Code

In essence, the history of the different patterns of reception in various countries and the reaction to the repeal of the Civil Code exemplify the significance of culture contact in understanding the pattern of legal change and show the relevance of explaining the formation of new legal identities and meanings in terms of a process of hybridisation. As was the case for colonialism, discussed in Chapter 2, the history of the diffusion of the Civil Code shows that binary classifications based on rigid schemes end up presenting a stereotypical and simplified reality.

1.3.2.4. Conclusions

It follows from the above that legal borrowing, even when imposed under hegemonic circumstances, involves complex processes of reception that need to be disentangled to give a proper socio-cultural contextualisation. This is the same idea at the heart of the ambivalent relationship between colonisers and colonised culture described in postcolonial theory. History demonstrates that the model of legal transplants is not a flexible paradigm and that it may possibly be misleading. It does not provide an accurate representation of the process of legal evolution, as it does not explain the tension and interaction with the existing legal traditions. The idea of pure transferable forms and transparent knowledge is largely an illusion. It is only by considering the process of hybridisation where an area of mediation peculiar to each specific contact situation is created (a hybrid paradigm) that an appropriate meaning can be given to legal borrowing and to the mechanism of reception.

2. The Test Case

2.1. General

The contribution of comparative jurisprudence[30] advanced in the previous chapters cannot be addressed appropriately only on theoretical grounds or by mere reference to examples of borrowing involving entire legal systems without coming at the expense of the accuracy and reliability of the analysis. A focus is necessary in order to explore its full significance and to clarify the meaning of the general episodes of borrowing based on the framework of hegemonic/non-hegemonic contacts presented above. In the following chapters, a test case is used for this purpose. This concerns the transfer of shares in England. It considers both the scenario where the shares are held directly by the owner (direct holding system) and the scenario of one or more persons being in the chain of ownership (indirect holding system).

30 This terminology is borrowed from W Ewald 'Comparative Jurisprudence (I): What Was It Like to Try a Rat?' (1995) 143 U Pa L Rev 1889.

2.2. *Rationale*

There are various reasons justifying the choice of the test case underlying this study. The three most relevant will be outlined below.

2.2.1. England

England represents a challenging case for examining the theory of legal transplants and for considering the pattern of legal evolution. British historians have often claimed that the development of English law has consisted in an autochthonous national achievement, independent from continental law.[31] Within Europe, England, it is argued in a leading textbook on English legal history, 'remained an island in law as well as in fact [...] As so, English law flourished in isolation from Europe'.[32] The common lawyer in the words of Maitland was someone who 'knew nothing and cared nothing for any system but its own'.[33]

This study, in line with others,[34] contends that this perception is a myth. England was never entirely isolated from continental culture. In very general terms, a number of circumstances and connections suggest that 'large areas of English law (in particular the law of contract) were inspired, characterized or influenced by the ideas and concept, the rules and institutions as well as the general intellectual undercurrents of the European *ius commune*.'[35] The force of the civilian ideas introduced at different times by the publications of Bracton, Blackstone[36] and Birks[37] and the influence of the 'treatise writers' in the eighteenth and nineteenth centuries in shaping the evolution of English law have been all well documented.[38] Further examples can be seen in the importance of canon law in influencing the formation of the jurisdiction of equity,[39] the diffusion of the legal literature produced by the English 'civilians'[40] and the use of the *lex mercatoria* in the Court of Admiralty[41] before commercial law was incorporated into the developing

31 See RC van Caenegem *The Birth of English Common Law* (CUP Cambridge 1988) 85.

32 JH Baker *An Introduction to English Legal History* (Butterworths London 2002) 29.

33 FW Maitland 'Why the History of English Law is not Written' in HAL Fisher (eds) *The Collected Papers of Frederic William Maitland*, vol 1 (CUP Cambridge 1911) 488.

34 See R Zimmermann 'A Change in Perspective' in Id (ed) *Roman Law, Contemporary Law, European Law* (OUP Oxford 2001) 111.

35 R Zimmermann 'Roman Law and European Legal Unity' in A Hartkamps, M Hesselink, E Hondious, C Joustra and E du Perron (eds) *Towards a European Civil Code* (Kluwer The Hague 1998) 34.

36 See A Watson 'The Impact of Justinian's Institutes on Academic Treaties: Blackstone's Commentaries' in Id (ed) *Roman Law and Comparative Law* (University of Georgia Press Georgia 1991).

37 See P Birks *Unjust Enrichment* (OUP Oxford 2005); and Id (ed) *English Private Law* (OUP Oxford 2000).

38 See Simpson 'The Rise and Fall of the Legal Treatise. Legal Principles and Forms of Legal Literature' (1981) 48 U Chi L Rev 632; and M Graziadei 'Changing Images of the Law in XIX Century English Legal Thought (The Continental Impulse)' in M Reinmann (ed) *The Reception of Continental Ideas in the Common Law World 1820–1920* (Duncker & Humlot Berlin 1993).

39 In general, see RE Helmholz *Canon Law and the Law of England* (Hambledon London 1987).

40 i.e. the graduates of English universities where Roman law was taught. See DR Coquilette *The Civilian Writers of Doctors' Commons* (Duncker & Humblot Berlin 1988) that gathers in one volume four articles published in the Boston Law Journal from 1986.

41 See JH Baker *An Introduction to English Legal History* (Butterworths London 2002) 123.

national legal system. Even the *Magna Carta*, it has been observed,[42] was influenced by the continental legal tradition. In short, English lawyers were familiar with international sources of law and it is beyond doubt 'that they borrowed from them, that they did so more than once in a great while, and that this borrowing has been important in the development of the common law'.[43]

This study contributes to the historical discussion sketched above by looking at certain areas of English commercial law, arguing that the mechanism of the reception of law in those contexts cannot be qualified in terms of legal transplants. It examines, in particular, the influence of the Italian legal tradition and the pattern of formation of supranational legal instruments in order to describe the characters of the process of hybridisation. Starting from an overview of the current legal framework, it first considers how it has been shaped by the interaction of imported models and by the force of pre-existing indigenous legal tradition. It then shows how a similar pattern of cultural interaction and hybridisation can be observed when reflecting on the modes of formation and implementation of certain supranational legal instruments.

2.2.2. Modes of Share Transfer

The transferability of interests is a distinguishing structural characteristic of modern company law. Together with other features, it explains the rise and success of the corporate form at the basis of modern industrial capitalism.[44] What is argued in this study is that the concept of transferable joint stock capital was not an English invention, but possibly the result of a complex evolution of certain schemes of commercial association well known in medieval Italy. These models were borrowed and employed in early English maritime partnerships in the sixteenth and seventeenth centuries. Hybridisation for the purpose of this study is the story of the process of colonisation and cultural integration of the Italian models as evolved from the *societas* within the pre-existing English legal framework. This has been, as will be explained in Part II, a process of commercial (non-hegemonic) contacts and indigenous reactions.

The point of significance for the inquiry is not the fact of transferability *per se*, but the meaning and the method of transfer. In other words, the reason why the paradigm formed at the time of the advent of the joint stock company and at the base of the modern legal characterisation of the circulation of registered shares (both certificated and uncertificated) evolved along the lines of the civilian concept of contractual novation rather than the one of negotiability or assignment. The aim is to find the possible pattern of borrowing and to understand the process of hybridisation as the origin for the formation and later evolution of the method of transfer of registered shares in England.[45]

42 See RE Helmholz 'Magna Carta and the Ius commune' (1996) 66 U Chi L Rev 297.

43 RH Helmholz 'Continental Law and Common Law: Historical Strangers or Companions?' (1990) 6 Duke L J 1208.

44 See R Kraakman, J Armour, P Davies, L Enriques, H Hansmann, G Hertig, K Hopt, H Kanda and E Rock *The Anatomy of Corporate Law* (OUP Oxford 2009) 11.

45 This is particularly interesting phenomenon, as the concept of novation for shares transfer never took root in the English legal discourse.

The peculiarity of the resulting (hybrid) scheme becomes even clearer when contrasting this with the different trajectory for share warrants to bearer.

2.2.3. Holding Patterns

There is a third reason that makes the chosen test case an interesting one for the scope of this study. This is related to the circumstance that the indirect system of holding shares is at the heart of various international law reform initiatives on post-trading.[46] These normative programmes have been set up at national and at international level under the influential impulse of a number of reports and contributions promoted by the industry, independent consultative groups[47] and international organisations[48] in response to issues of legal uncertainty that have dramatically arisen from the evolution in financial practice. For the purpose of this study, the significance of the ongoing law reform debate is the scheme of legal evolution, the circumstance that it involves a process of negotiations and cultural interactions among international participants. Contrary to the pattern in the evolution of state legislation either by independent creation or by borrowing, this model consists of a regulated mechanism of harmonisation set out by the contributions of delegates and national experts at international *fora*. The final outcome, it will be argued in Part III, is a common framework to be later implemented at national level under the force of its hegemonic authority. It follows that under this scenario the evolution of domestic legislation involves a process of hybridisation between the international instrument as enacted in the domestic jurisdiction and the pre-existing framework. This suggests that the notion of hybridity as originated in postcolonial theory and employed in the historical discussion on legal transplants is also a valid conceptual means to explain the pattern of legal evolution in prospective terms.

46 i.e. on the processes of delivery of securities in fulfilment of contractual obligation (settlement) and on the ways the risk during the interval between trading and settlement is managed (clearing).

47 Immediate reference goes to Group of *Thirty Clearance and Settlement in the World's Securities Markets* (1989) and Id *Global Clearing and Settlement: A plan of Action* (2003). See also the 'Giovannini Group' *Cross-Border Clearing and Settlement Arrangements in the European Union* (November 2001), available at <www.ec.europa.eu/internal_market/financial-markets/docs/clearing/first_giovannini_report_en.pdf> (accessed 7 August 2013); Id *Second Report on EU Clearing and Settlement Arrangements* (April 2003), available at <www.ec.europa.eu/internal_market/financialmarkets/docs/clearing/second_giovannini_report_en.pdf> (accessed 7 August 2013) (the 'Giovannini Group' was formed in 1996 to advise the European Commission on issues relating to EU financial integration and the efficiency of euro-denominated financial markets. It consisted of financial market participants and met under the chairmanship of Alberto Giovannini) and the Financial Markets Law Committee c/o the Bank of England *Property Interests in Investment Securities* – Issue 3 (5 July 2004), available at <www.fmlc.org/papers/fmlc1_3_july04.pdf> (accessed 7 August 2013). See the analysis in Part III below.

48 See IOSCO/BIS *Recommendations for Securities Settlement Systems* (November 2001), available at <www.bis.org/publ/cpss42.pdf> (accessed 7 August 2013) and UNIDROIT Study Group for the Preparation of Harmonised Substantive Rules on Transactions on Transnational and Connected Capital Markets (Restricted Group on Harmonised Substantive Rules regarding Securities Held with an Intermediary) *Position Paper* (August 2003) part of Study LXXVIII <www.unidroit.org/english/documents/2003/study78/s-78-008-e.pdf> (accessed 7 August 2013).

Summary

SUMMARY OF PART I

Part I outlined the *raison d' être* of this study. It addressed the significance of the concept of hybridity within the comparative debate on legal change. In doing so, it examined the theory that describes the movement of law from one country to another by using the metaphor of legal transplant. Two irreconcilable approaches were discussed. The first one suggested that the evolution of law is largely autonomous from society as it consists primarily of a function of rules being imported from another legal system. The second one established that the development of law cannot take place through borrowing because law mirrors, and is responsive to, situated linguistic, cultural and moral national frameworks. Both views were found to fall short: the first one ignores the relationship between legal comparison and sociology of law, and the second one over-simplifies the concepts of language and culture.

Chapter 1 offered a proposal to tackle the comparative conundrum. The inquiry opened with the observation that borrowing is not necessarily a legal phenomenon, but that it reflects a common trend of social life, a mechanism of culture diffusion. It applies to law because law is itself a form of culture. Building on this, it was, however, noted that the fact of borrowing *per se* has a mere descriptive value and says little about culture interaction and the assimilation process.

For this reason, Chapter 2 considered recent contributions on culture contact and culture change and concluded that they provide an interesting explanation for the process of borrowing and legal evolution. The analysis centred on the notion of hybridity, a fundamental theme in cultural and post colonialist studies that highlights the 'in-betweenness' of people and their actions in colonial situations. By complying with colonial norms and standards and at the same time maintaining the indigenous perceptions, colonial people develop new cultural norms and standards of their own. They create new traditions. The process of hybridisation was illustrated by reference to cases taken from archaeological studies. It was argued that the same dynamics can be used to explain the reception mechanism in law. As with colonial norms and standards, legal paradigms borrowed outside their original meanings become unsettled. They interact at different levels with local traditions, with certain indigenous perceptions, and do not survive in their original identities. Irrespective of whether this happens by way of imposition or as a result of a voluntary process (hegemonic and non-hegemonic contact situations) a new legal tradition, a third space that is peculiar to the specific contact situation is therefore created. Borrowed legal paradigms in the new environment become almost the same as the original ones, but not quite.

Chapter 3 concluded the theoretical analysis of Part I. It looked at the idea of hybridity outside the narrow boundaries of modern colonialism based on the imperialistic notion of dominance and focused on the legal debate on transplantation. In doing so, it briefly considered two well-known episodes of transfer of the entire legal system under hegemonic and non-hegemonic contact situations. It concluded that in both cases legal borrowing involves complex processes of reception similar to one described in postcolonial theory for the ambivalent relationship between colonisers and colonised culture. An appropriate meaning can be given to legal borrowing and to the mechanism of reception only by considering the process of hybridisation where an area of mediation peculiar to each specific contact situation is created. This introduced the more specific test case on the circulation of English shares, which will be developed in Parts II and III.

PART II

THE CIRCULATION OF SHARES

Introduction

INTRODUCTION TO PART II

This Part of the book considers the first leg of the case study on comparative jurisprudence according to the plan outlined at the end of Part I. It examines the historical evolution of the mechanisms by which shares in companies are transferred and refines Watson's thesis on legal transplants with arguments on cultural interaction originating in the postcolonial debate. In doing so, it shows that, contrary to certain preconceptions that claim the joint stock company and its structural elements of association to be 'Britain's most influential invention',[1] there is little that is inherently indigenous in its original form. The joint stock company emerged in the sixteenth century with the growth of British trade when certain commercial models borrowed from abroad were progressively integrated into the pre-existing national legal framework. It is argued below that this amounted to a process of hybridisation.

The analysis in this Part has two chapters, Chapters 4 and 5. They explain the mechanism of legal borrowing and the process of reception at the root of the current pattern for the transfer of registered shares and share warrants to bearer, respectively. The reason for the separate inquiry is dictated by the fact that, even if registered shares and share warrants to bearer have the same economic function as units of the corporate capital, they are distinct in terms of their legal nature, regulation and modes of circulation. While in the case of registered shares (unless dematerialised) the certificate is mere evidence of the shares held by the member and title is acquired through entry in the register of shareholders, title to share warrants to bearer is inherent in the physical control of the warrant and passes by manual delivery. It will be shown below that these differences have a historical explanation. More precisely, it will be pointed out that the model for the circulation of registered shares has its origin in the evolution of the scheme of the medieval partnership, and the one for share warrants to bearer has its roots in certain peculiar developments of nineteenth century corporate finance. Even if the seeds of both instruments were not indigenous, they adapted and evolved with peculiar (hybrid) characteristics in the English legal framework.

1 This thesis has been recently reiterated by J Micklethwait and A Wooldridge *The Company, A Short History of a Revolutionary Idea* (Phoenix Paperbacks London 2005).

Chapter 4

THE TRANSFER OF REGISTERED SHARES

The conventional view is that the genealogy of the modern English limited liability company (and the mechanism of transfer of registered shares) has its roots in the scheme of the partnership and of the unincorporated joint stock company formed by contract or under a deed of settlement.[1] This view identifies an important thread in explaining the history of the current legal framework and highlights the relevance of legal tradition in shaping legal change.[2] It is suggested in this chapter that this view offers, however, a partial representation of the process of legal evolution. This is done in three steps. Section 1 presents the founding elements and characteristics underlying the modern law of registered shares.[3] Section 2 sets out the orthodox interpretation of the immediate genealogy of the modern English company and of the techniques of transfer of membership. Building on this analysis, section 3 argues that the current legal characterisation of the circulation of registered shares has been shaped to a significant extent by legal borrowing from the Genoese model of maritime partnership (the *societas maris*) employed for part-ownership in ships in England starting from the seventeenth century. It also argues that the reception of that scheme did not occur in its original form, but that it was adapted through a process of hybridisation in accordance with the indigenous fellowship traditions of the guilds.

1. The Current Legal Framework

The paragraphs below set the boundaries and identify the subject matter of the inquiry. The investigation focuses on the legal nature and the (possible) physical manifestation of registered shares, establishing how legal title is transferred (sections 1.1 and 1.2).

1 See CA Cooke *Corporation, Trust and Company* (Manchester UP Manchester 1950) 45–47 and 86–88 and P Ireland 'Company Law and the Myth of Shareholder Ownership' (1999) 62 MLR 32 at 39.

2 The 'doctrinal path dependence' identified by E Micheler *Property in Securities – A Comparative Study* (CUP Cambridge 2007).

3 The peculiar cases of alienation of shares by operation of law are outside the scope of this study and are not considered in the following analysis (See section 773 of the Companies Act 2006 and Uncertificated Securities Regulations 2001 (SI 2001/3755) reg 27(6)). See also the provisions contained in the default articles of association for private limited companies by shares registered on or after 5 October 2009 – Companies (Model Articles) Regulations 2008 (SI 2008/3229), arts 27 and 28).

Although this necessarily involves separate studies of the law of certificated and uncertificated shares (section 1.3), the underlying legal characterisation of the nature of the transfer in terms of novation remains identical (section 1.4). Finally, some attention is dedicated to the '*bona fide* purchaser' defence as a fundamental rule for understanding the nature of transactions related to registered shares (section 1.5). This specific issue will be discussed again in Part III when comparing it with the protection available for innocent purchasers of intermediated shares.

1.1. Legal Nature

In order to describe how registered shares are transferred it is first necessary to establish what shares are and, in particular, what their legal nature is. The Companies Act 2006 states that shares are personal property.[4] They are not in the nature of real estate. Unlike the case of a partnership, shares do not give the shareholders any proprietary interest in the company assets. This follows from a long line of cases originating in the early nineteenth century,[5] which clarify that there is no direct proprietary link between the company's property and the member's rights in that property. Shareholders are not the owners at law or in equity of the company's property. In *Short v Treasury Commissioners* Evershed LJ conclusively stated the point, declaring that: 'shareholders are not, in the eye of law, part owners of the undertaking. The undertaking is something different from the totality of the share-holdings'.[6]

Issued (registered) shares are rather *choses* in action as opposed to *choses* in possession. In *Re VGM Holdings Ltd*, Lord Green clarified that 'a share is a *chose* in action. A *chose* in action implies the existence of some person entitled to rights which are rights in action as distinct from rights in possession'.[7] More precisely, shares are rights under a contract and 'each of them represents an indivisible collection of contractual and statutory rights,

4 With the exception of Scotland where shares are moveable property – section 541 of the Companies Act 2006. This normative qualification of a share as property in its own right has posed certain taxonomical concerns in setting the boundaries of the law of personal property within the scheme of the Justinian classification of property and obligation. Pretto (A Pretto-Sakmann *Boundaries of Personal Property* (Hart Oxford 2005), in particular, has recently attempted to define the boundaries of the law of personal property by employing shares and intermediated shares to test under different hypotheses where the frontier of personal property lies. Her conclusion has been that (personal) 'property in the strict sense cannot be stretched beyond rights *in rem locabilem*' (at 225) and that therefore shares and intermediated shares are not property as opposed to obligations, but merely property in the layman's understanding of property as wealth. Pretto's contribution represents a challenging proposal resulting from a sophisticated taxonomical exercise, but is not consistent with the existing law (see section 541 of the Companies Act 2006) and the conventional understanding of the legal nature of shares (see book reviews McGhee in (2006) LQR 525 and P Eden (2006) Conveyancer and Property Lawyer 309).

5 *Bligh v Brent* (1837) 2 Y&C Ex 268 at 294, 160 ER 397; *Myers v Perigal* (1851) 2 De GM&G 599 at 600, 42 ER 1006; *Watson v Spratley* (1854) 10 Ex 222 at 243, 156 ER 424; *Ashworth v Munn* (1880) 15 ChD 363 (CA) at 368, 372 and 375–6 *per* Cotton LJ.

6 [1948] 1 KB 116 (CA) at 122.

7 [1942] 1 Ch 235 (CA) at 241. See also a similar statement in *The Colonial Bank v Whinney* (1886) 11 App Cas 426 (HL).

each one of which is a legal *chose* in action';[8] a bundle of contractual and statutory rights against the company relating to dividends, winding up and voting;[9] a *sui generis* species of *choses* in action with their own rules, according to Millett J.[10] This notion is reflected in the *ratio* of section 33(1) of the Companies Act 2006 which establishes that the provisions of a company's constitution bind the company and its members to the same extent as if they were covenants on the part of the company and each member to observe those provisions.

Under English law, however, shares also present certain unique characteristics other than being a mere bundle of contractual rights and obligations between the company and its members. In particular, a shareholder also enjoys some proprietary interest in the company. Paraphrasing the often quoted dictum of Farwell J in *Borland's Trustee v Steel Bros & Co. Ltd*, a share does not consist only in a series of mutual covenants entered into by all shareholders *inter se* and the company and the shareholders. It is also 'the interest of a shareholder in the company measured by a sum of money, for the purpose of liability in the first place, and of interest in the second'.[11] As will be shown below, this peculiar proprietary nature of shares follows from the circumstances that, historically, companies held their property in trust for their members[12] and that shares were transferable at law at the time when other *choses* in action were not legally assignable.[13] Calling shares property is therefore possible under English law provided that it is clear that today they do not comprise any proprietary interest in the company's assets.

1.2. *Physical Manifestation*

A second preliminary inquiry before discussing how registered shares are transferred centres on the significance of their possible physical manifestation. As will be shown in Chapter 5, this is an important element of distinction between registered shares and share warrants to bearer.

8 RR Pennington *Pennigton's Company Law* (Butterworths London 2001) 398.

9 This point in presented in S Worthington 'Shares and Shareholders: Property, Power and Entitlement. Part 1' (2001) 22 Company Lawyer 260. See also G Barton 'The Legal Nature of a Share' in N Palmer and E McKendrick (eds) *Interests in Goods* (LLP London 1998) 111.

10 See *Macmillan Inc v Bishopsgate Trust (No 3)* [1995] 1 WLR 978 (ChD) at 992.

11 *Borland's Trustee v Steel Bros & Co. Ltd* [1901] 1 Ch 279 (ChD) at 288, cited with approval by Lord Russel in *IRC v Crossman* [1937] AC 26 (HL) at 66.

12 And, therefore, shares embodied members' equitable rights of property. See *Child v Hudson's* Bay (1723) 2 P Wms 207 at 208–9, 24 ER 702; *Harrison v Pryse* (1740) Barn Ch 324 at 326, 27 ER 664; and *Ashby v Blackwell and Million Bank* (1765) Amb 503 at 505, 27 ER 326.

13 See *Pinkett v Wright* (1842) 2 Hare 120, 67 ER 50 and, especially, *Poole v Middleton* (1861) 29 Beav 646 at 650, 54 ER 778 where Sir Romilly MR conclusively held that shares were *choses* in action capable of transfer ('shares in joint stock companies [...] are in fact in the nature of property, and according to the ordinary rule, every person possessed of property has the right, by law, to dispose of it, except to the extent that he may be fettered by any contract which diminishes or derogates from that right').

Unless dematerialised,[14] registered shares are represented by certificates and, as such, belong to the category of documented intangibles,[15] but the paper certificate does not carry the value of the intangible rights that it evidences.[16] This becomes clear when closely observing the mechanism whereby a share comes to be issued and transferred. On issue, when the allotment of shares is concluded, the purchaser has merely an unconditional right to be included in the company's register by virtue of the contractual process of offer and acceptance of shares between the issuer and the prospective shareholder. It is only the registration in the company's register of members[17] that confers membership of the company and title to the shares.[18] In the words of Lord Templeman in *National Westminster Bank plc v Inland Revenue Commissioners*, 'no person can be a shareholder until he is registered. A person who is not a shareholder by registration cannot claim that the share has been issued to him, but only that the company is bound by contract to issue a share to him'.[19] By the same principle, transfer of legal title in a share by an existing member is not complete until registration has occurred.[20]

1.3. Modes of Transfer

The manner in which legal title to shares is transferred is at the core of this section. The mechanism of transfer depends on whether registered shares are certificated or uncertificated (dematerialised). A description of the procedure for each case is outlined in turn under 1.3.1 and 1.3.2 below. This provides a comprehensive technical background for the discussion on the juridical nature of legal transfer that is set out in section 1.4.

1.3.1. Certificated Shares

The procedure for transferring legal title to English registered shares represented by paper certificates is for the transferor to execute a share transfer form by which he disposes for a consideration, if any, of a number of shares to the transferee provided the latter accepts the conditions set in the company's articles of association. More precisely, the transfer is conditional upon the delivery of a properly executed 'instrument of

14 By definition uncertificated shares are not represented by certificates. They exist in a pure electronic form. Section 769(2)(a) of the Companies Act 2006 allows companies to dispense with the issue of a share certificate by the terms of issue. See Uncertificated Securities Regulations in 2001 (SI 2001/3755) pursuant to section 784 of the Companies Act 2006.

15 See the analysis of A Pretto-Sakmann *Boundaries of Personal Property* (Hart Oxford 2005) 73, drawing from the classification in E McKendrick *Goode on Commercial Law* (Penguin London 2010) 51.

16 See *The Colonial Bank v Cady* (1890) LR 15 App Cas 267 (HL) *per* Lord Halsbury at 272, *per* Lord Hershell at 285 and *per* Lord Morris at 287.

17 Sections 113 and 771 of the Companies Act 2006.

18 Section 112 of the Companies Act 2006.

19 [1995] 1 AC 119 (HL) at 126.

20 See *Societe Generale de Paris v Walker* (1886) LR 11 App Cas 20 *per* Lord Selborne at 28; *Shropshire Union Railways and Canal Co v The Queen* (1875) LR 7 HL 496 *per* Lord Cairns at 509 and *per* Lord Hatherley at 512–13; *Roots v Williamson* (1888) LR 38 ChD 485 *per* Stirling J at 494; and *Macmillan Inc v Bishopsgate Trust (No 3)* [1995] 1 WLR (ChD) at 1001.

transfer'[21] together with the share certificate[22] from the transferor. This is subject to certain statutory exceptions.[23] The company, unless its articles impose restrictions on transferability,[24] ascertains that the documents are formally in order, bear the requisite stamp[25] and then amends the register by entering the transferee's name in the register of members as owner of the shares in place of the transferor.[26] There is authority for the proposition that nothing short of registration can be accepted to pass the legal title to the shares to the transferee.[27] Finally, as soon as is practicable and in any event within two months after the date on which the transfer is lodged with the company, a new share certificate is issued to the transferee.[28] The transferor's share certificate is then cancelled by the company.

The registration in the company's register of members and the issuance of the share certificate do not provide, however, conclusive evidence of ownership. They are only *prima facie* evidence of title.[29] Title to shares vests only in the person who can show a complete chain of title from the original issue by the company down to his acquisition. Consequently, if the transferor's title to shares registered in the company's register of members is defective for some reason, the transferee will not obtain a better title than the transferor had[30] and the company can be compelled by court order to rectify the

21 Section 770(1)(a) of the Companies Act 2006. The actual form of the instrument of transfer (not for listed shares) is often provided by the Stock Transfer Act 1963, unless the articles establish otherwise or the Act is not applicable (unlimited companies and companies limited by guarantee – section 1(4) of the Stock Transfer Act 1963) – section 554 of the Companies Act 2006.

22 In the absence of an *ad hoc* statutory provision in this respect, directors may refuse to register the transfer, unless it is delivered or the loss accounted for: see *Re East Wheal Martha Mining Co* (1863) 33 Beav 119.

23 e.g. the exemption of the Stock Transfer Act 1982 (section 770(1)(b)(i) of the Companies Act 2006) and regulations made under sections 784 *et seq* of the Companies Act 2006.

24 e.g. in the case of breach of rights of pre-emption or first refusal, the company has a power to refuse to register the transfer. See Companies (Model Articles) Regulations 2008 (SI 2008/3229) art 26(5) (Private Companies Limited by Shares). The limit to the powers attributed to the directors of the company is clearly stated in *Re Smith, Knight & Co, Weston's Case* (1868) LR 4 Ch App 20; *Re Copal Varnish Co Ltd* [1917] 2 Ch 349 at 353–354 *per* Eve J. See also *Greenhalgh v Mallard* [1943] 2 All ER 234 (CA) at 237 *per* Greene MR; *Re New Cedos Engineering Co Ltd* [1994] 1 BCLC 797 (ChD) at 806 *per* Oliver J. It follows that not all registrations necessarily mean that the transfers are valid. It is still possible for the directors of a company to exercise their right to decline the registration of a transfer. See section 771 of the Companies Act 2006 and *Re Hackney Pavilion Ltd* [1924] 1 Ch 276 (ChD) at 280 *per* Lord Astbury followed in *Moodie v W&J Shepherd (Bookbinders)* (1950) SC (HL) 60.

25 Sections 5 and 19 of the Stamp Act 1891.

26 Section 112 of the Companies Act 2006.

27 *Ireland v Hart* [1902] 1 Ch 522 at 526 *per* Joyce J.

28 Section 776 of the Companies Act 2006.

29 Sections 127 and 768 of the Companies Act 2006, respectively. As far as the significance of company's register in evidencing legal title, see also the *dictum* in *Reese River Silver Mining Co v Smith* (1869) LR 4 HL 64 at 77 *per* Lord Westbury and at 80 *per* Lord Cairns. With respect to share certificates, consider *Re Baku Consolidated Oilfields Ltd* [1993] BCC 653.

30 e.g. because it involved the use of a forged instrument of transfer. See *Welch v Bank of England* [1955] Ch 508, 1 ER 811 and *Taylor v Midland Rly Co* (1860) 28 Beav 287, 54 ER 872.

register.[31] This is in line with the general rule of property law which states that a person cannot confer a better title than he himself has (*nemo dat quod non habet*),[32] subject to the cases on title by estoppel discussed below. In the event of inconsistency/conflict between the evidence provided by the register of members[33] and a share certificate[34] the register of members prevails over what is stated in the share certificate.[35]

Notwithstanding this general rule on the transfer of shares when the transferor's title is defective, English law recognises certain cases in which the true owner of shares may be estopped by representation[36] from denying the validity of an unauthorised[37] or irregular transfer.[38] In force of these rules, the owner of legal title to shares may under very exceptional circumstances be estopped from proving his entitlement. For this to happen, it is essential that the transferee is unaware of the defect in his transferor's title to shares at the time of the transfer and that the creation of the apparent title is ascribable to the transferor.[39]

A different application of the doctrine of estoppel arises with respect to the representations contained in the share certificate. These are declarations by the company 'to all the world that the person in whose name the certificate is made out, and to whom

31 Section 125 of the Companies Act 2006. See *Barton v North Staffordshire Ry Co* (1888) 38 ChD 458 and *Barton v London and North Western Rly Co* (1888) 38 ChD 144. When substantial factual issues have to be investigated, the most appropriate course of action would be a claim for the declaration as to the ownership of the shares and consequential relief. See *Re Hoicrest Ltd, Keene Martin* [2000] 1 BCLC 194 CA at 199 *per* Mummery LJ.

32 A good outline of the issue is in provided by E McKendrick *Goode on Commercial Law* (Penguin London 2010) 61 and S Worthington *Personal Property Law: Text and Materials* (OUP Oxford 2000) 457.

33 Which is *prima facie* evidence of all the details recorded in it (section 127 of the Companies Act 2006).

34 Which is *prima facie* evidence of a member's title to the shares specified in it (section 768(1) of the Companies Act 2006).

35 This position reflects the conventional interpretation of the existing law as set out in PL Davies and S Worthington *Gower and Davies' Principles of Modern Company Law* (Sweet & Maxwell London 2012) 1003.

36 On the general principles of the doctrine of estoppel by representation, see P Feltham, D Hochberg and T Leech *The Law Relating to Estoppel by Representation – the Original Text by George Spencer Bower* (LexisNexis London 2004) 1–323, especially at 249–264.

37 This is rare. One of the most common cases could be the delivery by the transferor of the share certificate and the instrument of transfer duly executed with the name of the transferee in blank to an agent to whom is given limited authority to deal with the shares (see *Colonial Bank v Hepworth* (1887) 36 ChD 36 at 54; and *Société Generale de Paris v Walker* (1885) 11 App Cas 20 at 28–29 *per* Lord Selborne). However, even if the same agent later completes the transfer outside the scope of his authority, the transferor is not estopped from denying that the agent was not entitled to deal with the shares against a good faith purchaser for value. In other words, the principal is not estopped from setting up his title against the purchaser because he has left the certificate in the hands of an agent in such condition as to convey a representation to the rest of the world that the agent had authority to deal with them. See *Colonial Bank v Cady and Williams* (1890) LR 15 App Cas 267, *per* Lord Watson at 278; *Fuller v Glyn, Mills, Currie & Co* [1914] 2 KB 168 *per* Pickford J; and *Mercantile Bank of India Ltd v Central Bank of India Ltd* [1938] AC 287 PC *per* Lord Wright at 302.

38 See *Welch v Bank of England* [1955] Ch 508 [1955] 1 ER 811; and *Brown v Westminster Bank Ltd* [1964] 2 Lloyd's Rep 187.

39 *Barton v London and North Western Railway Co* (1889) 24 QBD 77.

it is given, is a shareholder in the company, and it is given by the company with the intention that it shall be so used by the person to whom it is given, and acted upon in the sale and transfer of shares'.[40] Accordingly, and except in cases of forgery,[41] the certificate operates as an estoppel against the company issuing it from denying the truth of the representation to an innocent transferee who relies on the statement as genuine.[42] However, in this case the transferee will only be entitled to indemnity from the company if registration is refused[43] or if the company rectifies the register in favour of the true owner.[44]

Building on the practical consequences of the doctrine of estoppel by representation, it has been suggested that in the cases when it operates, the protection of the innocent transferee of registered shares resembles the one available for the holder in due course who acquires a negotiable instrument. The acquisition of good title by estoppel against the true owner creates a pattern that has been termed 'quasi negotiability'.[45] More precisely, it has been argued that the possession of the certificate under certain circumstances places the bearer in a position similar to that of the holder of a documentary intangible, 'for they both have a certificate of ownership which will estop the signer of it; and both have a transfer of title which is intended to be acted upon by subsequent purchasers, and it is therefore a representation to them which will estop the transferor's assertion of any claim which he may have'.[46] This challenging functional analogy, however, is not always easy to square with the existing law.[47]

1.3.2. Dematerialised Shares

Since 15 July 1996, issues and transfers of dematerialised shares in UK and Irish markets are effected through the computer settlement system named CREST built by the Bank of

40 *Re Bahia and San Francisco Rly Co* (1868) LR 3 QB 584 *per* Cockburn CJ at 595.

41 See *Ruben v Great Fingall Consolidated* [1906] AC 439; *Simm v Anglo American Telegraph* (1879) 5 QBD 188; *Sheffield Corporation v Barclay* [1905] AC 392 per Lord Halsbury at 396; *Yeung Kai Yung v Hong Kong and Shanghai Banking Corp* [1981] AC 787 (PC); and *Royal Bank of Scotland v Sandstone* [1998] 2 BCLC 429.

42 *Balkis Consolidated Co Ltd v Tomkinson* [1893] AC 396. See also *Re Ottos Kopje Diamond Mines, Limited* [1893] 1 Ch 618; *Dixon v Kennaway & Co* [1900] 1 Ch 833; *Alipour v UOC Corp* [2002] 2 BCLC 770; and recently Lindsay J in *Cadbury Schweppes Plc v Halifax Share Dealing Ltd* [2006] BCC 707 at 714.

43 *Re Ottos Kopje Diamond Mines Ltd* [1893] 1 Ch 618.

44 *Re Bahia and San Francisco Rly Co* (1868) LR 3 QB 584; and *Hart v Frontino and Bolivia South American Gold Mining Co* (1870) LR 5 Exch 111.

45 See E Micheler 'Farewell Quasi-Negotiability? Legal Title and Transfer of Shares in a Paperless World' (2002) JBL 358 arguing from earlier doctrinal studies on estoppel made by JS Ewart 'Negotiability and Estoppel' (1900) 16 LQR 135 at 142 and Id *An Exposition of the Principles of Estoppel by Misrepresentation* (The Carswell Company Toronto 1900) 315–316.

46 JS Ewart *An Exposition of the Principles of Estoppel by Misrepresentation* (The Carswell Company Toronto 1900) 315.

47 See E Micheler 'Farewell Quasi-Negotiability? Legal Title and Transfer of Shares in a Paperless World' (2002) JBL 358 at 367–368 and the clear distinction made in *Colonial Bank v Hepworth* (1887) 36 ChD 36 at 53 *per* Chitty J.

England.[48] CREST superseded the paper-based settlement system named Talisman introduced in 1979 by the London Stock Exchange. With Talisman, once a trade was concluded on the London Stock Exchange, transfers were effected by physical delivery of the shares to SEPON (Stock Exchange Pool Nominee) which acted as a nominee between account days on behalf of member firms and their clients who maintained SEPON accounts.

The CREST system, which is now part of the Euroclear group, is operated by Euroclear UK and Ireland Ltd (EUI)[49] in London.[50] Shares that are not issued under the laws of a UK jurisdiction, the Republic of Ireland, Jersey, the Isle of Man or Guernsey are not eligible for settlement through CREST[51] unless repackaged in the form of depositary interest (DI), an instrument similar to a depositary receipt.[52] CREST is sometimes referred to as the UK Central Securities Depository (CSD). However, although CREST does provide administrative custodial services,[53] it is a settlement system but not a securities depository.[54] EUI does not hold securities or cash for participants in CREST. The CREST member is treated as holding securities directly from the issuer and cash balances are held with settlement banks.[55] This member alone is entitled to exercise voting, dividend and other rights relating to the shares and may act directly against the issuer. EUI is not a securities intermediary standing between its members and the issuers, but 'is more akin to a registrar who holds the primary records'.[56]

The legislative implementation of the new system of electronic settlement has its roots in the amendment of section 207 of the Companies Act 1989[57] which empowered

48 See the historical background provided by E Micheler 'Modernising securities settlement in the UK' (2002) 23 Company Lawyer 9. On the pre-existing electronic settlement system operated by the London Stock Exchange named Taurus, see S Wilkinson 'The collapse of TAURUS' (1993) Int'l Company & Com L Rev 207, and R Barnham 'CREST: the Phoenix from the Ashes of Taurus' (1993) JIBL 426.

49 Announced in Euroclear's Operational Bulletin No 1327 (6 July 2007).

50 EUI is recognised as a clearing house by the FCA (Pt XVIII of FSMA 2000) and therefore subject to the FCA Recognized Investment Exchanges Sourcebook (REC). The CREST system has also the benefit of designation for the purposes of the Settlement Finality Directive by the FCA pursuant to the Financial Markets and Insolvency (Settlement Finality) Regulation 1999 (SI 1999/2979) as amended.

51 See CREST Rule 7 and Rule 8, available at <https://my.euroclear.com/dam/EUI/Legal%20information/CRESTRules.pdf> (accessed 7 August 2013).

52 See CREST Rule 9, available at <https://my.euroclear.com/dam/EUI/Legal%20information/CRESTRules.pdf> (accessed 7 August 2013).

53 e.g. the processes to facilitate corporate actions, voting services, stock lending and repo, central counterparty services. On this issue, see Chapter 7 CREST Reference Manual, available at <https://my.euroclear.com/dam/EUI/Legal%20information/CREST-Reference-Manual.pdf> (accessed 7 August 2013) and M Yates 'UK Settlement' in M Blair and G Walker (ed) *Financial Markets and Exchanges Law* (OUP Oxford 2012) Chapter 12.

54 The idea that CREST is the UK CSD is wrong, but it in not rare in the literature. See, for example, A Pretto-Sakmann *Boundaries of Personal Property* (Hart Oxford 2005) 138. Recently, L Gullifer 'The Proprietary Protection of Investors in Intermediated Securities' in J Armour and J Payne (eds) *Rationality in Company Law – Essays in Honour of DD Prentice* (Hart Oxford 2009) 223; and R McCormick *Legal Risk in the Financial Markets* (OUP Oxford 2010) 333 footnote 10.

55 See CREST Rule 16, available at <https://my.euroclear.com/dam/EUI/Legal%20information/CRESTRules.pdf> (accessed 7 August 2013).

56 L Gullifer *Goode on Legal Problems of Credit and Security* (4th edn Sweet & Maxwell London 2008) 236.

57 Now section 784 of the Companies Act 2006.

the Secretary of State to make provisions for title to securities to be 'evidenced and transferred without a written instrument' and in the Uncertificated Securities Regulation 2001[58] (USR), which was enacted in order to amend some of the provisions of property[59] and company law[60] concerning the transfer of paper-based share certificates. Under the new legal framework, shares may be issued in a dematerialised form[61] and existing certificated shares may be dematerialised.[62] Conversely, dematerialised shares may be reconverted into paper-based shares.[63]

It is generally argued that the process of transfer of dematerialised shares is relieved by statute[64] from the requirement of writing.[65] The process operates on a delivery versus payment (DVP) basis to settle trades and works as follows.[66] CREST keeps separate accounts for each class of securities maintained for members and cash memorandum accounts[67] in the name of the members (users[68] or sponsored members).[69] Upon receiving matching instructions from participants, CREST settles the transactions by debiting the seller's account and crediting the purchaser's account with shares, and by debiting the buyer's cash memorandum account and crediting the sellers' cash memorandum account with the purchase price (via notification to the Bank of England's inter-bank payment system to transfer the agreed consideration from the transferee's to the transferor's settlement bank).[70]

58 USR 2001 (SI 2001/3755) (which repealed USR 1995 (SI 1995/3272) as amended by USR 2000 (SI 2000/1682)) as amended by the Uncertificated Securities (Eligible Debt Securities) Regulations 2003 (SI 2003/1633), the Uncertificated Securities (Amendment) Regulations 2007 (SI 2007/124) and the Companies Act (Consequential Amendments) (Uncertificated Securities) Order 2009 (SI 2009/1889).

59 See USR 2001 (SI 2001/3755) reg 38(5) disapplying section 53(1)(c) of the Law of Property Act 1925 as to the need for written instruments of transfer.

60 See USR 2001 (SI 2001/3755) regs 14–17, 38(2) and 38(3)(a) disapplying the rules of company on the issue of certificates evidencing title to shares.

61 Section 769(2)(a) of the Companies Act 2006.

62 USR 2001 (SI 2001/3755) reg 33.

63 USR 2001 (SI 2001/3755) reg 32(2), (3), (6) and (7).

64 USR 2001 (SI 2001/3755) reg 2(1). Consider also that section 53(1)(c) of the Law of Property Act 1925 disapplies in relation to financial collateral arrangements the Financial Collateral Arrangements (No 2) Regulations 2003 reg 4(2), as amended by the Financial Markets and Insolvency (Settlement Finality and Financial Collateral Arrangements) (Amendment) Regulations 2010.

65 Although the wording of USR reg 38(5) and (6) does not fully clarify whether in the case of equitable transfers the provision of section 53(1)(c) of the Law of Property Act 1925 should not apply. See the discussion in A Pretto-Sakmann *Boundaries of Personal Property* (Hart Oxford 2005) 146–149. This is also the interpretation offered in M Yates and G Montagu *The Law of Global Custody* (Tottel Publishing Haywards Heath 2013) 213 and recently endorsed by Lewison J in *Mills v Sportdirect.com Retail Ltd* [2010] EWHC 1072 (Ch) at 70–73.

66 USR 2001 (SI 2001/3755) reg 27(1)(a).

67 i.e. participants in CREST make payments through account entries by availing of the services of settlement banks previously appointed (USR 2001 (SI 2001/3755) reg 16).

68 i.e. members who have direct access to CREST.

69 i.e. members who connect to CREST by means of services provided by users (they require authorisation under FSMA 2000 (Regulated Activities) Order 2001, art 45).

70 M Yates and G Montagu, *The Law of Global Custody* (Tottel Publishing Haywards Heath 2012) 216 and CREST Reference Manual, Chapter 6, section 6, available at <https://my.euroclear.com/dam/EUI/Legal%20information/CREST-Reference-Manual.pdf> (accessed August 2013).

Legal title is acquired when the transfer is registered in EUI's register. It is now EUI's register[71] that constitutes the primary record of entitlement (*prima facie* evidence that the CREST member has legal title to) to uncertificated shares.[72] This is the same level 'of title as a shareholder obtains under English law upon registration of its name in the company register, and is the best title to registered securities available under English law'.[73] A share register must also be maintained by the issuer,[74] but in the event of inconsistency of the entries in the registers, the one recorded in the EUI's register prevails.[75]

As in the cases where the true owner of registered shares may be estopped from denying the validity of an unauthorised or an irregular transfer, the legal owner of uncertificated shares in CREST may be bound by a 'properly authenticated dematerialised instruction' (PADI).[76] More precisely, if the purchaser had no actual knowledge of this lack of authority, the legal owner will always be bound when the instruction has been sent from its computerised link with CREST even without its consent. In the case of an unauthorised instruction, EUI's liability is capped at £50,000,[77] provided that the person responsible has not been identified.[78]

1.4. *Legal Characterisation of the Transfer of Registered Shares*

Having clarified the operational mechanism for the transfer of certificated and uncertificated shares, this section examines its juridical characterisation. This is an essential inquiry for the scope this study. It will be put forward in sections 2 and 3 that the current juridical characterisation possibly has its origin in the scheme of the Genoese maritime partnership (*societas maris*) that took root and evolved in England at the beginning of the sixteenth century.

Historically, at common law *choses* in action could not be assigned.[79] A personal action enforcing an essentially personal right was regarded as inherently not transferable.[80] The historical rationale followed from the fear that the practice of

71 i.e. the operator's register.

72 USR 2001 (SI 2001/3755) reg 24(2) and (3).

73 M Yates 'UK Settlement' in M Blair and G Walker (ed) *Financial Markets and Exchanges Law* (OUP Oxford 2012) 302–316 where it is also observed that 'the wording in the CREST Regulations effectively duplicates for UK securities held through CREST the position regarding UK shares not held through CREST.'

74 USR 2001 (SI 2001/3755) regs 20–22.

75 USR 2001 (SI 2001/3755) reg 24(2) and (3).

76 USR 2001 (SI 2001/3755) reg 35.

77 USR 2001 (SI 2001/3755) reg 36(6). Unless EUI has been found guilty of wilful neglect or negligence (USR 2001 (SI 2001/3755) reg 36(9)).

78 USR 2001 (SI 2001/3755) reg 36(4).

79 See WW Cook 'The Alienability of *Choses* in Action' (1916) 29 Harv L Rev 816; and G Glenn 'The Assignment of *Choses* in Action: Rights of *Bona Fide* Purchaser' (1934) 20 Virgina L Rev 621. In general, see WS Holdsworth 'The History of the Treatment of Choses in Action by the Common Law' (1920) 33 Harv L Rev 997.

80 See the *Lampet's Case* (1612) 10 Co Rep 46b at 48a, 77 ER 994 at 998; *Master v Miller* (1791) 4 TR 329 at 340, 100 ER 1042; and *Picker v London & County Banking Co Ltd* (1887) LR 18 QBD 515 (CA) at 519. See also the comprehensive analysis contained in M Smith and N Leslie *The Law of Assignment* (OUP

assignment of *choses* in action could lead to the wrong of maintenance (or champerty) 'where a person maintains a litigation, having no interest in the subject-matter of it, nor any relation to the litigant which justifies him in doing so'.[81]

However, contrary to the general rule, shares were capable of being transferred well before the statutory interventions of the Judicature Act 1873–1875 which permitted legal assignment of *choses* in action at common law.[82] In *Poole v Middleton*, Romilly MR stated in very practical terms that shares in joint stock companies 'are in fact in the nature of property, and according to the ordinary rule, every person possessed of property has a right, by law, to dispose of it, except to the extent that he may be fettered by any contract which diminishes or derogates from that right'.[83]

The introduction of section 136 of the Property Act 1925[84] entitling an assignee of a debt or other *chose* in action to recover it by way of proceedings brought in his own name did not concern the technique for the transfer of shares. This is because of historical reasons possibly ascribable to path dependency mechanisms[85] and of the peculiar nature (within the *genus* of *choses* in action) of a share in a company. Notwithstanding the legislative intervention, other principles of contract law continued to apply. As a general rule, burdens cannot be transferred at law or in equity without the consent of the creditor.[86] Obligations cannot 'be shifted off the shoulders of a contractor on to those of another without the consent of the contractor'.[87] This affects shares because, even if they

Oxford 2013) 208; G Tolhurst *The Assignment of Contractual Rights* (Hart Oxford 2006) 11; and the historical contribution of OR Marshall *The Assignment of Choses in Action* (Pitman & Sons Ltd London 1950) 36 and JH Baker *An Introduction to English Legal History* (Butterworths London 2002) 97 ftn 4.

81 *Fitzroy v Cave* (1905) 2 KB 364 at 365. Or 'intermeddling in litigation that does not concern the meddler' – *Neville v London Express Newspaper Ltd* [1919] AC 368 at 404. By contrast, equity did not regard the assignee as an officious intermeddler, but as a person who obtained an interest in property. *Choses* in action were assignable in equity. See *Warmstrey v Tanfield* (1628) Rep Ch 29, 21 ER 498; *Squib v Wyn* (1717) 1 P Wms 378, 24 ER 498 and *Ryall v Rowles* (1750) 1 Ves Sen 348 (still a valuable consideration). Equity *de facto* created new property rights by way of trust. It 'ignored the common law distinction between *choses* in action and *choses* in possession and allowed many (although not all) legal and equitable *choses* in action to be freely transferable in Equity' – S Worthington *Equity* (OUP Oxford 2006) 60.

82 Section 25(6) of the Supreme Court of the Judicature Act 1873 which abandoned the equitable provision that imposed upon the assignee the burden to join the assignor as a party when seeking to enforce his rights against the debtor. See the analysis of Sargant J in *Re Westerton* [1919] 2 Ch 104 (ChD) at 112 and Channell J in *Marchant v Morton, Down & Co* [1901] 2 KB 829 (KBD) at 832, 54 ER 778.

83 (1861) 29 Beav 646 at 650, 54 ER 778.

84 Section 136 of the Law of Property Act 1925 (substantially) re-enacted section 25(6) of the Judicature Act 1873 mentioned above.

85 This happens when legal change is effected by adapting existing legal concepts rather than by introducing new ones. With specific reference to incumbent legal doctrine, see E Micheler 'English and German Securities Law: A Thesis in Doctrinal Path Dependence' (2007) LQR 254.

86 See J Kirby 'Assignment and Transfers of Contractual Duties: Integrating Theory and Practice' (2000) 31 VUWL Rev 319.

87 *Tolhurst v Associated Portland Cement Manufacturers* [1902] 2 KB 660 at 668 *per* Collins MR. See also *Linden Gardens Trust Ltd v Lenesta Sludge Disposal Ltd* [1994] 1 AC 85 at 103 *per* Lord Browne-Wilkinson; *Don King Productions Inc v Warren (No 1)* [1998] 2 Lloyd's Rep 176, 2 ER 609 *per* Lightman J at 194; affirmed [2000] Ch 291 and *Baytur SA v Finagrain Holdings SA* [1992] QB 610, 4 ER 129 per Lloyd LJ at 619.

are generally fully paid and no debt obligations are imposed on the holders, 'other restrictions may be imposed, such as limitations of liability and other waivers, or representations and warranties of residence or other issues of regulatory *status*'.[88] Hence, obligations/liabilities of shares in a company can be transferred only by way of novation in terms not dissimilar from the method by which liability owed by the existing partners is passed to the new partners when the composition of partnership changes.[89] A new contract comes into being, a transaction to which the creditor must be party.[90] As just mentioned, this is also the default rule for the introduction of a new partner in partnership law[91] where 'no person may be introduced as a partner without the consent of all existing partners'.[92] Technically, however, unlike assignment, novation does not involve the transfer of any property, but rather the annulment of one claim and the creation of a new claim in its place.[93] Moreover, novation provides that the transferee of the shares takes free of the obligations of a shareholder after the transfer was effected. The purchaser is not an assignee[94] and, therefore, he does not take 'subject to equities', to any defects in the assignor's title and subject to certain claims which the debtor had against the assignor.[95]

Pennington supports this analysis, also relying on the language of old case law.[96] Historically, the transfer of legal title in shares, he argues, involved a tripartite contract. It consisted of an agreement between the company, the transferor and the transferee whereby the transferee, assuming the same rights as the transferor and subject to the same obligations, should be substituted for the transferor as a member of the company. This resonates in the present statutory rules for the transfer of the legal estate in paper shares, as sketched above. Although the consent of the issuer is no longer an express requirement for the transfer of shares, it is *de facto* still implicit because legal title to shares passes to the transferee only when the company amends the register by entering the transferee's name in the register of members.

88 J Benjamin *Interests in Securities* (OUP Oxford 2000) 67.

89 Section 17(3) of the Partnership Act 1890.

90 This is demonstrated by the fact that apart from the need of appropriate contractual intention, consideration should also be provided. See *Rasbora Ltd v JCL Marine Ltd* [1977] 1 Lloyd's Rep 645 (QBD) at 659; *Custom & Excise Commissioners v Diners Club Ltd* [1988] STC 416, 2 ER 1016 at 1023; affirmed [1989] 1 WLR 1196, 2 ER 385; *Tatlock v Harris* (1789) 3 TR 174, 100 ER 517, at 180. In general, see G Treitel *The Law of Contract* (Sweet & Maxwell London 2003) 701.

91 Subject, of course, to possible contrary intention and contrary clause in the partnership agreement. See *Byrne v Reid* [1902] 2 Ch 735(CA) and *Re Franklin and Swaythling's Arbitration* [1929] 1 Ch 238.

92 Section 24(7) of the Partnership Act 1890.

93 *Re United Railways of Havana and Regla Warehouses Ltd* [1960] Ch 52 at 84 *per* Jenkins LJ; and *Scarf v Jardine* (1882) LR 7 App Cas 345 (HL) at 351 *per* Lord Selborne.

94 *Rasbora Ltd v JCL Marine Ltd* [1977] 1 Lloyd's Rep 645.

95 See *Ord v White* (1849) 3 Beav 357, 49 ER 140; and *Mangles v Dixon* (1852) 3 HLC 702, 10ER 278 at 731. In general, see also G Treitel *The Law of Contract* (Sweet & Maxwell London 2003) at 689.

96 RR Pennington *Pennigton's Company Law* (Butterworths London 2001) 398. Among the cases Pennington considered, see *Ashby v Blackwell* (1765) 2 Eden 299, 28 ER 913 at 302–303; and *Simm v Anglo-American Telegraph Company* (1879) 5 QBD 188 *per* Bramwell LJ at 204. This is also the position endorsed by E Micheler *Property in Securities – A Comparative Study* (CUP Cambridge 2007) 23 and J Benjamin *Interests in Securities* (OUP Oxford 2000) 64.

Transfer of uncertificated shares is also consistent with the novative model of transfer for certificated shares just outlined and it represents a development of that model in a 'paperless environment'. The legal record of entitlement to the uncertificated shares is determined by registration in the EUI's register.[97] As in the case of section 112 of the Companies Act 2006 where legal title to certificated shares vests in the transferee when his name is entered in the issuer's register, legal title to uncertificated shares vests in the transferee upon amendment of the operator's records.

1.5. *The Protection of an Innocent Purchaser of Registered Shares and Competing Claims to the Legal Estate*

This section concludes the analysis of the circulation of registered shares and looks at the commercial dynamics of transferability. It asks whether the current law protects a transferee from pre-existing interests in the registered shares that he purchases. By referring to possible remedies, it reconsiders some of the themes tackled above relating to the significance of the certificate for registered shares and on the way legal title is transferred. The themes addressed in this section are not only relevant in providing a comprehensive view of the current legal framework on the circulation of English registered shares. They will also have an impact in Chapter 7 when considering whether the innocent purchaser for value of intermediated shares is adequately protected against adverse claims under English law, and when addressing the related discussion on the process of law reform.

Under English law there is no general defence of good faith purchase for the innocent acquirer for value of title to property that the seller did not have to give. The system operates on the principle of *nemo dat quod non habet* (no one gives what he does not have, or, more accurately in the context of property law, no person can confer a better title than he himself has). At common law, security of ownership almost invariably takes priority over security of transaction. Hence, the transferee takes legal title to property subject to prior interests affecting the estate. It is irrelevant that the transferee purchased the securities in good faith. With reference to personality,[98] Cleasby J in *Hollins v Fowler* described this rule as follows: 'persons deal with property in chattels or exercise act of ownership at their peril.'[99]

97 USR 2001 (SI 2001/3755) reg 24. Although an issuer's register of members needs still to be maintained together with the operator's register of members, USR reg 25(2) establishes the particulars entered in the issuer's register of members are not considered *prima facie* evidence if they are inconsistent with the operator's register. In short, USR has *de facto* 'transformed the CREST records into the shareholder register' and 'downgraded the legal status of the register maintained by the company' – E Micheler *Property in Securities* (CUP Cambridge 2007) 78.

98 So far as realty is concerned, 'it is perhaps because the *nemo dat* principle is so fundamental that it is difficult to find examples of it at work in the case of common law interests' – W Swadling 'Restitution and *Bona Fide* Purchase' in W Swadling (ed) *The Limits of Restitutionary Claims: A Comparative Analysis* (United Kingdom Comparative Law Series London 1997) 80. See also L Merrett 'The importance of delivery and possession in the passing of title' (2008) 67 CLJ 376.

99 (1872) LR 7 QB 616 at 639; approved in *Hollins v Fowler* (1874–75) LR 7 HL 757. See also *Farquharson Bros & Co v King & Co* [1902] AC 325.

Apart from one significant exception relating to equitable claims that will be discussed in Chapter 7, the *nemo dat* rule also applies to the transfer of registered shares: a purchaser acquires no better title than the vendor himself has.[100] Shares, it has been authoritatively stated, are 'in this respect like other goods and chattels'.[101]

A number of isolated exceptional circumstances at common law confer to an innocent purchaser for value a title to property, which its vendor did not have to give.[102] In relation to share transfers, a *bona fide* purchaser is protected if the transfer is a PADI (properly authenticated dematerialised instruction)[103] sent to an innocent purchaser by the computer of the legal owner of uncertificated securities from his computerised link with CREST without his consent.[104] Moreover, there are cases where a shareholder is estopped from asserting his title because of his representations to the buyer or his negligent failure to act in order to prevent the seller from appearing as the owner.[105] The rules contained in the Factors Act 1889,[106] Sale of Goods Act 1979[107] and of negotiability[108] do not apply to registered shares.[109]

When the exceptions do not apply, the general approach for regulation of priorities in the transfer of the same *chose* as between legal estates and interests is that estate and interests rank in the order in which they are created.[110] There is authority for this. Millett J in *Macmillan v Bishopsgate Investment Trust plc (No 3)* clearly held that the order of

100 *Colonial Bank v Cady and Williams* (1890) LR 15 App Cass 267 at 288 *per* Lord Morris.

101 WB Lindley *Law of Companies* (Sweet & Maxwell London 1902) 658.

102 See the critical account of the rule and its exceptions contained in A Foster 'Sale by a Non-owner: Striking a Fair Balance Between the Rights of the True Owner and Buyer in Good Faith' (2004) 9 Cov LJ 1; and JWA Thornely 'Thives, Rogues, Innocent Purchasers and Legislatives Tangles' (1988) 47 Cam LJ 15. Particular consideration should also be given to the doctrinal analysis of T Weir 'Taking for Granted – the Ramifications of the *Nemo Dat*' (1996) 49 CLP 325; and I Davis 'Transferability and Sale of Goods' (1987) 7 LS 1.

103 SI 2001/3755 reg 35(3).

104 i.e. a subject who had no actual knowledge of the lack of authority.

105 See the case cited above *sub* Chapter 4, section 1.5.

106 i.e. section 2 of the Factors Act 1889. Buyers dealing with professional agents are protected in similar ways as the holder in due course of negotiable instruments according to sections 8 and 9 of the Factors Act 1889. See A Foster 'Sale by a Non-owner: Striking a fair Balance Between the Rights of the True Owner and Buyer in Good Faith' 9 (2004) Cov LJ 1 at 11.

107 i.e. sections 24 and 25 of the Sale of Goods Act 1979 ('sellers and buyers in possession') – when the purchaser/seller chooses to leave the seller/buyer in possession of the goods before property passes, he should be the one who bears the risk of the seller/buyer, not the innocent purchaser. See the explanation for the exception contained in section 24 of the Act provided by Lord Pearson in *Pacific Motor Auctions Ltd v Motor Credit (hire purchase)* [1965] AC 867 at 886. With respect to section 25 of the Act, see *Newtons of Wembley Ltd v Williams* [1965] 1 QB 560.

108 i.e. the case of documentary intangibles recognised at common law by mercantile usage where the document incorporates the right. Title to the document passes on delivery (or on endorsement and delivery) and the 'holder in due course' takes free from any defect in title of the seller. See E McKendrick *Goode on Commercial Law* (Penguin London 2010) 52.

109 The mercantile agency, seller in possession and buyer in possession are all based on the possession of goods or documents of title relating to goods. See AG Guest (ed) *Benjamin's Sale of Goods* (Sweet & Maxwell London 2006) ch 7, and M Bridge *The Sale of Goods* (OUP Oxford 2012) ch 5.

110 However, as mentioned above, in the case of registered shares, the register of the company and that of EUI provide a rebuttable *prima facie* evidence of title. Hence, in theory, priorities in competing claims

priority where both interests are legal is that 'the two interests rank in the order of their creation.'[111]

1.6. *Conclusions*

Section 1 analysed the current law for the circulation of registered shares. This was done for the benefit of the inquiry to be developed in sections 2 and 3 below. It is only by having a clear picture of the subject matter that the historical analysis can be appropriately developed, links identified and the pattern of the evolution of law accurately traced.

Section 1 showed that a share today is a bundle of contractual rights with certain unique proprietary characteristics, 'an interest measured by a sum of money and made up of various rights contained in the contract, including the right to a sum of money of more or less amount.'[112] The presence of the certificate (capable of possession) in the case of registered shares does not contradict this view. This is because title to registered shares is acquired by means of registration and the delivery of the certificate upon registration is only evidence of legal title. The only valid source of information to prove a member's title is the register of shareholders. In the context of dematerialised shares, of course, this issue does not even arise, as the title is evidenced and transferred without a written instrument.

The transferee of registered shares becomes a member of the company once he assents to do so and his name is entered in the company's register of members. Legal title passes upon the transferee's (name) entry in the members' register. The ordinary procedure of alienation consists, essentially, of a tripartite contract in which the transferee substitutes the transferor as member of the company. It is not an assignment of *choses* in action, but rather a novation. This technique of transfer of shares has practical consequences. Since novation is not subject to 'equities', when the issue of shares is defective in substance[113] and the purchaser for value without notice has been registered as a member of the company, it avoids some of the possible risks inherent in the assignment of *choses* in action, enhancing, therefore, the transferability of shares. The legislative rules introduced do away with the need for paper-based certificates and provide that transfers and settlement of dematerialised shares are effected through the CREST computer system operated by EUI. EUI maintains securities accounts in the name of the members (users or sponsored members) and settles the transactions by debiting the seller's account and crediting the purchaser's account upon receiving matching instructions from participants. The register of members held by the operator of the system constitutes *prima facie* evidence of title. The changes introduced by the new regulations are in line with the common law scheme for registered shares. What changes is only the legal significance of the records kept by EUI, which is now the register of uncertificated

to legal estate in registered shares may technically be determined only by investigating the complete chain of title.

111 [1995] 1 WLR 978 (ChD) at 999.

112 *Borland's Trustees v Steel Bros & Co Ltd* (1901) 1 Ch 288 *per* Farrell J.

113 e.g. when the contract of allotment is void because of a fundamental mistake.

securities. As in the case for certificated shares where legal title vests in the transferee when his name is entered in the issuer's register, legal title to uncertificated shares vests in the transferee upon amendment of the operator's records. Hence, legal title to uncertificated shares is also transferred by alteration of the operator's register according to the scheme of novation described above for the circulation of certificated shares.

Finally, section 1 pointed out that the cases which provide a defence for a good faith purchaser form an exception to the general principle of *nemo dat quod non habet*. As a general rule, therefore, security of ownership always takes priority over security of transaction. Apart from the binding PADI sent by the legal owner of uncertificated securities from his computerised link with CREST without his consent, the exceptions to the *nemo dat* rule operating in favour of the '*bona fide* purchaser' for value do not generally apply to the transfer of registered shares: a purchaser acquires no better title than his vendor himself has.

2. Historical Foundations

Having presented the subject matter of the chapter in section 1, section 2 focuses on the analysis of the modes of circulation of registered shares in a historical perspective. It examines the origin of the novative model outlined in section 1.4 above, and points out the relevance of legal tradition as a driver for shaping the evolution of law. As it has been for the regulations on uncertificated shares that have closely mirrored the scheme for certificated shares contained in the Companies Act 1985[114] (and now in the Companies Act 2006),[115] it argues that the evolution of transfer procedure for membership in joint stock companies has primarily reflected the pre-existing model of partnership law based on novation where a new partner may be introduced only with the consent of all existing partners.[116]

Section 2 also suggests that this finding is not conclusive for understanding the pattern of legal change. The fact that the mechanism of circulation of registered shares has evolved in the past few centuries in accordance with pre-existing legal tradition provides only a partial explanation. The broader historical investigation addressed subsequently in section 3 will show that the evolution of English law in this area has likely been the outcome of a process of reception and hybridisation from foreign models.

Section 2 has four sections. Section 2.1 is introductory. Section 2.2 explains the meaning of incorporation in the evolution of English company law. The inquiry shows that the enactment of the Joint Stock Companies Act of 1844[117] that gave companies a distinct corporate personality at its formation did not make a break with the past. Rather, it confirmed the existence of a close link with the law of partnership where members qualified as partners. Building on this, section 2.3 suggests that the current model of shares transfer grew in a path-dependent way. It finds that the novative scheme did not

114 See section 22 of the Companies Act 1985.

115 Section 112 of the Companies Act 2006.

116 Section 25(6) of the Partnership Act 1890.

117 7 & 8 Vict c 110.

change into negotiability or assignment in the middle of the nineteenth century when the concept of joint stock fund and corporate personality became inseparable and the registration of a joint stock company created a different legal entity from the partnership. Section 2.4 summarises the results of the analysis and introduces the historical discussion on legal change and hybridisation that will be carried out in section 3.

2.1. *Introduction*

The conventional interpretation is that the current legal characterisation of the modes of circulation of registered shares in England follows from the model of the partnership with transferable shares and the unincorporated joint stock company formed by contract or under a deed of settlement.[118] This origin should be self-evident when reflecting on the circumstance that until the beginning of the twentieth century, company law did not have academic autonomy as such. Rather, it was treated as an appendix to the studies on the law of partnership. Significantly, one of the most authoritative systematic works on company law until 1902 was entitled 'A Treatise on the Law of Companies considered as a branch of the Law of Partnership'.[119] This followed the 1860s 'Treatise on the Law of Partnership, including its Application to Companies' where company law was not considered to deserve separate treatment, but only an investigation by analogy with the law of partnership. The derivative nature of company law has been clearly epitomised in the preface of a late edition of the same work: the 'Law of Companies was being developed by legislative enactment and judicial decision out of the Law of Partnership'.[120]

This section grounds these references in an appropriate historical perspective as a first step for the discussion that will be addressed in section 3 below on the advent of the partnership model in England as the possible outcome of a process of borrowing and hybridisation.

2.2. *A Preliminary Clarification: the Meaning of Incorporation*

A superficial view of the current legal framework may suggest that English companies have always been formed by incorporation, starting from the granting of Royal Charter or as a result of an Act of Parliament, and that they have always been distinguished from partnerships because of the formality and the legal consequences involved in (and following from) the process of incorporation. This is misleading and historically inaccurate. Rather, the links between the development of the partnership model and the evolution of the company are strong and direct. The model of the corporate enterprise with legal personality distinct from that of its members as a privilege obtained by Royal

118 See FW Maitland 'The Unincorporated Body' and 'Trust and Corporation' in Id (ed) *Selected Essays* (CUP Cambridge 1936) at 128 and 141; AB Dubois *The English Business Company After the Bubble Act 1720–1800* (Commonwealth Fund New York 1938) 215; CA Cooke *Corporation, Trust and Company* (Manchester UP Manchester 1950) 83; and AH Manchester *Modern Legal History of England and Wales 1750–1950* (Butterworths London 1980) 350.

119 WB Lindley *Law of Companies* (Sweet & Maxwell London 1902).

120 From the preface of WB Lindley *A Treatise on the Law of Partnership* (Sweet & Maxwell London 1924).

Charter or Act of Parliament experienced a parallel life and played a negligible role in the process of foundation of the modern English company.[121]

The following analysis deals with the evolution of joint stock associations and, starting from their emergence as partnerships that imitated the corporate form under the impulse of trust law (under 2.2.1), it explains the meaning of incorporation in a historical perspective (under 2.2.2). This search makes it possible to identify the close links between the founding elements of joint stock associations and partnerships before addressing in greater detail the historical roots for the modes of shares transfer in section 2.3.

2.2.1. The Court of Chancery and the Rise of the (Unincorporated) Company

At the end of the seventeenth century, it was still common for business associations that started as large partnerships 'to get the corporate form and to carry on their business as a joint stock company'[122] under a Royal Charter or an Act of Parliament. Apart from the monopolistic economic privileges to engage in foreign trade, incorporation brought certain legal advantages to the members such as perpetual succession, governance by majority rule[123] and limitations on personal liability of the shareholders.[124] Clauses in the charters that allowed the free transferability of shares,[125] fiscal advantages in holding shares and bonds rather than land, investors' euphoria towards market shares in support of new ventures, together with lack of barriers to ownership by married women[126] and increased prosperity following the 'Glorious Revolution' of 1688, contributed at various levels to the success of company formation at the end of the seventeenth century in England and Scotland.[127] Notwithstanding the monetary crisis 1696–97 and the difficult economic conditions at the beginning of the eighteenth century,[128] such economic growth, linked with the idea that the activities of an incorporated joint stock company were not limited by the terms of the Royal Charter and statute[129] 'led to the advent of a

121 Quite surprisingly, however, apart from few minor differences (according to the classification set out by Pennington (R Pennington 'Can Shares in Companies Be Defined?' (1989) 10 Company Lawyer 140)), the rules that today govern the transfer of shares in registered companies are very similar to the ones applicable to companies incorporated by Royal Charter or by special Act of Parliament.

122 WS Holdsworth *A History of English Law* (Methuen & Co London 1925) vol VIII 208.

123 Rather than unanimity.

124 G Carruthers *City of Capital: Politics and Markets in the English Financial Revolution* (Princeton UP Princeton 1996) 130.

125 Under the control over admission vested in the directors. See KG Davies 'Joint Stock Investment in the Later Seventeenth Century' (1952) 4 Economic History Review 283 at 294.

126 See M Freeman, R Pearson and J Taylor '"A Doe in the City": Women and Shareholders in the Eighteenth and Early Nineteenth Century Britain' (2006) 16 Accounting, Business & Financial History 265 at 267.

127 See WR Scott *The Constitution and Finance of English, Scottish and Irish Joint-Stock Companies to 1720*, vol I (CUP Cambridge 1912) 326–33 and 345–46; and E Chancellor *Devil Take the Hindmost: A History of Financial Speculation* (Plume Books New York 1999) 34–35.

128 WR Scott *The Constitution and Finance of English, Scottish and Irish Joint-Stock Companies to 1720*, vol I (CUP Cambridge 1912) 352–356; and P Mirowski 'The Rise (and Retreat) of a Market: English Joint Stock Shares in the Eighteenth Century' (1981) 41 Journal of Economic History 559 at 594.

129 Not to mention the circumstance that the prerogative writs of *quo warranto* and *scire facias* were rarely implemented to dissolve operating enterprises without a charter or statutory authorisation. See B Cheffins *Corporate Ownership and Control* (OUP Oxford 2008) 135.

race to trade in Royal charters and statutes'.[130] This was the case of the South Sea Company, which similarly to the Bank of England and the East India Company before it, in 1719 abandoned trade with Spanish colonies in South America and started a scheme to finance national debt through stock offering, converting governmental debt into South Sea shares.[131] The market boom that began in late 1719 caused an irrational increase in share prices (trading as high as five and even ten times par value) of existing incorporated companies and of newly floated unincorporated companies, which had 'simply opened up share subscription books in the city and collected deposits or partial payments.'[132] A statute, later named the 'Bubble Act',[133] was therefore introduced in June 1720 to protect the public against fraud in the promotion of speculative enterprises,[134] or possibly to limit competition for investment capital.[135] This essentially forbade unincorporated companies from offering shares to the public and incorporated companies from selling their charters or to use them outside the limits of their acts of incorporation.[136] The newly enacted legislation, together with the pronouncement of the Treasury that it would apply the writ of *scire facias* to a series of duly incorporated companies,[137] caused legal uncertainties and a loss of public confidence in the scheme of the joint stock companies in general, leading to the market collapse by the end of 1720.[138] Following the burst of the speculative bubble, many chartered companies disappeared and few subsequently succeeded in obtaining charters on the basis of the more stringent requirements[139] and more difficult credit conditions.[140] As Scott puts it, 'in one that might have been established with a moderate outlay, which for any reason it was desirable to collect from a large number of persons, the trouble and cost proved prohibitive. Therefore, for upwards of a century, industry was deprived of the advantages of a certain amount of capital which would otherwise have been available'.[141]

130 See the cases cited in WR Scott *The Constitution and Finance of English, Scottish and Irish Joint-Stock Companies to 1720*, vol II (CUP Cambridge 1912) 418.

131 M Balen *A Very English Deceit: The Secret History of the South Sea Bubble and the First Great Financial Scandal* (HarperCollins London 2003) 36–38 and 90–91; and PGM Dickson *The Financial Revolution in England: A Study in the Development of Public Credit 1688–1756* (Macmillan London 1967) 65–66.

132 R Harris *Industrializing English Law* (CUP Cambridge 2000) 62.

133 6 Geo 1, c 18.

134 HA Shannon 'The Coming of General Limited Liability' (1931) 2 Economic History 267 at 268; and M Patterson and D Reiffen 'The Effect of the Bubble Act on the Market for Joint Stock Shares' (1990) 51 Journal of Economic History 163.

135 See J Carswell *The South Sea Bubble* (Sutton Publisher Limited University of California 1993) 129–130.

136 Consider the case of the South Sea Company as discussed in WR Scott *The Constitution and Finance of English, Scottish and Irish Joint-Stock Companies to 1720*, vol I (CUP Cambridge 1912) chapters XXI and XXII (and the graphical representation of the fluctuations in the shares contained vol III).

137 J Carswell *The South Sea Bubble* (Sutton Publisher Limited University of California 1993) 144; and M Balen *A Very English Deceit: The Secret History of the South Sea Bubble and the First Great Financial Scandal* (Harper Collins London 2003) 127.

138 See H Roseveare *The Financial Revolution: 1660–1760* (Longman London 1991) 57.

139 AB Dubois *The English Business Company after the Bubble Act 1720–1800* (The Commonwealth Fund New York 1938) 12.

140 See PM Garber *Famous First Bubble: The Fundamentals of Early Manias* (MIT Press MIT 2001) 119.

141 WR Scott *The Constitution and Finance of English, Scottish and Irish Joint-Stock Companies to 1720*, vol I (CUP Cambridge 1912) 438.

Nevertheless, the burst of the bubble did not affect the British economy in a significant way[142] and from 1750s, it experienced what is commonly referred to as the 'Industrial Revolution'.[143] Unincorporated joint stock companies increased in number after 1720[144] and 'many legal contrivances, generally associated with modern company law, were developed during this apparent dark age for technical innovation'.[145] Even if they were regarded as nuisance at common law and though they carried some practical and conceptual difficulties,[146] the unincorporated joint stock company provided an alternative model of commercial association, outside the rigid formalities of the pattern of incorporation.[147] This was essentially because, contrary to the common law ruling that an unincorporated group of persons could not own property, the Court of Chancery laid down that property could be held on trust for it. In other words, the organisation's real and personal property was placed in the name of the trustees who were also entitled in certain instances to act in the organisation's behalf.[148] The beneficiaries' interests were essentially limited to the expectations of 'receiving a share of the balance of the partnership's assets after discharging all its debts and liabilities on its dissolution and their right to be credited with their proper share of the partnership's realised and unrealised profits meanwhile'.[149] In its infancy, each partner also had an equitable right arising by operation of law (a lien, as it was rather improperly called)[150] on the property of the firm and on the shares of the other co-partners upon the dissolution of the partnership.[151] This was possibly a legal device employed by courts to compensate for the lack of an immediate proprietary right vested in each partner of the assets belonging to the partnership.[152]

142 J Hopitt 'The Myth of the South Sea Bubble' (2002) Transactions of the Royal History Society 141 at 152. Even the South Sea Company survived the 1720 crisis and its affairs were wound up only in 1855 – see B Baskin and PJ Miranti *A History of Corporate Finance* (CUP Cambridge 1997) 116.

143 J Mokyr 'Editor's Introduction: The New Economic History and the Industrial Revolution' in Id (ed) *The British Industrial Revolution: An Economic Perspective* (Westview Press Oxford 1999) 1 at 3; and J Wilson *British Business History 1720–1994* (Manchester UP Manchester 1995) 21.

144 Especially in the insurance and mineral fields and from 1790s by the public floatation of canal companies. See AB Dubois *The English Business Company after the Bubble Act 1720–1800* (The Commonwealth Fund New York 1938) 37 footnote 231; R Pearson *Insuring the Industrial Revolution: Fire Insurance in Great Britain, 1700–1850* (Aldershot Ashgate 2004); M Buchinsky and B Polak 'The Emergence of a National Capital Market in England 1710–1880 (1993) Journal of Economic History 1; and J Hoppitt *Risk and Failure in English Business 1700–1800* (Manchester UP Manchester 1987) 132.

145 R McQueen *A Social History of Company Law* (Ashgate Farnham 2009) 17.

146 R Harris *Industrializing English Law* (CUP Cambridge 2000) 152–156.

147 e.g. for the relative ease in the changing of the basis of association.

148 See, for example, the case of the Phoenix Assurance Company which refused a charter in 1783 and which operated under a deed of settlement as unincorporated joint stock association. C Trebilcock *Phoenix Assurance and the Development of British Insurance, vol I 1782–1870* (CUP Cambridge 1985) 69.

149 R Pennington 'Can Shares in Companies Be Defined?' (1989) 10 Company Lawyer 141.

150 This is the terminology used by WB Lindley *A Treatise on the Law of Partnership* (Sweet & Maxwell London 1924) 438.

151 *West v Skip* (1749) 1 Ves Sen 497, 27 ER 1006.

152 See R Pennington 'Can Shares in Companies Be Defined?' (1989) 10 Company Lawyer 140.

Briefly, the unincorporated joint stock association represented an efficient substitute for incorporated companies when incorporation by Royal Charter or Act of Parliament was very difficult and rare, when the incidents of incorporation remained 'either a dispensation or a favour within the special gift of Parliament or a carefully guarded bureaucratic concession'.[153] Promoters availed themselves of the loophole in the system that enabled them to carry out their plans without subjecting themselves to the cumbersome and slow processes of government.[154] It has been estimated that at the beginning of the nineteenth century about one thousand large unincorporated joint stock companies were operating in England.[155] In the often quoted statement of Maitland, equity trust *de facto* 'enabled men to form [unincorporated] joint stock companies with limited liability, until at length the legislature had to give way'.[156]

2.2.2. Incorporated/Unincorporated Companies

The subsequent passage from unincorporated companies to incorporated (registered) companies was not dramatic. The history of company law reform from 1840s onwards shows that it was a linear evolution. This is reflected in the contractual nature of the association and in the original legal notion of the shares as interests in the assets of the company. Shareholders of incorporated and unincorporated companies were not just 'the company'. They were the owners of the company's assets. While in incorporated companies the legal interest in the property was vested in the corporation, in unincorporated companies, constituted through deeds of settlement, the legal title was vested in trustees.

The underlying idea is that historically there is no necessary connection between incorporation and the joint stock fund. These two grew up independently and 'even when the great trading companies of the sixteenth century operated joint stock funds, these adventures were independent of their corporate *status*'.[157] The two concepts became inseparable only in the nineteenth century with the enactment of the Joint Stock Companies Act in 1844.[158]

Recent studies have shown that both the unincorporated and the incorporated joint stock companies in the eighteenth and nineteenth century were not entities different

153 BC Hunt *The Development of the Business Corporation in England, 1800–1867* (Harvard UP Cambridge MA 1936) 5; and GM Anderson and RD Tollison 'The Myth of the Corporation as a Creation of the State' (1983) 3 International Review of Law and Economics 107 at 100.

154 J Taylor *Creating Capitalism (Joint Stock Enterprise in British Politics and Culture (1800–1870)* (Boydell Press Woodbridge 2006) 94.

155 BC Hunt *The Development of the Business Corporation in England 1800–1867* (Harvard UP Cambridge MA 1936) 87.

156 FW Maitland 'The Unincorporate Body' in Id (ed) *Selected Essays* (CUP Cambridge 1936) 135. In the same line, see also LC Gower 'Some Contrasts Between British and American Corporation Law' (1956) 69 Harv L Rev 1371–72; CA Cooke *Corporation, Trust and Company* (Manchester UP Manchester 1950) 85; and JW Hurst *The Legitimacy of the Business Corporation in the Law of the United States* (University Press of Virginia Charlottesville 1970) 6.

157 CA Cooke *Corporation, Trust and Company* (Manchester UP Manchester 1950) 18.

158 7 & 8 Vict c 110.

from the sum of the individual shareholders.[159] Both were understood to consist of the shareholders as a body. This can be seen by reference to the language used in the Companies Act 1856 and 1862. In the Companies Act 1856,[160] section 3 identifies the company with its members. It states, 'seven or more persons […] may form themselves into an incorporated company'. In contrast, the Companies Act of 1862,[161] section 6 omitted the words 'themselves into' in the same definition. It reads 'seven or more persons […] may form an incorporated company'. This suggests that from 1862 onwards people did not form themselves into companies but, instead, they formed companies. The old perception is also evidenced by a series of cases[162] where the incorporated joint stock company is referred to as 'they', rather than 'it', in 'the view that the shareholders of such a company possessed a direct equitable interest in the company's assets, and in the view that the directors of such a company were the agents of its shareholders, subject to their direct control – a rule which persisted until the end of the nineteenth century'.[163]

As a consequence, the incorporation of a joint stock company did not create a different legal entity from the partnership composed of individuals. A joint stock company was a joint stock company whether it was incorporated or not.[164] There was no conception of the company as completely separate from its shareholders. The distinction was economic rather than legal. It also followed that the principles of the law of partnership, slightly modified, 'were thought to be applicable to companies, and as the early texts make clear this was considered true of incorporated, as well as unincorporated [joint stock companies]'.[165] In short, until the nineteenth century all joint stock companies, irrespective of their legal *status* (i.e. incorporated or unincorporated), were conceptualised as aggregates of individuals, as types of extended partnerships. The meanings attached to incorporation were very different from the ones that are ascribed to it today.

Although it has been argued that the law of priorities based on interpersonal credit developed by the Court of Chancery allowed from the sixteenth century the formation of a veil between investors and traders,[166] the conventional position maintains that the

159 See P Ireland, I Grigg-Spall and D Kelly 'The Conceptual Foundations of Modern Company Law' (1987) 14 Journal of Law and Society 150. And until the railway boom in the mid-1840s companies did not have sizeable shareholder base. See B Cheffins *Corporate Ownership and Control* (OUP Oxford 2008) 157–163; and HG Lewin *The Railway Mania and its Aftermath 1845–1852* (David & Charles Newton Abott 1968) 261.

160 19 & 20 Vict c 47.

161 25 & 26 Vict c 89.

162 As incorporated companies are concerned, see *Bligh v Brent* (1837) 2 Y&C 268 at 293, 160 ER 397 *per* Alderson B ('they were to have the power of purchasing lands'). With regard to unincorporated companies, see *Myers v Perigal* (1851) 2 De GM&G 599, 42 ER 1006.

163 J Armour 'Companies and Other Associations' in P Birks (ed) *English Private Law* (OUP Oxford 2007) 174.

164 P Ireland 'The Rise of the Limited Liability Company' (1984) 12 Int J of the Soc L 240.

165 P Ireland 'Company law and the Myth of Shareholder Ownership' (1999) 62 MLR 32 at 39. See also *Ridley v The Plymouth, Stonehouse and Devenpor Grinding and Baking Co* (1848) 2 Ex 711 at 716, 154 ER 676, *per* Parke B.

166 J Getzler and M Macnair 'The Firm as an Entity before the Companies Act' in P Brand, K Costello and WN Osborough (eds) *Adventures of the Law. Proceedings of the Sixteenth British Legal History*

advent of the doctrine of corporate personality was achieved only at the end of the nineteenth century. This 'was reflected in the changed consequences attributed to incorporation, but incorporation was not its source'.[167] Instead, signs of the development should be sought in the changing economic nature of the joint stock company following the industrial revolution, particularly in the railways sector. Railways required massive investments and the aggregation of large capitals unaffordable except by wealthy individuals on incorporation. The growth in the volume of railway shares resulting from a significant widening of the investor base[168] played an important part in enlarging the London Stock Exchange[169] and in placing a new emphasis on company shares 'at a time when the volume of British government debt was declining, and when investors were distrustful of overseas investment. The railway boom was also largely responsible for the creation of national financial and investment press, and in creating widespread interest in new investment opportunities',[170] not to mention its contribution to the formation of institutionalised stock exchanges and the decline in the operations of provincial stock exchanges.[171] This inevitably involved not only dramatic quantitative changes in the number of shareholders[172] who acted more as *rentiers*[173] than partners, but also qualitative consequences on shares (usually of high denomination)[174] which became liquid assets, a form of profitable[175] and marketable commodity which could be easily converted into money. The economic changes and the advent of high transferability on the shares were reflected in turn in their legal characterisation. Shares became the

Conference – Dublin 2003 (Four Courts Press Dublin 2005) 288.

167 P Ireland, I Grigg-Spall and D Kelly 'The Conceptual Foundations of Modern Company Law' 14 (1987) JLS 151.

168 TR Gourvish *Railways and the British Economy 1830–1914* (Palgrave Macmillan Basingstoke 1980) 17.

169 In 1853 railways shares accounted for 16 per cent of the nominal value of all securities listed in the London Stock Exchange (and about 67 per cent if domestic and foreign bond are not included). See C Michie *The London Stock Exchange: A History* (OUP Oxford 1999) 88–89.

170 MC Reed 'Railways and the Growth of the Capital Market' in Id (ed) *Railways in the Victorian Economy* (David & Charles Newton Abbot 1969) 182; Id *Investment in Railways in Britain: 1820–1844 – A Study in the Development of the Capital Market* (OUP Oxford 1975).

171 The number of stock exchanges in Britain increased from three to eighteen in the mid-1850s. See C Michie *The London Stock Exchange: A History* (OUP Oxford 1999) 63. See also WA Thomas *The Provincial Stock Exchanges* (Frank Cass London 1973).

172 Including early institutional investors such as investment trusts and insurance companies. See TL Alborn *Conceiving Companies: Joint Stock Companies in Victorian England* (Routledge London 1998) 241–242.

173 See R Pearson 'Shareholder Democracies? English Stock Companies and the Politics of Corporate Governance During the Industrial Revolution' (2002) 117 English Historical Review 840; and P Ireland 'Limited Liability, Rights of Control and the Problem of Corporate Irresponsibility' (2010) 34 Camb J Econ 837.

174 Following the Limited Liability Act in 1855, shares of high denomination tended to provide a security against the fear of speculation and kept the composition of the shareholders stable. With the spread of limited liability in the 1870s and 1880s and with the increase in the effectiveness of methods used to reach the investors, the shares denomination tended to fall' – JB Jefferys *Business Organisation in Great Britain, 1856–1914* (Arno Press New York 1977) 177.

175 A number of railways delivered dividends of 6 per cent per annum and some up to 10 per cent. See H Pollins *Britain's Railways: An Industrial History* (David & Charles Newton Abbot 1971) 35.

constitutive elements of the corporate capital and ceased to be the portions of the property owned by the company. By the mid-nineteenth century, shares of joint stock companies were treated as legal objects in their own right, as forms of property separate from the assets of the company, and divorce of ownership from control was achieved by the formation of a professional managerial elite.[176] After the railway boom, the links between shares and the assets of the company were therefore severed. Shares were no longer regarded as realty or part of the assets of the undertaking, but rather as personalty. In *Bligh v Brent* (1837)[177] it was held that shareholders had no (legal/equitable) direct interest in the property owned by the company, but only a right to dividends and a right to assign their shares for value. Notwithstanding the legislative interventions from 1844[178] to 1862,[179] it took another fifty years to conclusively establish that directors were no longer to be regarded as agents of the shareholders.[180] It follows that the source of the modern principle of separate personality is not incorporation, 'but the historical processes whereby the joint stock company share emerges as a form of fictitious money capital'.[181]

2.3. *Historical Basis for the Transfer of Registered Shares*

The analysis above suggests that the legal paradigm around which the model of joint stock companies grew, follows primarily from the contractual relationship of the law of partnership.[182] Incorporation *per se*, up until the industrial revolution in the mid-nineteenth century when the 'railway mania' resulted in significant widening of the investor base, did not determine significant qualitative differences between the law of (joint stock) companies and the law of ordinary partnerships.

Building on the above introductory remarks, a more precise explanation of the growth of the legal techniques for the transfer of registered shares in England is presented below. The analysis describes the model for early chartered and statutory companies, its similarities with the one developed later for unincorporated joint stock companies (under 2.3.1 and 2.3.2), before dealing with the nineteenth century advent of the scheme for registered companies (under 2.3.3). It shows that in all circumstances the transfer procedure for membership was based on novation.

176 TR Gourvish 'A British Business Elite: The Chief Executive Managers of the Railway Industry, 1850–1922' (1973) 47 Business History 289 at 290.

177 2 Y&C 268 at 273, 160 ER 397.

178 Companies Act 25 & 26 Vict c 89.

179 Joint Stock Companies Act 7 & 8 Vict c 110.

180 *Salomon v Salomon & Co Ltd* [1897] AC 22. See also *Automatic Self-Cleansing Filter Syndicate Co Ltd v Cuninghame* [1906] 2 Ch 34.

181 P Ireland, I Grigg-Spall and D Kelly 'The Conceptual Foundations of Modern Company Law' (1987) JLS 160.

182 Until late into the nineteenth century 'extremely complex and capital intensive concerns involving multi-site operations and combining manufacturing, merchanting and even banking could and did operate as partnerships' – PL Cottrell *Industrial Finance 1830–1914* (Methuen London 1980) 10.

2.3.1. Chartered and Statutory Companies

Prior to the enactment of the Joint Stock Companies Act of 1844[183] which facilitated the access to the corporate *status* with the filing of a deed of settlement without the need of a grant by Statute or Crown Charter, chartered and statutory companies were the only type of companies recognised by English law. They were formally different from other existing commercial associations because royal and parliamentary grants of incorporated *status*[184] gave the firm a legal personality distinct from that of its members.[185]

The amount of capital raised by chartered and statutory companies was determined by statute and divided into shares. From the nineteenth century, English courts began not to treat shares as portions of the underlying company's assets.[186] The nature of the assets of a corporation ceased to determine the property classification of its shares[187] and shares were conceptualised as personal property even when the company was holding land.[188] Litigation at the time of the East India Company has shown that shares were transferable by registration in a 'stock book' kept by the company or by the holder of shares executing an instrument of transfer, usually under seal, which was noted in the company's stock register of stock book.[189]

2.3.2. Partnership and Unincorporated Joint Stock Companies

It has been seen above that the law of unincorporated companies developed from the law of partnership, modified and adapted to the needs of a large and fluctuating number of members. The partnership property was held on trust by the partners or by trustees appointed by the partners in accordance with the covenants established in a deed of settlement, which also set out the joint stock capital of the company, the number of shares and their transferability. As the property was vested in the trustees, shareholders had no direct interest in the company's property, but relied on the provisions contained

183 7 & 8 Vict c 110.

184 The King was inclined to grant them under certain circumstances because the control which could be exercised by the incorporated company over its members was of great assistance to the State 'in the international complications which often arose out of the various mercantile activities of its subjects' – WS Holdsworth *A History of English Law*, vol VIII (Metheuen & Co London 1925) 199.

185 See M Lobban 'Commercial Law' in W Cornish, JS Anderson, R Cock, M Lobban, P Polden and K Smith (eds) *The Oxford History of the Laws of England, Volume XII 1820–1914 – Private Law* (OUP Oxford 2010) 613. On this issue, see also J Taylor *Creating Capitalism: Joint Stock Enterprise in British Politics and Culture, 1800–1870* (Royal Historical Society London 2006) 137 and 141.

186 Occasionally, the statutory and chartered corporation's joint stock was regarded as trust fund (see *Child v Hudsons Bay Co* (1723) 2 P Wms 207; *Ashby v Blackwell* (1765) Amb 503) especially 'in order to protect the ownership of shares and to enable the title of a shareholder to be asserted against a chartered or a statutory company which had accepted a transfer of his shares to a third person made without his authority' – R Pennington 'Can Shares in Companies Be Defined?' (1989) 10 Company Lawyer 140 at 141. This notion was completely abandoned before the end of the nineteenth century (*Edwards v Hall* (1855) 6 De GM&G 74, 43 ER 1158 and *Bligh v Brent* (1837) 2 Y&C 268, 160 ER 397).

187 See R Harris *Industrializing English Law* (CUP Cambridge 2000) 118.

188 *Edwards v Hall* (1855) 6 De G M & G 974.

189 Evidence of this is provided by R Pennington 'Can Shares in Companies Be Defined?' (1989) 10 Company Lawyer 140.

in the deed of settlement. Moreover, when a special provision of limitation was inserted into the deed of settlement, the possibility to sue the unincorporated company in the names of the trustees avoided a typical constraint of partnership that could initiate and answer lawsuits only through use of the names of all partners, 'which was a problem if share tradability kept the roster of partners in constant flux'.[190]

The circulation of shares in unincorporated joint stock companies was subject to rules similar to those of partnerships. They were transferable by means of a deed of bargain and sale, 'a method of transfer reminiscent of a small partnership'.[191] Deeds often used the terminology of the law of real property and hardly referred to shares as being *choses* in action. The registration in the company's books was not regarded as a copy of a deed of assignment, but the process of transfer itself. As Dubois explained in his detailed historical study of English company law after the Bubble Act, 'the purchaser might receive a receipt verifying the sale from the seller, but evidence of title would be the entry in the books in the possession of the company. A permanent record was thus insured'.[192]

The fact that in unincorporated joint stock companies legal title was transferred by registration replicated the legal scheme of members' consent at the centre of the process to replace a partner in small partnerships. The model was preserved in substance, albeit under inferred terms.[193] It was not like the assignment of the (proceeds of personal rights arising from a)[194] partnership share that, unless otherwise agreed, assigns the rights in the partnership's assets to the assignee without making the assignee partner in the assignor's place.[195] The replacement of a shareholder in unincorporated joint stock companies involved an agreement with other members, as is the case for the replacement of a partner in partnership law. In other words, in unincorporated companies a new contract came into being – an agreement between the company, the transferor and the transferee whereby the transferee, assuming the same rights as the transferor and subject to the same obligations, was substituted for the transferor as a member of the company. This novative scheme required the consent of the parties involved in a way that is not far from the consent at the basis of the formation of the partnership agreement as set out in section 24(7) of the Partnership Act 1890.

2.3.3. From Unincorporated Joint Stock Companies to Registered Companies

Following the legislation that repealed the Bubble Act,[196] the formation of unincorporated joint stock companies with transferable stock acting under a deed of settlement through

190 H Hansmann, R Kraakman and R Squire 'Law and the Rise of the Firm' (2006) 119 Harv L Rev 1383.

191 AB Dubois *The English Business Company after the Bubble Act 1720–1800* (The Commonwealth Fund New York 1938) 359.

192 Ibid 360.

193 See *Lovegrove v Nelson* (1834) 3 M&K 1, 40 ER 1 as cited by Lord Lindley *A Treatise of the Law of Partnership* (Sweet & Maxwell London 1924).

194 See *Public Trustee v Elder* [1926] Ch 776 at 779.

195 See section 31 of the Partnership Act 1890.

196 1825 6 Geo IV c 91.

trustees continued to rise steadily.[197] The advent of an active market for companies' shares[198] under the impulse of the railway boom referred to above[199] and the pressure of a new middle class of investors[200] rendered, however, a legislative intervention unavoidable. This was to settle the legal uncertainties about the formation, distinction between management, ownership and limited liability in unincorporated joint stock companies. The shareholders/beneficiaries, who had limited say in the policy of the business and restricted access to the records of the commercial association, were in effect 'shouldering a burden of liability out to their mere ownership of theoretical fractions of the business'.[201] As a consequence, in 1841 a select committee was set up under the chairmanship of Gladstone and in 1844 the Joint Stock Companies Act was enacted following the recommendations of the Board of Trade. The core of the legislative intervention was the introduction of the concept of registration as a substitute for a petition to the Parliament or to the Crown. This was the end of unincorporated joint stock companies that employed deeds of settlement and the trust device, and set out clearly the distinction between joint stock companies and partnerships.[202] With the exception of limitation of liability,[203] from 1844, a registered company enjoyed all the features of incorporation. Amongst these were, of course, separate personality and free transferability of shares.[204]

Following the 1855 Limited Liability Act,[205] the Joint Stock Companies Act enacted in 1856[206] consolidated the existing legislation by succeeding in fusing the equitable company with the common law company and introduced a general system of limited liability incorporation (to the par value of the shares owned by the shareholders) to England.[207] As far as the circulation of shares is concerned, section 20 of the same Act established, in line with the past, that the transferor remained the legal holder of the shares until the name of the transferee had been entered in the register of shareholders.

197 See, for example, *Garrard v Hardey* (1843) 5 Man and Gr 471, 134 ER 648.

198 See M Patterson and D Reiffen 'The Effect of the Bubble Act on the Market for Joint Stock Shares' (1990) 50 J Econ Hist 163.

199 RW Kostal *Law and English Railway Capitalism 1825–1875* (OUP Press Oxford 1994) chapter 1.

200 See JB Jefferys *Business Organisation in Great Britain, 1856–1914* (Arno Press New York 1977) and R McQueen *A Social History of Company Law* (Ashgate Farnham 2009) 96.

201 CA Cooke *Corporation, Trust and Company* (Manchester UP Manchester 1950) 111.

202 All new companies with more than 25 members had to be registered. J Taylor *Creating Capitalism (Joint Stock Enterprise in British Politics and Culture 1800–1870)* (Boydell Press Woodbridge 2006) 135.

203 The Gladstone Committee was unconvinced of the suitability of limited liability 'for firms not engaged in the tasks requiring large capital or involving high risk' – M Lobban 'Commercial Law' in W Cornish, JS Anderson, R Cock, M Lobban, P Polden and K Smith (eds) *The Oxford History of the Laws of England, Volume XII 1820–1914 – Private Law* (OUP Oxford 2010) 621.

204 BC Hunt *The Development of the Business Corporation in England 1800–1867* (Harvard UP Cambridge MA 1936) 116–159; CA Cooke *Corporation, Trust and Company* (Manchester UP Manchester 1950) 127–169; and AB Levy *Private Corporations and Their Control*, vol I (Routledge London 1950) 64–70, 75–79 and 82–84.

205 18 & 19 Vict c 133.

206 19 & 20 Vict c 47.

207 See M Lobban 'Commercial Law' in W Cornish, JS Anderson, R Cock, M Lobban, P Polden and K Smith (eds) *The Oxford History of the Laws of England, Volume XII 1820–1914 – Private Law* (OUP Oxford 2010) 627.

Moreover, the scheme of the statutory contract that comes into existence at the time of registration pursuant section 18 of Joint Stock Companies Act 1856[208] is a repetition of the express covenants that the members of an unincorporated joint stock company used to enter into with each other when the company was formed. This was because, for unincorporated joint stock companies, 'the execution of the deed of settlement was essential to give contractual cohesion to the rights and obligations of the shareholders, because the company had no legal personality itself and its affairs were not regulated by charter, Act of Parliament or other legislative instrument. When under the Companies Acts, registered companies became incorporated on being registered, and their memoranda and articles of association thereupon became binding on their members, the execution of those instruments by members (other than the seven, or, later, two subscribers of the memorandum and articles) became unnecessary and the so called statutory contract became nothing more than a legal fiction'.[209]

As already suggested, the process was completed without significant changes[210] with the enactment of the Companies Act of 1862. At that stage the concept of joint stock fund and corporate personality became inseparable and the registration of a joint stock company created a different legal entity from the partnership composed of individuals.[211]

2.4. *Conclusions*

This section has focused on the historical background of the circulation of registered shares. Building on the legal framework outlined earlier in section 1 it has established the links between the growth of the legal tradition and the present characterisation. The critical discussion on the concept of incorporation, in particular, has shown that the historical connections between the development of the partnership model and the company form are strong and direct. Until the enactment of the Joint Stock Companies Act 1862, companies were conceptualised in terms of aggregates of individuals, as types of extended partnership. As with partnerships, shareholders of incorporated and unincorporated companies were not just 'the company', they were the owners of the company's assets.

This connecting thread became perhaps clearer when the mechanism of transfer of legal title to shares both for incorporated and unincorporated companies was explored. It was found, in particular, that, in line with the current legal characterisation, the model for the circulation of shares was based on registration in the company books. This novative scheme did not change into negotiability or assignment later in time when the concept of joint stock fund and corporate personality became inseparable and the

208 And in identical wording in the following: section 16(2) of the Companies Act 1908, section 13(2) of the Companies Act 1929 and section 13(2) of the Companies Act 1945.

209 R Pennington 'Can Shares in Companies Be Defined?' (1989) 10 Company Lawyer 140 at 142.

210 The default set of articles of 1856 was re-enacted under Table A – M Lobban 'Commercial Law' in W Cornish, JS Anderson, R Cock, M Lobban, P Polden and K Smith (eds) *The Oxford History of the Laws of England, Volume XII 1820–1914 – Private Law* (OUP Oxford 2010) 630.

211 See the summary of this process provided in P Ireland 'The Triumph of the Company Legal Form, 1856–1914' in J Adams (ed) *Essays for Clive Schmitthoff* (Professional Books Limited Abingdon 1983) 29.

registration of a joint stock company created a different legal entity from the partnership composed of individuals. In short, what emerges from this section is that the formation of the current legal characterisation for the transfer of registered shares is the outcome of the evolution of the pre-existing legal tradition.

What will be argued in the following section is that reference to (doctrinal) path dependence[212] alone does not provide a comprehensive and satisfactory explanation for the pattern of legal change. The significance of legal tradition becomes weaker and less convincing outside a national and temporally restricted context. It lacks historical depth and offers superficial results. Section 3, in this respect, shows that the current legal characterisation of the circulation of registered shares, crystallised in the Companies Act 2006, as evolved from partnership law, is not an indigenous creation, but the outcome of legal borrowing to a significant extent from Italy and implemented in England through a process of hybridisation. Historical evidence suggests that the embryonic paradigm of particular Italian partnership models evolved from a close scheme into a more sophisticated and open pattern of transferable capital at the time of the growth in trade of the medieval *comuni/città marinare*. This result was at first a consequence of the effort to escape from the operation of usury law in ordinary business life. It was then employed in more sophisticated forms for part-ownership in ships and as such was later exported to other countries, including England, from the beginning of the sixteenth century. This should become apparent when reflecting upon certain historical circumstances such as the importance of the shipping industry in early English mercantile economy, the intensity, volume and value of trade between Italy and England and the fact that it was in the sector of shipping that the concept of joint stock was first employed in England. From the sixteenth century onwards, the Italian law of partnership was gradually assimilated into English law with the incorporation of merchant trading companies and the granting of monopolies to license overseas trade by virtue of royal prerogative. As suggested earlier, it was because of the procedural rigidity of the common law system and various historical circumstances[213] that joint stock companies later evolved independently within the realm of equity, allowing them *de facto* to meet the commercial needs arising from the mercantile community. That said, it is argued below that the suggested pattern of borrowing (and hybridisation) is still at the foundation of the paradigm for partnership and unincorporated joint stock companies described above.

3. Legal Borrowing and Hybridisation

Apart from some rather isolated opinions,[214] it is agreed among historians that the commercial/banking mechanisms that were first adopted in Italy to meet the needs of

212 The force of path dependency in driving the evolution of this area of law is even clearer when considering the peculiarity of the English model with respect to the growth of the law in the countries influenced by the Napoleonic Code (e.g. Italy) or in German law – see E Micheler *Property in Securities* (CUP Cambridge 2007).

213 e.g. the enactment of the Bubble Act 1720 (6 Geo, I, c 18).

214 MM Postan 'Italians and the Economic Development of England in the Middle Ages' in Id (ed) *Medieval Trade and Finance* (CUP Cambridge 1973) 335.

the medieval trading centres[215] spread, with the development of international commerce, first to the commercial cities of the Netherlands and then to England.[216] It follows that any sound analysis on the evolution of medieval commerce ought to have as its focus 'the leading towns of Italy, even as all research on the origins of the Industrial Revolution must centre on England'.[217] Italian commercial statutes and documents are the original authorities for the early history of medieval commercial law, the prototype of modern commercial economy. In the words of Mitchell, they throw 'a flood of light upon the origin and development of commercial rules and customs that then or afterwards found their way into the commercial laws of Europe'.[218] On more fundamental and far-reaching grounds, it has also been suggested that the same legal doctrines devised by the medieval canonist and civilians to give expression to the forms and working of the commercial mechanism adopted for solving commercial needs in the great medieval trading centres of Italy, were received in England, 'together with the commercial mechanism, to which they owed their origin and development'.[219]

All of the above are general statements. They may not be correct under all circumstances and need, therefore, to be carefully grounded and tested by assessing the specific cases of borrowing and the various schemes of legal reception. Without attempting to provide a comprehensive survey of the history of the law merchant,[220] the pattern of reception of the early models of commercial associations in England is addressed below. By placing special emphasis on the analysis of the techniques of transfer of membership, it is shown that this pattern consisted of a process of hybridisation.

The analysis is structured as follows. Section 3.1 presents a historical picture of the significance of foreign trade in medieval England. Building on that, in sections 3.2 and 3.3 it is suggested that the advent of the joint stock company has not been the result of a mere transplantation of models employed by foreign merchants operating in England, but the outcome of a long and complex process of hybridisation. The discussion of the origin of medieval commercial associations and their progressive reception provides some support to this view. In section 3.4 the inquiry into the advent of the joint stock model in England is specifically addressed. It is shown how the initial scheme of Genoese origin adapted, albeit in limited respects, in accordance with the indigenous legal tradition founded on the fellowship relations of the trading guilds. By looking at the techniques of transfer of membership based on novation and on its later evolution under the jurisdiction of equity, it is argued that such interaction amounted to a process of hybridisation. Finally, section 3.5 summarises the observed historical themes by referring to the current English legal framework presented in sections 1 and 2 above.

215 See the overview provided by D Waley *The Italian City-Republics* (Longman London 1988).

216 See RL Reynolds 'Origins of Modern Business Enterprise: Medieval Italy' (1952) 12 Journal of Economic History 350.

217 IW Raymond and RS Lopez (eds) *Medieval Trade in the Mediterranean World* (Columbia UP New York 2001) 9.

218 W Mitchell *An Essay on the Early History of the Law Merchant* (CUP Cambridge 1904) 30.

219 WS Holdsworth *A History of English Law*, vol VIII (Methuen & Co London 1937) 99.

220 For a rapid outline of the history of the *ius mercatorum*, see F Galgano *Storia del Diritto Commerciale* (Il Mulino Bologna 1976) 29–55.

A clarification on the use of the legal sources and breadth of the research should be made from the outset. The following discussion is carried out by employing secondary sources and to a significantly lesser extent original documents (mainly notaries *protocolli*,[221] entries in the mercantile *libri di commercio*,[222] certain business correspondence such as the *lettere private*[223] and the *lettere di compagnia*[224] and the ledgers of the *massari*[225]).[226] For more in-depth analysis of the general context, reference is necessarily made to the authoritative contributions of Mitchell,[227] Ashley,[228] Scott,[229] Holdsworth,[230] Hunt,[231] Dubois[232] and Harris.[233]

3.1. *Commercial Contacts*

Part I of this study argued that the notion of colonialism should be restricted to the dominance assumptions of modern European experience, of political, military and economic domination by intrusive foreign groups over indigenous people. Instead, the term 'pseudo-colonialism' refers to a broader concept of the 'absence from home and being in a foreign country' (*apoikiai*). Following this reading, therefore, 'pseudo-colonialism' includes in its sphere of application all trading contacts/settlements/economic networks without foreign occupation and without submission of the host community.

Building on this awareness, what follows is a historical analysis of certain 'pseudo-colonial' issues in medieval England. It clarifies, in particular, the mechanisms of reception and the significance of the Italian mercantile culture in shaping the evolution of early English commercial law.

221 i.e. books in which the notaries transcribed their contracts or *imbreviature*.

222 i.e. commercial registers.

223 i.e. private letters sent by branch managers to the head offices of the *compagnia*.

224 i.e. letters of the *compagnia* that dealt with business routine matters such as information for the bookkeeper about drafts and remittances.

225 i.e. ledgers of the municipal treasurers.

226 This is, for example, the case of the vast collection of Italian maritime documents contained in R Zeno *Documenti per la Storia del Diritto Marittimo nel secoli XIII e XIV* (Lattes Editori Torino 1936); in M Chiaudano and M Moresco *Il Cartolare di Giovanni Scriba*, vols I and II (Istituto Storico Italiano per il Medio Evo Roma 1935); and the sources on merchant law (mainly in Italian) gathered in the work of IW Raymond and RS Lopez (eds) *Medieval Trade in the Mediterranean World* (Columbia UP New York 2001).

227 W Mitchell *An Essay on the Early History of the Law Merchant* (CUP Cambridge 1904).

228 WJ Ashley *An Introduction to English Economic History and Theory* (Longmans, Green and Co London 1906).

229 WR Scott *The Constitution and Finance of English, Scottish and Irish Joint-Stock Companies to 1720* (CUP Cambridge 1912).

230 WS Holdsworth *A History of English Law*, vol VIII (Methuen & Co London 1937) 99–300.

231 BC Hunt *The Development of the Business Corporation in England 1800–1867* (Harvard UP Cambridge MA 1936).

232 AB Dubois *The English Business Company after the Bubble Act 1720–1800* (The Commonwealth Fund New York 1938).

233 R Harris *Industrializing English Law* (CUP Cambridge 2000).

This introductory section presents a general historical picture of Italian trade in medieval England (under 3.1.1) and, with specific emphasis on the wool trade, it discusses the importance of ('pseudo-colonial') maritime settlements (under 3.1.2). Lastly, some likely patterns of cultural/commercial interaction are sketched (under 3.1.3).

3.1.1. Relevance of the Italian Merchants in Medieval England

Until the early Tudor period, foreign merchants controlled more than half of the London export trade[234] and 'had successfully preserved their near monopoly over certain categories of imports'.[235] Foreign merchants lived under a measure of self-government.[236] Starting from the fifteenth century a jury *de medietate linguae* (or 'half tongue') composed of half-aliens was introduced for trial of cases where they were parties. Baker reports that most of the cases involved Italians,[237] reflecting the large number of Italians in London. Among the Italians, one of the most prominent communities was the one formed by the Genoese. This is indirectly proved by the fact that Genoese merchants 'are frequently encountered as litigants in the plea rolls'.[238]

In general terms, the Italian merchant community was regarded as a commercial and financial aristocracy within the alien communities in London. Drawing on superior business organisation, significant capital resources and often under Papal patronage, the Italians progressively penetrated into English commercial life during the early Middle Ages. By the end of the thirteenth century, the presence of Italian bankers was extremely significant.[239] This was also because 'the expulsion of the Jews by Edward I in 1290 had given the Italians the opportunity to make their financial services indispensable to the English Crown, and in the intervening centuries the leading Italian families succeeded in cornering a substantial proportion of London's import and export trade'.[240] The Florentines were the first Italians who settled in London and, as well as being bankers, they operated as goldsmiths, pawnbrokers and merchants.[241] They also 'accommodated the kings of England with loans of money; but they were more fortunate than the Jews, for they received many marks of favour and approbation'.[242] Edward I found them indispensable.[243] In similar ways to how the *comuni* borrowed from their citizens,

234 F Pollock and FW Maitland *The History of English Law*, vol I (CUP Cambridge 1968) 464.

235 A Pettegree *Foreign Protestant Communities in Sixteenth-Century London* (OUP Press Oxford 1986) 10.

236 Reference to a judgement of the council of the nation of Venetians in London (*Orio v Trono* – c 1490) is made by J Baker *The Oxford History of the Laws of England, vol VI 1483–1558* (OUP Oxford 2007) 613 footnote 138.

237 'Juries half Genoese, half Florentine, and half Venetian, which not only appeared in court, but proceeded to find against the Italian defendants': ibid 613.

238 Ibid 613.

239 See WE Rhodes 'The Italian Bankers in England and their Loans to Edward I and Edward II' in TF Toot and J Tait (ed) *Historical Essays by Members of the Owens College, Manchester* (London 1902) 137.

240 A Pettegree *Foreign Protestant Communities in Sixteenth-Century London* (OUP Press Oxford 1986) 10.

241 See M Phillips *A History of Banks, Bankers and Banking* (Effingham Wilson & Co 1894) 2.

242 WJ Lawson *The History of Banking* (Richard Bentley London 1855) 31.

243 M Powicke *The Thirteenth Century 1216–1307* (OUP Oxford 1953) 639.

English kings became large borrowers from Italian banking houses,[244] as during the Welsh wars under Edward I (1287) which were financed almost exclusively by the Ricciardi 'who provided £8,288 out of a total expenditure of £10,600'.[245] This allowed Italian bankers to live in England as privileged citizens exempt from aids, tallage and local services, with a freedom greater than the *Carta mercatoria*.[246] The normal technique of repayment of the loans was from the proceeds of custom duties, thus allowing the spreading of the cost of expensive campaigns over longer periods. Massive loans to the Crown gave the financial machinery of the government strength and flexibility, although, as Prestwich claims, 'the successive failure of the Ricciardi, the Frescobaldi, the Bardi and the Peruzzi showed the danger of extending credit too far to improvident rulers'.[247]

The level of expertise and reliability in structuring financial transactions by Italian bankers[248] who had emigrated to London is likely to have influenced the growth of English business practice.[249] As has been authoritatively submitted by Cunningham, by the end of the thirteenth century, the Italians *de facto* 'were left to carry on nearly all the financial operations of the country'[250] and this is likely to have allowed them to take up a powerful position in English trade.

It is also likely that they had a considerable influence over the growth of English commercial law. There is significant historical evidence that from the fourteenth century English merchants were familiar with some of the legal techniques of Italian businessmen and were employing some of these in their own affairs. English merchants, in particular, used the Italian facilities for the documentary transfer of money, including the letter of credit,[251] for an efficient method of bookkeeping and accountancy and for a modern technique of maritime insurance.[252] As will be will explained in greater detail in the sections below, English merchants, in line with the pattern of the development of the Italian *societas*, operated at first under a sort of rudimentary occasional partnership. It usually began with the purchase 'of a certain merchandise and ended with its division or

244 See the history of the loans made to Edward III and the impact of his refusal to repay the borrowed money to the Peruzzi and Bardi of Florence in A Sapori *La Crisi delle Compagnie Mercantili dei Bardi e dei Peruzzi* (Oschki Florence 1926).

245 M Prestwich 'Italian Merchants in the Late Thirteenth and Early Fourteenth Century England' in R Lopez (ed) *The Dawn of Modern Banking* (Yale UP New Haven 1979) 79.

246 There is evidence showing that from 1224 onward safe-conducts and export licences were issued to Florentines. See R de Roover 'The Organization of Trade' in MM Postan and EE Rich (eds) *Cambridge Economic History of Europe* (CUP Cambridge 1963) vol iii, 71.

247 M Prestwich 'Italian Merchants in the Late Thirteen and Early Fourteenth Century England' in *The Dawn of Modern Banking* (Yale UP New Haven 1979) 78.

248 Among the most important 'families' of bankers: the Frescobaldi (from the time of Edward I until circa 1311 – A Sapori *La Compagnia dei Frescobadi in Inghilterra* (Oschki Florence 1926)) and the Bardi and the Peruzzi (from the time of Edward III – see A Sapori *La Crisi delle Compagnie Mercantili dei Bardi e dei Peruzzi* (Oschki Florence 1926)) were from Florence. The Ricciardi were from Lucca (from the time of Henry III until circa Edward I).

249 C Johnson 'An Italian Finance House in the 14th century' (1903) 1 Transactions of St Albans and Hertfordshire Architectural and Archaeological Society 320.

250 W Cunningham *Alien Immigrants to England* (Cass London 1969) 75.

251 MM Postan 'Italians and the Economic Development of England' in Id (ed) *Medieval Trade and Finance* (CUP Cambridge 1973) 338.

252 On the origin and early history of maritime insurance, see HO Nelli 'The Early Insurance Contract. A New Discovery' (1972) 39 Journal of Risk and Insurance 215.

joint sale. Each time a transaction was carried out jointly by two or several partners, the partnership had to be formed anew even if the partners and the terms of sharing remained the same'.[253] Following maritime advancements and the growth of commerce linked to the colonial expeditions, the model evolved into partnerships of joint stock along the lines of the development observed for the Genoese *societas maris* and the model of the division of contributions adopted for *loca navis*.

3.1.2. 'Pseudo-Colonial' Settlements

In addition to their influence in banking/financial practice, the physical presence of Italian settlements in England further supports the argument that Italians had a prominent role in shaping the evolution of early English commercial law. Several large *compagnie* of Italian merchants had branches in England in the Middle Ages. Further, numerous Italian maritime *commendae* and *societates* operated from English ports.

It was principally the excellence of English wool, unrivalled in Europe in the thirteenth century for its strength and quality,[254] that brought the Italian merchants to England for the purpose of trade. English wool was a valuable asset in the Middle Ages. The barons of England sitting in Parliament 'asserted in 1297 that wool represented half of England's wealth or, as they put it, half the value of the whole land'.[255] When the Italian involvement in the wool trade increased in the course of the thirteenth century, a growing number of merchants established themselves in England. They were well acquainted with the English sources of supply. In particular, they often utilised their relations with the wealthy landowning religious communities of England and entered into contracts with them to buy all their wool.[256] As a consequence of the Italians' presence in England, the northern industry 'came to depend in large measure upon distant Mediterranean markets, both for some raw materials such as dyestuffs and for outlets in which the finished products could be sold. By the close of the following century the Italians were second to none in the wool commerce'.[257] They also developed a woollen industry at home, finishing the shipped cloths from Flanders.[258] The Italians operated across the Channel from the Low Countries, landing small amounts of spices, silks and other luxuries at Dover, Sandwich and London, and shipping in return samplers of English wool back to Italy through the Low Countries. In early times, the Genoese prevailed in this business because the Florentines were not a seafaring nation until the capture of Pisa and, therefore, could not independently carry out the wool transactions

253 MM Postan 'Partnership in English Medieval Commerce' in *Studi in Onore di Armado Sapori* (Istituto Editoriale Cisalpino Milano 1957) 540.

254 See E Power *The Wool Trade in English Medieval History* (OUP Oxford 1941).

255 MM Postan 'The Medieval Wool Trade' in Id (ed) *Medieval Trade and Finance* (CUP Cambridge 1973) 342. To limit it to a few examples, wool (fifty thousand sacks) was also used to pay Richard I's ransom when he was captured abroad and taxes on wool or loans on wool entirely bore the costs of the early stages of the Hundred Years War.

256 FR Sanborn *Origins of the Early English Maritime and Commercial Law* (The Century Co London 1930) 360.

257 RW Kaeuper *Bankers to the Crown. The Riccardi of Lucca and Edward I* (Princeton UP Princeton 1973) 5.

258 See TH Lloyd *The English Wool Trade in the Middle Ages* (CUP Cambridge 1977).

with the English producers. In the thirteenth and fourteenth century the Genoese merchants were the most sophisticated traders in shipping, not just in the Mediterranean Sea.[259] The technical development in shipbuilding stimulated by the crusades[260] made voyages from Genoa to England possible, probably starting from 1278.[261] The Genoese established themselves as one of the predominant groups of Italians in England in the latter half of the fourteenth century (especially) after the decline of the Florentines. Commercial treaties and privileges and protection repeatedly assured to Genoese merchants were entered into between Edward III and Genoa, mainly to secure the naval aid of the Genoese against France.[262] Following the changes in the character of trade and shipping, with the abandonment of merchant galleys for larger and cheaper carracks, a large part of the Genoese trade in England chose Southampton as the main centre of commerce. Southampton rapidly became one of the principal depots for the Mediterranean trade, served as it was with good road connections with Winchester and London.[263] It is beyond the scope of this investigation to provide a detailed account of the complex history of the development of Genoese colonies and trade in England up until the decline of Southampton in the sixteenth century.[264] What is important to emphasise is the close interaction between English merchants and Italian trade, especially from the beginning of the fifteenth century. There are official records[265] that numerous English merchants made use of Genoese carracks to carry their merchandise between Southampton and the Low Countries in the reign of Henry VI, entering *de facto* into the carrack and galley trade. Over the course of the fifteenth century the relative importance of foreign shipping declined. As English merchants developed the ability to supply the Italian market themselves, the number of ships owned by Englishmen either in partnership or alone increased.

3.1.3. Commercial Contacts and Borrowing

The above analysis emphasised the intensity of the trading contacts between Italy and England and the significant presence of Italian settlements in England in the Middle

259 There was no commander in the northern seas 'like the Genoese admiral and merchant Benedetto Zaccaria, who helped to conquer Gibraltar from the Moors, drew up Philip the Fair a plan for the blockade of English trade, commanded the French fleet which sailed for Flanders in 1299, and ended his life as Lord of Chios, with its profitable alum mines' – FM Powicke *The Thirteenth Century 1216–1307* (OUP Press Oxford 1953) 639.

260 See EH Brine *Genoese Shipping in the Twelfth and Thirteenth Centuries* (Medieval Academy of America Cambridge MA 1930) 19.

261 When 'a group of merchants hired three galleys, the Sanctus Joannes, Sanctus Anthonious and the Alegrancia, to bring a cargo of alum to England' – AA Ruddock *Italian Merchants and Shipping in Southampton 1270–1600* (University College Southampton 1951) 19.

262 A Beardwood *Alien Merchants in England, 1350 to 1377. Their Legal and Economic Position* (The Medieval Academy of America Cambridge MA 1931) 5.

263 See JD Mackie *The Earlier Tudors 1485–1558* (OUP Oxford 1952) 219; and A Beardwood *Alien Merchants in England, 1350–1377* (The Medieval Academy of America Cambridge MA 1931) 155.

264 See J Herres 'Les Genois en Angleterre: La Crise de 1458–1466' in *Studi in Onore di Armado Sapori* (Istituto Editoriale Cisalpino Milano 1957) 809.

265 e.g. the brokerage books at Southampton.

Ages. The cultural prominence of Italian business techniques also suggests that English merchants learned the techniques of business practice directly from Italians and, in particular, from the ones established or naturalised in England.

This position is strongly endorsed by Ruddock who claims that it was by practical experience rather than from translation of foreign business manuals that English merchants laid the foundations of methods of business. He reports that English merchants acquired their knowledge of financial instruments and business techniques 'not from books, but from Italians living in their own community, buying and selling with them, acting as their factors overseas, sometimes entering their households and marrying into their families, and in Southampton, if not elsewhere holding municipal offices and exercising a very real influence on the lives of their English neighbours'.[266]

3.2. *Patterns of Borrowing and Reception*

Having ascertained the importance of Italian mercantile culture in the commercial life of medieval England, this section focuses on the evolution of the partnership and of the joint stock company. It examines whether (and in what terms) these models of business association have been imported from Italy. Historians broadly distinguish between two explanations for the advent of the joint stock company: transplantation and, although the term is never used, *de facto* hybridisation. It will be shown that the latter provides a more convincing representation of the complexities involved in the process of reception and legal change.

3.2.1. The 'Direct Bodily Transplantation' Theory

It has been suggested that the method of formation, organisation and membership of commercial associations in England has been imported wholly from Italy. Once the relevance of Italian commercial presence in England before the middle of the fifteenth century is remembered, 'allowance must be made for the possibility that, when the time was ripe, the method of constituting a company might have been copied, and that, when an organisation of this type was at length founded, it would be, in its main essentials, an importation from abroad and not an indigenous product'.[267]

266 AA Ruddock *Italian Merchants and Shipping in Southampton 1270–1600* (University College Southampton 1951) 205. From an extensive research on a large number of primary sources, Ruddock reports the case of the Italian Christopher Ambrose who took English apprentices into his household. His story serves as one of the many example of transplantation. A Florentine by birth, Ambrose had received his early training as an Italian clerk and factor before establishing himself as a naturalised Englishman in Southampton. It is unlikely that he would have abandoned the efficient methods of bookkeeping and accountancy he learned as a Florentine and adopted the indigenous English system in his private ledgers. It is reasonable to assume instead that James Harrison and other apprentices and his own son, Robert, who also established himself as an English merchant in Southampton, all benefited from his instruction in the Italian methods of bookkeeping and other business techniques.

267 WR Scott *The Constitution and Finance of English, Scottish and Irish Joint-Stock Companies to 1720*, vol I (CUP Cambridge 1912) 1.

Although not to be excluded in principle, this radical possibility should, however, be regarded as remote once it is noted that at the time joint stock companies came into existence in England, direct commercial relations with Italy had already declined.[268]

3.2.2. The Conventional View

The conventional historical view holds that the partnership and the joint stock undertakings with freely transferable shares have evolved through a long process of transition primarily from the Italian medieval partnership and, to a lesser extent, from the Anglo-Saxon guilds[269] – a process of hybridisation, according to the terminology of this study.

Guilds were closed 'fellowships' formed for various purposes (religious, social, commercial) with strict conditions for membership,[270] organisation[271] and ceremonial forms.[272] In the *gilda mercatoria*,[273] similar to the Italian trade protection associations of the *Arte della Lana* and *Arte di Calimala*,[274] trading usually involved a monopoly and was carried out individually subject to the rules of the guild. Expression of an embryonic form of the corporate character was given by the use of the common seal.[275] Although medieval guilds lost significance with the expansion in the scale of business and the appearance of maritime trading, Scott claims that some of their characteristics such as the conception of 'perpetual succession' and framing of by-laws 'many of which related to the exercise of the monopoly'[276] have probably affected and influenced the embryonic organisational structure of trading companies in the sixteenth and seventeenth century.

268 Consider, for example, the reduced influence of the Italian bankers in London at the end of the fourteenth century. See W Cunningham *Alien Immigrants to England* (Swan Sonneschein London 1897) 76.

269 For a preliminary introduction, see the essay 'On the History and Development of Gilds and the Origin of Trade-Unions' by L Brentano in T Smith *The Original Ordinances of More Than One Hundred Early English Gilds* (Early Eng Text Society London 1870). A more analytical description is offered by JM Lambert *Two Thousand Years of Gild Life* (Brown Hull 1891).

270 Membership came generally by birth or apprenticeship and the members had to take an oath of fidelity. See T Smith *The Original Ordinances of More Than One Hundred Early English Gilds* (Early Eng Text Society London 1870) 316–319.

271 There was usually a chief official (an alderman), 'one or more wardens and stewards, who had charge of the property, a dean or clerk, who summoned the brethren to the meetings and kept the register of members' – WR Scott *The Constitution and Finance of English, Scottish and Irish Joint-Stock Companies to 1720*, vol I (CUP Cambridge 1912) 3.

272 e.g. mandatory festive gatherings and processions. See T Smith *The Original Ordinances of More Than One Hundred Early English Gilds* (Early Eng Text Society London 1870) 19, 25, 30, 38, 43, 72, 141, 148, 232, and 446.

273 See C Gross *The Gild Merchant: a Contribution to British Municipal History* (OUP Press Oxford 1890) 14, 34, 61.

274 Both guild houses were involved in the manufacturing and sale of cloth. See the work on the *Compagnia di Calimala* in Florence by A Sapori *Una Compagnia di Calimala ai Primi del Trecento* (Olschki Editore Firenze 1932).

275 See the thirteenth and fourteenth centuries gilds reported in T Smith *The Original Ordinances of More Than One Hundred Early English Gilds* (Early Eng Text Society London 1870) 201, 207 and 250.

276 WR Scott *The Constitution and Finance of English, Scottish and Irish Joint-Stock Companies to 1720*, vol I (CUP Cambridge 1912) 8.

This link will become apparent when discussing the case of the Russia Company in the following section.

It is, however, generally maintained that it is from the original forms of commercial partnerships, namely the *commenda*, the *societas* and, to a lesser extent, the *compagnia* that the roots of the English partnership and joint stock company are more neatly traceable.[277]

In the light of that purported relevance, before dealing specifically with the process of reception of the joint stock company, a brief historical overview of the rise of the medieval partnership and its progressive advent in England will be outlined in section 3.3 below. It is timely to inquire this at this stage, not least to give a comprehensive account of the complexities of the process of hybridisation that will be discussed in section 3.4. It will be shown that, well before the introduction of the joint stock company, incomplete forms of the *commenda*, the *societas* and the *compagnia* were already in place in England, and it will be argued that their presence is likely to have facilitated the process of reception and hybridisation of the Italian model.

It is, however, difficult to assess their exact relevance or to identify conclusively the role they played in the later evolution of the joint stock company. Boundaries of borrowing and patterns of reception are hard to establish, especially given the fact that the relevance of partnerships in the organisation and finance of English medieval commerce 'is almost wholly by-passed by English economic historians. Even Sir William Ashley, who was well acquainted with the medieval *societas* and fully aware of its importance, described it with hardly any reference to English doctrine and practice'.[278]

3.3. *Early Forms of Commercial Association*

It is still uncertain,[279] and fundamentally a matter of conjecture,[280] whether partnerships existed under Roman law as a separate entity,[281] or whether they merely amounted to a

[277] This is the position supported by WS Holdsworth *A History of English Law*, vol VIII (Methuen & Co London 1937) 99; and L Neal *The Rise of Financial Capitalism* (CUP Cambridge 1990) 44. It is also implicitly endorsed in the 'classical' account of the history of company law to 1825 in PL Davies *Gower and Davies' Principles of Modern Company Law* (Sweet & Maxwell London 1997) 19.

[278] MM Postan 'Partnership in English Medieval Commerce' in *Studi in Onore di Armando Sapori* (Istituto Editoriale Cisalpino Milano 1957) 521.

[279] The *Lex Iulia de collegiis* which is supposed to have been the basis of the classical law of private corporations and the numerous *senatus consulta* on the matter have not been preserved to us. See WW Buckland *A Textbook of Roman Law from August to Justinian* (CUP Cambridge 1950) 175.

[280] Classical lawyers rarely dealt with the law of (business associations and) corporations as it was regarded to a considerable extent a question of public law. Corporation-like associations under Roman law were created for public rather than for commercial interest. Consider the case of the *societates publicanorum* in public monopolies as examined by V Arangio-Ruiz *La Società in Diritto Romano* (Jovene Napoli 1950) 80 and 159. This circumstance in itself probably prevented the development of a full theory of the law of corporations as suggested by F Schulz *Classical Roman Law* (OUP Press Oxford 1951) 89. *Contra*, see PW Duff *Personality in Roman Private Law* (CUP Cambridge 1938) and, more recently, A Borkowski and P du Plessis *Textbook on Roman Law* (OUP Oxford 2005) 286.

[281] Above all, as T Mommsen maintains in his paper on Roman corporation at the beginning of the twentieth century, 'in the whole sphere of Roman law there is hardly a problem so obscure and vexing

complex set of obligatory relations among members (*socii*) of no concern to third parties.[282] A recent contribution in the area has argued that the possible undeveloped status of the Roman partnership may be 'attributable at least in part to Rome's reliance on other forms of organisation for most business activity'[283] such as the *familia* (*communi iure*)[284] and the *peculium*.[285]

What is certain is that maritime partnerships were numerous in the Middle Ages in the cities in the western part of the Mediterranean, and in Italy in particular.[286] Partnerships supplied the most popular and least objectionable method of financing trade.[287] Their growth was greatly influenced by the canonist doctrine on the use of capital, which discouraged loans and encouraged partnerships. More precisely, by employing the model of partnership the commercial practice of loans at interest avoided the occurrence of the wrong (sin) of usury, as interest was legitimised by converting it into dividend.[288] As Ireland suggests, many inactive providers of money were legally qualified as partners rather than lenders because they put their capital at risk. Thus, 'lenders' who received interest (a 'certain and defined' return) were distinguished from 'partners' who received a share in profits (a return that was 'casual, indefinite and depending on the accidents of trade'), although both received the return on their capital in the same form – 'as a reward for the mere ownership of money'.[289]

In addition to this, closer attention should also be given to the variety of primitive organisation of medieval trade. This could in effect be another element that contributed to the success of partnerships in medieval Europe. The medieval merchant was not always necessarily a 'travelling merchant'[290] involved in maritime commerce. He was often an artisan who could employ little more than his labour. The necessary capital, therefore, had to be 'supplied not by the merchant himself but by nobles, ecclesiastics and

as that concerning so-called legal persons', cited in F Schulz *Classical Roman Law* (OUP Press Oxford 1951) 87.

282 See V Arangio-Ruiz *La Società in Diritto Romano* (Jovene Napoli 1950); and Id *Istituzioni di Diritto Romano* (Jovene Napoli 1957) 349.

283 H Hansmann, R Kraakman and R Squire 'Law and the Rise of the Firm' 119 (2006) Harv L Rev 1333 at 1358.

284 The Roman family was an entity formed of a large number of members including the ones bearing only the same *nomen* and as such was sufficiently solid to finance a typical commercial firm independently. See T Frank *An Economic History of Rome* (Jonathan Cape London 1927) 222 and V Arangio-Ruiz *Istituzioni di Diritto Romano* (Jovene Napoli 1957) 427.

285 It was a set of assets provided by the master to the slave (or for a son – see *peculium castrenses*) for use in business ventures. The *peculium* remained the property of the master and upon default on the *peculium* the master was liable as against third parties (only up) to the value of the *peculium*. See V Arangio-Ruiz *Istituzioni di Diritto Romano* (Jovene Napoli 1957) 50 and 58.

286 RS Lopez *The Commercial Revolution of the Middle Ages: 950–1350* (CUP Cambridge 1976) 18 and M Weber *The History of Commercial Partnerships in the Middle Ages* (Rowman & Littlefield Publishers Lanham 2003) 63.

287 WJ Ashley *An Introduction to English Economic History and Theory* (Longmans London 1906) 413.

288 See W Cunningham *The Growth of English Industry and Commerce during the Early and Middle Ages* (CUP Cambridge 1905) 367; and J Noonan *The Scholastic Analysis of Usury* (Harvard UP Cambridge MA 1957) 133.

289 P Ireland 'Company Law and the Myth of Shareholder Ownership' (1999) 62 MLR 32 at 37.

290 See below *sub* Chapter 4, section 3.4.

rich townsmen who were not merchants, and whose association with professional traders took, as a rule, the form of partnership'.[291]

Although still largely unsettled in its precise boundaries,[292] the conventional historical classification of medieval partnerships distinguishes between three different forms: the *commenda*, the *societas* and the *compagnia*.

3.3.1. The *Commenda*

The *commenda* was a temporary arrangement of Muslim origin,[293] not rare in Italy[294] in the eleventh century for financing maritime trade. Under it, one party (the *commendator* or *stans*) lent capital, either money or goods, to another party (*commendatarius* or *tractator*) without personally taking an active part in the operations of the commercial association. Although it had a number of variations, which sometimes closely resembled the structure of a loan agreement[295] or the modern agency agreement,[296] the *commenda* was fundamentally a contract of 'sleeping partnership'.[297] In exchange for a greater percentage of the profits and without supplying capital, the *commendatarius* agreed to conduct the actual trade of the partnership. The *commendator* enjoyed full liability (*risucum maris et gentium*) up to the limit of his original investment.[298]

291 MM Postan 'Partnership in English Medieval Commerce' in *Studi in Onore di Armando Sapori* (Istituto Editoriale Cisalpino Milano 1957) 522.

292 See U Santarelli *Mercanti e Società fra Mercanti* (Giappichelli Torino 1992) 121 and 159.

293 The *muqarada*. See M *Cizakca A Comparative Evolution of Business Partnerships: Islamic World and Europe, With Specific Reference to the Ottoman Archive* (Brill Leiden 1996) 11; AL Udovitch 'At the Origins of the Western Commenda. Islam, Israel, Byzantium' (1962) 37 Speculum 198; and Id *Partnership and Profit in Medieval Islam* (Princeton UP New Jersey 1970). In more general terms, AE Lieber 'Eastern Business Practices and Medieval European Commerce' (2) 21 Economic History Review 230. Contra see JH Pryor 'Origins of the Commenda Contract' (1977) 52 Speculum 33.

294 See the geographical analysis of the diffusion of the *commenda* provided in M Weber *The History of Commercial Partnerships in the Middle Ages* (Rowman & Littlefield Publishers Lanham 2003) 71.

295 See docs IV, VI, XV, XLV, LXVII, CXV, CX in R Zeno *Documenti per la Storia del Diritto Marittimo nel secoli XIII e XIV* (Lattes Editori Torino 1936) and, in general terms on this issue, U Santarelli *Mercanti e Società fra Mercanti* (Giappichelli Torino 1992).

296 i.e. a contract where the commission agent buys and sells goods in his name on the account of the principal. See M Weber *The History of Commercial Partnerships in the Middle Ages* (Rowman & Littlefield Publishers Lanham 2003) 66.

297 See docs II, III, VII, XI, XII, XVII, XIX, XXXIII, XXXV, XXXVII, XXXVIII, XXXIX, XL, XL, XLII, LI, LXXXVI, LXXXVIII, LXXXIX, XCIII, XCIV, CVI, CXVII, CXX, CXXXVI, CXLVI, CLI, CLIX, CLXX in R Zeno *Documenti per la Storia del Diritto Marittimo nel secoli XIII e XIV* (Lattes Editori Torino 1936); docs VI, XXVII, LXVIII, LXIX, CV, CCIX, CDLV and DCCCL in M Chiaudano and M Moresco *Il Cartolare di Giovanni Scriba*, vols I and II (Istituto Storico Italiano per il Medio Evo Roma 1935); and the ones gathered in IW Raymond and RS Lopez (eds) *Medieval Trade in the Mediterranean World* (Columbia UP New York 2001) 174. In general terms, see the analysis in G Astuti *Origini e Svolgimento Storico della Commenda Fino al Secolo XIII* (Utet Torino 1933).

298 See docs II, VII, XI, XVII, XIX, XXIII, XXV, XXVII, XXXVIII, XL, LI in R Zeno *Documenti per la Storia del Diritto Marittimo nel secoli XIII e XIV* (Lattes Editori Torino 1936). Consider also the analysis in M Weber *The History of Commercial Partnerships in the Middle Ages* (Rowman & Littlefield

This older and simpler form of *commenda* under the force of the law merchant was extensively used throughout Europe[299] and evolved in France in the seventeenth century[300] into more complex forms for terrestrial use. Later, these led to the formation of the modern *société en accomandite*[301] where two classes of members existed, one with a responsibility limited to the amount of the capital they contributed and the other 'with an unlimited liability for the debts of the society, the administration of which lies solely in their hands'.[302]

Although occasionally adopted in its simplest forms in the fifteenth century,[303] it was only with the Limited Partnerships Act 1907[304] that this type of commercial association was formally recognised in England. According to Scott,[305] the reason for this was the late development of trade and commercial law when compared with the continent and with Italy in particular.[306] In the second part of the sixteenth century, the emergence of the joint stock company incorporated by charter as an alternative and more efficient vehicle for investing capital was a likely cause for the *commenda* to be surpassed. Not to mention, of course, the fact that the concept of a partner immune to claims essentially 'conflicted with basic common law forms of action and with tort, contract and agency doctrines'.[307] There is, however, still some controversy over this reasoning. Postan,[308] in particular, claims in strong terms that the commercial scheme had a parallel in medieval England. The 'narrower application of the term partnership by English courts, and the absence of an English *terminus techinicus* for the *commenda*', he argues, 'have led the historians to overlook many of the arrangements that fulfilled the same economic function and was put to the same use as an ordinary *commenda*. *Commenda*-like arrangements, employed for the function of service were assimilated to ordinary relationships of master and servant; *commenda*-like arrangements for the power to loan were assimilated to ordinary loans, but *commenda* partnerships they nevertheless were'.[309] It is, however, impossible to establish beyond doubt whether the fourteenth

Publishers Lanham 2003) 68; and H Hansmann, R Kraakman and R Squire 'Law and the Rise of the Firm' (2006) 119 Harv L Rev 1333 at 1372–1373.

299 See the comprehensive survey by R de Roover 'The Organization of Trade' in MM Postan and EE Rich (eds) *Cambridge Economic History of Europe*, vol III (CUP Cambridge 1963) 68.

300 Immediate reference is made to Colbert's Ordinance in 1673.

301 See CM Cipolla *European Society and Economy before the Industrial Revolution: 1000–1700* (Routledge London 1993) 194 and CE Freedman *Joint-Stock Enterprise in France 1807–1869: From Privileged Company to Modern Corporation* (University of North Carolina Press 1979) 3.

302 W Mitchell *An Essay on the Early History of the Law Merchant* (CUP Cambridge 1904) 129.

303 WS Holdsworth *A History of English Law*, vol VIII (Methuen & Co London 1925) 196.

304 7 Edw VII c 24.

305 WR Scott *The Constitution and Finance of English, Scottish and Irish Joint-Stock Companies to 1720*, vol I (CUP Cambridge 1912) 11 and 270.

306 This is also consistent with the explanation provided by Cooke who argues that the *commenda* never took root in England because England lagged behind the continent, particularly the Italians and the Dutch, in bookkeeping technique – CA Cooke *Corporation, Trust and Company* (Manchester UP Manchester 1950) 46.

307 R Harris *Industrializing English Law* (CUP Cambridge 2000) 20.

308 In general terms, see MM Postan *Medieval Trade and Finance* (CUP Cambridge 1973) 73.

309 MM Postan 'Partnership in English Medieval Commerce' in *Studi in Onore di Armado Sapori* (Istituto Editoriale Cisalpino Milano 1957) 540.

century transactions contained in the yearbook cases that have profit-sharing elements in them and where one of the parties was an Italian merchant did in fact involve the *commenda* or rather a general partnership, as 'these transactions were litigated within the framework of the writ of account that gave rise only to disputes between partners, not to disputes between partners and third parties'.[310]

3.3.2. The *Societas*

The *societas maris*, or *collegantia* to use the Venetian nomenclature,[311] reflected 'the transition from a unilateral *commenda* to a partnership with bilateral contribution of capital'.[312] The *societas* was a kind of partnership employed in Italy in which partners were close members of an association that shared the same privileges and responsibilities for carrying out commercial enterprises under a collective name. Solidarity in sharing the risk and often a higher degree of permanence were distinguishing elements from the unilateral *commenda*. In its later development, separate accounts no longer existed for the partnership property. A joint fund was established at the beginning of the venture. Each partner, as they appeared in the books of the firm, was an agent of the others[313] and personally liable for the loss of capital in proportion to his investment.[314]

As reported in the earliest Recognisance Rolls in the City of London Records,[315] with regard to the transactions carried out by London merchants for the purchase of commodities from the continent,[316] certain elements of the scheme of the Italian *societas* were well known in England in the fourteenth century.[317] The partnership was that of

310 R Harris 'The Institutional Dynamics of Early Modern Eurasian Trade: The *Commenda* and the Corporation' 16–17, working paper available at <www.papers.ssrn.com/sol3/papers.cfm?abstract_id=1294095> (accessed 7 August 2013).

311 G Astuti 'Note sulla collegantia veneta' in G Diurni (ed) *Tradizione Romanistica e Civiltà Giuridica Europea: Raccolta di Scritti di Guido Astuti*, vol II (Edizioni Scientifiche Italiane Napoli 1984) 1375.

312 M Weber *The History of Commercial Partnerships in the Middle Ages* (Rowman & Littlefield Publishers Lanham 2003) 68.

313 See docs CLXXII, CLXXIII, CLXXIV, CLXX, CLXXXVI and CLXXXVII in R Zeno *Documenti per la Storia del Diritto Marittimo nel secoli XIII e XIV* (Lattes Editori Torino 1936) and, among others, see docs IX, XXXIV, XXXVm XLVIII, LIX, LXXI, XCIII, XCVII, CXLI in M Chiaudano and M Moresco *Il Cartolare di Giovanni Scriba* (Istituto Storico Italiano per il Medio Evo Roma 1935) vols I and II.

314 This element has been clearly pointed out by de Roover in his fundamental contribution in the area. See R de Roover 'The Organization of Trade' in MM Postan and EE Rich (eds) *Cambridge Economic History of Europe*, vol III (CUP Cambridge 1963) 53.

315 Notably in Roll 1.

316 These cases have been studied by Postan and usually refer to 'groups of Londoners, often chaloners, acknowledging jointly a debt to an importer' – MM Postan 'Partnership in English Medieval Commerce' in *Studi in Onore di Armado Sapori* (Istituto Editoriale Cisalpino Milano 1957) 541.

317 See WJ Ashley *An Introduction to English Economic History and Theory* (Longmans, Green and Co London 1906) 414. The Italian forms of partnership were also matched by parallel arrangements in Germany. According to Postan, the North German towns distinguished two types of partnership or pseudo-partnership: the *Sendeve* (i.e. a *commenda*-like partnership employed for the purposes of investment) and the *Wederlegginge* (i.e. parallel to the Italian *societas maris*) – MM Postan 'Partnership in English Medieval Commerce' in *Studi in Onore di Armado Sapori* (Istituto Editoriale Cisalpino Milano 1957) 527.

'joint sale and purchase'. This was an occasional partnership confined to one transaction which began with the purchase of 'certain merchandise', usually wool exports,[318] and concluded with its division or sale. The principle of representation, although originally by way of reciprocal 'procuration' between partners to represent and bind the firm, was also recognised so that each partner 'could represent the rest and make contracts upon the whole firm'.[319]

3.3.3. The *Compagnia*

The model of the *compagnia*, primarily employed by the Italian merchant bankers in the thirteenth and fourteenth centuries, responded to the needs of a permanent commercial association operating with branches abroad.[320] It represented the evolution from the schemes suitable for 'travelling merchants' (such as the *commenda* and the *societas*) to the ones suitable for 'sedentary merchants', to schemes more in line with a stable and capitalised organisation that operated primarily in industry rather than exclusively in trade. In the classic characterisation provided by Gras, 'while the travelling merchant spent his best energies in moving from place to place, the sedentary merchant used his abilities in the administration of business. While the travelling merchant was largely subject to a single great risk (though he tried to remedy this), the sedentary merchant diversified his risk over a wide front'.[321]

Although the *compagnia* probably originated in line with the guilds as a very closed joint economic household (*stare ad unum panem et vinum*)[322] essentially characterised by the community of labour, the membership gradually ceased to coincide with that of a specific family. This was the result of the growth of business and the consequent need to involve non-family members in the commercial activities.[323] The case of the association in the artisan profession of the Florentine Alberti and Peruzzi families belonging to the *Arte di Calimala* who set up permanent branches abroad provides a good example of this evolution.[324]

318 The reason why in wool accounts partnerships occur more frequently than in other custom accounts 'is the fact that the custom and subsidy for wool seem to have been generally paid in instalments, and the shipper was obliged to deliver to the customers obligation for the amount still due from him. It was therefore natural that if partners shared in financial responsibility for the business, as they did in mutual partnerships, the names of both partners were declared to the customer and a joint bond entered into' – MM Postan 'Partnership in English Medieval Commerce' in *Studi in Onore di Armado Sapori* (Istituto Editoriale Cisalpino Milano 1957) 542.

319 W Mitchell *An Essay on the Early History of the Law Merchant* (CUP Cambridge 1904) 134.

320 See R de Roover *Money, Banking and Credit in Medieval Brugges* (Harvard UP Cambridge MA 1948) 34 on the organisation of the Italian mercantile and banking houses with branches in Bruges.

321 NS Gras *Business and Capitalism, an Introduction to Economic History* (FS Crofts New York 1939) 67.

322 Share the bread and the wine.

323 See ES Hunt and JM Murray *A History of Business in Medieval Europe 1200–1550* (CUP Cambridge 1999) 62.

324 See A Sapori 'La famiglia e la compagnia degli Alberti del Giudice' in *Studi in Onore di Armado Sapori*, vol II (Istituto Editoriale Cisalpino Milano 1957) 975; and R de Roover 'The Story of the Alberti Company, 1302–1348, as revealed in its Account Books' (1958) 23 The Business History Review 14.

Registration of partners in a *compagnia* was usual because notoriety was not sufficient to prove the partnership, and from the fourteenth century onwards 'such registers were kept not merely by the gilds, but by the city authorities'.[325] Members of the *compagnia* were bound together in joint and unlimited liability as a firm.[326] Even if each branch of the firm lacked limited liability it has been suggested that, contrary to the modern rules on partnerships, creditors at one branch enjoyed priority of claim to the assets held in the specific location.[327] This was the case whilst the *compagnie* were 'organized not as single partnerships, but rather on a hub-and-spoke system with branch offices formed as separate partnerships, and with central partnership (or individual) that held a controlling interest in each subpartnership and exercised company-wide executive authority'.[328] The most well-known example of the change in the structure of a partnership relates to the Medici conglomerate (a holding company) in the fifteenth century where the parent company controlled the branches by holding more than half of the capital and closely supervising their commercial activities.[329]

As will be discussed in detail below, branches of Italian *compagnie* existed in England from the thirteenth century.[330] Italian bankers originally resided in the country as agents of the Pope (the *camsores domini papae*) to collect tithes for the Crusades or other revenues owed to the Church by princes, ecclesiastic orders or laymen. At the time of Martin IV (1281–1285) the Spigliati, the Spini, the Cerchi, the Alberti, the Scali and the Frescobaldi of Florence were entrusted with the receiving of contributions. These agents, who could dispose of considerable sums of money, also used them for their personal affairs and some *compagnie*[331] progressively became the largest moneylenders to the Crown. It is difficult, however, to assess the extent to which this model of partnership had direct influence in the evolution of the English partnership and joint stock company. It seems reasonable to suggest that it probably played a very limited role, as the joint stock company (at least in its infancy) was confined to enterprises different in kind from the work of the sedentary merchant.[332]

A very accurate investigation into the *compagnia dei Bonsignori* is provided by M Chiaudano *Studi e Documenti per la Storia del Diritto Commerciale Italiano* (Università di Torino Torino 1930).

325 W Mitchell *An Essay on the Early History of the Law Merchant* (CUP Cambridge 1904) 131.

326 U Santarelli *Mercanti e Società fra Mercanti* (Giappichelli Torino 1992) 132; Id *Per la Storia del Fallimento nelle Legislazioni Italiane dell'età intermedia* (Cedam Padova 1964) 187; RS Lopez *The Commercial Revolution of the Middle Ages: 950–1350* (CUP Cambridge 1976) 74; and see ES Hunt and JM Murray *A History of Business in Medieval Europe 1200–1550* (CUP Cambridge 1999) 106.

327 See F Galgano *Lex Mercatoria* (Il Mulino Bologna 2001) 63.

328 H Hansmann, R Kraakman and R Squire 'Law and the Rise of the Firm' (2006) 119 Harv L Rev 1333 at 1366.

329 See R de Roover *The Rise and Decline of the Medici Bank* (Harvard UP Cambridge MA 1963).

330 See the accurate outline in A Sapori *The Italian Merchant in the Middle Ages* (Norton & Company New York 1970 transl by Patricia Ann Kennen) 65–91.

331 i.e. the Riccardi from Lucca and the Frescobaldi, Bardi and Peruzzi of Florence.

332 See NS Gras *Business and Capitalism, an Introduction to Economic History* (FS Crofts New York 1939) 105.

3.3.4. Conclusions

The above inquiry has presented the founding characteristics of medieval partnerships. It has suggested that while these originated and primarily operated in Italy, their structural elements were surely also in place in England from the end of thirteenth century.

This evidence is significant for the scope of this study on legal change. It reveals the complexity of the process of growth of the Italian joint stock model from different schemes of partnerships and allows us to clarify the level of commercial interaction between Italy and England in the Middle Ages. On more general terms, it supports the argument advanced in section 3.2 above (to be fully developed in section 3.4 below) that the presence of the *commenda*, the *societas* and the *compagnia* as part of the English indigenous tradition facilitated the process of reception of the Genoese joint stock model in the sixteenth century.

3.4. *The Advent of the Joint Stock Company in England*

Building on the analysis developed above, this section deals with the historical discussion on the origin of the joint stock company and its advent in England. It first considers the Genoese model of the *loca navis* as the original legal structure for joint stock companies. In particular, it outlines the conventional interpretation for its growth, presenting the transition from the *commenda/societas* arrangements (under 3.4.1). The terms of the emergence of the joint stock company and the possible pattern of reception in England of the Genoese model are subsequently discussed (under 3.4.2). The conclusion is that this pattern was the outcome of a process of hybridisation (under 3.4.3).

3.4.1. On the Origin of the Joint Stock Company

There are two views as to the origin of the joint stock principle whereby the company trades as a single person with joint stock capital contributed by its members and the company has transferable interests.

One view, the orthodox view, considers that it originated in the history of public debt in Genoa.[333] This interpretation has been questioned, as it offers only a partial explanation for the movement towards the formation of the corporate joint stock. It neglects, in particular, the significance of the growth of commerce among the Italian maritime cities starting from the twelfth century.[334] A second view maintains that the joint stock model was the spontaneous outcome of the increase in the partnership groups together with the

333 W Mitchell *An Essay on the Early History of the Law Merchant* (CUP Cambridge 1904) 138; and M Cizakca *A Comparative Evolution of Business Partnerships: Islamic World and Europe, with Specific Reference to the Ottoman Archive* (Brill Leiden 1996) 27–31. The same conclusions, although in passing, have been recently endorsed by H Hansmann, R Kraakman and R Squire 'Law and the Rise of the Firm' (2006) 119 Harv L Rev 1333 at 1376.

334 Or possibly even before. According to the Tavola d'Amalfi, at Amalfi already in the eleventh century, 'the owners, the captain and even the common sailors all had a share in the profits of the voyage and

increase in the volume and scope of mercantile ventures. In other words, it represented the gradual evolution from earlier legal commercial maritime structures such as the *commenda* and the *societas*. Both views are analysed below.

3.4.1.1. The Orthodox Position

The orthodox interpretation argues that the early joint stock company originated as a device employed by the Republic of Genoa to borrow financial resources from their citizens. The story is rather convoluted.[335] It has its roots in 1149 when the Republic of Genoa assigned as a loan to a group of investors the right to collect tax revenues for fifteen years to finance a war in Spain (Almeria and Tortosa).[336] The lenders formed a joint stock company of eighteen members for the exploitation of the tax monopoly.[337] This scheme was later replicated in several other cases. The Republic of Genoa occasionally also provided certain forms of security for the capital and interest. This sometimes even consisted in a *dominium utile* (i.e. *usufructus*) of the conquered land, as was the case of the loan raised to cover the cost of the conquest of Chios and Phocaea (1346).[338]

The debt instrument issued (*compera*) was treated as an annuity.[339] It was generally divided in units called *luoghi* (in Latin, '*loca*') with nominal value. The *luoghi* were not documentary intangibles, but merely documented intangibles. The names of the lenders (*luogatari*) were registered in special books called *cartulari*. The *luoghi* passed to the heirs in case of the owner's death and could be freely bought and sold by registration in the *cartulari*. Given that interest on *luoghi* was not guaranteed, that profit was uncertain and that *luogatari* registered in the *cartulari* were explicitly named participants (*partecipi*), it is reasonable to assert that the investors were shareholders in the current sense of the word.[340] The Republic of Genoa consolidated its growing public debt in 1407 in the Casa di San Giorgio. San Giorgio's shareholders purchased the entire previous *compere* issued by the Republic and 'performed what today would be called a debt-for-equity swap'.[341] Although a secondary market for *luoghi* had existed since the middle of

formed an association whose liability was strictly limited' – W Mitchell *An Essay on the Early History of the Law Merchant* (CUP Cambridge 1904) 138.

335 See the contribution of M Fratianni and F Spinelli 'Did Genoa and Venice Kick a Financial Revolution in the Quattrocento?' working paper 2005 (no 112), available at <www.oenb.at/en/img/wp112_tcm16-38081.pdf> (accessed 7 August 2013).

336 D Gioffrè *Il Debito Pubblico Genovese: Inventario delle Compere Anteriori a San Giorgio o non Consolidate nel Banco* (Giuffrè Milano 1967) 12.

337 E Marengo, C Manfroni and G Pessagno *Il Banco di San Giorgio* (A Donath Editore Genova 1911) 22.

338 See PP Argenti *The Occupation of Chios by the Genoese and their Administration of the Island 1346–1566* (CUP Cambridge 1958) 107.

339 E Marengo, C Manfroni and G Pessagno *Il Banco di San Giorgio* (A Donath Editore Genova 1911) 19–26. See also the episodes cited in SA Epstein *Genoa and the Genoese 958–1528* (University of North Carolina Press Chapel Hill 1996) 233–34.

340 See E Marengo, C Manfroni and G Pessagno *Il Banco di San Giorgio* (A Donath Editore Genova 1911) 87.

341 M Fratianni 'The Evolutionary Chain of International Financial Centres', working paper Mofir available at <www.dea2.univpm.it/quaderni/pdfmofir/Mofir006.pdf> (accessed 7 August 2013).

the thirteenth century,[342] with the consolidation of public debt, the secondary market for *luoghi* became very active and sophisticated. There was no restriction against foreign ownership and *luoghi* were often used as collateral by bankers, borrowers and tax collectors.[343]

3.4.1.2. Critique of the Orthodox View

As suggested earlier, traces of the joint stock company can be found in Genoa in the shipbuilding sector independently from any reference to public debts. According to this interpretation, in the early times the Genoese joint stock company expressed nothing else than the division of a (interest in the) ship between investors who enjoyed equal status *vis-à-vis* each other. The management of the commercial association was generally entrusted to a captain who was an employee.[344]

The financial parts (*loca navis*) were transmissible *mortis causa* and *inter vivos* by amending the register (*cartulari*), although in the latter circumstance subject to the consent of the other associates.[345] Shares in the ownership of the vessels, or better in a company operating the vessel, 'were […] the subject of business transactions'[346] as they were considered property and, therefore, bought and sold or pledged as security, like other commercial commodities. *Luoghi* were regarded as particularly good security 'for one of the favourite forms of investment across the sea, the sea loan (*foenus nauticum*) which permitted a high interest, 20 per cent to 50 per cent in view of the risk, and which was repaid only if the ship arrived safely at the prescribed destination'.[347] From a purely economic perspective, the transition from the *commenda/societas* arrangements to the joint stock model was essentially driven by commercial necessity, by the need to meet the huge costs of the ships and armaments which required a larger number of investors and the indispensable use of shares (*luoghi*) to raise capital. Investors, including the entire merchant class, 'were thus enabled to participate in the profits of shipping, lesser individuals, men, women and minors also found here an encouragement for their money across the seas, all with safety in view of the divided risk'.[348] The Genoese joint stock company also allowed a system of risk diversification. Rather than buying a whole ship by himself, an investor could invest small amounts in various ships. Ownership by *loca* remained a typical feature of Genoese shipping until the middle of the thirteenth century

342 SA Epstein *Genoa and the Genoese 958–1528* (University of North Carolina Press Chapel Hill 1996) 147.

343 M Fratianni 'Government Debt, Reputation and Creditors' Protection: The Tale of San Giorgio' (2006) 10 Review of Finance 492.

344 See docs CXXXI, CLXXI, CLXXIII, CLXXIV, CLXXV, CLXXXVI in R Zeno *Documenti per la Storia del Diritto Marittimo nel secoli XIII e XIV* (Lattes Editori Torino 1936).

345 IW Raymond and RS Lopez (eds) *Medieval Trade in the Mediterranean World* (Columbia UP New York 2001) 175.

346 E Byrne 'Commercial Contracts of the Genoese in the Syrian Trade of the Twelfth Century'(1916–1917) 31 Quarterly Journal of Economics 129 at 135.

347 E Byrne *Genoese Shipping in the Twelfth and Thirteenth Centuries* (The Medieval Academy of America Cambridge MA 1930) 14.

348 Ibid.

when the wealth accumulated by families and individuals together with the increased security of overseas trade caused them to become outdated.

That said, it is tempting to suggest that the widespread system of *loca* which originated in the shipbuilding sector may have exercised a significant influence on the creation and development of the scheme employed by the purchasers of the *compere* in the public debt of the Republic of Genoa and in the formation of the vast commercial associations aimed at the exploitation of the natural resources at Ceuta and Chios in the fourteenth century (the so-called *maone*).[349]

3.4.2. The Rise of the Joint Stock Model

Having clarified the origin of the joint stock company in the history of the shipbuilding sector in Genoa, the following analysis explains the terms according to which this scheme of association was exported in England. This is preliminary to the assessment, dealt with further below under 3.4.3, of the pattern of reception of the original model in the pre-existing legal framework.

In England, the essential features of the joint stock company have many similarities to the ones observed in the evolution of the Genoese *societas maris*. In England too they were the product of overseas trade and mercantilist environment. Although still controversial among historians[350] who support the idea of a natural evolution of the *gilda mercatoria*,[351] this study argues that it was primarily from the legal framework of business organisation of ship ownership that the embryonic idea of corporate joint stock found its roots in England. Above all, this explanation reflects the transition to a large scale of business that was primarily centred on maritime ventures and enterprises.

As seen in Genoa, the property in a ship was divided into freely transferable (by registration)[352] financial portions belonging to a large partnership of members. Early English joint stock companies did not typically provide a system of terminable stock, as had been the case for the 'regulated corporations'[353] where each member under a common infrastructure traded on his own account, taking risks and liabilities individually. This allowed partnerships to avoid the technical difficulties of obtaining sufficient capital, as had been the case of the East India Company who failed to float a

349 A vast commercial organisation that managed the monopoly of alum and employed its own armed forces. See the description in PP Argenti *The Occupation of Chios by the Genoese and their administration of the island 1346–1566* (CUP Cambridge 1958) 107.

350 See WR Scott *The Constitution and Finance of English, Scottish and Irish Joint-Stock Companies to 1720*, vol I (CUP Cambridge 1912) 12.

351 The suggested interpretation of this study is also opposed by Harris who claims that the shipping business organisation had a unique legal framework outside the realm of the common law. It was a 'pseudo joint stock partnership', *de facto* an alternative scheme to the joint stock company. See R Harris *Industrializing English Law* (CUP Cambridge 2000) 186–190. *Contra* CA Cooke *Corporation, Trust and Company* (Manchester UP Manchester 1950) 47–48.

352 JW Smith *A Compendium of Mercantile Law* (Sweet & Maxwell London 1843) 169.

353 Mainly formed under the shield of common privileges for the government of the single trade. See WS Holdsworth *A History of English Law* (Metheuen & Co London 1925) vol VIII, 206.

stock for a second voyage to India in October 1601.[354] The part-ownership of the ship was inspired by the property law concept of tenancy in common. The affairs of the association were managed on behalf of the members 'by one or two partners or, even, in some cases, by a ship's master who was not a partner'.[355]

Whilst the Genoese model was originally adopted to solve the problem of the scarcity of capital in shipbuilding industry, the fundamental reason for the emergence of this system of ship-owning in England has to be associated with the necessity of risk diversification, of reducing the financial exposure in the event of loss of the ship. This should be clear when reflecting on the fact that, although in seventeenth-century England it was in the capacity of individual merchants to own the ships themselves, they still opted to own only small shares in them.[356] The argument also finds significant support in the fact that until the 1710s maritime insurance did not exist and that it was not until around the 1720s that it developed sufficiently 'to provide a reasonable alternative to the method of risk spreading by the division of ownership into small parts'.[357] While the size of ships continued to increase, the subdivision of ownership reached its peak in the decades before 1700 and stopped there.[358] During the eighteenth century the rapid decline in the number of owners can be closely linked with the growing use of insurance 'which made it less necessary for the shipping entrepreneur to spread his risk and to share his profits with sleeping partners'.[359]

As in Genoa, the development of the English joint stock association in the period before 1720 was driven by the needs of the State and by the rise in the scale of maritime trade following the technical advances in the theory and practice of navigation.[360] It was fundamentally the grants of the privileges of incorporation by the sovereign for the financing of foreign trade and the foundation of new colonies[361] that were at the basis of the success of the joint stock model in England. From the point of view of the Crown, the revenues acquired from granting monopolies allowed it to reduce the gap between the declining land revenues and growing military expenses.[362] In short, contrary to the policies adopted in Portugal and Spain, which responded to the unprecedented growth

354 WR Scott The Constitution and Finance of English, Scottish and Irish Joint Stock Companies to 1720 (CUP Cambridge 1912) vol II, 95–98.

355 R Davis *The Rise of the English Shipping Industry* (David & Charles Newton Abbot 1972) 82.

356 While the cost of building and equipping the largest merchant ship in the seventeenth century (the Charles II of 800 tons) for her first voyage was £15,680, the fortunes of the Childs, the Riders or the Heathcotes amounted to hundreds of thousands of pounds.

357 R Davis *The Rise of the English Shipping Industry* (David & Charles Newton Abbot 1972) 88.

358 M Cizakca *A Comparative Evolution of Business Partnerships: Islamic World and Europe, with Specific Reference to the Ottoman Archive* (Brill Leiden 1996) 33.

359 R Davis *The Rise of the English Shipping Industry* (David & Charles Newton Abbot 1972) 89.

360 See G Callender and FH Hinsley *The Naval Side of British History 1458–1945* (Christophers London 1952).

361 e.g. the Virginia Company founded in 1609 and New England Company founded in 1620 ('the joint stock company would arrange for the raising of capital, for the transportation of planters, and for the survey and divisions of land' – WR Scott *The Constitution and Finance of English, Scottish and Irish Joint-Stock Companies to 1720*, vol II (CUP Cambridge 1912) 249.

362 See MJ Braddick *The Nerves of State: Taxation and the Financing of the English State, 1558–1714* (Manchester UP Manchester 1996) 131.

in trade opportunities in the sixteenth century 'by organizing and funding intercontinental trade through the state, the Dutch and especially the English followed the Genoese examples of combining private investment with state-granted monopoly privileges'.[363]

Although the force of the State needs and of the mercantile expansion represent the *leitmotive* in justifying the common economic rationale for the growth of the joint-stock principle in Genoa and in England, this is *per se* of little help in explaining the surprising similarities in the legal response.[364] It would strain credulity to suppose that the almost identical outcome follows from the mere circumstance that 'substantially the same causes were at work in England at this period [i.e. the sixteenth and seventeenth centuries] as those which had been at work in Italy in the Middle Ages'.[365] This interpretation would in fact overlook (or at least greatly underestimate) the historical perspective, the physical presence and the cultural influence of 'alien merchants'[366] in the development of the English commercial law. Not to mention the possible impact of certain forms of Italian commercial associations (*commenda*, *societas* and *compagnia*) existing in England from the end of the thirteenth century.

It is argued therefore that to a large extent, the advent of the joint stock association in England is the result of legal borrowing, of the reception (although not necessarily direct)[367] of the model of partnership employed by the Italian merchants in the Middle Ages (the *societas*) and, in particular, of peculiar legal schemes of Genoese (the *luoghi*). The great historian de Roover has endorsed this connection in the past. He maintained:

> 'did not the first joint-stock companies arise in overseas trade? It is true that they were set up by the Dutch and the English, but their promoters were certainly familiar with Italian precedents in the financing and management of collective colonial enterprises, such as the maone of Chios and Ceuta. Was not a Genoese Pallavicini among the shareholders of the Virginia Company; and did not Tomas Mun reside for many years in Leghorn and Pisa before he returned to London and became one of the first directors of the East India Company? Moreover, let us not overlook the fact that, even in the East Indian trade, a permanent company was not created at the beginning. The first voyages were each separate ventures, much like the temporary partnership in the pioneering days of Genoese and Venetian shipping'.[368]

363 H Hansmann, R Kraakman and R Squire 'Law and the Rise of the Firm' (2006) 119 Harv L Rev 1333 at 1376.

364 i.e. internal structure/formation of capital/members' participation.

365 WS Holdsworth *A History of English Law*, vol VIII (Metheuen & Co London 1925) 208.

366 i.e. persons born outside the realm to parents also born outside the realm. See K Kim *Aliens in Medieval Law* (CUP Cambridge 2000) 23 with specific reference to alien merchants.

367 It has been suggested that borrowing could also have been the result of an indirect process involving the translation of French and Flemish works published in the Low Countries in the sixteenth century: thus argues R de Roover 'Discussion on NSB Gras' paper 'Capitalism –Concepts and History' (1942) 16 Bulletin of the Business Historical Society 37.

368 R de Roover 'The Organization of Trade' in MM Postan and EE Rich (eds) *Cambridge Economic History of Europe*, vol III (CUP Cambridge 1963) 58.

Although there is no conclusive and incontrovertible primary evidence on the matter, certain historical data suggest that de Roover's interpretation of legal change based on borrowing is not a mere conjecture. Italian models have represented one of the major sources of legal evolution for the joint stock company. Two significant examples related to the formation of early English joint stock associations for the discovery of new trades are mentioned below. They illustrate specific episodes of borrowing of great relevance and they represented models of reference for the evolution of English business enterprises. These are the cases of the Russia and the Levant Companies in the sixteenth century:

The Russia Company (also known as the Muscovy Company)[369] was the first English joint stock company of importance[370] and it represented the evolution from 'regulated' to 'joint stock' company. In the light of the great wealth obtained by the Spanish and Portuguese in similar ways, the trading expedition at the foundation of the company started with the idea of discovering a north-east passage to China and new countries to trade with. In 1553, the adventurers' subscribed capital was £6,000 by calls of £25 on each share. This was used to buy three ships and the equipment for the trading expedition. Instead of each person participating by trading his own capital, as it had been the case for the African adventurers in that same year, a joint stock was formed for the first time. One of the most convincing explanations for the change in the participation to the commercial association and in the method of raising the stock from the past is ascribable to the cultural influence of the Genoese Sebastiano Caboto,[371] one of the founders of the venture and later its governor for life. This is because 'it may have been through his knowledge of the joint-stock system in Italy that it was decided there should be one common stocke of the company, and that no member or servant might trade on his own account'.[372] The same internal constitution prescribed in the Royal Charter points to the Italian origin of the scheme of the body. The evidence consists of the fact that among the persons who controlled or influenced the conduct of the company's affairs, besides the 'governor' and the 'assistants', was the 'consul'. This was the prototype of the English 'deputy governor' which did not exist at all or was extremely rare in English companies.[373] The office of 'consul' was instead very common in Genoa for supervising the administration of the finances at the beginning of the debt. Hence, 'there can be little doubt that this temporary introduction of the term consul as applied to a deputy governor, was of Italian origin'.[374]

369 A detailed account of the history of this company is provided by TS Willan *The Early History of the Russia Company 1553–1603* (Manchester UP Manchester 1956).

370 WR Scott *The Constitution and Finance of English, Scottish and Irish Joint-Stock Companies to 1720*, vol I (CUP Cambridge 1912) 17.

371 Caboto later became a citizen of Venice in 1476.

372 WR Scott *The Constitution and Finance of English, Scottish and Irish Joint-Stock Companies to 1720*, vol I (CUP Cambridge 1912) 18.

373 The only other case was that of the Company of Kathai, incorporated in 1577, which was formed by members of the Russia Company. See WR Scott *The Constitution and Finance of English, Scottish and Irish Joint-Stock Companies to 1720*, vol I (CUP Cambridge 1912) 20.

374 Ibid vol I, 20.

The second example is the case of the Levant Company (also known as the Turkey Company).[375] This example differs from that of the Russia Company, but a study of its history also supports the view that Italian merchants had a direct cultural influence in the promotion of the legal form of English joint stock associations. The Levant Company had its origin in the commerce of English merchants with Italy and in the ventures that from 1511 consistently carried out trading with the Levant. Bearing in mind that in the Middle Ages it was through the markets of Italy that the rich products of the East found their way into Christendom, it is easy to see that Italian merchants played a crucial role in the first part of the Levant commerce.[376] The Genoese and later the Venetians had the monopoly for exporting currants from the Mediterranean 'having been granted by Syndics to a fellow-countryman of their own'.[377] On the basis of the monopoly, they could simply not be excluded from the Levant trade and a mixed association had to be formed. This led Italian merchants and the new (English) adventurers to the Levant to join 'in a petition for incorporation [before Elizabeth I], with exclusive privileges, and on September 11th, 1581, a charter was signed'.[378] By the end of the sixteenth century, however, the Venetian trade with England had gradually declined because of the commercial and naval policy of Henry VII[379] and because the League of Cambrai crippled the power of the Republic of Venice.[380] These events had a very beneficial influence on the promotion of the enterprise of English merchants in trade with the Levant,[381] but they did not alter the founding structure of the company. While the Levant trade was originally formed only by English merchants organised under the schemes of a partnership based on the *societas* or by every merchant independently, with the growth of commerce and the participation of Venetian merchants as described above, trade was carried out on a joint stock basis.[382] Although there is no conclusive primary evidence of the influence of the Italian commercial practice in driving the structure of the organisation of the early Levant Company, it seems very likely that this was the case. At the time of incorporation, the strength of the joint stock model adopted by Venetians for their profitable commercial trades in the Levant since the time of the Crusades prevailed over the less efficient and less sophisticated commercial structure of English merchants.

375 A detailed account of the history of this company is offered by AC Wood *A History of the Levant Company* (Frank Cass & Co London 1964).

376 M Epstein *The Early History of the Levant Company* (George Routledge & Sons Ltd London 1908) 2.

377 See WR Scott *The Constitution and Finance of English, Scottish and Irish Joint-Stock Companies to 1720*, vol II (CUP Cambridge 1912) 84.

378 Ibid vol II, 84.

379 M Epstein *The Early History of the Levant Company* (George Routledge & Sons Ltd London 1908) 4. Henry VII wanted English ships to have a share in the wine trade (which was a Venetian monopoly) and retaliated against the levies imposed by the Venetian exports from Candia in foreign ships.

380 Ibid 5.

381 'In 1513 an English consul was established in the island of Chios, and in 1522 a mercantile settlement was made at Candia, while in 1533 began the English currant trade with Zante' – M Epstein *The Early History of the Levant Company* (George Routledge & Sons Ltd London 1908) 6.

382 See WR Scott *The Constitution and Finance of English, Scottish and Irish Joint-Stock Companies to 1720*, vol II (CUP Cambridge 1912) 85.

3.4.3. Hybridisation

The analysis above suggested that in addition to the general arguments about the Italian influence in the development of English commercial law put forward in section 3.1, there is evidence that the introduction of the joint stock company was the likely result of legal borrowing from an Italian model. The case of the formation of the Russia Company, in particular, showed that the Genoese structure of the joint stock association not only influenced, but also provided, the legal specimen for the commercial ventures of English merchants from the sixteenth century onwards. This link is even clearer when observing the mechanism for the circulation of Genoese *luoghi* and how this was reflected in the novative model of (chartered corporations and) unincorporated joint stock companies observed in section 2 above.

The evidence of borrowing as such, however, may be misleading at times and not conclusive in explaining the pattern of legal change. It may offer a superficial view of the process of the development of law, as it identifies specific facts and circumstances without properly taking into account the historical context and the social implications involved. It does not consider, in particular, the mechanism of interaction between the purported borrowed models with the pre-existing legal/economic framework. In other words, it says little on whether the borrowed model under different economic and historical conditions was reproduced verbatim or whether it was adapted according to the existing local traditions.

The analysis below suggests that although certain significant elements were clearly successfully borrowed from Italian models, the English joint stock company was also shaped in accordance with the English legal tradition and that it later evolved in original ways in response to peculiar national legal and economic circumstances. All this, it is suggested, was the result of a process of hybridisation.

The most straightforward way to illustrate that exclusive reference to transplantation/borrowing of legal rules greatly oversimplifies the historical reality is by reference to the case of the Russia Company mentioned above.

3.4.3.1. Complexities in the Pattern of Borrowing and Legal Reception

It was put forward in the preceding section that the internal constitution of the Russia Company provided for three different organs to be involved in the management of the business. Besides the governor and the assistants, there was an intermediate order appointed to supervise the administration of finances: the consul. This was clearly of Italian origin and, even without relying on other strong indirect elements, it provides evidence that significant founding rules of the organisation of the English joint stock company were borrowed from Italy. Other circumstances, however, should be carefully considered before reaching a final conclusion on the pattern of legal change and claiming that it was merely the result of borrowing. A more careful consideration of the process of formation of the Russia Company may help to explain the point.

According to its charter, the undertaking was described as 'one bodie and perpetuall fellowship and communaltie'.[383] This is consistent with the terminology in force in the early guilds marked by the analogy to the family where the members of the fellowship were pictured as 'bretheren' and 'sisteren'. In this respect, it suggests a direct influence of the model developed in the guild merchant for the organisation of the regulation of by-laws of the Russia Company. The fact that from 1446 the men associated with the alderman (the governor) and responsible for the management of the guild in general were named associates (assistants, in the Russia Company) also seems to point in the same direction. The alderman and those associated with him were in fact typically responsible for the management of the old guild merchants.[384] Even the organisation of convivial meetings indicates strong links with the activities of the guilds. Scott notices for example that 'the gilds arranged processions with no little pomp and ceremony, and the same feature reappears at the beginning of the history of the Russia company – there, just as in the social fraternities at the funeral of a member.'[385] These parallels are, of course, to be seen having also in mind the perspective of the existing medieval partnership models mentioned before.[386]

It follows from the above that the advent of the joint stock company in England was not just the outcome of legal borrowing, but most likely the product of three blurred and differently weighted lines of development. Namely, the pre-existing forms of medieval partnerships, the structure for the organisation of corporate activity provided by the *gilda mercatoria* and the method of constituting joint stock companies that originated in maritime commerce in Genoa.

3.4.3.2. The Impact of Borrowing on Legal Evolution

Even allowing for the idea that the introduction of the joint stock company in England was the direct result of legal borrowing, significant historical circumstances suggest that this element is *per se* unhelpful for understanding the complexities of the process of legal evolution. In particular, when considering that the financial structure of a permanent joint stock in the Russia Company was retained only for 31 years from the time of its formation, its relative historical impact as a direct transplant should be clear. Given the expenses and costs of establishing the new trade, the Russia Company was in fact reorganised in 1586 by using short-term capital (as opposed to perpetual capital) and individual accounts. The underlying plan was to raise more capital from a greater number of investors and to allow for the possibility to pay dividends more frequently. The Russia

383 WR Scott *The Constitution and Finance of English, Scottish and Irish Joint-Stock Companies to 1720*, vol I (CUP Cambridge 1912) 19.

384 Ibid vol I, 7.

385 Ibid vol I, 5.

386 With a slightly different emphasis, Harris is more inclined to follow path-dependence theories. He supports the view that the advent of business corporations with the organisational form of the joint stock in England in the second half of the sixteenth century had its foundations in medieval guilds and municipal corporation when they became 'increasingly used for profit-oriented organization of business' – R Harris *Industrializing English Law* (CUP Cambridge 2000) 39.

Company was therefore reorganised[387] along the lines of the old guilds that regulated the business activities of its members. The Levant Company was similarly reorganised in 1592. Apart from the East India Company and 'highly adventurous one-time voyages to the remotes shores of Africa and the Atlantic',[388] permanent joint stock simply proved to be an unappealing feature for early business associations. It was only in 1670 that the Hudson's Bay company was chartered (again) as a joint stock corporation with trade monopoly over the Hudson Bay drainage basin[389] and only in the 1690s that new joint stock companies were formed in domestic manufacture and trade.[390]

3.4.3.3. Hybrid Paradigms

In more general terms, it should finally be noted that the Genoese model, which has been argued to be at the foundation of the English company as adapted by the influence of the Anglo-Saxon guilds, did not survive in its original form but developed consistently with the evolution of the pre-existing legal framework.

It has been suggested in section 2 that the scheme at the basis of the current mechanism of circulation of registered shares is the one resulting from mid-nineteenth century reforms in company law. This, in turn, largely consolidated the law for unincorporated joint stock companies. That model, it was seen, grew successfully after the enactment of the Bubble Act, because it provided a distinct and alternative form of business organisation from chartered and statutory joint stock companies at a time when incorporation was difficult to achieve. Unincorporated joint stock companies grew within the peculiar bounds of equitable jurisdiction. In the words of Maitland, equity trust 'in effect enabled men to form [unincorporated] joint stock companies with limited liability, until at length the legislature had to give way'.[391]

This historical reference intends to show that it was not the Genoese model that directly formed the basis of the current legislation on companies. Instead, it was an adaptation of that original model in accordance with the existing legal tradition through a process of hybridisation. The process of the constitution of joint stock companies in the form of a deed of settlement, although it replicated in functional terms the model of commercial association (for the significant parts) of Italian origins, was very different from the borrowed one. It was the expression of the peculiar environment of the jurisdiction of equity, offering in this way an original model for the development of large- scale concerns when incorporation by Parliament or Royal Charter was difficult to obtain. This was a hybrid paradigm in the terms outlined in Part I where postcolonial studies were considered.

387 i.e. not a joint stock. See TS Willan *The Early History of the Russia Company 1553–1603* (Manchester UP Manchester 1956) 211.

388 R Harris *Industrializing English Law* (CUP Cambridge 2000) 45.

389 See AM Carlos and S Nicholas 'Agency Problems in Early Chartered Companies: The Case of the Hudson's Bay Company' (1990) 50 J Econ Hist 853.

390 WR Scott *The Constitution and Finance of English, Scottish and Irish Joint-Stock Companies to 1720*, vol II (CUP Cambridge 1912) 330.

391 FW Maitland 'The Unincorporate Body' in Id *Selected Essays* (CUP Cambridge 1936) 135.

3.5. Conclusions

The conclusion of the inquiry in this chapter is that the current legal characterisation of the circulation of registered shares, as crystallised in the Companies Act 2006, has followed directly from the development of the principles of the joint stock company. The historical analysis above has shown that the embryonic paradigm of the Italian partnership model evolved from a very close scheme into a more sophisticated and open pattern of transferable capital at the time of the growth in trade starting from the time of the Crusades. This, it was suggested, was at first a consequence of the effort to escape from the operation of the usury law in ordinary business life. It was also argued that the Italian model of maritime partnership (the *societas maris*), as refined in the scheme of a joint stock fund in Genoa, was transplanted and employed for part-ownership in ships in England from the beginning of the sixteenth century. The reception was probably facilitated by the commercial interaction originated by the existence of commercial Italian settlements involved in the wool trade in the South of England, by the cultural influence of the Italian mercantile community and by the widespread employment of certain Italian forms of business association in England (*commenda*, *societas* and *compagnia*). Shareholding in the *societas navis* was evidenced by the inscription of the ownership of the shares in the common stock in the company's register. Upon other members' consent, the transfer of membership required an amendment of the same register arrangements in line with the scheme of partnership law. The underlying rule was novation. Along the terms of the technique of circulation of the Genoese *luoghi* within the scheme of the vast commercial association (*maone*) where 'the shares could be freely bought and sold'[392] and the names of the owners were registered in special books (*cartulari*), English shares in chartered and joint stock companies were freely transferable and title was determined by registration. By referring to a 1568 case that surprisingly echoes the modern instruction that a shareholder gives to his broker, it has been suggested that from the sixteenth century shares were sold and bought with a considerable degree of freedom 'outside personal acquaintances and without limiting conditions'.[393] Nevertheless, the Genoese model was not received in its original form. Rather, it was adapted, albeit in limited respects, in accordance with the indigenous legal tradition founded on the fellowship relations typical of the trading guilds. The borrowed model later developed in an original way in the realm of the jurisdiction of equity consistently with the growth of unincorporated joint stock companies. The role of the Court of Chancery in shaping the law of partnership and trust provided for the unique evolution of the paradigm of the English joint stock company when incorporation was not easily available. A hybrid paradigm was therefore progressively formed out of the interaction of the original model and the indigenous legal tradition.

392 W Mitchell *An Essay on the Early History of the Law Merchant* (CUP Cambridge 1904) 138.

393 WR Scott *The Constitution and Finance of English, Scottish and Irish Joint-Stock Companies to 1720*, vol II (CUP Cambridge 1912) 416.

In short, as with colonised subjects, the reproduced model 'is almost the same, but not quite'.[394] It is a hybrid paradigm or in postcolonial discourse, the effect of 'a flawed colonial mimesis in which to be Anglicised is emphatically not to be English'.[395] This was outlined in section 2 above, where it was also seen that the same model was later consolidated in statutes. It was also argued in that context that the recent development of law has been the result of the path dependency and that incorporation did not affect the law of transfer for registered shares. A simple comparison with the overview provided in section 1 shows that the same rules have been replicated in the existing ones for the transfer of English registered shares under both the Companies Act 2006 and the Uncertificated Securities Regulation 2001 as far as uncertificated shares are concerned. The company's register, and in similar terms the operator's register under CREST, is *prima facie* evidence of title, and registered shares (both certificated and uncertificated) do not qualify as negotiable instruments. Share certificates are merely documented intangibles as was the case for the early part-ownership in ships and the Genoese *loca navis*.

The key issue in this chapter is that the choice for 'an off-the-shelf set of laws governing investment and commercial transactions'[396] has represented a very significant pattern in the evolution of English commercial law. The historical evidence in support of this statement, however, provides only a descriptive and rather superficial understanding of the pattern of legal change. It was only by considering the process of legal reception that it has been possible to assess the success of such choice, the significance of the interaction between the borrowed and the indigenous legal traditions and to observe the emergence of hybrid models.

394 H Bhabha 'Of Mimicry and Men' in Bhabha H (eds) *The Location of Culture* (Routledge London 1994) 123. In general, see also B Parry 'Problems in current discourse theory' (1987) 9 Oxford Literary Review 27.

395 H Bhabha 'Of Mimicry and Men' in H Bhabha (eds) *The Location of Culture* (Routledge London 1994) 125.

396 R Goode, H Kronke and E McKendrick *Transnational Commercial Law* (OUP Oxford 2007) 183.

Chapter 5

THE TRANSFER OF SHARE WARRANTS TO BEARER

Registered shares and share warrants to bearer express the same economic function as units of the corporate capital. They differ in terms of their legal nature and modes of circulation. It has already been pointed out that this has an historical explanation.

Within the theoretical boundaries of this study, Chapter 5 investigates the historical evolution of the transfer of share warrants to bearer. It shows that some of the roots of the current legal characterisation can be found in certain Italian notarial exchange contracts used to obviate the risk of physical transport of money for long-distance trade in the Middle Ages. These instruments were received in English commercial practice in the fifteenth century and developed later on through a process of hybridisation.

This chapter is organised as follows. Section 1 establishes where the law related to share warrants to bearer currently stands. As was the case in Chapter 4 with respect to registered shares, the goal of this chapter is to offer a coherent overview of the subject matter before embarking on a historical discussion.

The fundamental finding in section 1 is that share warrants to bearer are negotiable instruments. Building on this, section 2 examines the origin and development of the concept of negotiability. It discusses the Italian contract of *cambium* and then deals with the gradual process of recognition of the alienability of rights *in personam* embodied in the documents in England.

Section 3 assesses the significance of market practice as the medium for exporting the Italian scheme for negotiable instruments and traces the history of the bills of exchange within the debate on the role of merchant law for the development of the common law. The arguments on the possible incorporation of the law merchant into common law by adapting old legal principles to new commercial necessities are tackled in some detail so as to show how legal growth has occurred via hybridisation. Section 3 also offers additional arguments for assessing the extent of borrowing and the pattern of legal change. In particular, it considers the precise position of the innocent purchaser for value of negotiable instruments, suggesting that the holder in due course doctrine has not been a key element of the law in that area from its earliest stages, but it has been a later indigenous achievement.

After an overview of the nineteenth century legislative consolidation, the last section of this chapter discusses how scrip certificates may be regarded as the ancestors of the modern share warrants to bearer within the theory of negotiability. This is linked to the historical analysis carried out in the preceding sections 2 and 3, and reiterates the nature of the legal evolution of share warrants to bearer as a process of hybridisation.

1. The Current Legal Framework

Share warrants to bearer, although not very popular,[1] have not completely fallen out of use in England.[2] It seems unlikely that they will be of widespread use in the future as it is difficult to square their rationale with the need to serve the commercial needs for rapid and efficient transfer of shareholdings. The advent of dematerialisation at the end of the 1990s and the growth of intermediation[3] more generally have rendered obsolete and an intolerable burden the recourse to the existence and transfer of physical documents.[4] In addition to that, their use needs to consider the great disadvantages in managing the proxy voting machinery, the risk of theft and the high stamp duties, all well known by practitioners.[5] Nevertheless, share warrants to bearer are still available to English companies, as the provisions contained in the Companies Act 2006 confirm.

In setting the boundaries for the following historical analysis on hybridisation, this section looks at the legal nature and at the physical manifestation of share warrants to bearer (sections 1.1 and 1.2) as a preliminary inquiry to establish how legal title is transferred (section 1.3) and in order to assess its underlying legal characterisation (section 1.4). In symmetric contrast to the *bona fide* purchaser defence addressed in Chapter 4, section 1.5, when dealing with the circulation of registered shares, devotes some attention to the holder in due course doctrine as the distinguishing element of negotiability.

1.1. Legal Nature

In order to understand how share warrants to bearer are transferred, it is first necessary to establish what they are. As for their ultimate legal nature, they are like registered shares. For the purpose of this inquiry reference is therefore made to the analysis already carried out in Chapter 4, section 1.1. The rationale for this direct reference is grounded in legislation itself. Under section 779(1) of the Companies Act 2006, a company limited by shares, if authorised by its articles, may issue share warrants instead of share certificates in respect of any paid-up shares stating that the bearer of the warrant is entitled to the shares specified in it.[6]

1 In contrast with practice on certain continental jurisdictions. See references to German and Austrian law in E Micheler *Property in Securities – A Comparative Study* (CUP Cambridge 2007) 145.

2 e.g. see the recent case *AMG Global Nominees (Private) Ltd v SMM Holdings Ltd* [2008] EWCA Civ 1278.

3 See below *sub* Chapter 6, section 1.1.

4 A broader critical analysis on negotiable instruments in general is put forward by JS Rogers *The End of Negotiable Instruments* (OUP Oxford 2012).

5 As already noted more than 30 years ago by LCB Gower *Gower's Principles of Modern Company Law* (Stevens & Sons London 1979) 442.

6 See the default articles of association for a public companies registered on or after 5 October 2009 – Companies (Model Articles) Regulations 2008 (SI 2008/3229) art 51. There seems to be no restrictions in principle for private companies even if share warrants to bearer are often unsuitable for private companies when there are provisions in the articles that restrict the transferability of shares.

Share warrants to bearer may now be issued on the allotment of shares[7] without the need to create the shares in certificated form first[8] and then convert them.[9] Until the 2006 Act that was not possible. Moreover, section 122(3) of Companies Act 2006, against the general principle on acquisition of membership,[10] provides that the articles of a company may deem the bearer of a share warrant to be a member of the company either to a full or a limited extent as defined in the articles.[11]

1.2. *Physical Manifestation*

What essentially distinguishes share warrants to bearer from registered shares is that when a share warrant is issued, the register of members must state that fact and the date of issue, but the identity of the holder is not declared on the register. No entry of the owner of the warrants needs to be made in the register of members when the transfer is effected. Possession of the certificate establishes the entitlement to the shares represented by it and substitutes for the register as *prima facie* evidence of title. Unlike registered shares, share warrants to bearer are documentary intangibles as the paper is seen as having the value of the right in which it is embodied.[12]

More accurately, share warrants to bearer are negotiable instruments. At the beginning of the twelfth century, Lord Alverstone CJ, Kennedy and Ridley JJ in *Webb, Hale & Co v Alexandria Water Co Ltd*[13] held that a share warrant to bearer issued by a company registered in England under the Companies Act[14] was by mercantile usage a negotiable instrument.[15] The Court in that circumstance conclusively solved an uncertain matter[16] and felt bound by the authority of *Rumball v The Metropolitan Bank*.[17] The decision distanced itself from the outcome of an earlier case where it had

7 Sections 122(1)(b), 769(2)(c) and 779(1) of the Companies Act 2006.

8 Section 776(3)(c) of the Companies Act 2006.

9 Section 620 of the Companies Act 2006.

10 Section 112(2) of the Companies Act 2006.

11 See section 779(3) of the Companies Act 2006 for the case of payments of dividends by coupons or otherwise. Consider also the cases of the attendance and vote at the general meetings. See also the default articles of association for a public companies registered on or after 5 October 2009 – Companies (Model Articles) Regulations 2008 (SI 2008/3229) art 51(6).

12 AP Bell *Modern Law of Personal Property in England and Ireland* (Butterworths London 1989) 384; E McKendrick *Goode on Commercial Law* (Penguin London 2010) 52; FH Lawson and B Rudden *The Law of Property* (OUP Oxford 2002) 31 and 33; and MG Bridge *Personal Property Law* (OUP Oxford 2002) 74. See *MCC Proceeds Inc v Lehman Brothers International (Europe)* [1998] 4 All ER 675 (CA).

13 (1905) 21 TLR 572.

14 Namely sections 27, 28 and 29 of the Companies Act 1867.

15 On the ratio that allows a court to recognise an instrument as negotiable through mercantile usage, see *Goodwin v Robarts* (1875) LR 10 Ex Ch 337 *per* Cockburn CJ as approved by the House of Lords (1876) 1 App Cas 476 (HL).

16 In general, see F Tillyard *Banking and Negotiable Instruments* (Adam & Charles Black London 1908) 231.

17 (1877) 2 QBD 194 *per* Mellor J following the *ratio* established in *Goodwin v Robarts* (1876) 1 App Cas 476 (HL).

been declared that 'share warrants in English companies are not negotiable and cannot be made so by usage'.[18]

1.3. *Transfer of Title in Share Warrants to Bearer*

As just suggested, share warrants to bearer, unlike registered shares, are negotiable instruments.[19] Title is evidenced by possession of the document. This fact is essential for understanding their circulation. The share warrant embodies the right of the holder and passes by manual delivery[20] without the need for a written instrument of transfer or of the transfer to be registered by the company.[21]

As negotiable instruments, the three characteristic features of negotiability under English law apply,[22] namely (a) transferability of the instrument by delivery without intimation to the debtor; (b) presumption of money received; and (c) good title acquisition for the onerous *bona fide* tranferee.[23] These features adapt/innovate the general law of contract and property for the needs of safe, easy and rapid circulation of claims.[24] In the clear picture provided by Holdsworth, negotiability borrows from the law of property 'the easy method of assignment by means of an endorsement and delivery or delivery merely of the instrument. It borrows from the law of contract the principle that the person primarily liable is personally bound by his contract to pay the endorsee or bearer producing the bill; and that, therefore, no defence, which he might have had to claims by other persons, and no question of title to the bill, can be any answer to the endorsee or bearer producing the bill, who has acquired it in good faith and for value. In addition, it borrows from mercantile custom the principle that, normally, good faith and value will be presumed.'[25]

As a corollary of the above, a purchaser of a forged share warrant has no claim against the company[26] unless he has been induced (even by silence or inaction)[27] to complete

18 *Little v London Joint Stock Banking Company* [1891] 1 Ch 270 at 296. A similar position had been also endorsed in 1896 by W Willis QC in an introductory conventional work on the subject – W Willis *The Law of Negotiable Instruments (six lectures delivered at the request of the Council of Legal Education)* (Stevens & Haynes London 1896) 49.

19 *Webb, Hale & Co v Alexandria Water Co* (1905) 21 TLR 572 (CA).

20 Section 779(2) of the Companies Act 2006. See also the default articles of association for a public companies registered on or after 5 October 2009 – Companies (Model Articles) Regulations 2008 (SI 2008/3229) art 51(3).

21 See *AMG Global Nominees (Private) Ltd v SMM Holdings Ltd* [2008] EWCA Civ 1278.

22 On the general distinction between negotiable and non-negotiable instruments, see E McKendrick *Goode on Commercial Law* (Penguin London 2010) 514; and DW Cowen and L Gering *Cowen's Law of Negotiable Instruments in South Africa* (Juta Cape Town 1985) 31.

23 The so-called holder in due course.

24 See *Nova (Jersey) Knit Ltd v Kammgarn Sinnerei GmbH* [1977] 1 Lloyd's Rep 463 *per* Lord Russel of Killowen at 732.

25 WS Holdsworth *A History of English Law*, vol VIII (Metheuen & Co London 1925) 146.

26 See *Morris v Bethell* (1869) LR 5 CP 47; and *Brook v Hook* (1871) LR 6 Exch 89.

27 See *Polak v Everett* (1876) 1 QBD 669 at 673 *per* Blackburn J; and *Greenwood v Martins Bank Ltd* [1933] AC 51 at 57 *per* Lord Tomlin.

the acquisition following a specific representation from the company.[28] As in the case of registered shares, the company is estopped (by representation) from asserting the forgery.[29]

Finally, the peculiar characteristics governing negotiable instruments and, in particular the autonomy of the right embodied in the document from the underlying contract giving rise to the payment obligation, excludes any rights of set-off of the company against a transferee for value. This is because, unlike the assignee of a contractual right, the transferee of a negotiable instrument does not take it subject to equities.[30] It follows that a company that has issued a share warrant can only 'exercise its right to set off a debt owed to it against dividends and repayments of capital only if the debt is owed by the present holder of the warrant or by a person from whom he acquired it gratuitously.'[31]

1.4. *Nature of Transfer of Share Warrants at Common Law*

The mechanism for the transfer of share warrants to bearer just described has clarified that they circulate in accordance with the rules of negotiable instruments. Thus, the legal nature of transfer of share warrants at common law is negotiability.

The absence of a requirement to involve the company in the transfer of the document[32] (and the rights embodied in it) for the validity of transaction clearly prevents the legal characterisation to be novation. Moreover, *choses* in possession are not technically assignable at common law.

1.5. *The Protection of an Innocent Purchaser of Share Warrants to Bearer*

A good faith purchaser for value[33] of share warrants to bearer, which have been duly delivered to him (the 'holder in due course'), obtains good title notwithstanding defects in the title of his transferor of which he was unaware.[34] The requirement of good faith is defined according to the holder's honesty and not negligence.[35] A holder in due course[36] must simply have no actual or imputed notice of a defect in the transferor's title. It follows

28 See by way of analogy what established under section 24 of the Bills of Exchange Act 1882 in respect of forged or unauthorised signatures.

29 *Brown v Westminster Bank Ltd* [1964] 2 Lloyd's Rep 187 where actual knowledge gave rise to a duty to speak founding an estoppel.

30 See *Miller v Race* (1758) 1 Burr 452, 97 ER 398.

31 R Pennington *Pennington's Company Law* (Butterworths London 2001) 406.

32 i.e. no instrument of transfer is required.

33 There is a presumption that the holder has given value for the instrument – see section 27(2) of the Bills of Exchange Act 1882.

34 For the fundamental rule applying to bearer instruments, see section 29(1) of the Bills of Exchange Act 1882 (negotiable bills of exchange) and *Garey v Dominion Manufacturers Ltd* [1925] 1 DLR 99 (bearer bonds).

35 See section 90(1) of the Bills of Exchange Act 1882.

36 Only a transferee for value can be a holder in due course, unless the 'shelter principle' under section 29(3) of the Bills of Exchange Act 1882 applies.

that a constructive notice of a defect in the transferor's title does not preclude a holder from taking an instrument as a holder in due course. So, it is not relevant if the holder was negligent and would have found the defect in the transferor's title had acted with greater care.[37]

From a more practical perspective, if a warrant has been stolen or obtained fraudulently from the company or from any intermediate holder, a subsequent good faith holder who purchases it will take perfect title to it and can enforce all its rights against the company. Contrary to the common law rule that property rights do not survive dispositions by non-owners, even where the transferee is an innocent purchaser for value, the transferor of a share warrant can give a better title than he himself has. Hence, unlike the case of registered shares examined in Chapter 4, this is one of the cases where the maxim *nemo dat quod not habet* has no application.

1.6. Conclusions

Section 1 has outlined the current legal framework for share warrants to bearer. Emphasis has been placed on the fact that they are negotiable instruments. This element and the following corollaries on circulation have been presented primarily for the benefit of the historical analysis on legal change and hybridisation that will be carried out in the next sections.

In particular, it has been suggested in this section that in the case of share warrants to bearer, possession, as opposed to registration, is an alternative method of evidencing title to company shares. It substitutes the entitlement for the register as *prima facie* evidence of title. The register of members merely states the fact of the existence and the date of issue of a warrant.[38] Given their nature as negotiable instruments, the method of transfer of share warrants to bearer is by delivery without written instrument of transfer and without the transfer being registered by the company. Legal title to the warrant passes from one person to another by delivery of the warrant without the need to make entries in the register of members when the transfer is executed. Consequently, it was argued that no novation agreement is involved between the new purchaser and the company.

Starting from their current legal characterisation, the inquiry below on the process of legal change looks at the history of share warrants to bearer, focusing, inevitably, on the roots of the law of negotiable instruments and the concept of negotiability. It shows that the advent and the evolution of negotiable instruments in England has been the outcome of a process of hybridisation.

As has been seen with registered shares, the inquiry draws mainly from secondary sources. Repeated reference is made to the seminal work of Jenks[39] on the clauses of

37 Even if it might be questioned whether he can be characterised as being in good faith.

38 Warrant holders' names cannot be registered – sections 122(2), (4) and (6) of the Companies Act 2006.

39 E Jenks 'The Early History of Negotiable Instruments' (1893) LQR 70.

early medieval documents and to the historical studies of Holden[40] and Rogers.[41] The contributions of Holdsworth,[42] de Roover,[43] Baker,[44] Postan[45] and Grisoli[46] will also be discussed in detail.

2. Notes on the Early History of Negotiable Instruments

It seems surprising that until the end of the nineteenth century there had not been any serious scientific attempt to trace the origin of negotiable instruments. This is well documented by Jenks, who once argued that 'institutions which are the very heart of modern business life, the fountain heads of not ungrateful streams of litigation, are accepted as though, like the image of Ephesus, they fell direct from heaven for the benefit of a deserving profession. The legal question to which they give rise are studied with minute care, the legal relationship, which they create are made the occasion of microscopic analysis. But the subject itself, the really interesting and important matter, is left untouched. No example is better than negotiable paper'.[47]

The historical perspective has radically changed in the twelfth century up to the point where Postan observed that 'the medieval *tratta* (bill of exchange), its origin and diffusion, has been a special favourite with the students, and we know more about its legal and diplomatic evolution in the Middle Ages than we do of its fortunes in modern times'.[48]

Such renewed attention has brought a consensus among historians that negotiable instruments originated and developed in the thirteenth century from a variation[49] of certain Italian notarial exchange contracts and the contract of *cambium* as effected under the machinery of the bill of exchange (*tratta*, to use Italian terminology).[50] In its

40 JM Holden *The History of Negotiable Instruments in English Law* (Athlone Press London 1955).

41 JS Rogers *The Early History of the Bills and Notes* (CUP Cambridge 1995); Id 'The Myth of Negotiability' (1990) 31 BCL Rev 265; and Id 'Negotiability, Property and Identity' (1990) 21 Cardozo L Rev 471.

42 WS Holdsworth 'Origins and History of Negotiable Instruments' (1915) 31 LQR 12, 173 and 376 (3 parts); Id *A History of English Law*, vol VIII (Metheuen & Co London 1925).

43 R de Roover *L'Evolution de la Lettre de Change XIV-XVIII siécles* (Librairie Armand Colin Paris 1953).

44 JH Baker 'The Law Merchant and the Common Law Before 1700' (1978) 38 Cam LJ 295.

45 MM Postan 'Private Financial Instruments in Medieval England' in Id (ed) *Medieval Trade and Finance* (CUP Cambridge 1973) 28.

46 A Grisoli *La Cambiale nel Diritto Inglese* (Cedam Padova 1957).

47 E Jenks 'The Early History of Negotiable Instruments' (1893) LQR 70 at 71.

48 MM Postan 'Private Financial Instruments in Medieval England' in Id (ed) *Medieval Trade and Finance* (CUP Cambridge 1973) 28 at 30.

49 i.e. different from the *cambium minutum* (a contract by which A bargains to give coins of one denomination to B in return for coins of another denomination) and the *cambium siccum/cambium fictivum* (a loan at usurious interest, disguised under the form of a sale of goods 'in return for a price which, being supposed to have been borrowed abroad, was therefore enhanced by the costs of exchange') – WS Holdsworth *A History of English Law*, vol VIII (Methuen & Co London 1925) 127. In general, see TW Blomquist 'The Dawn of Banking in an Italian Commune: Thirteenth Century Lucca' in R Lopez (ed) *The Dawn of Modern Banking* (Yale UP New Haven 1979) 69.

50 See R de Roover *L'Evolution de la Lettre de Change XIV-XVIII siécles* (Librairie Armand Colin Paris 1953).

essence, the *tratta* consisted of an instrument (*instrumentum ex causa cambii*) specifically devised by the 'sedentary merchants'[51] for long-distance trade to obviate the risk of the physical transport of money from one fair to another or from one country to another. Besides the function of funds transfer and exchange transactions, it also served as a means of lending.[52] Financing trade by exchange became, in the fifteenth century, one of the most profitable businesses of Italian banking firms such as the Medici.[53]

Following the plan set out at the beginning of this chapter, this section looks at this original Italian scheme for exchange transactions (section 2.1) and then considers its diffusion in England (section 2.2).

2.1. The Initial Scheme for the Circulation of Negotiable Instruments

According to the Italian medieval commercial practice, in its infancy the letter of exchange or *tratta* involved four parties[54] as it was easier for creditors who wished to collect, and debtors who wished to pay, to appoint exchangers to do it for them. The letter was 'addressed by B [the drawer – often an exchanger] to C [the drawee/acceptor – often an exchanger], asking C to pay to a third person D [the payee] a sum of money, which A [the payor] has entrusted to B for this purpose. This letter is handed by B to A, who sends it on to D; and D presents it for payment to C'.[55] In short, the *tratta* provided that the drawee (C) who had accepted the bill was bound to the instruction of the drawer (B) and the payee (D) could sue the drawee to recover his property. Some of the peculiar characteristics of the current forms of the negotiable instruments were not yet present in such earlier schemes. This is because:

- the payee (D) could not assign his rights under the bill to a third party;
- the drawee (C), even if he had accepted the bill, could successfully plead the fact that he had not received funds from the drawer (B) as a defence against the payee (D); and, above all,
- the drawee (C) 'could urge any other defence against the payee which could have been urged by the drawer'.[56]

51 See NS Gras *Business and Capitalism, an Introduction to Economic History* (FS Crofts New York 1939) 37–44.

52 TFT Plucknett *A Concise History of the Common Law* (The Lawyers Co-Operative Publishing Company Rochester NY 1929) 229. On the functions of exchange transactions, see the economic analysis of R de Roover *Money, Banking and Credit in Medieval Bruges: Italian Merchant-Bankers, Lombards, and Money-Changers* (Medieval Academy of America Cambridge MA 1948) 48–75 and AP Usher *The Early History of Deposit Banking in Mediterranean Europe* (Harvard UP Cambridge MA 1943) 61.

53 R de Roover *The Rise and Decline of the Medici Bank, 1397–1494* (Harvard UP Cambridge MA 1963) 108.

54 The drawer (B), the drawee (C), the payee (D) and 'a presenter, or recipient on behalf of the payee' (A) – E Jenks 'The Early History of Negotiable Instruments' (1893) LQR 70 74.

55 WS Holdsworth *A History of English Law*, vol VIII (Methuen & Co London 1925) 131.

56 Ibid vol VIII, 140.

The *tratta*, in its infancy, was therefore a letter of payment, a mandate by a written command to pay.[57] That the *tratta* possessed full negotiability is largely a myth. It was freely transferable, but not fully negotiable. As will be observed in the analysis below, this clarification is crucial for the purpose of this study on legal change. Early negotiable instruments did not correspond to their modern English equivalent.[58] The term negotiable has not always been as settled as it seems to be today. It did not always embody the legal doctrine of the holder in due course rules; it obtained that characterisation through a process of hybridisation.

2.2. *The Advent of the Exchange Transactions in England and its Economic Rationale*

The Italian *tratta* was occasionally received in English mercantile practice even in the fourteenth century.[59] It is in particular evident from the cases reported in the Calendar of the early rolls of the Mayor's Court in the City of London that the Italian merchants in England were making use of this machinery.[60] It was not however until about the middle of the fifteenth century that instruments similar to the modern bills of exchange were used by English merchants.[61] The Italian merchants probably exported the legal device for giving effect to the contract of *cambium* in England at the time of the development of the wool trade.[62]

The borrowing is proved by the fact that the earliest specimens of bills of exchange came from Italy and that 'their wording, when they appear in England in the sixteenth and early seventeenth century, is almost identical with the wording of the Italian bills of the fourteenth century'.[63]

Another circumstance that points to an early Italian influence in bills of exchange is that, apart from the case where Italian merchants were directly involved,[64] the bills were often written in Italian even if none of the parties to the bill were Italians or had an Italian domicile.[65]

57 MM Postan 'Private Financial Instruments in Medieval England' in Id (ed) *Medieval Trade and Finance* (CUP Cambridge 1973) 57.

58 This interpretation, instead, has generally been the conventional historical position. See TE Scrutton *The Elements of Mercantile Law* (William Clowes and Sons London 1891) 22; WS Holdsworth *A History of English Law*, vol VIII (Methuen & Co London 1925) 114; and FK Beutel 'The Development of Negotiable Instruments in Early English Law' (1938) 51 Harv L Rev 831.

59 And possibly even in the thirteenth century as maintained by MM Postan 'Private Financial Instruments in Medieval England' in Id (ed) *Medieval Trade and Finance* (CUP Cambridge 1973) 59.

60 AH Thomas (ed) *Calendar of Early Mayor's Court Rolls Preserved among the Archives of the Corporation of the City of London at the Guildhall, AD 1298–1307* (CUP Cambridge 1934) 94 (Roll D) and 200 (Roll G).

61 JM Holden *The History of Negotiable Instruments in English Law* (Athlone Press London 1955) 22.

62 See above *sub* Chapter 4, section 3.1.

63 WS Holdsworth *A History of English Law*, vol VIII (Methuen & Co London 1925) 132.

64 M Rotondi, preface to A Grisoli *La Cambiale nel Diritto Inglese* (Cedam Padova 1957) xi.

65 E Jenks 'The Early History of Negotiable Instruments' (1893) LQR 70 at 74.

The above explanation for the advent of the bills of exchange is supported by a logical and economic rationale that has its roots in the principles of trade and mercantile theory. The argument is as follows. The need in England for an instrument suited to the settlement of foreign accounts such as the bill of exchange was primarily determined in the fifteenth century by the unprecedented growth of English foreign trade. When English merchants became the principal dealers in commodities (wool and cloth exports), they found that a very efficient and reliable model already existed in international market practice. Hence, when they became the principal dealers in exchanges, they imported the scheme of the bill of exchange adopted by the Italian banking houses. In the words of Postan, 'the rise of the letter of exchange was due to the rise and development of that type of commercial organisation of which the Italian banking houses were a *specimen*: we mean the appearance of firms with permanent connections abroad'.[66]

3. The Pattern of Reception of Negotiable Instruments

Building on the above points, the analysis that follows assesses the process of reception of negotiable instruments and the advent of negotiability in England. It shows that this process was not a mere transplantation of existing models, but that it involved the adaptation of old principles to the changing commercial necessities. It also shows that negotiable instruments and the concept of negotiability have not always been part of the same historical phenomenon and that distinguishing between the two is essential in order to explain the pattern of legal change until the enactment of the Bills of Exchange Act in 1882.

In carrying out this analysis the debate on the role of merchant law in shaping the development of English law will be tackled. Although the conventional account of the history of negotiable instruments maintains that their use and modes of transfer originated within the 'law merchant' in response to the needs of medieval merchants,[67] recent studies have found this perspective to be flawed. These recent studies do not regard the law merchant as a distinct and independent body of law and claim that negotiable instruments developed within the system of the common law in response to changes in commercial and financial practice.[68] It will be suggested below that the arguments supporting both views are not irreconcilable.

This section is organised as follows. Section 3.1 introduces the main arguments of the debate just mentioned on the nature of the law merchant. Section 3.2 reconciles the different positions from an historical perspective, arguing for the existence of a process of hybridisation in the reception of the Italian models, which later in time lead to the

66 MM Postan 'Private Financial Instruments in Medieval England' in Id (ed) *Medieval Trade and Finance* (CUP Cambridge 1973) 63.

67 TE Scrutton *The Elements of Mercantile Law* (William Clowes and Sons London 1891) 1; WS Holdsworth *A History of English Law*, vol VIII (Methuen & Co London 1925) 99; and JM Holden *The History of Negotiable Instruments in English Law* (Athlone Press London 1955).

68 JS Rogers *The Early History of the Bills and Notes* (CUP Cambridge 1995) 2. Along the same lines, see also JH Baker 'The Law Merchant and the Common Law before 1700' (1979) 38 Cam LJ 295; and Id *The Law's Two Bodies* (OUP Oxford 2003) 25.

advent of the concept of negotiability in England. Finally, section 3.3 employs the suggested pattern for explaining the growth of the bills of exchange and promissory notes until the enactment of the Bills of Exchange Act in 1882.

3.1. The Condition of Law Merchant and Common Law before the Eighteenth Century

The precise *status* of the law merchant and the possible nature of the process by which it became fused with common law are intensely disputed among historians.[69] Interestingly, this is not a new debate. In 1845, Blackburn observed that there is 'no part of the history of English law more obscure than the one connected with the maxim that the law merchant is part of the law of the land'.[70]

3.1.1. The Conventional Interpretation

The orthodox view sees the law merchant as an independent set of laws of an autonomous jurisdiction operating alongside state law.[71] It originated in the practice and law of the Italian merchants and bankers in medieval *comuni* and spread first to the Low Countries and later to England.[72] It was based on mercantile customs consisting in a codification of special commercial techniques.[73]

In England, in particular, the law merchant was uncluttered by the technicalities of the common law and administered by special commercial courts[74] in which the merchants themselves were judges.[75] It was only by the end of the sixteenth century that English common law courts began to recognise the rules of law merchant as authentic

69 See C Donahue 'Medieval and Early Modern Lex Mercatoria. An Attempt at the *Probatio Diabolica*?' (2004) 5 Chicago J Int'l Law 21; and A Cordes 'The Search for a Medieval Lex mercatoria' in V Piergiovanni (ed) *From* Lex Mercatoria *to Commercial Law* (Dunker & Humblot Berlin 2005) 53.

70 C Blackburn *A Treatise on the Effect of the Contract of Sale* (William Benning and Co London 1845) 207.

71 FM Burdick 'What is the Law Merchant' (1902) Colum L Rev 470. See also the different views of TE Scrutton *The Influence of Roman Law on the Law of England* (CUP Cambridge 1885) 177 (law merchant as the direct expression of Roman Law tradition) and HJ Berman and C Kaufman 'The Law of International Commercial Transactions (*Lex Mercatoria*)' (1978) 19 Harv Int'l LJ 221 (law merchant as expression of universal *ius gentium*).

72 See C Donahue 'Benvenuto Stracca's *De Mercatura*: Was There a *Lex Mercatoria* in Sixteenth Century Italy?' 109 and A Wijffels 'Business Relations Between Merchants in Sixteenth-Century Belgian Practice-Oriented Civil Law Literature' 255 in V Piergiovanni (ed) *From* Lex Mercatoria *to Commercial Law* (Duncker & Humblot Berlin 2004).

73 See E Kadens 'Order within Law, Variety within Customs. The Character of Mediaeval Merchant Law' (2004) 5 Chicago J of Int'l Law 39.

74 Sea port towns had their own maritime courts (e.g. Cinque Ports) before being centralised under the jurisdiction of the Courts of Admiralty, held in the name of the Lord High Admiral who was appointed by the Crown. Mercantile courts, originally independent (e.g. the courts of piepowder) were later centralised under the staple courts. See TFT Plucknett *A Concise History of the Common Law* (The Lawyers Co-Operative Publishing Company Rochester NY 1929) 223.

75 See TE Scrutton *The Elements of Mercantile Law* (William Clowes and Sons London 1891) 1–39; and the economic discussion on reduced transaction costs put forward by PR Milgrom, DC North and

principles of law.[76] This process was the outcome of a deliberate policy of the judiciary. In the words of Holden, 'unless the courts were prepared to give recognition to what the mercantile community, as a whole, felt to be right, they would never succeed in commanding the respect of that community'.[77] The result was often achieved by adapting old principles to the commercial necessities through a process of hybridisation, as in case of the action of *assumpsit* or, more accurately, of the action of trespass in the case of an *assumpsit*. This provided remedies for breach of contract by means of a tortious action when the payee could not sue the acceptor because of the common law provision that 'the only person who can sue on a promise is the person from whom the consideration moves'.[78] Outside the strict rules on contractual pleadings at common law, it allowed the payor (A in the example above) as the injured party to sue the drawer (B in the example above) in the case the *tratta* had been dishonoured by the drawee (C in the example above). The first recorded example of *assumpsit* in actions on bills of exchange can be found in an updated precedent from the 1590s in *Rastell's Entries*.[79] The process of incorporation of the law merchant into the common law was eventually completed by the end of the seventeenth century during the tenure of Holt as Chief Justice when English courts took judicial notice of mercantile custom and treated it as part of the law (applicable to non-merchants in any place).[80]

3.1.2. The Centrality of the Common Law

Baker[81] and Rogers[82] have challenged this conventional explanation.[83] They argue, together with others,[84] that the traditional incorporation theory is misleading. In particular, their search into primary sources indicates that the law merchant was not a distinct body of substantive law and that 'the apparent absence of commercial cases from

BR Weingast 'The Role of Institutions on the Revival of Trade, Part I: The Medieval Law Merchant' (1990) 2 Economics and Politics 1.

76 See the overview of a similar patter occurred in France offered by AD Kessler *A Revolution in Commerce. The Parisian Merchant Court and the Rise of Commercial Society in Eighteenth-Century France* (Yale UP New Haven 2008) 100.

77 JM Holden *The History of Negotiable Instruments in English Law* (Athlone Press London 1955) 52.

78 Ibid 27.

79 A book on pleadings first published in 1566 by William Rastell. See JH Baker 'The Law Merchant and the Common Law before 1700' (1978) 38 Cam LJ 295 at 296.

80 *Woodward v Rowe* (1666) 2 Keb 106, 84 ER 67; and *Pinkney v Hall* (1697) 1 Ld Raym 175, 91 ER 1013. See TA Street *The Foundations of Legal Liability: A Presentation of the Theory and Development of the Common Law*, vol II (Edward Thompson Company Northport 1906) 334.

81 JH Baker 'The Law Merchant and the Common Law before 1700' (1978) 38 Cam LJ 295.

82 JS Rogers *The Early History of the Bills and Notes* (CUP Cambridge 1995).

83 See also JS Ewart 'What is the Law Merchant?' (1903) 3 Colum L Rev 135; and DR Coquillette *The Civilian Writers of Doctors' Commons, London: Three Centuries of Juristic Innovation in Comparative, Commercial and International Law* (Dunker & Humblot Berlin 1988) 149–158 and 215–55.

84 HJ Berman *The Formation of the Western Legal Tradition* (Harvard UP Cambridge MA 1983) 333; and LE Trakman *The Law Merchant. The Evolution of Commercial Law* (Colorado Legal Publishing Littleton 1983) 7.

the records of the common law courts is largely an illusion'.[85] There was not an exclusive and mandatory independent jurisdiction for merchants. Mercantile courts were not specialised commercial courts characterised by the commercial nature of the disputes, but 'simply local courts of general jurisdiction held at places where a great deal of trade took place'.[86] Moreover, the records of the cases involving city tradesmen and merchants as reported in the rolls of the Common Pleas for the fourteenth and fifteenth century suggest that merchants, instead of resorting to their 'own' courts, did not disdain the use of common law courts.[87] Baker maintains that what is claimed to be the medieval law merchant in its origin was nothing more than an expeditious procedure adapted for the needs of merchants. The substantive mercantile law 'had no existence as a coherent system of principles before the common law itself developed the means of giving it expression'.[88] There were no doctors in *lege mercatoria* and that subject was not taught in universities. Above all, the law merchant in England was simply a refinement of the common law, which had always governed mercantile affairs. The growth of English commercial law during the Renaissance was not primarily the result of the borrowing of ready-made set of laws from outside the common law, but rather the judicial crystallisation of principles of the common law in response to developments in commercial and financial practice. In short, the mercantile procedures were not incorporated into the common law as a body of law akin to foreign law, but rather they were used by common law courts to create the law merchant.

3.2. *The Significance of the Debate on the Nature of Law Merchant on the Process of Hybridisation*

The preceding section presented the essential terms of the debate. This section argues that the two interpretations, when placed in the appropriate historical perspective, are not irreconcilable, as they appear to be at first. Rather, they complement each other in explaining different stages of the process of reception and hybridisation of negotiable instruments: incorporation theory emphasises the fact that the original model was imported from abroad, and the 'non-incorporation' theory clarifies the foundations of the peculiar evolution of negotiability within the English legal framework.

3.2.1. Borrowing and Incorporation

The underlying position of the incorporation theory is that the initial reception of the Italian *tratta* in England[89] necessarily predicates the independence of the law merchant

85 JS Rogers *The Early History of the Bills and Notes* (CUP Cambridge 1995) 12. See, for example *Dane v Holbein* (1388) YB 11 Rich II (Ames Ser) 238; and *Scottow v Birkeleghe* (1312) YB 5 Edw II 33 SS 205 (involving the use of the writ of account in commercial disputes between merchants).

86 JS Rogers *The Early History of the Bills and Notes* (CUP Cambridge 1995) 25.

87 *Dederic v Abbot of Ramsey* (1315) in C Gross and H Hall (ed) *Selected Cases Concerning the Law Merchant, AD 1239–1633*, vol 46 (Bernard Quatrich London 1930) SS 86.

88 JH Baker 'The Law Merchant and the Common Law before 1700' (1978) 38 Cam LJ 295 at 321.

89 See above *sub* Chapter 5, section 2.1.

from the common law. Italian commercial techniques are at the foundation of the early history of the law of negotiable instruments as part of a well-identifiable formal set of rules under the heading of 'merchant law'.

That said, the employment of old principles to deal with changed commercial necessities, such as the action of *assumpsit*, showed that incorporation was not a radical imposition, but rather the result of a process of hybridisation between the imported models and the pre-existing legal tradition. It was not a case of pure transplantation of legal rules from abroad.

3.2.2. Legal Reception and Negotiability

Having clarified the mechanism of initial reception, it is however only by referring to the non-incorporation theory that the subsequent evolution of English law can be properly understood. It is not in fact from borrowing or incorporation that, for example, the doctrine of negotiability grew in England in absolute autonomy and independence from the evolution of continental law.

Contrary to the 'incorporation' view that explains the history of negotiable instruments as the struggle against the common law principle that *choses* in action are not assignable, 'non-incorporation' writers argue that common law courts had already accommodated the practice of transferring negotiable instruments by the seventeenth century.[90] In their origin, negotiable instruments were in effect transferable, but not negotiable. The need to protect a *bona fide* holder for value was not significant at all. That this is so follows from reflecting on the rationale of the commercial practice that gave rise to the use of the *tratta*. The typical transactions were not the cases of credit sales of goods where instruments circulated as payment media free form adverse claims. Legal disputes before Mercantile and Admiralty courts generally concerned actions by the holder against the person on whom the bill was drawn (the drawee)[91] or by the payor[92] against the drawer.[93] As suggested for the above four-parties model of the *tratta*, negotiable instruments in their infancy were simply 'means of making use of balances that one person held for the account of the other. Even the inland bill of exchange was a bill of exchange, not simply a bill. A merchant who had shipped goods to a factor for sale would draw a bill on the factor when he had occasion to use the balances that he had built up in the factor's location'.[94] This account of the significance of negotiability is further supported by the fact that the legal treaties published in the eighteenth and nineteenth century (in contrast with the ones published in the twentieth century) hardly mention

90 Reference is often made to *Dashwood v Lee* (1667) 2 Keb 303, 84 ER 189, and *Tercese v Geray* (1677) Finch 301, 23 ER 165.

91 *Burton v Davy* (1437) in C Gross and H Hall (ed) *Selected Cases Concerning the Law Merchant, AD 1239–1633*, vol 49 (Bernard Quaritch London 1930) SS 117. On this specific case, see the analysis provided by JS Rogers *The Early History of the Bills and Notes* (CUP Cambridge 1995) 45–48.

92 The debtor of the underlying obligation.

93 *Fuller v Thorne* (1533) in H Jenkinson and B Formoy (eds) *Select Pleas in the Court of Admiralty*, vol 6 (Selden Society London 1894) SS 38–41.

94 JS Rogers *The Early History of the Bills and Notes* (CUP Cambridge 1995) 171.

the concept of negotiability or the peculiar nature of the rights of the holders in due course.[95] None of them 'had an introductory passage or chapter explaining the concept of negotiability in the sense of freedom from claims and defences', 'a passage contrasting negotiability with mere assignability' or 'a separate chapter on the rights of *bona fide* holders'.[96] If the conventional understanding that sees negotiability as the definitional characteristic of the law of negotiable instruments from its origin was correct, exactly the opposite outcome should have been found.[97] Although a number of sixteenth century English cases implicitly contemplated the practice of negotiability,[98] there is no clear evidence that such cases stretched the contractual rights of transfer beyond agency concepts as well recognised in continental Europe.[99] It is significant to note that in *Martin v Boure*,[100] often reported as the first case decided by the Exchequer Chamber on bills of exchange concerning an action by the drawer against the acceptor (drawee), the action of *assumpsit* was still employed. The decision is founded on an ordinary action in special *assumpsit* on a promise that was made in relation to exchange dealing, rather than on an action 'to enforce either an exchange contract or a bill of exchange'.[101]

Holden[102] claims that the issue of the protection of the good faith of a holder's position has been originally raised in England by a public notary who practiced at the Royal Exchange in London named Marius[103] in relation to the loss of a bill of exchange payable to the bearer. The matter was treated as a corollary of the principle of the transferability of bills of exchange discussed above. Although Marius was familiar with European law and practice, he concluded in 1651 that in a conflict with the original holder, the *bona fide* holder for value of a bill would be the loser.

Negotiability theories first developed in England at the end of the eighteenth century, probably in response to the business practice of employing negotiable instruments in the credit system to raise finance 'for those who were unable to secure credit directly from banks'.[104] Bills of exchange were often discounted by their holders: 'the trader who needed cash could indorse his bill to a bank or discount house, which would charge the seller a sum representing interest on the time remaining before the bill was to be paid, as well as a commission'.[105] Alternatively, it could have been from the growth in the market for

95 J Bayley *A Short Treatise on the Law of Bills of Exchange, Cash Bills, and Promissory Notes* (E Brooke London 1789); S Kyd *A Treatise on the Law of the Bills of Exchange and Promissory Notes* (Thomas, Andrew and Penniman Albany 1800) and J Chitty *A Treatise on the Law of Bills of Exchange, Checks on Bankers, Promissory Notes, Bankers' Cash Notes, and Bank-Notes* (E&R Brooke London 1799).

96 JS Rogers *The Early History of the Bills and Notes* (CUP Cambridge 1995) 7.

97 i.e. it would have been included in the legal treaties mentioned above.

98 See FK Beutel 'The Development of Negotiable Instruments in Early English Law' (1938) 51 Harv L Rev 835.

99 See AP Usher *The Early History of Deposit Banking in Mediterranean Europe* (Harvard UP Cambridge MA 1943) 107.

100 (1602) Cro Jac 6, 79 ER 6.

101 JS Rogers *The Early History of the Bills and Notes* (CUP Cambridge 1995) 136 footnote 24.

102 JM Holden *The History of Negotiable Instruments in English Law* (Athlone Press London 1955) 42.

103 Advice Concerning Bills of Exchange (London 1651).

104 JS Rogers *The Early History of the Bills and Notes* (CUP Cambridge 1995) 121. See also DM Dailey 'The Early Development of the Note-Brokerage Business in Chicago' (1938) 46 J of Political Economy 202.

105 M Lobban 'Commercial Law' in W Cornish, JS Anderson, R Cock, M Lobban, P Polden and K Smith (eds) *The Oxford History of the Laws of England,Volume XII 1820–1914 – Private Law* (OUP Oxford

investment securities that the concept of negotiability took root in England. This perspective is supported by the case law where the most frequent cases involving the concept of negotiability[106] are about government bonds rather than bills of exchange. The leading case concerned the negotiability of bank notes,[107] and during Lord Mansfield's tenure as Chief Justice of the Kings' Bench, the same rule was applied to an inland bill of exchange.[108] In *Peacock v Rhodes*[109] the difference between assignability and negotiability was clearly established: 'the holder of a bill of exchange or promissory note is not to be considered in the light of an assignee of the payee. An assignee must take the thing assigned subject to all the equity to which the original party was subject. If this rule applied to bills and promissory notes, it would stop their currency. The law is settled that a holder, coming fairly by a bill or note, has nothing to do with the transaction between the original parties. I see no difference between a note indorsed blank and one payable to bearer'.[110] Later decisions of the courts before the enactment of the Bills of Exchange Act 1882 focused on the test for notice for the *bona fide* transferee. In *Raphael v Bank of England* (1855)[111] Willes J identified a 'purely subjective test' where notice meant not merely notice, but knowledge, or the means of knowledge of the fact that the seller had no title.

Finally, the Bills of Exchange Act 1882 consolidated the pre-existing case law. It defined a 'holder in due course' in similar terms to the good faith purchaser without notice. In fulfilling certain requirements set forth under section 29(1), the holder in due course acquires a title to the bill free from equities and defects in title of his transferor. In particular, although value is presumed,[112] he must be in good faith[113] and have no notice of any defects in the title of the transferor.

3.2.3. Hybridisation

It follows from the above that it was probably by employing the action of *assumpsit*[114] that common law courts incorporated the Italian mercantile rules for enforcing the rights of the parties to a negotiable instrument and established the basis for the advent of

2010) 729. On the decline in the process of rediscounting bills at the beginning of the twelfth century, see S Nishimura *The Decline of Inland Bills of Exchange in the London Money Market, 1855–1913* (CUP Cambridge 1971).

106 See *Goodwin v Robarts* (1876) 1 App Cas 476; and *Crouch v The Credit Foncier Ltd* (1873) LR 8, QB 374.

107 *Miller v Race* (1758) 1 Burr 452, where it was established that although bank notes were not goods, nor securities, nor documents for debts, they were 'treated as money, as cash, in the ordinary course and transaction of business, by the general consent of mankind; which gives them the credit and currency of money, to all intents and purposes' *per* Lord Mansfield at 457.

108 See LS Pressnell *Country Banking in the Industrial Revolution* (OUP Press Oxford 1956) 105.

109 (1781) 2 Doug 633, 99 ER 402.

110 *Peacock v Rhodes* (1781) 2 Doug 633 at 636.

111 (1855) 17 CB 161, 139 ER 1030.

112 Sections 31(1) and 27(2) of the Bills of Exchange Act 1882.

113 Section 90(1) of the Bills of Exchange Act 1882.

114 i.e. an action for the recovery of damages by reason of the breach or non-performance of a simple contract. As suggested earlier, the use of *assumpsit* in actions on bills of exchange 'is clearly illustrated in Rastell's Entries a book of pleading first published in 1566' – JM Holden *The History of Negotiable Instruments in English Law* (Athlone Press London 1955) 28.

the principle that the custom of merchants concerning bills of exchange was part of the common law.[115]

When liability of the parties to a negotiable instrument came to be rationalised in terms of common law forms of action rather that of mercantile custom, 'courts rarely used the consideration doctrine to undo the work of the law merchant. Rather, the shibboleth of consideration was adapted to fit commercial needs already recognized by the rules of the law merchant'.[116] Later,[117] following the development dictated by changed commercial necessities linked to the rise of trading credits (and the transfer of claims), the peculiar doctrine of negotiability involving, among other things, the protection of the holder in due course for value emerged.[118]

It has therefore been from the interaction of the common law and the borrowed Italian mercantile rules that the English law of negotiable instruments has been progressively shaped. Apart from the early documents authorising the debtor to pay the creditor or his nominee, the process of evolution did not consist of a pure transplantation of legal rules, nor did it simply reflect just a spontaneous indigenous creation as the study of negotiability may suggest. Rather, as was also the case for its later evolution, it has been the outcome of an original process of hybridisation.

3.3. *Normative Consolidation*

The last step of the process of legal growth for negotiable instruments is sketched below. This is the normative development of the bills of exchange and promissory notes into negotiable instruments that have economic significance independent from the early exchange transactions. In the light of the analysis on legal change, the discussion below also considers the relationship with the pre-existing rules and the legal consequences following the enactment of the Bills of Exchange Act in 1882.

3.3.1. Bills of Exchange

Bills of exchange became recognised independently from older forms of exchange dealings only in the late seventeenth century[119] when judges and lawyers spoke explicitly of actions on bills of exchange, 'and it was well established that people who drew, accepted, or

115 See *Williams and Williams* (1694) Carthew 269, 90 ER 759.

116 G Gilmore 'On the Difficulties of Codifying Commercial Law' (1948) 57 Yale LJ 1341 at 1409.

117 And unlike Scotland and continental Europe. See RG Anderson *Assignation* (Edinburgh Legal Education Trust Edinburgh 2008) 4–56 and 5–11.

118 According to Grisoli, the characterisation of the modes of transfer shaped in accordance to the rules on equitable assignment – A Grisoli *La Cambiale nel Diritto Inglese* (Cedam Padova 1957) 96.

119 The earliest evidence of explicit order papers (later used on bills of exchange) comes from certain loose documents of the sixteenth century found in the Archives of Naples where the Italian word *girata* is used for the technical English term of endorsement. More precisely, from the study of the Neapolitan documents it can be inferred that when the *girata* is 'full', it contains declaration that consideration has been received. In this case, the new holder is not an agent of the principal, but a new principal. The new holder becomes an *adjectus in rem suam*. This was the revolutionary achievement of the ingenuity of the Italian mercantile community. See AP Usher *The Early History of Deposit Banking in Mediterranean*

endorsed bills of exchange incurred enforceable legal obligations independent of obligations that might have arisen in the underlying transaction in which the bills were used'.[120] Pleadings lost any reference to specific facts of the action and about the relationship between the drawer and drawee,[121] suggesting therefore a clear independence from the obligation in which the bill was issued. From the late seventeenth century, the bill of exchange simply ceased to reflect transactions that necessarily involved four parties.[122]

The development followed the dramatic changes in volumes of commercial practice. Bills of exchange became frequently used through the intervention of middlemen[123] for the needs of domestic trade (inland bills)[124] and operated as an efficient payment device to provide credit. In essence, they were 'a flexible and convenient means by which credits arising out of trade – whether in the form of collected balances held in the hands of one's factor, debts due from customers, or merely the willingness of trading correspondents to provide accommodation – could be used to make payments and to obtain credit'.[125] This evolution in trading credits was possible because of the parallel growth of specialised banking institutions.

3.3.2. Promissory Notes

The history of promissory notes stems from the history of bills of exchange. While there is a common perception among historians that documents containing promises to pay and authorising the debtor to pay the creditor or his nominee, or the creditor or the holder of the document were probably present in embryonic forms in early mercantile transactions,[126] it is beyond doubt that well into the seventeenth century they did not have any of the negotiable characteristics.[127] This was because, in line with the legal orthodoxy of Roman law, medieval and renaissance lawyers found it difficult to qualify the creditor's nominee/the bearer of the document differently from agents of the creditor. He had no independent right of action. It was felt that the nominee/bearer of the document could not possibly sue upon the contract in his own rights unless he proved 'either that he has been appointed the agent if the creditor, or that the creditor has transferred to him his rights by making him a *procurator in rem suam*'.[128]

The reception in the common law of the bill of exchange as the type and model for negotiable instruments in the sixteenth century, however, led to a revival of older forms

Europe (Harvard UP Cambridge MA 1943) 100; and R de Roover *L'Evolution de la Lettre de Change XIV-XVIII siécles* (Librairie Armand Colin Paris 1953) 83.

120 JS Rogers *The Early History of the Bills and Notes* (CUP Cambridge 1995) 99.

121 *Oaste v Taylor* (1612) Cro Jac 306, 79 ER 262.

122 See *Edgar v Chut* (1663) 1 Keb 592, 83 ER 1130.

123 WJ Ashley *An Introduction to English Economic History and Theory*, vol II (Putnam's Sons New York 1893) 218–237.

124 i.e. bills drawn and made payable upon a person resident in England.

125 JS Rogers *The Early History of the Bills and Notes* (CUP Cambridge 1995) 124.

126 See above *sub* Chapter 5, section 2.1.

127 FK Beutel 'The Development of Negotiable Instruments in Early English Law' (1938) Harv L Rev 830; and WS Holdsworth *A History of English Law*, vol VIII (Methuen & Co London 1925) 114.

128 WS Holdsworth *A History of English Law*, vol VIII (Methuen & Co London 1925) 124.

of transferable bonds.[129] The re-emergence was gradual. Up until the 1698 Act[130] that required a protest in the event of non-payment of an inland bill of exchange, the promissory notes and the inland bills of exchange closely resembled each other and they were not often clearly distinguished by law reporters.[131] By the beginning of the eighteenth century, promissory notes were 'transferred frequently and indorsed as bills of exchange'[132] and still treated by merchants interchangeably with bills of exchange. Even the goldsmiths' notes, which were promissory notes – sometimes to the bearer, sometimes to order – signed by the goldsmiths in exchange for the deposit of money, were often confused with inland bills of exchange. Notwithstanding the strong opposition from Holt CJ,[133] who considered on several occasions the heresy that 'Lombard Street would give laws to Westminster Hall',[134] the 1704 Promissory Notes Act[135] clearly established[136] that the notes whether to the payee/to order or to the bearer were negotiable instruments. They were 'assignable or indorsable in the same manner and with the same legal effects if they were inland bills of exchange'.[137]

3.3.3. The Bills of Exchange Act 1882

The common law rules relating to bills of exchange, cheques and promissory notes, developed and established at the time of Lord Mansfield's resignation from the office of Chief Justice in 1788, were codified in the Bills of Exchange Act as drafted by Sir Mackenzie Chalmers.[138] Knowledge of pre-existing law was still necessary because, as the Act itself expressly stated, 'the rules of common law including the law merchant save in so far as they are inconsistent with the express provisions of this Act, shall continue to apply to bills of exchange, promissory notes, and cheques'.[139]

The Bills of Exchange Act 1882, subject to amendments largely related to cheques, provided a code for the creation and enforcement of bills, cheques and promissory notes. It remains in force today. The principles enunciated in it are usually derived by analogy from cases involving other types of negotiable instruments.[140] The Act did not in fact establish a normative closed list of negotiable instruments (*numerus clausus*). Under

129 Ibid vol VIII, 114.

130 Payment of Bills Act (1698) 9 Will 3 c 17.

131 See the complaint on the promiscuity in the use of the words 'note' and 'bill' delivered by Lord Mansfield in *Grant v Vaughan* (1764) 3 Burr 1525, 97 ER 957.

132 *Buller v Crips* (1703) 6 Mod 29, 87 ER 793 at 794 per Holt CJ.

133 See Holt CJ's decision in *Clerke v Martin* (1702) 2 Ld Raym 757, 92 ER 6 where it was refused to allow an endorsee to sue on a promissory note.

134 *Clerke v Martin* (1702) 1 Ld Raym 758, 92 ER 6.

135 3&4 Ann c 9.

136 See the Preamble of the Promissory Notes Act 1704 in Appendix C of JM Holden *The History of Negotiable Instruments in English Law* (Athlone Press London 1955).

137 WS Holdsworth *A History of English Law*, vol VIII (Methuen & Co London 1925) 173.

138 MD Chalmers *A Digest of the Law of the Law of Bills of Exchange, Promissory Notes and Cheques* (London 1878); and Id 'An Experiment in Codification' (1886) 3 LQR 125. In general, see JM Holden *The History of Negotiable Instruments in English Law* (Athlone Press London 1955) 199.

139 Section 97(2) of the Bills of Exchange Act 1882.

140 J James *Richardson's Guide to Negotiable Instruments* (Butterworths London 1991) 37.

English law, commercial practice can develop new types of negotiable instruments. The law merchant is not a 'closed book, nor is it fixed or stereotyped'.[141] Before the enactment of the Bills of Exchange Act 1882, Cockburn CJ in *Goodwin v Robarts*,[142] in particular, strongly argued for a foreseeable expansion of the law merchant in order to meet the varying circumstances and needs of commerce. The same position with specific respect to negotiable instruments was later followed in *Bechuanaland Exploration Co v London Trading Bank Ltd*[143] and *Edelstein v Schuler & Co.*[144]

Unless there is a special provision created by an Act of Parliament, the test to decide whether a given instrument is negotiable has been provided by Blackburn J in *Crouch v The Crédit Foncier Co.*[145] In particular, the instrument must be transferable according to the custom of trade in the English market by delivery and be capable of 'being sued upon by the person holding it *pro tempore*'.[146] A good illustration of the application of the rule outlined by Blackburn J can be found in *London and County Banking Company Ltd v London and River Plate Bank Ltd*[147] with reference to certain types of shares certificates related to American companies which were issued in favour of a specified registered holder, but which incorporated (on the back) a form of transfer and power of attorney for execution in blank by the registered holder.[148] Although the certificates by usage of English bankers were transferable by delivery, Mainsty J held that they were not negotiable instruments because they could not be sued upon by the person holding them *pro tempore*.[149] When the requirements set out by Blackburn J in *Crouch v The Crédit Foncier Co.*[150] are not clearly satisfied, it is for the court to establish conclusively the nature of negotiable instruments. This has been the case in the past as the cases of bank post bills,[151] exchequer bills[152] and, as will be seen below, for share warrants to bearer.[153]

4. The Advent of Share Warrants to Bearer

The analysis above has clarified that, although the class of negotiable instruments and the concept of negotiability progressively converged on one another, they have not always coincided. Historically, they developed at different stages in response to changing commercial necessities and they developed along different legal patterns. More precisely,

141 From the Privy Council decision in *Bank of Baroda Ltd v Punjab National Bank Ltd* [1944] AC 176 *per* Lord Wright at 183.
142 (1875) LR 10 Ex Ch 337.
143 (1898) 2 QB 658.
144 (1902) 2KB 144.
145 (1873) LR 8 QB 374. See also *Lang v Smyth* (1831) 7 Bing 284, 131 ER 109.
146 *Crouch v The Crédit Foncier Co* (1873) LR 8 QB 374 *per* Blackburn J at 381.
147 (1887) 20 QBD 232.
148 JM Holden *The History of Negotiable Instruments in English Law* (Athlone Press London 1955) 265.
149 *London and County Banking Company Ltd v London and River Plate Bank Ltd* (1887) 20 QBD 232 at 239.
150 (1873) LR 8 QB 374 at 381.
151 *Forbes v Marshall* (1855) 11 Ex 166, 156 ER 788.
152 *Wookey v Pole* (1820) 4 B&Ald 1, 10 ER 839. See also *Brandao v Barnett* (1846) 3 CB 519 at 530, 136 ER 206.
153 *Webb, Hale & Co. v Alexandria Water Co. Ltd* (1905) 93 LT 339.

while in their infancy negotiable instruments adapted the four-party scheme of the *tratta* borrowed from Italian merchants, they later developed through a process of hybridisation into negotiable forms that embodied an obligation binding the drawee (after acceptance) to pay the payee or other successive holders.

What is argued in this section is that the same pattern of legal growth applies to share warrants to bearer, as they originated as a species of the *genus* of negotiable instruments at a time when the concept of negotiability had already become an essential aspect of the law of negotiable instruments.

4.1. *From Scrip Certificates to Share Warrants to Bearer*

The present legal characterisation of share warrants to bearer in terms of negotiable instruments follows directly from the evolution of the rules for scrip certificates. This is clear when considering that the ratio of *Webb, Hale & Co v Alexandria Water Co Ltd*[154] is based on *Rumball v The Metropolitan Bank*,[155] which concerned scrip certificates shares. These are provisional certificates very similar to share warrants to bearer as they give the bearer the right to certain shares when all instalments upon such shares have been paid. Scrip certificates, although never particularly popular with English companies or investors, were probably of some importance in the past because it was also possible to create companies constituting only scripholders where 'scrip and shares are synonymous, there being in fact no difference between scripholders and shareholders'.[156] It was only with the decision in *Rumball v The Metropolitan Bank*[157] that scrip certificates came to be considered as negotiable instruments and that it was established that 'any infirmity in the title of the person from whom he has taken them'[158] could be recovered from a *bona fide* holder for value without notice.

More precisely, in *Webb, Hale & Co v Alexandria Water Co Ltd*[159] dividends were awarded to *bona fide* purchasers of six share warrants, each payable to bearer, that had been previously stolen. The main contention put forward in the case was whether the Companies Act 1867,[160] which allowed, for the first time, a company to issue share warrants to bearer, simply did away with the need for transfer by deed or whether there were more serious implications for negotiability. Although share warrants to bearer were not covered by any decided case, the Court relied on the usage proved in *Rumball v The Metropolitan Bank* where, referring to *Goodwin v Robarts*,[161] the *bona fide* holder for value successfully resisted an action to recover four scrip certificates fraudulently deposited by an intermediary as security for his own debt. The alternative route to

154 (1905) 93 LT 339.
155 (1877) LR 2 QBD 194.
156 WB Lindley *Law of Companies* (Sweet & Maxwell London 1902) 84.
157 (1877) LR 2 QBD 194.
158 WB Lindley *Law of Companies* (Sweet & Maxwell London 1902) 85.
159 (1905) 93 LT 339.
160 Sections 27, 28 and 29 of the Companies Act 1867 (30 & 31 Vict c 131 to amend the Companies Act 1862 (25 & 26 Vict c 89)).
161 (1876) 1 App Cas 476 (HL).

negotiability of characterising the issuance of a document representing a share as estoppel by representation against the company[162] was not followed in *Webb, Hale & Co v Alexandria Water Co Ltd*.[163]

It is clear how the bipartite paradigm based on an unconditional undertaking made by one party (company) to another (the holder),[164] and mechanics of circulation by delivery, mirrors the scheme of promissory notes briefly described above. This is different from the tripartite scheme of the bill of exchange.[165]

4.2. Conclusions

To a large extent, the findings in this last section are a corollary of the pattern of reception outlined in the earlier sections of the chapter. Share warrants to bearer involving the concept of negotiability were introduced in response to the business practice using the same flexible rationale adopted for the development of other negotiable instruments.

Historical evidence supports the view that the old Italian model of the contract of *cambium*, as effected under the machinery of the *tratta*, was exported at different stages to various European countries. This was primarily in response to the commercial need to avoid the physical transportation of money from one fair/town to another for the purchase of goods. The document was originally written in Italian (or translated *verbatim* from an Italian specimen) even when the parties involved in the transaction were not Italians. The reception and development of the bill of exchange in England coincided with the growth of foreign trade. As Pluckett significantly puts it, 'the history of bills of exchange in English law is the history first of the reception of Italian practice among English merchants in the sixteenth century.'[166]

At first, the borrowed Italian model amounted to a four-party transaction and was not centred on the modern concept of negotiability. The original model was adapted to the English legal framework by the use of the action of *assumpsit* and this already testifies to the existence of a process of hybridisation. Negotiability was a later achievement. The assertion that the law of negotiable instruments developed from its origin 'in response to a universal mercantile need for debt instruments that could circulate as payment media free from defences and claims is nothing but a myth.'[167] In other words, the orthodox explanation of the process by which the common law accommodated the merchant theory of negotiability is flawed in its historical foundations. It was only at the beginning of the nineteenth century that the commercial practice needed debt instruments capable of being transferred as a means of payment in accordance with the rules of negotiability.

162 See *Crouch v The Credit Foncier Co* (1873) LR 8QB 374 at 384; and *Re Bahia and San Francisco Rly* Co (1868) LR 3 QB 584. See above *sub* Chapter 4, section 1.5.

163 (1905) 93 LT 339.

164 According to the definition contained in section 83 of the Bills of Exchange Act 1882.

165 Which involves a written order by the drawer to the drawee to pay money to the payee. See the definition contained in section 3 of the Bill of Exchange 1882.

166 TFT Plucknett *A Concise History of the Common Law* (The Lawyers Co-Operative Publishing Company Rochester NY 1929) 231.

167 JS Rogers 'The Myth of Negotiability' (1990) 31 BCL Rev 314.

Judges and lawyers carried the process of reconceptualisation of new commercial transactions into the existing legal framework and provided solutions to legal problems found in mercantile practice. It follows that the Italian model, adapted by the employment of the action of *assumpsit*, evolved from the original paradigm in accordance with the changing economic, legal and social circumstances in a distinct scheme, similarly to the process of hybridisation observed in postcolonial studies in Part I.

The case of share warrants to bearer fits in well with the above scenario even if, as suggested in the preceding section, the history of legal characterisation concerns only the last part of the evolution of negotiable instruments. More precisely, the scheme for promissory notes followed from the original model of the bill of exchange and, in the terms codified in the Bills of Exchange Act 1882, formed the basis of reference for the following development of certain categories of negotiable instruments. This was the case of scrip certificates for shares, the legal ancestors of share warrants to bearer as conclusively established by the court's decision in *Webb, Hale & Co v Alexandria Water Co Ltd*.[168]

[168] (1905) 93 LT 339.

Summary

SUMMARY OF PART II

Part II investigated the historical evolution of the mechanisms by which shares in English companies are transferred. In line with the themes presented in Part I, it redefined Watson's thesis on legal transplants with arguments on cultural interaction originated in the postcolonial debate. More precisely, it suggested that contrary to the conventional interpretation, the original form of the joint stock company and its structural elements of association were not a spontaneous indigenous creation. They were borrowed from abroad and progressively integrated through a process of hybridisation in the pre-existing English legal framework starting from the sixteenth century with the growth of international trade.

The inquiry distinguished between the transfer of registered shares and share warrants to bearer. Although they both enjoy the same economic function of units of the corporate capital, they are nevertheless different in terms of legal nature, regulation and modes of circulation. The explanation is historical.

Chapter 4 examined registered shares. Section 1 identified the subject matter of the inquiry by describing where the law currently stands. It found that a share today is a bundle of contractual rights with certain unique proprietary characteristics and that the certificate (capable of possession) in the case of registered shares is not evidence of legal title. Legal title[1] passes upon the entry of the transferee into the register of members[2] according to a tripartite scheme of transfer akin to novation. Section 2 focused on the modes of circulation of registered shares from an historical perspective. Building on the legal framework outlined in section 1, it set out the links between the growth of the legal tradition and the present characterisation. The analysis on the concept of incorporation, in particular, suggested that the historical connections between the development of the partnership model and the evolution of the company form were very strong at least until the enactment of the Joint Stock Companies Act of 1844. The discussion on the mechanism of transfer of legal title to shares, both for incorporated and unincorporated companies, supported this view, evidencing among other things, the similarities with the current legal characterisation based on novation. In sum, section 2 pointed out that the existing legal framework for the circulation of registered shares has been greatly

1 Both certificated and uncertificated shares.

2 The operator's register in the case of uncertificated shares.

influenced by pre-existing legal tradition. Section 3 intervened in that inquiry and clarified that reference to path dependence alone does not provide a comprehensive and satisfactory explanation for the pattern of legal growth. It argued that while it is incontrovertible that the current legal characterisation of the circulation of registered shares as crystallised in the Companies Act 2006 follows from the development of the principles of the joint stock company and partnership law, the historical analysis suggests that the embryonic paradigm is not English. It was in fact the model of maritime partnership (the *societas maris*), as refined in the scheme of a joint stock fund in Genoa that (most likely) was borrowed and employed for part-ownership in ships in England starting from the beginning of the sixteenth century. The reception was facilitated by the commercial interaction deriving from the existence of commercial Italian settlements involved in the wool trade in the south of England, from the cultural influence of the Italian mercantile community and from the widespread recourse in practice to certain Italian forms of business association. However, these elements did not lead to the univocal conclusion that the Genoese model was received in its original form. Rather, the Genoese model was adapted in accordance with the indigenous legal tradition founded on the fellowship relations typical of the trading guilds. The role of the Court of Chancery in shaping the law of partnership and trust later provided for the unique evolution of the paradigm of the English joint stock company when incorporation was not easily available. The conclusion of section 3 was that, in line with the arguments on postcolonial discourse developed in Part I, a hybrid paradigm was progressively formed as a result of the interaction of the original Genoese model and the indigenous legal tradition of the guilds. Briefly, as for colonised subjects, the reproduced model 'is almost the same, but not quite'.[3]

Chapter 5 investigated the historical evolution for the transfer of share warrants to bearer. Section 1 outlined the current legal framework, placing special emphasis on the finding that they qualify as negotiable instruments. It suggested that in the case of share warrants to bearer, possession, as opposed to registration, is the method of evidencing title to company shares and that legal title passes from one person to another by delivery of the warrant. Starting from their current legal characterisation, section 2 looked at the history of share warrants to bearer, focusing, inevitably, on the evolution of the law of negotiable instruments and the concept of negotiability. It found that negotiable instruments originated and developed in the thirteenth century from a variation of certain Italian notarial exchange contracts and the contract of *cambium* as effected under the machinery of the bill of exchange (*tratta* – when using the Italian terminology). In its essence, the *tratta* consisted of an instrument specifically devised by sedentary merchants for long distance trade to obviate the risk of the physical transport of money from one fair to another or from one country to another. The Italian *tratta* was received in English commercial practice when English merchants became the principal dealers in commodities (wool and cloth exports) in the fifteenth century. Section 3 looked more carefully at the process of reception thorough hybridisation and at the resulting advent of negotiability in England. It clarified in particular that, although they progressively

3 H Bhabha 'Of Mimicry and Men' in Id (ed) *The Location of Culture* (Routledge London 1994) 123.

converged, the class of negotiable instruments and the concept of negotiability have not always coincided. Historically, they developed at different stages in response to changing commercial necessities and along different legal patterns. A more robust view is that mercantile conditions changed over centuries and it was only at the beginning of the nineteenth century that the commercial practice needed debt instruments capable of being transferred as a means of payment in accordance with the rules of negotiability. From this finding, it followed that the Italian *tratta* evolved in England from the original paradigm in accordance with the changing economic, legal and social circumstances in a distinct scheme. This pattern is consistent with the process of hybridisation observed in postcolonial studies in Part I. Section 4 finally examined the specific case of share warrants to bearer. It argued that the scheme for promissory notes followed from the original model of the bill of exchange and, in the terms codified in the Bills of Exchange Act 1882, formed the basis of reference for the subsequent development of certain categories of negotiable instruments. This was the case for scrip certificates, the legal ancestors of share warrants to bearer.

PART III

THE TRANSFER OF (INTERESTS IN) SHARES

Introduction

INTRODUCTION TO PART III

This Part focuses on the second leg of the case study on comparative jurisprudence according to the scheme outlined at the end of Part I. By looking at the evolution of the methods by which shares are transferred in financial markets, it considers prospectively (*de iure condendo*) certain themes on cultural interaction originated in the postcolonial debate. In essence, Part III examines the limits of current practice of holding and disposition of shares through intermediaries and discusses the initiatives for modernising the existing legal framework. In doing so, it suggests that the concept of hybridisation presented in Part I and discussed in Part II with respect to the non-hegemonic scheme of borrowing, also applies outside that specific context.

The inquiry is specifically grounded on the process of formation and possible implementation in the UK of the UNIDROIT Convention on Substantive Rules for Intermediated Securities adopted by the diplomatic conference in Geneva on 9 October 2009 (hereinafter, the 'Geneva Securities Convention') as the most advanced and sophisticated legislative achievement in the area of the circulation of indirectly held securities. It is argued in this Part that, by analogy to the pattern of legal change based on borrowing, the model arising from a regulated mechanism of harmonisation set out by the contributions of delegates and national experts at international sessions and diplomatic conferences also involves a form of hybridisation. This pattern (unlike the one based on borrowing) consists of a two-step process where cultural interactions occur both at the formation of the international instrument and at the time of its hegemonic implementation in the domestic legal framework. In the light of the existing uncertainty on whether the Geneva Securities Convention will be ratified in the UK, only the first step can be properly addressed in this study. With respect to the second one, supportive reference to the arguments on hybridisation will be made by referring to comparable paradigms.

Part III is divided into two chapters. They consider at different levels and with a variety of emphases the evolution of law in the area of holding and transfer of shares in financial markets.

Chapter 6 takes a broad perspective. As a preliminary matter it tackles the economic themes underlying the evolution of market practice. Building on that inquiry, it evaluates the possible sources of legal risk at a national and international level and discusses the need to enhance legal certainty for the promotion of market confidence and efficiency in the area of post-trading. In doing so, it focuses primarily on the English legal characterisation for indirectly held shares and on certain conflict of laws themes. Building on that analysis the law reform proposals are evaluated and it will be shown in particular that the negotiations underlying the Geneva Securities Convention involved a process of hybridisation, which eventually led to the formation of a hybrid legal instrument.

Chapter 7 is narrower and more specific in its scope. It departs from the general scenario outlined in Chapter 6 and concentrates on one of the most controversial issues in the transfer of intermediated shares: the protection of the innocent purchaser from adverse claims. The condition of English law is addressed at first in the light of the criticisms made in a pioneering report by the Financial Market Law Committee c/o Bank of England (the 'FMLC')[1] and subsequently reiterated by the Law Commission.[2] This framework is then contrasted with the law currently in force in Italy and with the model described under Article 8 UCC. The aim of the comparative exercise is to provide a comprehensive map of possible legal scenarios before discussing how the Geneva Securities Convention treats the innocent purchasers of intermediated securities and arguing that the specific enacted provisions represent the effect of a process of hybridisation.

1 *Property Interests in Investment Securities* – Issue 3 (5 July 2004) and available at <www.fmlc.org/papers/fmlc1_3_july04.pdf> (accessed 7 August 2013). The remit of the FMLC is to identify issues of legal uncertainty or misunderstanding (present and future) in the framework of the wholesale financial market which might give rise to material risk and to consider how such issues should be addressed.

2 Law Commission *Unidroit Convention on Substantive Rules Regarding Intermediated Securities – Further Advice to HM Treasury* (May 2008) available at <www.lawcom.gov.uk/docs/intermediated_securities_advice_May2008.pdf> (accessed 7 August 2013)..

Chapter 6

INDIRECT HOLDING AND THE PROCESS OF LEGAL EVOLUTION

This chapter looks at the process of legal change in the area of post-trading following the growth of intermediation in financial markets.

Section 1 analyses the meaning of the move from direct to indirect (book-entry) holdings, from the pattern of holding shares to the one of holding interests/entitlements in shares. It then discusses some of the most significant sources of legal risk arising from the evolution of financial practice by placing special emphasis on certain deficiencies and ambiguities in English law and argues for law reform. Given the interconnection between financial markets, it finds that it makes little sense to promote legal change merely at a national level and proposes that coordinated international action to address legal uncertainties is preferable.

Building on this, section 2 assesses the responses to legal uncertainty provided by two of the most important existing normative projects on the transfer of indirectly held securities: the Geneva Securities Convention and the EU Commission project on clearing and settlement. It is, in particular, by looking closely at the preparatory works and at certain issues of the final text of the Geneva Securities Convention that the pattern of growth of English law is examined and the process of hybridisation revealed.

1. Underlying Themes

At the heart of the law reform debate on post-trading is the ubiquitous commercial practice of intermediation, the fact that investors do not physically hold investment securities any more. Today in capital markets it is customary for securities[1] to be held and circulated through financial intermediaries and to employ local sub-custodians in cross-border transactions. Investors purchase and sell, and provide collateral to secured lenders on their holdings by means of book-entries made in the securities account kept with the intermediary. Intermediated securities are intangibles evidenced in electronic records of the intermediary, usually on an unallocated basis,[2] commingled with those of other investors.[3] This holding pattern is operationally convenient as it reduces administration

1 Shares, of course, belong to this *genus*. See eg *Citibank NA v MBIA Assurance SA* [2007] EWCA Civ 11.

2 There is no link between particular participants and particular securities.

3 So-called 'pooling'.

and allows transfers of securities from one customer to another to be effected through the books of the intermediary.[4] It also allows for the smooth performance of complex brokerage and investment management services even when dealing with large securities portfolios.[5]

The holding scenario just described is legally distinct from the traditional holding system observed in Part II where an investor's right to the underlying security represented by a definitive paper certificate is given by the possession of the document or by a separate record in the issuer's registry. Although the underlying securities and the interests in securities of the investor are the same in economic terms, in the case of intermediated securities there are not usually[6] earmarked assets (segregated) and they (if issued in the form of paper certificates at all) are not transferred according to the mechanism provided in companies' constitutions.

The following sections offer a picture of the evolution of the indirectly holding system. This provides the background that is fundamental for the analysis of hybridisation addressed in the second part of section 2. Giving emphasis to English law, the following sections describe the existence of domestic sources of legal uncertainty and cross-border inconsistencies, which are, of course, unwelcome in financial markets. Clarity at national level and harmonisation at international level are needed. While section 1.1 introduces the fundamental technological changes in settlement systems that facilitated intermediation and paperless dealing, section 1.2 addresses certain legal concerns at the root of the movement for law reform in the area of post-trading. This inquiry is carried out by focusing on three examples of substantive English law and by sketching the major causes of ambiguity in the area of conflict of laws. Section 1.3 concludes the general picture and finds the method to which rights arising from intermediated securities can be enforced against the issuer to be the major conceptual obstacle to the formation of a common international legal framework.

1.1. Electronic Settlement Systems

The practice of intermediation was prompted by the growth in securities transactions and securitisation techniques[7] and has been made possible by the improvements in information technologies[8] and, in particular, by the introduction of book-entry systems of settlement.[9]

4 Avoiding, therefore, all the formal requirements involved in direct transfer of shares. See above *sub* Chapter 4, section 1.3.

5 See S Schwartz and J Benjamin 'Intermediary Risk in the Indirect Holding System for Securities' (2002) 12 Duke J Comp & Int'l L 312.

6 i.e. it is not customary for intermediaries to hold shares separately for each investor.

7 Driven by the practical benefits for the issuers and investors. See the description of the 'practical advantages' outlined by the Law Commission *The UNIDROIT Convention on Substantive Rules Regarding Intermediated Securities – Updated Advice to HM Treasury* (May 2007) 17. See also L Gullifer 'The Proprietary Protection of Investors in Intermediated Securities' in J Armour and J Payne (eds) *Rationality in Company Law – Essays in Honour of DD Prentice* (Hart Oxford 2009) 224–225.

8 See R Knott and A Mills 'Modelling Risk in Central Counterparty Clearing Houses: a Review' (2002) Bank of England Financial Stability Review 162.

9 J Benjamin 'Negotiability and Computerisation' (1995) 10 JIBFL 253.

These originated from the need to replace paper certificates with electronic records following the technical problems experienced during the 'paper crunch' in the 1970s in the US[10] and in the 1980s in the UK.[11] In short, the traditional process of delivering paper-based shares[12] against payment in order to fulfil contractual obligations arising out of trading could not keep pace with the increase in the number of transactions. Severe delays in the settlement interval became frequent and 'backlogs of unsettled trades threatened the integrity of the securities market'.[13] Further to this, the physical handling and movement of paper-based shares (and transfer forms) was labour-intensive[14] and risky.[15]

With the advent of electronic settlement systems, the interests of the participants (or their agents) are recorded by credit/debit entries in securities/cash accounts maintained in their names by the operator of the system. Following the instruction of the participants to the system, the transaction is executed by debiting and crediting those securities/cash accounts. Efficient settlement is obtained by allowing the synchronisation of the delivery of securities with the payment of the cash sum.[16] In other words, in electronic settlement systems a link between a securities transfer system and a fund transfer system is created in order to ensure that delivery occurs if and only if payment occurs.[17]

Two different approaches to electronic settlement have generally been employed, either separately or together:[18] immobilisation and dematerialisation.

10 See E Ledrut and C Upper 'The US Paper Crunch' (2007) BIS Quarterly Review; RB Smith 'A Piece of Paper Revisited' (1971) 25 Bus Law 1769; and, recently, D Donald 'The Rise and Effects of the Indirect Holding Systems – How Corporate America Ceded its Shareholders to Intermediaries' working paper available at <www.papers.ssrn.com/sol3/papers.cfm?abstract_id=1017206> (accessed 7 August 2013).

11 The topic is comprehensively covered in M Yates and G Montagu *The Law of Global Custody* (Tottel London 2013) Chapter 8. A similar description is provided in various articles written by J Benjamin. See J Benjamin 'Overview of Post-Trade Infrastructure. Part 1' (2003) JIBFL 127; Id 'Overview of Post-Trade Infrastructure. Part 2' (2003) JIBFL 171–177; and Id 'Overview of Post-Trade Infrastructure. Part 3' (2003) JIBFL 223–228.

12 In the case of registered shares, the seller had to deliver the paper certificate and transfer form before re-registration with the issuer.

13 M Yates and G Montagu *The Law of Global Custody* (Tottel London 2013) 205.

14 As it required a high number of settlement clerks.

15 See MJ Aronstein 'The Decline and Fall of the Stock Certificate in America' (1978) 1 J Comp L & Sec Reg 273; and Id 'A Certificateless Article 8? We Can Have it Both Ways' (1976) 31 Bus Law 727.

16 The so-called DVP ('delivery versus payment').

17 This has been driven by guidance of industry participants such as the International Securities Services Association (*Recommendations* 2000) and the Group of Thirty (*Global Clearing and Settlement: A Plan for Action* 2003).

18 In line with the authoritative suggestions contained in 1988 Group of Thirty Report entitled *Clearance and Settlement in the World's Securities Markets*, available at <www.group30.org/rpt_43.shtml> (accessed 7 August 2013).

1.1.1. Immobilisation

In the case of immobilisation,[19] paper certificates, generally issued in global form (a global note), are retained either under compulsory or optional[20] terms by a depositary on behalf of a settlement system[21] (CSD[22] or ICSD[23] depending on whether the nominee who holds directly for the issuer is a depositary for domestic or international issues) and are represented by entries in the securities account maintained by the participants in the settlement system. Immobilisation necessarily involves intermediation. Following the transfer by way of book entries in the participants' accounts, changes of ownership of the immobilised shares are effected in the account kept by the depository (or its nominee).

The world's largest depository is the Depository Trust Corporation (DTC),[24] which holds most US-issued shares. UCC Article 8 governs the accounts maintained by DTC through its nominee (Cede & Co) for its participants.[25]

1.1.2. Dematerialisation

Under a dematerialised settlement system, physical certificates are not required and the electronic records themselves represent the securities. However, under certain settlement systems,[26] a person holding uncertificated securities may have them reconverted into certificated securities by arranging for its members to issue an instruction to the operator to that effect.[27] Dematerialisation does not affect the relationship between investor and issuer. It remains the same as in the case of issuance of certificated securities. Transfers of securities consist in electronic entries in the account kept by the operator of the system.

It was shown in Part I that the UK settlement system, named CREST, which settles securities in uncertificated form, follows this approach. The operator of the CREST system[28] is not a central securities depositary. The operator does not hold dematerialised shares for account holders, but it merely constitutes a legal record of entitlement to the shares.[29]

19 For a general overview, see N Papaspyrou 'Immobilisation of Securities: Part 1 Proprietary Rights of Indirect Holders' (1996) 10 JIBL 430; and Id 'Immobilisation of Securities: Part 2 Personal Rights of Indirect Holders' (1996) JIBL 459.

20 Depending on whether the securities deposited with a custodian can be withdrawn at any time.

21 See F Christie and H Dosanjh 'The Practical Elements of Settlement and Custody' in F Oditah (ed) *The Future for the Global Securities Market – Legal and Regulatory Aspects* (OUP Oxford 1996).

22 Central securities depositary.

23 International central securities depositary. Euroclear Bank and Clearstream Bank Luxembourg operate as ICSD and settlement systems for international bonds, equities and investment funds. Their ICSD operations are governed by Belgian and Luxembourg laws, respectively.

24 DTC is a limited-purpose trust company organised under the New York Banking Law, a 'clearing corporation' within the meaning of the New York Uniform Commercial Code and a 'clearing agency' registered pursuant to the provisions of section 17A of the Securities Exchange Act of 1934.

25 See F Coogan 'Security Interests in Investment Securities Under Revised Article 8 of the Uniform Commercial Code' (1979) 92 Harv L Rev 1018.

26 e.g. the English settlement system (CREST) pursuant to USR 2001 reg 32(2)(b) and (3)(b).

27 L Gullifer *Goode on Legal Problems of Credit and Security* (Sweet & Maxwell London 2008) 237.

28 EUI. See above *sub* Chapter 4, section 1.3.

29 USR 2001 reg 24.

1.2. Sources of Legal Risk

As already suggested, the growth of financial intermediation created areas of legal uncertainty at national level and generated unpredictable effects for cross border transfers of securities. These issues are at the foundation of the law reform debate and, inevitably, of the discussion on hybridisation addressed in section 2. An overview of some of the major legal concerns in both cases is presented below.

1.2.1. Unsound National Law

Even if the applicable law for indirectly held securities has been designated under the rules of conflict of laws (see below), the substantive law thus identified may itself not be settled, sound or clear. Apart from certain taxonomical difficulties,[30] traditional concepts adapted from other contexts have often proved difficult to square with the market practice of intermediation. At times, a different set of commercial law concepts and rules has been regarded as indispensable.

This emerges from the experience of revision of Article 8 UCC where the 1978 rewriting of the law in 'media neutral' terms[31] did not eliminate the uncertainties related to the current securities holding practices where transfers were performed by computerised entries in the records of intermediaries and not of the issuers.[32] The radical revision of UCC Article 8 consisting of an *ad hoc* set of new commercial concepts and rules[33] was adopted in 1994 (mainly in response to robust academic criticisms)[34] and stands out as a Copernican revolution in promoting a new flexible concept of property suitable for the new holding mechanism.[35] The 1994 UCC reform, and its peculiar drafting technique ('first describe it, then name it'),[36] remains, however, a somewhat

30 See the doctrinal debate on the concept of 'equitable property right' in Chapter 7.

31 i.e. the introduction of 'uncertificated securities' in the 1978 revision of UCC Article 8 to address the problems caused by the inefficient paper-based securities trading system.

32 See JS Rogers 'An Essay on Horseless Carriage and Paperless Negotiable Instruments: Some Lessons from the Article 8 Revision' (1995) 31 Idaho L Rev 691. See also K Kettering 'Repledge Deconstructed' (1999) 61 U Pitt L Rev 45; and SL Schwarcz 'Intermediary Risk in a Global Economy' (2001) 50 Duke LJ 1541.

33 In particular, the property concept of 'securities entitlement' which comprises both personal rights against the intermediary and the property rights concerning the underlying assets (as defined in UCC §8–102(a)(17) and specified under UCC §8–501–511). See the outline provided by CS Bjerre and SM Rocks *The ABC of the UCC: Article 8, Investment Securities* (American Bar Association Chicago 2004).

34 See CW Mooney 'Beyond Negotiability: A New Model for Transfer and Pledge of Interests in Securities Controlled by Intermediaries' (1990) 12 Cardozo L Rev 305; JL Schroeder 'Is Article 8 Finally Ready This Time? The Radical Reform of Secured Lending on Wall Street' (1994) 3 Columbia Bus L Rev 291 at 303; and PH Coogan 'Security Interests in Investment Securities under Revised Article 8 of the Uniform Commercial Code' (1979) 92 Harvard L Rev 1013.

35 See JS Rogers 'Policy Perspectives on Revised UCC Article 8' (1996) 43 UCLA L Rev 1431; Id 'An Essay on Horseless Carriages and Paperless Negotiable Instruments: Some Lessons from Article 8 Revision' (1995) 31 Idaho L Rev 689.

36 JS Rogers 'Policy Perspectives on Revised UCC Article 8' (1996) 43 UCLA L Rev 1451.

isolated example.[37] While legislation for dematerialisation has been enacted in many countries,[38] the need for a radical modernisation of concepts rooted in legal tradition has not always been regarded as indispensable.[39] A new set of rules has not been introduced in many legal systems simply because the existing framework has been considered flexible enough to accommodate the scheme of the modern system of holding through intermediaries.

In England, the pioneering report of the FMLC published in 2004[40] suggested that even though legislation for uncertificated securities has been in place since 1995, the existing legal framework does not address all the practical problems arising from the circulation of indirectly held securities. Although subject to academic criticisms,[41] the FMLC report still represents the conventional position under English law.[42] Legislative intervention is highly desirable 'to clarify existing law and reflect market developments',[43] especially at a time when competition among different systems of commercial law is strong. The Law Commission[44] examined the same issues to advise on the work of the European Commission in the area of post-trading and, by rejecting a purely parochial solution, reached similar conclusions in its final advice submitted to HM Treasury in 2008.[45]

37 With the exception of the Canadian Uniform Securities Transfer Act as approved at the Uniform Law Conference of Canada in August 2004. See WD Grayand and M Scavone 'A Primer on the Uniform Securities Transfer Act' (2004) Ontario Branch of the Canadian Bar Association 1, available at <www.mcmillan.ca/Upload/Publication/2A.pdf> (accessed 7 August 2013). See also J Rogers 'The Revision of Canadian Law on Securities Holdings Through Intermediaries: Who What, When, How and Why?' (2007) 45 CBLJ 49.

38 e.g. in France (art 94(2) of the Loi de Finances of 31 December 1981 entered into force on 5 November 1984 implemented by Decret no 83-359 of 2 May 1993), Italy (Decreto Legislativo 24 giugno 1998 no 213, *Disposizioni per l'introduzione dell'euro nell'ordinamento nazionale, a norma dell'art 1, comma 1, della legge 17 dicembre 1997, n 433* art 28 para 1, in accordance to the *Regolamento* agreed between Consob and Banca d'Italia, enacted through Consob Regulation no 11768 of 23 December 1998, as amended, art 23 paras 1 and 3) and United Kingdom (USR 1995 (SI 1995/3272) now replaced by USR 2001 (SI 2001/3755) and subsequent amendments).

39 This has been the case in Belgium (Belgian Royal Decree 62, as co-ordinated by Royal Decree of 27 January 2004) and Luxembourg (Law of 1 August 2001 on the circulation of securities and other fungible Instruments. Articles 7.7 and 15). See FMLC *Property Interests in Investment Securities (International Overview)* (June 2004) and available at <www.fmlc.org/papers/fmlc2_3_july04.pdf> (accessed 7 August 2013).

40 FMLC *Property Interests in Investment Securities – Issue 3* (5 July 2004) and available at <www.fmlc.org/papers/fmlc1_3_july04.pdf> (accessed 7 August 2013).

41 See the analysis by B McFarlane and R Stevens 'Interest in Securities – Practical Problems and Conceptual Solutions' in L Gullifer and J Payne (eds) *Intermediated Securities – Legal Problems and Practical Issues* (Hart Oxford 2010) 33.

42 See the contribution to the debate (a reply to McFarlane and Stevens paper cited above) by G Moss 'Intermediated Securities: Issues Arising from Insolvency' in L Gullifer and J Payne (eds) *Intermediated Securities – Legal Problems and Practical Issues* (Hart Oxford 2010) 61.

43 FMLC *Property Interests in Investment Securities – Issue 3* (5 July 2004) and available at <www.fmlc.org/papers/fmlc1_3_july04.pdf> (accessed 7 August 2013) 18.

44 As part of its 9th Programme of Law Reform.

45 Law Commission *UNIDROIT Convention on Substantive Rules Regarding Intermediated Securities – Further Advice to HM Treasury* (May 2008) available at <www.lawcom.gov.uk/docs/intermediated_securities_advice_May2008.pdf> (accessed 7 August 2013) 32.

The practical concerns addressed by FMLC are of great relevance for the scope of this study on legal change and hybridisation, especially when confronted with the approach taken by the Geneva Securities Convention. This is for two reasons. First is because the analysis of the Convention shows whether and how the FMLC issues have been tackled in legislation. The second reason relates to the (possible) transposition of the Convention into the English legal framework in the near future. It is in this comparative light that three of the most significant concerns considered by FMLC are examined below and further discussed in section 2 when dealing with law reform initiatives and the pattern of legal change. Following a brief introduction on the legal characterisation for indirect holding under English law, the analysis will specifically look at (ii) the way an account holder is protected from the (relevant) intermediary's credit risk; (iii) the consequences of a shortfall in the assets held by the intermediary; and (iv) the availability of direct claims against any higher tier intermediaries, or against the issuer.

1.2.1.1. Legal Arrangement for Indirect Holding

There is a consensus among academics and practitioners[46] that, outside what is otherwise provided in a written agreement,[47] an intermediary that operates an account regulated by English law for (the benefit of) an account holder holds assets on trust.[48] Or, for a more accurate description that considers the reality of the pattern of intermediation in financial markets, reference should be made to the concept of sub-trust and to the system of holding as a series of sub-trusts.

Supported by a solid economic rationale,[49] this characterisation allows the protection of the account holders' assets from the claims of the intermediary's creditors. Assets held on trust are simply outside the trustee's estate. They are ring-fenced from the liability of the intermediary. On the intermediary's insolvency, the beneficiary would have a proprietary right, which could not be defeated by the intermediary's creditors.[50] The alternative interpretation of the custodial relationship in terms of bailment (or sub-

46 See generally J Benjamin *Interests in Securities* (OUP Oxford 2000) 40; M Yates and G Montagu *The Law of Global Custody* (Tottel London 2009) 23; and AO Peters *Custody of Investments: Law and Practice* (OUP Oxford 2000) Chapters 1 and 2.

47 e.g. pure contractual right to redelivery, equity of redemption and, under certain circumstances, bailment. See the overview contained in FMLC *Property Interests in Investment Securities – Issue 3* (5 July 2004) available at <www.fmlc.org/papers/fmlc2_3_july04.pdf> (accessed 7 August 2013) 10.

48 See, the analysis on this issue presented by J Benjamin *Interests in Securities* (OUP Oxford 2000), reiterated, following the Lehman Brothers collapse in J Smethurst and J Benjamin 'Restatement of the Law Relating to Client Securities' (2009) 4 Capital Markets LJ 311.

49 As well described by the Law Commission *Project on Intermediated Investment Securities – Second Seminar (Issues Affecting Account Holders and Intermediaries)* (23 June 2006) available at <www.lawcom.gov.uk/docs/investment_securities_seminar_paper_2.pdf> (accessed 7 August 2013) 11, the intermediary is a mere conduit for 'for the capital, income and other economic benefits that flow from the underlying securities. Its economic interest lies solely in the fees it receives for the custody and other banking services it provides to account holder'. Allowing the intermediary's creditors to have an equal claim to securities that the intermediary holds on behalf of its account holder would *de facto* entitle the intermediary's creditors to obtain a windfall.

50 In the case of a corporate insolvency see *Barclays Bank Ltd v Quistclose Investment Ltd* [1970] AC 567.

bailment)[51] should be dismissed as flawed.[52] Bailment arrangements are in fact restricted to tangible assets[53] and available only where possession is possible.[54] As already suggested, this is not the case of indirectly held shares[55] where there is nothing that can be physically possessed even when the underlying assets are tangibles.[56]

1.2.1.2. The Protection of the Account Holders' Assets from the Claims of an Intermediary's Creditors

The conventional legal characterisation of intermediated securities suggested above is based on the assumption that a valid trust is created notwithstanding the fact that the intangible assets held by the intermediary for investors are aggregated into one commingled holding (i.e. they are held on an unallocated or fungible basis).[57] This is because, contrary to the credit balances of cash accounts,[58] the fundamental principle of

51 Under a bailment relationship, legal title to the deposited assets is not transferred to the intermediary, but remains with the client. As the intermediary, the bailee is not the owner of the assets bailed with him, but he is entitled only to possession. He is a mere custodian and he must refrain from denying the bailor's title (*Biddle v Bond* (1865) 6 B&S 225, 122 ER 1179).

52 Contrary to this conventional view, Beaves argues that the law of bailment 'has […] evolved beyond the strict confines of Lord Holt CJ's classic analysis in *Coggs v Bernard*' (AW Beaves 'Global Custody: A Tentative Analysis of Property and Contract' in N Palmer and E McKendrick (eds) *Interests in Goods* (LLP London 1998) 125) and that principles akin to those of bailment should also govern the any custodial relationship involving dematerialised or immobilised securities and fungible accounting. Beaves' argument is grounded on three main themes: (1) as authorities (*Moukataff v British Overseas Airways Corporation* [1967] 1 Lloyd's Rep 396 and *Belvoir Finance Co Ltd v Stapleton* [1971] 2 QB 210) do suggest, the critical element in a bailment relationship is not physical possession of the securities in question, but the ability of the client to direct or control an entitlement to those securities through actions of the global custodian being carried out to the client's order: 'it is the authority from the client to the intermediary that enables the intermediary to deal with those securities, in effect "as owner", in its relations with any sub-custodian, central or common depositary, or indeed the issuer of the securities concerned' (AW Beaves 'Global Custody: A Tentative Analysis of Property and Contract' in N Palmer and E McKendrick (eds) *Interests in Goods* (LLP London 1998) 125 at 126); (2) certain court decisions have also evidenced that there is no longer any inconsistency between fungibility and the existence of bailment provided that certain conditions are met; this is different from the past – in short, pooling does not preclude *per se* a bailment relationship; and (3) by analogy to other areas of law where intangible rights are protected by proprietary remedies (in respect of confidential information, Beaves mentions *Boardman v Phipps* [1967] 2 AC 46, 3 ER 721), an extension of bailment to a series of documented rights should not be treated as unreasonable.

53 *Re Hallett's Estates, Knatchbull v Hallett* (1879) 13 ChD 696 *per* Jessell at 708 with respect to bearer bonds.

54 The conventional characterisation under English law is based on the decision of Holt CJ in *Coggs v Bernard* (1703) 2 Ld Raym 909.

55 i.e. they do not attach to any tangible asset. See the analysis in J Benjamin *Interests in Securities* (OUP Oxford 2000) 40.

56 e.g. in the case of share warrants to bearer.

57 When a sub-trustee is involved, there will be only a designated account in the name of the original trustee.

58 *Foley v Hill* (1848) 2 HL Cas 28. Unless the credit balances represent the proceeds of sale of trustee's assets (*Re Hallett's Estate, Knatchbull v Hallett* (1880) 13 ChD 696) or income derived from trust's assets

the need for certainty of subject matter for a valid trust to arise[59] is considered to be redundant in the context of a commingled pool of securities. There is authority on this. The Court of Appeal in *Hunter v Moss*[60] stated that the requirement of 'certainty of subject matter' does not necessarily entail the segregation of assets when an intangible asset is not distinguishable from another. Mr Moss, who was the owner of 950 shares in a private company, declared a trust of 50 of those shares for Mr Hunter. Mr Moss later sold the 950 shares, keeping all the proceeds for himself. Mr Hunter claimed a proportion of the proceeds of the sale, but Mr Moss argued that the lot of 50 shares of the 950 had never been clearly identified and that, therefore, the trust failed for want of certainty of subject matter. Upholding Rimer QC's first instance decision[61] based by way of analogy on the Missouri case *Rollestone v National Bank of Commerce in St Louis*,[62] Dillon LJ[63] held for Mr Hunter and established that the trust attached to the defendant's shareholding. In his reasoning, he employed a heavily criticised analogy[64] between declarations of trusts and bequests under a will so that Mr Moss could also be entitled to create an *inter vivos* trust of 50 of his 950 shares without previously segregating them.[65] Dillon LJ also distinguished from the rule in *Re London Wine Co (Shippers) Ltd*,[66] later endorsed by the Privy Council in *Re Goldcorp Exchange Ltd*,[67] on the basis that the case concerned intangible property and not tangibles. In the case of certain fungible intangible property such as shares of one class in one company, the rule requiring the settlor to identify the specific trust assets does not apply. The trust does not fail for want of ascertainment because the identification of shares of a particular issue is both irrelevant and impossible. Notwithstanding strong academic criticisms[68] and the existence of inconsistent

(*Swain v Law Society* [1981] 3 ER 797 *per* Oliver LJ at 813). Along the same lines, see *Re Lehman Brothers International (Europe), Lomas v RAB Market Cycles (Master) Fund Ltd* [2009] EWHC 2545 (Ch) 17.

59 *Knight v Knight* (1840) 3 Beav 148. See *Re Goldcorp Exchange* [1994] 2 ER 806 *per* Lord Mustill at 814.

60 [1994] 1 WLR 452, 3 ER 215.

61 *Hunter v Moss* [1993] 1 WLR 934.

62 (1923) 252 SW 394. This element in itself would deserve more attention as a clear example of legal borrowing.

63 With whom Mann and Hirst LJJ agreed.

64 See D Hayton 'Uncertainty of subject matter of trusts' (1994) 110 LQR 335.

65 *Hunter v Moss* [1994] 1 WLR 452 *per* Dillon LJ at 459.

66 [1986] PCC 121 *per* Oliver J, relying on the authority of *Re Wait* [1927] 1 Ch 606.

67 [1995] 1 AC 74. Establishing, implicitly, that *Hunter v Moss* should not be followed.

68 Most of the criticisms relate to the rationale in distinguishing the need for identification between shares, wine or gold and to the possible dealing with the 950 shares by Mr Moss. If it is assumed that the trust is in existence, it could easily happen that the shares sold by Mr Moss would be the ones belonging to Mr Hunter. In this case there would be a clear breach of trust. It is, however, impossible to know whether a breach has occurred because it is impossible to identify the property in the shares. According to Penner (J Penner *The Law of Trusts* (OUP Oxford 2006) 184), the better view is that Moss 'has not properly created a trust at all, and while he might have been contractually obliged to do so (under a term of Hunter's employment contract with him), it is conceptually confused to deal with his failure to make himself a trustee by treating him as a trustee in breach'. The suggested right response to *Hunter v Moss* should have been the imposition of an equitable charge on Mr Moss's shares in favour of Mr Hunter to the value of 50 shares (D Hayton 'Uncertainty of subject matter of trusts' (1994) 110 LQR 335). Alternatively, the imposition of a constructive trust on Moss 'over the whole 950 shares, to hold them in shares 1/19 for Hunter and 18/19 for himself, thus creating an equitable co-ownership of the shares

authorities on the possibility of creating property rights under a trust without attaching to any particular asset,[69] this *ratio* has been followed with a variety of accents in *Re Harvard Securities*,[70] in *Re CA Pacific Finance Ltd*,[71] *White v Shortall*[72] and more recently in *Re Lehman Brothers International (Europe), Lomas v RAB Market Cycles (Master) Fund Ltd*[73] and *Re Lehman Brothers International (Europe), Pearson v Lehman Brothers Finance SA and Others*[74] (not disagreed with in the Court of Appeal judgment).[75] It has also found some *ex post* doctrinal support. Professor Goode, in particular, strongly argues that a requirement for segregation is futile for shares. Unlike bottles of wine, gold bars or potatoes, shares of the same issue cannot be segregated from the bulk 'in the sense of cutting the buyer loose from an interest in the remainder of the issue'.[76] They are of fungible character, undivided, unnumbered[77] and incapable of ascertainment. Assuming that a transfer of part of the bulk amount to transfers of a proportion of the bulk and not to identifiable units of the bulk, it follows that any discussion on certainty of subject matter is redundant.[78]

until such time as Moss segregated 50 for Hunter': J Penner *The Law of Trusts* (OUP Oxford 2006) 184. See, however, the supportive view of the case based on the possible employment of the rules of tracing proposed by J Martin 'Certainty of Subject Matter: a Defence of *Hunter v Moss*' (1996) Conv 223, and S Worthington 'Sorting out Ownership Interests in a Bulk: Gifts, Sales and Trusts' (1999) JBL 1.

69 See, for example, the cases that require segregation of cash for certainty when holding cash on trust. *Mac-Jordan Construction Ltd v Brookmount Erostin Ltd* [1992] BCLC 350; *Russell-Cooke Trust Company and another v Richard Prentis and Co Ltd* [2002] EWHC 2227; and *Re BA Peters plc (in administration)* [2008] ER 392.

70 [1998] BCC 567 *per* Neuberger J at 388 (where it was also held that the principle in *Hunter v Moss* does not apply to Australian law).

71 [2000] BCLC 494 *per* Yuen J.

72 [2006] NSWSC 1379 *per* Campbell J at para 212 in symmetrical contrast with *Re Wait* [1927] 1 Ch 606.

73 [2009] EWHC 2545 (Ch) 12 at para 56. See the critical remarks of M Bridge 'Security Financial Collateral Transfers and Prime Broker Insolvency' (2010) LFMR 189 at 192.

74 [2010] EWHC 2914 (Ch) *per* Briggs J at paragraphs 225–248.

75 *In the matter of Lehman Brothers International (Europe) (in administration)* [2011] EWCA Civ 1544.

76 R Goode 'Are intangible assets fungible?' in A Pretto and P Birks (eds) *Themes in Comparative Law* (OUP Oxford 2002) 102. The same position is shared by B McFarlane and R Stevens 'Interest in Securities – Practical Problems and Conceptual Solutions' in L Gullifer and J Payne (eds) *Intermediated Securities – Legal Problems and Practical Issues* (Hart Oxford 2010) 40. Similar conclusions based on the peculiar nature and function of financial instruments (along a different path based on comparative legal history) have been put forward by E Micheler 'The Legal Nature of Securities: Inspirations from Comparative Law' in L Gullifer and J Payne (eds) *Intermediated Securities – Legal Problems and Practical Issues* (Hart Oxford 2010) ch 5.

77 Currently, section 543 of the Companies Act 2006.

78 J Benjamin *Interests in Securities* (OUP Oxford 2000) 56 has put forward an alternative explanation that may help to circumvent the need for allocation in the case of fungible custody arrangements. This is to suppose that the trust property comprises the entire holding in the pool and that account holders are equitable tenants in common of the pool of shares held by the intermediary. They own fractional shares in the pooled account rather than individual equitable proprietary interests over allocated securities with the pool and provided that shares (or intermediated shares if the holder is a lower tier intermediary) are not commingled with the ones belonging to the intermediary, as it would otherwise be impossible to identify the shares which are held on trust for the clients and the shares belonging to the intermediary. This analysis is consistent with *Re Stapylton Fletcher Ltd* [1995] 1 WLR 1181, 1 ER 192 *per* Baker QC at 210 and it has been recently endorsed by L Gullifer 'The Proprietary Protection of Investors in

Against the above pragmatic decision of the Court of Appeal in *Hunter v Moss* and in line with the existing scenario in other jurisdictions,[79] the FMLC and the Law Commission argued for the need to clarify once and for all in legislation that 'securities credited on an account holder's account should be considered outside the intermediary's estate without need to consider further whether or not they can be allocated for the purpose of a trust'.[80]

1.2.1.3. Shortfalls in the Assets Held by the Intermediary

The FMLC report also considered the situation where, even if the account holders' assets are ring-fenced from the claims of the intermediary's creditors,[81] a shortfall arises in the intermediary's account. This circumstance occurs when the securities credited in the books of the relevant intermediary fall short of the aggregate of the investor's entitlements recorded with the lower-tier intermediary in the chain. The imbalance does not necessarily result from the intermediary's fraud or mistake. It may also arise for operational reasons, including possible inefficiencies associated with cross-border settlement, insolvency displacement related to investors' purchases and sub-custodian insolvency.

Under English law the problem of the allocation of a shortfall among the different investors is relevant only when the intermediary is insolvent. A solvent intermediary, if he does not 'decide voluntarily to make up the shortfall for relationship and reputation reason',[82] is under a legal duty to make good the shortfall, to replace the missing securities or pay damages. He must account for the assets held on trust and he can be required to restore any deficiency in the trust assets to the trust.[83] Even outside the cases of strict liability when the shortfall is the result of a positive act of the intermediary,[84] his duty cannot *de facto* be contracted out.[85] Intermediaries who operate in financial markets are regulated by the FCA and must comply with its rules on safeguarding of trust assets

Intermediated Securities' in J Armour and J Payne (eds) *Rationality in Company Law – Essays in Honour of DD Prentice* (Hart Oxford 2009) 234–236. See also the contribution on the specific English law debate made by E Johansson *Property Rights in Investment Securities and the Doctrine of Specificity* (Springer Berlin Heidelberg 2009) 73.

79 e.g. under art 8 of the UCC where the 'securities entitlement' is a *pro-rata* property interest held with all other entitlement holders with respect to a specific type of financial asset held by the intermediary (UCC §8–503).

80 Law Commission *Project on Intermediated Investment Securities – Second Seminar* (Issues Affecting Account Holders and Intermediaries) (23 June 2006) available at <www.lawcom.gov.uk/docs/investment_securities_seminar_paper_2.pdf> (accessed 7 August 2013) 17.

81 i.e. a valid trust is in place.

82 J Benjamin *Financial Law* (OUP Oxford 2008) 435.

83 *Re Dawson* [1966] 3 ER 63 and *Target Holdings Ltd v Redferns (a firm) and another appellants* [1996] AC 421 at 434. See also P Millett 'Equity's Place in the Law of Commerce' (1998) 114 LQR 214 at 225.

84 e.g. fraud.

85 Under general principles of trust law, the liability of the intermediary in the course of business is high, but not strict. It can hardly be modified or excluded by agreement. See *Armitage v Nurse* [1998] Ch 214, [1997] 2 ER 705.

established in the High Level Principles[86] and in the Business Standards (CASS) rules.[87] In addition, the trustee's duty to account concerns the same subject matter of the trust, a duty on which the investor has relied. If it is contracted out, the trust is inevitably destroyed.[88]

When the intermediary is insolvent, various methods of allocating the shortfall among account holders are available. This is a source of legal uncertainty. Apart from the case of segregated accounts where shortfall loss affecting a particular account holder is borne entirely by the same account holder, it cannot be predicted whether competing claims to assets in a pooled fund should be resolved according to traditional tracing rules, to the 'first in, first out rule' applied in Clayton's case,[89] to a 'rolling charge approach'[90] or to a rateable distribution in proportion to the size of each account holder's holding with the relevant intermediary.[91] This last approach is the one favoured by the FMLC and by the Law Commission. It allows all investors to share the risk of the intermediary's insolvency undertaken at the time of the investment. Considering the arbitrary way in which administrative errors or frauds may affect individual accounts, the *pro rata* rule better captures the commercial expectations as it 'reflects the common venture of holding securities in a pooled account and the common risk taken by the account holders as to their intermediary's integrity and solvency'.[92]

However, although the *pro rata* solution seems to be the most practical and least arbitrary, 'it would be open to a particular customers to claim that the shortfall should be passed to other particular customers by applying the traditional rules of equitable tracing. Such a claim may be likely where a shortfall is significant, and attributable to problems associated with one customer's transactions'.[93] The possible coexistence of the two regimes for dealing with a shortfall has received academic support,[94] but following the Lehman Brothers collapse it has also attracted strong criticism for being an unworkable approach in practice.[95] Greater clarity on the consequences of a shortfall, the

86 FCA Handbook 'Principles for Business' (PRIN 2.10).

87 FCA Handbook 'Business Standards' (CASS, Custody Rules – Client Assets Rules 6.1).

88 See B McFarlane *The Structure of Property Law* (Hart Oxford 2008) 551; and *Armitage v Nurse* [1998] Ch 214 *per* Lord Millett at 253.

89 i.e. the first assets into a fund are deemed to have been the first out. *Devaynes v Noble* (1816) 1 Mer 529 at 572, 35 ER 781, *per* Sir William Grant MR at 798 'the first drawings out are attributed to the first payments in'.

90 See the discussion on this approach (or 'North American method') in *Barlow Clowes International Ltd v Vaughan* [1992] 4 All ER 22 *per* Woolf LJ at 35.

91 *Barlow Clowes International Ltd v Vaughan* [1992] 4 All ER 22.

92 Law Commission *Project on Intermediated Investment Securities – Second Seminar* (Issues Affecting Account Holders and Intermediaries) (23 June 2006) available at <www.lawcom.gov.uk/docs/investment_securities_seminar_paper_2.pdf> (accessed 7 August 2013) 34.

93 FMLC *Property Interests in Investment Securities – Issue 3* (5 July 2004) available at <www.fmlc.org/papers/fmlc2_3_july04.pdf> (accessed 7 August 2013) 11.

94 B McFarlane and R Stevens 'Interest in Securities – Practical Problems and Conceptual Solutions' in L Gullifer and J Payne (eds) *Intermediated Securities – Legal Problems and Practical Issues* (Hart Oxford 2010) 43–44.

95 G Moss 'Intermediated Securities: Issues Arising from Insolvency' in L Gullifer and J Payne (eds) *Intermediated Securities – Legal Problems and Practical Issues* (Hart Oxford 2010) 67 drawing from

FMLC argues, is desirable. This is still the case notwithstanding that recent statutory intervention[96] ensured the application of the *pari passu* principle in cases involving distribution of client assets where there is a shortfall, as the reform does not apply to CSDs, but only in cases where the account provider is an 'investment bank'.[97]

1.2.1.4. The No Look-Through Principle

The last issue addressed by FMLC that is considered here as background to the analysis explaining the process of legal change and hybridisation in this area of law, relates to the principle that prohibits an account holder from 'looking through' its immediate intermediary to make a claim in its own name against another intermediary higher up in the chain. The principle responds to practical difficulties and aims to promote market efficiency by limiting the possibility of tracing through the chain of intermediaries from which the ultimate investor acquired his interest. This exercise may in fact be extremely difficult, if not impossible, and costly. Correspondingly, there will be uncertain costs for the upper-tier intermediary to control the validity, as it is unlikely that he would have any record or knowledge of the lower-tier account holder. The advantages of the principle should be clear when considering that 'the principle allows an intermediary to quantify and manage its risk by reducing most of its system risks to bilateral risk assessments',[98] avoiding being exposed to responsibilities of an uncertain number of unknown persons.

The rationale underlying the no look-through principle to upper-tier intermediaries is reflected in the model of English trust where the rights of a beneficiary under a sub-trust are enforceable against the relevant trustee and not against the trustee higher up in the chain.[99] There are, however, exceptions to the rule (apparently against the very nature of a trust)[100] and this, inevitably, raises concerns of legal uncertainty and risk.

1.2.2. Conflict of Laws

Choice of law has also been singled out as one of the main sources of legal risks for post-trading activities in financial markets.[101] This is because, apart from jurisdictional

complicated cases (eg. *Re CA Pacific Finance Ltd* [2000]) where thousands of investors had individual trust rights and where the tracing process could have taken many years. See also J Marshall and N Herrod 'Lehman Brothers Insolvency – Client Assets' (2009) 3 LFMR 145.

96 Investment Bank Special Administration Regulations 2011 (SI 2011/245) reg 12(2).

97 On this specific issue, see D Turing *Clearing and Settlement in Europe* (Bloomsbury Professional Haywards 2012) 225.

98 Law Commission *Project on Intermediated Investment Securities – Second Seminar (Issues Affecting Account Holders and Intermediaries)* (23 June 2006) available at <www.lawcom.gov.uk/docs/investment_securities_seminar_paper_2.pdf> (accessed 7 August 2013) 57.

99 See *Bradstock Trustee Services Ltd v Nabarro Nathason* [1995] 1WLR 1405, 4 ER 888.

100 e.g. when a special responsibility towards beneficiary is owed by a third party. See *White v Jones* [1995] 2 AC 207, 1 ER 691; *Smith v Eric Bush* [1990] 1 AC 831; and *Henderson v Merrett Syndicates Ltd (No 1)* [1995] 2 AC 145.

101 See the report prepared by the Committee on Payment and Settlement Systems of the central banks of the Group of Ten Countries at Cross Border Securities Settlement (BIS) *Cross Border Securities Settlement* (March 1995), available at <www.bis.org/publ/cpss12.pdf> (accessed 7 August 2013).

issues,[102] it is often complicated to establish what system of laws applies to cross-border transactions regarding the sale, perfection and enforcement of intermediated securities. Moreover, consistent conflict of laws rules do not provide *per se* a completely satisfactory answer to legal uncertainty[103] and do not always make a great deal of commercial sense: even if the relevant choice of law rules are established, the cost involved in knowing the different doctrinal framework and approaches, depending on where the intermediaries/ intermediated securities are located, may still be significant.[104]

The traditional approach adopted to determine the law applicable to proprietary issues[105] (i.e. the *lex rei sitae*)[106] is highly unsatisfactory in relation to indirect holding systems. It may lead to practical impossibilities given the complexities involved in materially locating intermediated securities.[107]

The 'look-through approach' which considers the location of the certificate or the issuer's jurisdiction of incorporation along the chain of intermediation to determine the

102 i.e. choice of forum.

103 i.e. they do not eliminate the risk that different domestic rules governing intermediated holdings affect different aspects of the same transaction. This may pose severe challenges in cross-border situations where the failure to combining effectively becomes a source of legal uncertainty in itself. A very simple example may help to address this issue. When an investor holds in country X, through his intermediary, certified shares issued by a company incorporated in country Y, two different sets of laws apply: (a) the law governing the intermediary's holdings either in the form of a securities account with country Y's central securities depository (CSD) or through the services of a sub-custodian; and (b) the law governing the investor's holdings with the intermediary. According to all the most common rules on conflict of laws, it follows that country's X law governs the investor's acquisition and disposition of shares through the intermediary and country's Y law governs the rights acquired by the intermediary either through the credit of shares to his account with the sub-custodian in country Y or directly with the CSD in country Y. It is clear that two different laws govern the holding and disposition of shares at two different tiers of intermediation. It cannot be excluded that they are incompatible. For example, there can be a possible mismatch in the definition of the securities eligible to be credited to a securities account or it can happen that the two laws reflect different legal traditions. The addition of sub-custodians and tiers of intermediation in patterns of cross-border arrangements increase the degree and complexity of the problem. See P Paech 'Harmonising Substantive Rules of the Securities Held with Intermediaries as Collateral' (2002) Uniform Law Review/Revue de droit uniforme 1154.

104 In general, see the overview offered by C Chun *Cross-Border Transactions of Intermediated Securities* (Springer Heidelberg 2012) Chapter 8.

105 Approved in *Macmillan Inc v Bishopsgate Investment Trust plc (No 3)* [1995] 1 WLR 978 at 999 *per* Millett J. See MS Ooi *Shares in the Conflict of Laws* (OUP Oxford 2003) 87. The underlying assumption of the above analysis is that the issue is not characterised in contractual terms. Article 12(2) of the Rome Convention on the Law Applicable to Contractual Obligations (implemented in the UK by the Contracts (Applicable Law) Act 1990), as replaced for all contracts made on or after 17 December 2009 by the EU Rome I Regulation (Regulation 593/2008/EC of the European Parliament and of the Council of 17 June 2008 on the law applicable to contractual obligations) would apply under that circumstance and the applicable law would be the governing law of the claim. This, of course, does not concern shares as shares (it has been observed in Part II above) cannot technically be assigned under English law, but only novated.

106 The place where the securities are located.

107 In an intermediated system, the location of certificates, the issuer's records and jurisdiction of incorporation are not sufficient to identify the holder of intermediated securities. See J Rogers 'Of Normalcy and Anomaly: Thoughts on Choice of law for Indirect Holding System' (1998) 9 JIBFL (special supplement) 47.

applicable law is inappropriate under a fungible custody structure.[108] This is primarily because the issuer's records do not usually identify the investor as member. The only record of the investor's interest in intermediated shares is to be found in the books of the intermediary with which the investor has a direct relationship.[109] In addition, there are certain practical problems when collateral is provided with respect to a diversified portfolio of securities issued in a number of different jurisdictions.[110]

Various innovative solutions have been proposed to address the choice of law problems arising from transactions in intermediated securities.[111] They are inspired primarily by commercial need.

Among these,[112] the approach that considers the place where the intermediary holds the account to which the securities are credited (PRIMA) in order to determine the proprietary aspects of collateral transactions has gained widespread attention internationally.[113] It has become the cornerstone of European legislation[114] and it has been adopted, expressly or implicitly, in several countries.[115]

PRIMA, however, does not address all the circumstances where it is necessary to establish the applicable law for intermediated securities as it is 'transaction specific and applies only to determine the rights of holders of collateral security'.[116] Moreover, it is not the default rule of the international instrument prepared by the Hague Conference on Private International Law, as adopted by diplomatic conference in December 2002.[117]

108 See J Benjamin 'Determining the situs of Interests in Immobilised Securities' (1998) 47 Int Comp L Q 923. Note, however, that this approach has *de facto* been applied by Neuberger J in *Re Harvard Securities Ltd (in liquidation)* [1997] 2 BCLC 369.

109 See C Bernasconi, R Potok and G Morton 'General Introduction: Legal Nature of Interests in Indirectly Held Securities and Resulting Conflict of Laws Analysis' in R Potok (ed) *Cross Border Collateral: Legal Risk and the Conflict of Laws* (Butterworths London 2001) 28.

110 See RD Guynn and NJ Marchand 'Transfer of Pledge of Securities held through Depositories' in H Van Houtte (ed) *The Law of Cross-Border Securities Transactions* (Sweet & Maxwell London 1999) 60.

111 See the analysis offered by MS Ooi *Shares in the Conflict of Laws* (OUP Oxford 2003) 101 ff.

112 i.e. the 'law of the *situs* of the interest' (where the pool of fungibles is located), the 'law of the place of the transaction *(lex loci actus)*' (as determined by the last relevant transaction), the 'law which governs the contract (*lex contractus*)' (the law of the assignment), the 'law of the depository system' and the 'law under which the thing was created' (*lex creationis*) (the law under or by reference to which the thing which is the object of the transaction was itself created). See the comprehensive overview in MS Ooi *Shares in the Conflict of Laws* (OUP Oxford 2003) 101–155.

113 See R Potok 'Legal Certainty for Securities Held as Collateral' (1999) 18 IFL Rev 12; R Goode 'Security Entitlements as Collateral and the Conflict of Laws' (1998) 9 JIBFL (special supplement) 22; and Id 'Security in Cross-Border Transactions' (1998) 33 Texas Int'l LJ 47.

114 Directive 98/26/EC on settlement finality in payment and securities settlement systems (Settlement Finality Directive) [1998] OJ L166/45 as amended by Directive 2009/44/EC – Article 9(2) and Directive 2002/47/EC on financial collateral arrangements (Financial Collateral Directive) [2002] OJL168/43 as amended by Directive 2009/44/EC – Article 10.

115 e.g. France (art 29 of Law no 83–1of 3 January 1983) and *de facto* followed in England. See J Benjamin 'Cross-Border Proprietary Rights' (1997) 1 JIBFL 6 at 10.

116 M Ooi 'Intermediated Securities – The Choice of Choice of Law Rule' in L Gullifer and J Payne (eds) *Intermediated Securities – Legal Problems and Practical Issues* (Hart Oxford 2010) 222.

117 The Hague Convention on the Law Applicable to Certain Rights in Respect of Securities held with an Intermediary (not in force) and available at <www.hcch.net/upload/conventions/txt36en.pdf> (accessed 7 August 2013). For a background discussion, see C Bernasconi *Report on the Law Applicable*

The choice of law rule in the Hague Securities Convention is the law agreed by the account holder and the intermediary[118] or, where no such choice has been made, the law adopted to govern the account agreement,[119] provided in both cases that the intermediary maintaining the account has some factual links with the state whose law is chosen.[120] This *de facto* allows for party autonomy on proprietary issues. Whether this approach will be followed internationally[121] or whether it will prevail among European Member States over the PRIMA rule is at the present a matter of conjecture.[122]

1.3. Irreconcilable Conceptual Characterisations

Besides the legal uncertainties on substantive law and private international law referred to earlier, the main obstacle to the creation of a common (or even consistent) international legal framework for intermediated securities is probably a conceptual one. The difficulty concerns the legal characterisation of the account holder's rights and the method by which these rights can be enforced against the issuer. With a certain degree of approximation, the fundamental and irreconcilable divide on these matters is between 'direct and indirect' systems of enforcement, between systems where the account holder can or cannot enforce his rights directly against the issuer. The term 'indirect' in this context does not, of course, relate to the holding pattern, which remains in both cases indirect. Nor does it relate to the way in which an account holder's interests in securities are recorded along the chain of intermediation.[123]

to Dispositions of Securities Held through Indirect Holding Systems (Prel. Doc No 1 of Nov 2000) and the summary provided by C Chun *Cross Border Transactions of Intermediated Securities* (Springer Heidelberg 2012) Chapter 9.

118 Similarly, UCC §8–110(e)(1).

119 Similarly, UCC §8–110(e)(2).

120 Hague Convention on the Law Applicable to Certain Rights in Respect of Securities held with an Intermediary art 4(1). See R Goode, H Kanda and K Kreuzer *Hague Securities Convention Explanatory Report* (HCCH Publications 2005); H Sigman and C Bernasconi 'Myths about the Hague Convention Debunked' (2005) 24 IFLR 31; and JS Rogers 'Conflict of Laws for Transactions in Securities Held Through Intermediaries' (2005) Boston College Law School Faculty Research Paper 108.

121 Only United States, Mauritius and Switzerland signed the Hague Convention on the Law Applicable to Certain Rights in Respect of Securities held with an Intermediary (not in force) (5 July 2006). The Status table is available at <www.hcch.net/index_en.php?act=conventions.status&cid=72> (accessed 7 August 2013).

122 Following the concerns of ECB regarding systemic risk and the possible growth on the litigation of securities in which courts will have to apply foreign law, the European Parliament on 14 December 2006 reiterated its commitment to PRIMA and qualified as highly inadequate Article 4(1) of the Hague Securities Convention. In the same occasion, the European Parliament called on the Commission to submit to Parliament a comprehensive impact study on the implications of accession to the Hague Securities Convention, available at <www.europarl.europa.eu/sides/getDoc.do?pubRef=-//EP//TEXT+TA+P6-TA-2006–0608+0+DOC+XML+V0//EN> (accessed 7 August 2013). On 25 March 2009, the Commission withdrew its proposal for a Council Decision concerning the signing of the Hague Convention, available at <www.eur-lex.europa.eu/LexUriServ/LexUriServ.do?uri=OJ:C:2009:071:0017:0018:EN:PDF> (accessed 7 August 2013).

123 The so-called 'transparency' of the system or the possibility that the names of the investor are recorded not only in the books of the relevant intermediary, but also in the books of the intermediaries above, up

1.3.1. Direct Enforcement Systems

In most civil law jurisdictions,[124] investors are the legal owners of the securities deposited with the intermediary and, for operational reasons, they exercise their rights by relying on the cooperation of the intermediary. Investors are *pro rata* owners of the pool of securities held in fungible accounts and intermediaries are mere bailees. This structure distinguishing between ownership and possession supports the rationale for the protection of investors' and collateral takers' assets against intermediary's insolvency.[125] In short, no matter how many tiers of intermediation are in place, the bailment of the securities with the intermediary does not disrupt the investor's legal title and does not alter his contractual/corporate rights against the issuer.

1.3.2. Indirect Enforcement Systems

The scenario is different in common law jurisdictions where an investor is able to exercise his rights in the underlying securities only against its intermediary, but not directly against the issuer. Under English law, as suggested above, the legal characterisation of the custody relationship is usually a trust. The account holder will have to rely on contractual and fiduciary obligations of its intermediary as set out in the trust instrument to enforce its claims against the issuer. The issuer in turn will have a direct relationship only with the first tier intermediary, generally through its nominee. As most of the transactions among investors will not require a change of nominee in the issuer's register, they will go unnoticed from an issuer's perspective. Legal title to securities is vested in the upper-tier intermediary and the account holder's interests in securities qualify as equitable tenancy in common. As suggested above, the protection of the account holder's interests against the insolvency of the intermediary is achieved by way of trust law or, alternatively, by means of special legislation as in the case of the entitlement holder's rights under UCC §8–503 (1) and (2). It follows that in common law jurisdictions, account holder's interests in securities are of proprietary nature only when asserted against third parties.[126]

until the level of the CSD. Although it is possible that in jurisdictions where there is a direct relationship between investor and issuer, the system is also transparent (e.g. Spain), it is not necessarily always the case (e.g. France and Germany). It is, however, always true that all transparent systems are also direct systems. See the discussion on transparent systems in the CGE for the Preparation of Harmonised Substantive Rules regarding Intermediated Securities (third session) *Report from the Transparent Systems Working Group* Doc. 88 part of Study LXVIII <www.unidroit.org/english/documents/2007/study78/s-78-088-e.pdf> (accessed 7 August 2013).

124 e.g. France, Germany and Italy. Consider also the ambivalent case of the UK settlement system where the operator (EUI) offers to individual investors the possibility to hold uncertificated securities in their own name.

125 So-called 'ring-fencing'.

126 See J Benjamin *Interests in Securities* (OUP Oxford 2000).

1.4. Conclusions

Section 1 described the operational changes underlying the development of the modern system of holding through intermediaries with a view to providing the background for the analysis on legal change that is to be addressed in section 2 below and in Chapter 7.

In essence, section 1 discussed and qualified the great commercial advantages arising from the advent of electronic settlement and from the employment of intermediaries in financial markets (section 1.1). By focusing on three examples taken from English law, the inquiry also suggested that traditional legal concepts did not always keep pace with the rapid evolution of market practice. In the context of indirectly held securities, the application of existing legal rules sometimes proved to be ambiguous and, inevitably, a source of legal uncertainty and potential legal risk.[127] The concerns were not restricted to the national level. Even in the case of a sound and modernised domestic legal framework, the unpredictable consequences arising from the lack of a harmonised set of rules for solving conflict of laws issues within interconnected financial markets represented *per se* an additional source of legal risk (section 1.2). The final section 1.3 argued that the greatest obstacle for the creation of a sound legal framework for cross-border holding and transfer of intermediated securities was the irreconcilable conceptual compatibility of enforcement methods between civil law and common law legal systems.

2. The Process of Legal Evolution

Section 2 builds on the analysis above. Focusing on the economic benefits of the practice of intermediation, it makes the case for the desirability for a harmonised framework of substantive law. Following an overview of the rationale for law reform (section 2.1), it describes the most significant normative initiatives in the area (section 2.2) and focuses specifically on the three examples of legal uncertainty in English law that were examined in section 1 above *vis-à-vis* the provisions of the Geneva Securities Convention, the 2008 LCG Advice and EC Consultation Document (section 2.3). The scope of the comparative exercise is to identify the pattern of legal change in the transfer of intermediated securities and to show how it amounts to a process of hybridisation (section 2.4).

2.1. The Need for Law Reform

Not addressing the uncertainties associated with domestic/cross-border transfers of intermediated securities and the legal risk arising from the conceptual incompatibilities sketched in section 1 above may leave investors in a weaker position than when they hold the securities directly from the issuer. This is an unwelcome scenario. It may undermine the attractiveness of the indirectly holding system and, possibly, the efficiency of financial markets.[128]

[127] On the relation between legal risk and legal uncertainty, see R McCormick *Legal Risk in the Financial Markets* (OUP Oxford 2010) 183.

[128] See the overview of the main issues presented by L Thevenoz 'Intermediated Securities, Legal Risk, and the International Harmonization of Commercial Law' (2007) 13 Stanford Journal of Law, Business and Finance 384.

Reviewing the validity and enforceability of custody and collateral agreements under the relevant domestic law[129] is not an economically efficient option, as this exercise, whenever possible,[130] is likely to cause an intolerable increase in transaction costs. Moreover, it will not eliminate the possible domino effect, the effect that the failure of one institution to meet its financial obligation to third parties may trigger a systemic crisis in the financial system.[131] Given the international diversification of securities portfolios and the volumes of cross-border trading, an insular response has only a negligible effect on reducing legal uncertainty. It runs fundamentally against the general policy objectives of restoring market confidence and efficiency.[132]

It follows that the only way to reduce uncertainty and to achieve modernisation and harmonisation of the substantive law in the area is by simultaneously promoting sound domestic rules[133] and predictable outcomes where the laws of one or another legal system are applied to cross-border settlement of securities.[134]

This is a very challenging task in both regards. As the Law Commission clearly stated when commenting on the UNIDROIT project on intermediated securities, 'internal soundness and cross-border compatibility will not always go hand in hand. Improvements in one may come at the expenses of the other. A settlement system that achieves internal soundness through clear and modern settlement rules may nevertheless be incompatible with other systems. Likewise, a common legal framework will be counter-productive if implementing it has the effect of damaging the legal coherency and stability of national settlement systems'.[135]

129 e.g. legal opinions on the validity and enforceability of custody and collateral arrangements under the relevant national law.

130 It might be difficult when an internationally diversified portfolio of securities is taken as collateral.

131 In other words, the inability of one financial institution to meet its obligations when due may cause other financial institutions to be unable to meet their obligations when due. In general, and on the role of the law in reducing systemic risk, see SL Schwarcz 'Systemic Risk' (2008) 97 Geo LJ 194. With specific reference to the analysis of systemic risk justifying the adoption of UCC Article 8 in 1994, see the eleven-page discussion put forward by J Rogers 'Policy Perspectives on Revised UCC Article 8' (1996) 43 UCLA L Rev 1431. A critical analysis on the limits of Rogers' explanation is provided by FJ Facciolo 'Father Knows Best: Revised Article 8 and the Individual Investor' (2000) 27 Fla St U L Rev 615 at 616.

132 These concerns are well put by P Paech and K Lober 'Interconnecting Law of Securities Holding and Transfer – a chance for seamless international improvements' (2007) 1 JIBFL 9; and and P Paech 'Market Needs as Paradigm – breaking-up the thinking on EU securities law' in P Conac, U Segna and L Thevenoz (eds) *Intermediated Securities – The Impact of the Geneva Securities Convention and the Future European Legislation* (CUP Cambridge 2013) 23.

133 i.e. 'internal soundness'. See UNIDROIT Study Group for the Preparation of Harmonised Substantive Rules on Transactions on Transnational and Connected Capital Markets (Restricted Group on Harmonised Substantive Rules regarding Securities Held with an Intermediary) *Position Paper* (August 2003) at 13, part of Study LXXVIII <www.unidroit.org/english/documents/2003/study78/s-78–008-e.pdf> (accessed 7 August 2013).

134 i.e. 'cross-border compatibility'. See UNIDROIT Study Group for the Preparation of Harmonised Substantive Rules on Transactions on Transnational and Connected Capital Markets (Restricted Group on Harmonised Substantive Rules regarding Securities Held with an Intermediary) *Position Paper* (August 2003) at 13, part of Study LXXVIII <www.unidroit.org/english/documents/2003/study78/s-78–008-e.pdf> (accessed 7 August 2013).

135 Law Commission *Project on Intermediated Investment Securities – First Seminar (Objectives for a Common Legal Framework)* (22 March 2006) available at <www.lawcom.gov.uk/investment_securities.htm> (accessed 7 August 2013) 8.

2.2. *The (Substantive) Law Reform Projects*

Two major concurring law reform initiatives have been recently set up with a view to creating a harmonised international regime: the UNIDROIT project on intermediated securities[136] and the EU Commission project on clearing and settlement.[137] While the first one has been recently finalised with the adoption of the Geneva Securities Convention by the diplomatic Conference on 9 October 2009, the latter is still under way.

2.2.1. The Geneva Securities Convention

2.2.1.1. Chronology

The UNIDROIT project on 'Harmonised Substantive Rules Regarding Securities Held with an Intermediary' began in 2001 when the UNIDROIT Governing Council and General Assembly agreed to include it in its Work Programme. It was officially launched in 2002 as a follow-up to the Hague Securities Convention[138] with a view to creating a legal framework in the form of substantive rules for securities holding, transfer and collateralisation for intermediated securities in cross-border situations. The project was originally undertaken by a group of experts (the 'Study Group')[139] composed of sixteen experts from twelve countries and three international organisations which, after five sessions and consultations with practitioners and scholars, produced in August 2003 a Position Paper[140] and a 'Draft Convention on Substantive Rules Regarding Intermediated Securities' together with a set of Explanatory Notes. The latter was adopted by

136 UNIDROIT Project on *Substantive Rules regarding Intermediated Securities*, part of Study LXXVIII <www.unidroit.org/english/conventions/2009intermediatedsecurities/study78-archive-e.htm#NR2> (accessed 7 August 2013).

137 See Commission of the European Communities *Clearing and Settlement in the European Union: The Way Forward* (final draft of the Communication to the Council and the Parliament) COM (2004) 312 final (28 April 2004).

138 See above *sub* Chapter 6, section 1.2.

139 UNIDROIT Project on *Substantive Rules regarding Intermediated Securities*, part of Study LXXVIII <www.unidroit.org/english/conventions/2009intermediatedsecurities/study78-archive-e.htm#NR2> (accessed 7 August 2013). See the chronology of the project in Uniform Law Review (2005) 112–115. A primer on the fundamental themes of the Geneva Securities Convention is offered by CW Mooney 'The (Unidroit) Geneva Securities Convention on Intermediated Securities' (2009) 10 JIBFL 596; CW Mooney and H Kanda 'Core Issues under the UNIDROIT (Geneva) Convention on Intermediated Securities: Views from the United States and Japan' in L Gullifer and J Payne (eds) *Intermediated Securities – Legal Problems and Practical Issues* (Hart Oxford 2010) 69; and L Thevenoz 'The Geneva Securities Convention: Objectives, History and Guiding Principles' in P Conac, U Segna and L Thevenoz (eds) *Intermediated Securities – The Impact of the Geneva Securities Convention and the Future European Legislation* (CUP Cambridge 2013) 3.

140 UNIDROIT Study Group for the Preparation of Harmonised Substantive Rules on Transactions on Transnational and Connected Capital Markets (Restricted Group on Harmonised Substantive Rules regarding Securities Held with an Intermediary) *Position Paper* (August 2003) at 13, part of Study LXXVIII <www.unidroit.org/english/documents/2003/study78/s-78–008-e.pdf> (accessed 7 August 2013).

UNIDROIT's Governing Council and submitted on 23 December 2004 to the governments of UNIDROIT Member States for approval.[141] At the conclusion of four sessions of negotiations of the Committee of Governmental Experts, involving thirty-nine delegations and seventeen observer organisations, held in Rome from May 2005 to May 2007,[142] the UNIDROIT Governing Council approved the transmission of the text to a Diplomatic Conference. This was held at the invitation of the Swiss Government in two different sessions in Geneva: the first in September 2008 and a final one in October 2009 where representatives of government of fifty States and thirteen international organisations and groups were present. The Convention was eventually adopted by the Diplomatic Conference on 9 October 2009 and, on the same day, thirty-seven States signed the Final Act together with the European Commission. The Convention is now open for signature at the UNIDROIT in Rome.

2.2.1.2. Contents

Although the Geneva Securities Convention does not contain a traditional provision on its scope, its rules concern the recognition of book-entry accounts and 'the constitutive nature of credits to an account for any right or obligation'.[143] It does not distinguish in a neat way between domestic and cross-border transactions. As with the assets in the 2001 'Cape Town Convention on International Interests in Mobile Equipment and Equipment Specific Protocols',[144] it has been considered unhelpful to distinguish between international and domestic indirectly held securities. It is the same nature of the daily transactions involving the intermediated securities that exclude the need to treat differently domestic and international patterns.

Without specifically looking at the details of the structure, the Geneva Securities Convention provides the fundamental rules for indirect holding. It deals with the acquisition/disposal of rights and interests of account holders in intermediated securities, the rights and obligations of the relevant intermediary *vis-à-vis* the account holder, the

141 UNIDROIT – CGE for the Preparation of Harmonised Substantive Rules regarding Intermediated Securities (first session) *Preliminary Draft Convention and CGE Report to the Preliminary Draft Convention* (November/December 2004) Docs. 18 and 19, part of Study LXVIII <www.unidroit.org/english/documents/2004/study78/s-78–018.pdf> and <www.unidroit.org/english/documents/2004/study78/s-78–019-e.pdf> (accessed 7 August 2013).

142 UNIDROIT – CGE for the Preparation of Harmonised Substantive Rules regarding Intermediated Securities (second, third and fourth session) *Preliminary Draft Convention and Explanatory Notes to the Preliminary Draft Convention* (March 2006/November 2006/May 2007) Docs. 42, 43, 57, 58, 94 and 95, part of Study LXVIII <www.unidroit.org/english/documents/2004/study78/s-78–019-e.pdf>; <www.unidroit.org/english/documents/2006/study78/s-78–043-e.pdf>; <www.unidroit.org/english/documents/2006/study78/s-78–057-e.pdf>; <www.unidroit.org/english/documents/2007/study78/s-78–058-e.pdf>; <www.unidroit.org/english/documents/2007/study78/s-78–094-e.pdf> and www.unidroit.org/english/documents/2007/study78/s-78–095-e.pdf> (accessed 7 August 2013).

143 H Kronke 'The Draft Unidroit Convention on Intermediated Securities: Transactional Certainty and Market Stability' (2006) IMF Seminar on Current Development in Monetary and Financial Law, available at <www.imf.org/external/np/seminars/eng/2006/mfl/hk.pdf> (accessed 7 August 2013) 12.

144 P Thorne 'Goodbye Geneva '48, Hello Cape Town '01' (2006) 10 JIBFL 439.

protection of innocent purchases and the priority provisions that settle claims in intermediated securities.

2.2.2. The Advice of the Legal Certainty Group and the Consultation Document

2.2.2.1. Scope

The second initiative is part of a larger project undertaken by the EU Commission to enhance the efficiency and safety of post-trading arrangements across Europe. In essence, it consists of a set of normative recommendations for a harmonised European legal framework presented by the Legal Certainty Group (LCG) in August 2008.[145] The LCG, an advisory group formed of thirty-six legal experts from academia, industry and practice, was appointed by the European Commission in early 2005[146] with the mandate to give advice on a number of legal issues on inefficiency in post-trading infrastructure for securities and derivatives transactions raised in the 'First Giovannini Report' in 2001[147] and further addressed in the proposals contained in the 'Second Giovannini Report' in 2003.[148] The mandate did not replicate all the legal issues that created obstacles to efficient and safe cross-border clearing and settlement in the EU as identified in the First Giovannini Report. While it included issues concerning the absence of an EU-wide framework for the legal treatment of book-entry securities (Barrier 13), corporate action processing (Barrier 3) and restrictions on the location of securities (Barrier 9), it did not consider the treatment of bilateral netting (Barrier 14) and the uncertain application of international private law rules (Barrier 15). The reasons for the exclusions are straightforward. In the case of netting (Barrier 14), the legal obstacle found by the Giovannini Group was removed by the enactment of the Financial Collateral Directive,[149] which recognised close out netting. It was the possible adoption of the Hague Securities Convention that prompted the EU Commission not to ask for an immediate specific advice from LCG on conflict of laws rules (Barrier 15).

145 Second Advice of the Legal Certainty Group *Solutions to Barriers related to Post-Trading within the EU* (August 2008), available at <www.ec.europa.eu/internal_market/financial-markets/docs/certainty/2ndadvice_final_en.pdf> (accessed 7 August 2013). A comprehensive commentary on the results is provided by P Paech and K Lober 'Post-trading of Securities: Shaping the European Response to Legal Barriers' (2009) 4 JIBFL 211.

146 Following *Clearing and Settlement in the European Union – The way forward*, Communication from the Commission to the Council and the European Parliament, COM(2004) 312 final <www.eur-lex.europa.eu/LexUriServ/LexUriServ.do?uri=COM:2004:0312:FIN:EN:PDF> (accessed 7 August 2013).

147 The 'Giovannini Group' *Cross-Border Clearing and Settlement Arrangements in the European Union* (November 2001), available at <www.ec.europa.eu/internal_market/financial-markets/docs/clearing/first_giovannini_report_en.pdf> (accessed 7 August 2013).

148 The 'Giovannini Group' *Second Report on Clearing and Settlement Arrangements in the European Union* (April 2003) available at <www.ec.europa.eu/internal_market/financial-markets/docs/clearing/second_giovannini_report_en.pdf> (accessed 7 August 2013).

149 Directive 2002/47/EC on financial collateral arrangements (Financial Collateral Directive) [2002] OJL168/43, as amended by Directive 2009/44/EC.

2.2.2.2. Contents

The LGC carried out a comparative survey of the relevant laws of the twenty-five Member States and produced an Advice in 2006, later refined in 2008. As already suggested, the 2008 LCG Advice calls for new legislation. This would involve a set of rules such that: (a) the acquisitions and dispositions effected through an account have a harmonised effect within the EU financial market (Recommendations 1–11); (b) legal obstacles to corporate action processing arising from cross-border holdings of securities through chains of account providers are dismantled (Recommendations 12–14); (c) securities constituted under the law of a Member State are capable to be initially entered into holding and settlement systems governed by the law of another Member State and the law of Member States allows an issuer to arrange for its securities to be initially entered into holding and settlement structures in or governed by the law of any Member State (Recommendation 15). These normative recommendations will need, of course, to be integrated with the existing EU framework for holding and settlement of securities through book entries and, in particular, with the Settlement Finality Directive,[150] the Financial Collateral Directive[151] and MiFID.[152]

In response to the 2008 LCG Advice, the ECOFIN at its 2 December 2008 meeting in Brussels invited 'the Commission to present its response to the Legal Certainty Group advice as a matter of urgency, including an outline of proposed legislative measures, accompanied by precise timelines for their effective submission to the European legislator, bearing in mind the benefits of maintaining global compatibility with other jurisdictions'.[153] The European Commission then decided to undertake a new legal initiative, and a consultation document was issued in April 2009 to obtain 'information from Member States, market participants and other stakeholders, in particular investors, on the necessity to improve the EU-wide legal framework for securities holding and transaction and on how future EU legislation in this field could address the issue'.[154] On the basis of the results, the Commission was supposed to prepare a set text for a Securities Law Directive to be discussed with Member States' experts in early 2010.[155] In November 2010, the European Commission published a second consultation document titled

150 Directive 98/26/EC on settlement finality in payment and securities settlement systems (Settlement Finality Directive) [1998] OJ L166/45 as amended by Directive 2009/44/EC.

151 Directive 2002/47/EC on financial collateral arrangements (Financial Collateral Directive) [2002] OJL168/43 as amended by Directive 2009/44/EC.

152 Directive 2004/39/EC Markets in Financial Services Directive [2004] OJL 145/1 as amended by Directive 2006/31/EC.

153 Available at <www.consilium.europa.eu/uedocs/cms_data/docs/pressdata/en/ecofin/104530.pdf> (accessed 7 August 2013).

154 'Legislation on Legal Certainty of Securities Holding and Disposition' consultation document available at <www.ec.europa.eu/internal_market/consultations/docs/2009/securities-law/hsl_consultation_en.pdf> (accessed 7 August 2013). A summary of the results are available at <www.ec.europa.eu/internal_market/financial-markets/docs/securities-law/first_consultation_summary_en.pdf> (accessed 7 August 2013).

155 For introductory comments on the project, see D Turing and C Meinertz 'The Securities Law Directive: Implications for Account Provisions, Custody and Collateral Arrangements' (2011) 4 JIBFL 198.

'Legislation on Legal Certainty of Securities Holding and Dispositions' (the 'Consultation Document').[156] The Consultation Document contains twenty-two principles intended to cover the full scope of the possible legislative approach governing the holding and disposition of securities held through securities account (covering substantive law as well as conflict of laws).[157] In September 2011 the European Commission published a summary of the responses received to the Consultation Document.[158] It is difficult to predict the legislative outcome (if any) of the initiative, which remains very controversial: a detailed commentary of the Consultation Document would surely be rash at this stage and, in any case, well beyond the scope of the inquiry carried out in this book.

2.2.3. Comparison

Although the two projects described are different in terms of the nature of the instrument involved and in terms of their international/regional scope, they address similar issues. They intersect and overlap on some of the themes tackled.[159] Although the scope of the UNIDROIT initiative is more ambitious, the search for clarity and harmonisation in the legal framework underlying the use of book-entries in securities account is at the heart of both projects. The work submitted by the LCG on Barrier 13 mentioned above, 'addresses probably around 70% of the issues covered by Unidroit and, inversely, nearly all of the Barrier 13 issues dealt with by the Legal Certainty Group are in one or the other way included in the Unidroit draft'.[160]

The two projects share identical methodologies. In general terms, they recognise the diversity of legal concepts underlying securities holding and settlement among the variety of participants and, therefore, the complexities of the process to obtain fully harmonised rules for intermediated securities. Both aim to achieve sound technical solutions within a reasonable timeframe. In the light of those concerns, both promote a restrictive approach to harmonisation in order to accommodate different legal systems and legal traditions within a unitary framework (and, similarly, under Principles 1 and 14 of the Consultation Document). Only the elements that are essential to establish

156 EU Commission, Legislation on Legal Certainty of Securities Holding and Disposition, Consultation Document of the Services of the Directorate-General Internal Market and Services (November 2010) DG Markt G2 MET/OT/acg D (2010) 768690, available at <www.ec.europa.eu/internal_market/consultations/docs/2010/securities/consultation_paper_en.pdf> (accessed 7 August 2013).

157 See H Motani 'The Proposed EU Legislation on Securities Holding' in P Conac, U Segna and L Thevenoz (eds) *Intermediated Securities – The Impact of the Geneva Securities Convention and the Future European Legislation* (CUP Cambridge 2013) 65.

158 Available at <www.ec.europa.eu/internal_market/consultations/2010/securities_en.htm> (accessed 7 August 2013).

159 It should also be remembered that the EU Commission and EU Member States participated at the UNIDROIT project as observers and delegates.

160 Second Advice of the Legal Certainty Group *Solutions to Barriers related to Post-Trading within the EU* (August 2008) 27 <www.ec.europa.eu/internal_market/financial-markets/docs/certainty/2ndadvice_final_en.pdf> (accessed 7 August 2013).

internal soundness and cross-border compatibility need to be addressed.[161] The existing domestic law[162] should cover all of the other issues. As far the drafting is concerned, both initiatives adopt a functional approach,[163] an approach 'that uses neutral language in consideration of the various legal traditions involved and formulates rules by reference to facts, with a view to facilitate the accommodation of the different legal concepts in place in different jurisdictions'[164] as it has been successfully adopted in several international Conventions.[165] The idea is to refer to facts rather than legal principles. This is to allow operative economic results to be considered without any attempt to override the underlying domestic legal traditions and doctrine, and without disrupting the domestic property law with respect to the structure and characterisation of investors' interests in securities. In short, uniform rules will prescribe certain results, but it will be the responsibility of domestic lawmakers to apply their technical legal solutions to achieve that result.[166]

161 UNIDROIT Study Group for the Preparation of Harmonised Substantive Rules on Transactions on Transnational and Connected Capital Markets (Restricted Group on Harmonised Substantive Rules regarding Securities Held with an Intermediary) *Position Paper* (August 2003) 14, part of Study LXXVIII <www.unidroit.org/english/documents/2003/study78/s-78–008-e.pdf> (accessed 7 August 2013); and Second Advice of the Legal Certainty *Group Solutions to Barriers related to Post-Trading within the EU* (August 2008) 39 <www.ec.europa.eu/internal_market/financial-markets/docs/certainty/2ndadvice_final_en.pdf> (accessed 7 August 2013).

162 The 'non-Convention law' according to the UNIDROIT jargon (i.e. 'the law in force in the State whose law is applicable [...] other than the provisions of this Convention' – Article 1(m) of the Geneva Securities Convention) and the 'national law' according to Second Advice of the Legal Certainty Group Solutions to Barriers related to Post-Trading within the EU (August 2008) 39 <www.ec.europa.eu/internal_market/financial-markets/docs/certainty/2ndadvice_final_en.pdf> (accessed 7 August 2013). On this specific topic, see M Deschamps 'The Geneva Securities Convention – Selected Issues Left to Law Outside the Convention' (2010) Uniform L Rev 703.

163 See the UNIDROIT – CGE for the Preparation of Harmonised Substantive Rules regarding Intermediated Securities (first session) *Preliminary Draft Convention and CGE Report to the Preliminary Draft Convention* (November/December 2004) Doc 19, part of Study LXVIII <www.unidroit.org/english/documents/2004/study78/s-78–019-e.pdf> (accessed 7 August 2013) 19; and Second Advice of the Legal Certainty Group *Solutions to Barriers related to Post-Trading within the EU* (August 2008) 10 <www.ec.europa.eu/internal_market/financial-markets/docs/certainty/2ndadvice_final_en.pdf> (accessed 7 August 2013).

164 UNIDROIT Study Group for the Preparation of Harmonised Substantive Rules on Transactions on Transnational and Connected Capital Markets (Restricted Group on Harmonised Substantive Rules regarding Securities Held with an Intermediary) *Position Paper* (August 2003) 14, part of Study LXXVIII <www.unidroit.org/english/documents/2003/study78/s-78–008-e.pdf> (accessed 7 August 2013).

165 See J Wool 'Rethinking the Notion of Uniformity in the Drafting of International Commercial Law: A Preliminary Proposal for the Development of a Policy-based Unification Model' (1997) 2 Uniform Law Review 45; and Id 'Economic Analysis and Harmonized Privatisation of Private Law' (2003) 8 Uniform Law Review 389.

166 See CW Mooney Jr 'Law and System for Intermediated Securities and the Relationship of Private Property Law to Securities Clearance and Settlement: United States, Japan and the UNIDROIT Draft Convention' Discussion Paper No 2008-E-7 IMES Bank of Japan <www.ideas.repec.org/p/ime/imedps/08-e-07.html> (accessed 7 August 2013) 3.

2.3. *The Pattern of Legal Change and Hybridisation*

The analysis set out in sections 2.1 and 2.2 above pointed out the need for law reform in the area of indirectly held securities and presented the two most relevant international initiatives in the area.

Building on that, and also considering the general themes outlined in section 1, the following inquiry looks more closely at certain elements of the pattern of legal change. It re-examines in particular the three issues of legal uncertainty raised by the FMLC report and described earlier to see how they have been addressed in the Geneva Securities Convention and in the 2008 LCG Advice/Consultation Document (*sub* 2.3.1). By considering the pattern of legal evolution that led to the final text and estimating its (possible) implementation in England, it shows the existence of a process of hybridisation. It is argued that this scenario of cultural interaction is not dissimilar to the one observed for the formation of hybrid models at the centre of the postcolonial debate tackled in Part I (*sub* 2.3.2 and 2.3.3).

2.3.1. *Ad Hoc* Response to Legal Uncertainty

2.3.1.1. The Protection of the Account Holders' Assets from the Claims of an Intermediary's Creditors

It was seen above that the conventional legal characterisation of intermediated securities is based on the device of trust, notwithstanding the fact that the intangible assets held by the intermediary for investors are unallocated. It was also seen that, although there is support for the view that the requirement of certainty of subject matter for a valid trust to arise is met even in the case of fungible accounts, its reasoning has been criticised as lacking a convincing conceptual basis. A normative clarification on the matter has been invoked by the FMLC.

Intermediated securities are qualified by the Geneva Securities Convention as the rights conferred on the account holder by the credit of securities to a securities account.[167] Albeit that there is no reference to the legal nature of the rights and interests arising from the credit of securities to a securities account, these rights are effective against third parties.[168] This means that, similarly to the beneficiaries under a trust, account holders share a *pro rata* property interest against other account holders of the same intermediary.

Moreover, the Geneva Securities Convention, in line with Recommendation 9.b of the 2008 LCG Advice and Principle 10 of the Consultation Document, establishes a clear framework for the treatment of account holders' rights where both intermediary and customer securities are held in the same account. Unless a Contracting State declares that the securities held by the intermediary are in segregated form,[169] the general rule is that there is no need to segregate the securities that are credited to customer accounts

167 Article 9(1). An intermediary may receive these rights only if he is 'acting for its own account' (Article 9(1)(a)(i)) or 'if so provided by the non-Convention law' (Article 9(1)(a)(ii)).

168 Article 9(2).

169 Article 25(5).

from those held by the intermediary for its own account. When securities are mixed in a single account, they are simply allocated first to account holders[170] in accordance with non-Convention law[171] and they do not form part of the intermediary's estate available for creditors.[172] This is particularly relevant in the case of insolvency of the intermediary.

If the Convention is ratified and the intermediary has complied with the obligation to hold sufficient securities,[173] the investor's protection in relation to intermediated securities held by the intermediary is the same as that of a beneficiary under a trust. The concern in English law of holding securities in a fungible account does not arise by imposition of law. There is no need to identify whether particular securities in the account belong to individual customers for a valid trust to be created. Lack of segregation between 'house' securities and those held for other account holders would also cease to be an issue under English law.[174] This is because, as noted above, under the Convention, unless a Contracting State contracts out,[175] securities held in a fungible account are first allocated to the rights of the account holders to the extent required to reach the amount of the credits in their accounts.[176]

2.3.1.2. Shortfalls in the Assets Held by the Intermediary

The inquiry carried out in the preceding section also pointed out that under English law the allocation of a shortfall when the intermediary is insolvent is a source of legal uncertainty. This is because various methods of allocating the shortfall among account holders are available, and, otherwise, the case of segregated accounts where shortfall loss affecting a particular account holder is borne entirely by the same account holder, there is not a specific provision on how competing claims to assets in a pooled fund should be resolved.

In general terms, the Geneva Securities Convention establishes that it is the duty of the intermediary to hold or have available securities of a particular description to meet the total credited to the account it maintains for its account holders.[177] This rule greatly reduces the possibility of a shortfall arising. That said, the Convention also establishes a precise loss distribution method when there is a shortfall in the number of unallocated securities held by the intermediary and the intermediary falls insolvent before restoring the credit or reversing the transfer.[178] Losses are allocated *pro rata* among account holders to whom the relevant securities had been allocated.[179] This is subject to the

170 Article 25(1).

171 Article 25(3) and, similarly, Principle 10(2) of the Consultation Document.

172 Article 25(2).

173 Article 24(1).

174 See, for example, the conflicting authorities for the relevance of keeping trust moneys separate from trustee's own money (*R v Clowes* [1994] 2 All ER 316 at 325; and *In Re Kayford Ltd* [1975] 1 WLR 279 at 282).

175 Article 25(5).

176 Article 25(1).

177 Article 24(1). This obligation can be fulfilled according to the methods set out in Article 24(2).

178 If the intermediary is solvent, securities are restored according to Article 24(4).

179 Article 26(1).

allocation of any 'house' securities held in the account which are first allocated to the rights of the account holders mentioned above[180] and to any conflicting rule applicable in the insolvency proceeding.[181]

When securities are allocated to a single account holder, however, it is that account holder who bears the risk of the shortfall.[182] He is left as an unsecured creditor with only a personal claim against the intermediary. The other exception to the *pro rata* solution applies when the intermediary is an operator of a securities settlement system and the rules of the system contain provisions in the case of a shortfall, those provisions apply instead of the *pro rata* rule.[183]

The 2008 LCG Advice is silent on the issue. In the last part of Recommendation 9.b it is merely stated that in the case of a shortfall a rule will be needed on how the insufficient assets held by the account provider are to be shared among its account holders, but 'the exact parameters of the loss sharing can be left to the applicable law or the rules of a securities settlement system as far as permitted by the applicable law.'[184] Similarly, under Principle 10(2) of the Consultation Document, even if the response summary shows some support for a default harmonised rule based on a *pro rata* mechanism,[185] it would be left to Member States to determine whether to apply rateable distribution of assets in the event of a shortfall.

It follows from the above that if the Convention is ratified, English courts will resolve the conflict between competing claims to assets in a pooled fund in accordance with the *pro rata* apportionment amongst account holders depending on the size of their entitlements allowed by *Barlow Clowes International Ltd (in liquidation) v Vaughan.*[186] Under these circumstances, the rule in the Clayton's case[187] will be disapplied.

2.3.1.3. The No Look-Through Principle

Finally, it was also observed in section 1 above that the principle that prohibits an account holder from 'looking through' its immediate intermediary to make a claim in its own name against another intermediary higher in the chain is reflected in the model of English trust. There, the rights of a beneficiary under a sub-trust are enforceable against the relevant trustee and not against the trustee higher in the chain.[188] There are, however,

180 Article 25(1).

181 Article 26(1). This latter element, in particular, confirms the Convention's approach of leaving the characteristics and nature of an account holder's property right to the non-Convention law.

182 Article 26(2)(a).

183 Article 26(3).

184 Second Advice of the Legal Certainty Group *Solutions to Barriers related to Post-Trading within the EU* (August 2008) 72 <www.ec.europa.eu/internal_market/financial-markets/docs/certainty/2ndadvice_final_en.pdf> (accessed 7 August 2013).

185 See H Motani 'The Proposed EU Legislation on Securities Holding' in P Conac, U Segna and L Thevenoz (eds) *Intermediated Securities – The Impact of the Geneva Securities Convention and the Future European Legislation* (CUP Cambridge 2013) 87.

186 [1992] 4 All ER 22.

187 (1816) 1 Mer 572.

188 See *Hayim v Citibank NA* [1987] AC 730.

exceptions to this rule, namely when a third party owes special responsibility towards the beneficiary.[189] These circumstances have suggested the urgent need for a normative clarification.

Subject to a declaration mechanism[190] to accommodate the concerns raised by transparent settlement systems,[191] the Geneva Securities Convention prevents an attachment order in relation to securities credited to a securities account maintained by an intermediary which is not the account holder's relevant intermediary.[192] This clearly removes the issues of legal uncertainty raised by the FMLC with respect to the possibility of enforcing rights in securities above the level of an account holder's own intermediary.

Along similar lines, the 2008 LCG Advice (Recommendation 11) states that book-entry rights are not enforceable, nor is an attachment in respect to such rights permitted, against any upper-tier intermediary. In the same vein, according to Principle 12 of the Consultation Document, attachment at a level other than that of the account provider to the account holder is to be prohibited.

2.3.2. Hybridisation

It should be clear at this stage that although the Geneva Securities Convention, together with the 2008 LCG Advice/Consultation Document, adopts a functional approach by referring to facts and employing neutral legal concepts in the attempt to reach minimal harmonisation, its provisions will have a significant impact on the evolution of domestic law. They address some of the issues of legal uncertainty of current English law put forward by the FMLC and provide precise guidelines for legal change.

In very preliminary terms, and before looking more in detail at the specific case of the protection of the innocent transferee of intermediated shares in the next chapter, it can already be argued that the pattern of formation of the international instrument and the way it will be possibly implemented in England is part of a process of cultural interaction and hybridisation along the lines observed for postcolonialist studies in Part I. This becomes evident when the rules on fungible (commingled) accounts, on the *pro rata* allocation of losses in the case of shortfall in the securities held by the intermediary and on the no look-through principle are confronted with the existing paradigm of trust law, the unpredictable scheme of resolving competing claims to assets in a pooled fund and the possible exceptions to the no look-through principle. Even if no reference to trust law is made, it is clear that the final results address the specific concerns of legal uncertainty raised by the FMLC as reported by the English delegates

189 See *White v Jones* [1995] 2 AC 207, 1 ER 691; *Smith v Eric Bush* [1990] 1 AC 831; and *Henderson v Merrett Syndicates Ltd* (No 1) [1995] 2 AC 145.

190 Article 22(3).

191 i.e. settlement systems that allow attachment to be made either against a person other than the relevant intermediary. This is often the case of holding patterns where the relevant intermediary shares its functions with a third person (see Article 6).

192 Article 22(1).

during the debates and drafting sessions of the Geneva Securities Convention and of the 2008 LCG Advice/Consultation Document. That said, the provisions of the Geneva Securities Convention and the recommendations contained in the 2008 LCG Advice/Consultation Document are not the outcome of a univocal dominant scheme resulting from a single legal tradition, nor do they reflect the only possible normative option available. Other solutions could also have possibly been reached at national level by way of legislation or case law. Other schemes for universal reference could have been borrowed from jurisdictions where *ad hoc* legal regimes designed for intermediated securities holding are in place. Instead, they are a compromise, representing the optimal model for the harmonisation of the law on the circulation of intermediated securities among the Contracting States. They constitute a new (hybrid) framework in its own right.

The fact that the chosen approach is primarily functional should not be misleading in this respect. The idea that the Geneva Securities Convention does not override the underlying property law doctrine does not imply that it leaves the existing law unchanged. It is in fact the opposite. Notwithstanding the force of the interpretative tool provided by the Official Commentary,[193] the national implementation will inevitably produce an original hybrid paradigm in the regulation of intermediated securities that is different from the pre-existing one.[194] The results will vary from jurisdiction to jurisdiction not least because of the frequent deference to the non-Convention law in the Geneva Securities Convention and by the different techniques of implementation (depending on whether a further transposition for it to become domestically binding is required the 'dualist' and 'monist' approach of international law).[195] As noted by Mooney and Kanda when comparing US and Japanese law in the Convention context, this is a risk of optimal harmonisation: 'if the differences are within a reasonable range, the most important goals may be obtained, but there is no guarantee that in all cases the range of differences will be reasonable'.[196]

In short, during the complex process of negotiations held during four meetings of CGE in Rome and in two diplomatic sessions in Geneva,[197] national models lost their

193 H Kanda, C Mooney, L Thevenoz and S Beraud with the assistance of T Keijser on behalf of the UNIDROIT Secretariat *Official Commentary on the UNIDROIT Convention on Substantive Rules for Intermediated Securities* (OUP Oxford 2012).

194 In this way greatly influencing the evolution of national law and doctrine. An analytical view on the impact of the Geneva Securities Convention on certain European jurisdiction (Belgium, Spain, Switzerland and Germany) is provided in Part II of the volume P Conac, U Segna and L Thevenoz (eds) *Intermediated Securities – The Impact of the Geneva Securities Convention and the Future European Legislation* (CUP Cambridge 2013).

195 On this latter issue, see the analysis of H Kronke 'Remarks on the Geneva Securities Convention's Development and its Future' in L Gullifer and J Payne (eds) *Intermediated Securities – Legal Problems and Practical Issues* (Hart Oxford 2010) 248.

196 C W Mooney and H Kanda 'Core Issues under the Unidroit (Geneva) Convention on Intermediated Securities: Views from the United States and Japan' in L Gullifer and J Payne (eds) *Intermediated Securities – Legal Problems and Practical Issues* (Hart Oxford 2010) 76.

197 Well presented in the history of the preparatory works contained in the Draft Official Commentary to the Convention – UNIDROIT *Draft Official Commentary the Draft Convention on Substantive Rules regarding Intermediated Securities* following the first session of Diplomatic Conference, October 2009

peculiar doctrinal meanings in their interaction with each other. They distanced themselves from the original property-related national paradigms. Delegates and governmental experts contributed at various levels and with different weight to the shaping of a final 'hybrid' harmonised model, sometimes following a purely functional approach[198] and sometimes more inclined to endorse a complete harmonisation of legal doctrine.[199] As observed for three issues of English law, the Geneva Securities Convention did not reproduce pre-existing national law, nor can the final framework be characterised as the mere fusion of identifiable contributions. It is rather a new (hybrid) model. This is clearly consistent with the pattern observed for the formation of colonial culture in Part I.

The hegemonic force of the possible implementation of the Geneva Securities Convention on the pre-existing national legal framework and its impact on domestic legal traditions also suggests the existence of a second step of hybridisation for legal change. The transposition of the Convention will not be identical in all jurisdictions. It will vary in different (hybrid) schemes from jurisdiction to jurisdiction. Even in this case, the mechanism of legal change is comparable to the colonial context where neither colonial norms nor indigenous traditions survive, but both give way to an entirely new system of doing things and perceiving meanings that is peculiar to each colonial situation.

2.3.3. A Broader Perspective

The two-step process just identified should not be restricted to the Geneva Securities Convention or merely to the area of the transfer of indirectly held shares. It can also be extended to the formation of other supranational normative instruments, including EU Directives. From this perspective, reference to certain aspects of the formation and the English implementation of the Directive 2002/47 on financial collateral arrangements as discussed in the reasoning of the Judicial Committee of the Privy Council in *Cukurova Finance International Limited v Alfa Telecom Turkey Ltd*[200] may possibly help to further clarify the arguments on legal change and hybridisation addressed in this section.

In an attempt 'to improve the integration, efficiency and stability of financial markets by simplifying enforcement procedures, eliminating or reducing difficulties arising from the insolvency laws of different member states, and eliminating re-characterisation of

at 99, 105 and 110, available at <www.unidroit.org/english/conventions/2009intermediatedsecurities/conference/conferencedocuments2009/conf11-2-005-e.pdf> (accessed 7 August 2013); and H Kanda, C Mooney, L Thevenoz and S Beraud with the assistance of T Keijser on behalf of the UNIDROIT Secretariat *Official Commentary on the UNIDROIT Convention on Substantive Rules for Intermediated Securities* (OUP Oxford 2012) 1–8.

198 e.g. the legal characterisation of the rights conferred to the account holder by the credit of securities is left by Article 9 to the non-Convention law.

199 e.g. the legal doctrine concerning the innocent acquisition of intermediated securities under Article 18 – see the chapter below.

200 [2009] 1 CLC 701. On the judgment of the High Court of the British Virgin Islands, 2007, Claim Nos. 072, 119, Joseph-Olivetti J; see J Benjamin and F Maher 'Lessons from Cukurova' (2008) 3 Capital Markets LJ 126.

repurchase arrangements (repos) as merely security interests',[201] Directive 2002/47 allows, among other things, that, on the occurrence of an enforcement event, the collateral taker shall be able to realise the financial collateral by appropriation.[202] The Directive has been implemented in the United Kingdom by the Financial Collateral Arrangements (No. 2) Regulations 2003[203] and Regulation 17 expressly allows the power for the collateral taker to appropriate the collateral.

The possibility of appropriation by unilateral act without a court order[204] has been an absolute novelty in legal framework for most of the European countries. It is the result of the first step of a process of hybridisation, ultimately established by the contributions/negotiations of national representatives at the level of the European Parliament and the Council of the European Union. Contrary to the case of civil law countries, however, the implementation of the notion of appropriation contained in the Directive proved not only to breach the rule against the clog on equity of redemption,[205] but also to have a peculiar and a far-reaching impact on English law. As the reasoning of the Judicial Committee of the Privy Council in *Cukurova Finance International Limited v Alfa Telecom Turkey Ltd* points out, this was because the possibility of co-existing equitable rights over property together with legal rights is simply inconsistent with the univocal notion of appropriation adopted in the Directive. A significant part of the discussion of the case was centred on whether the power of appropriation could be validly exercised outside the case of full ownership, on whether the charges governed by English law (equitable mortgages) and the right of appropriation could be effective under the Financial Collateral Arrangements, even if the collateral taker had not become the registered (legal) owner of the shares. In line with the ratio of the ECJ in earlier cases, the Privy Council argued that the notion of appropriation in the Directive must be given an autonomous Community meaning and that the Regulations must be construed in order

201 *Cukurova Finance International Limited v Alfa Telecom Turkey Ltd* [2009] 1 CLC 701 at 704.

202 Subject to an earlier agreement between the parties on this specific manner of realisation of the financial collateral and on the valuation of the financial instruments (Directive 2002/47/EC on financial collateral arrangements (Financial Collateral Directive) [2002] OJL168/43 as amended by Directive 2009/44/EC – Article 4).

203 SI 2003/3226 (made under section 2(2) of the European Communities Act 1972), now amended by the Financial Markets and Insolvency (Settlement Finality and Financial Collateral Arrangements) (Amendment) Regulations 2010.

204 That is, on different grounds from the mortgagee's right of foreclosure where a court order is necessary. See W Clark *Fisher and Lightwood's Law of Mortgage* (OUP Oxford 2010) Chapter 32.

205 'Whenever a transaction is in reality one of mortgage, equity regards the mortgaged property as security only for money, and will permit of no attempt to clog, fetter, or impede the borrower's right to redeem and to rescue what was, and still remains in equity his own': *Marquess of Northampton v Pollock* (1890) 45 Ch D 190 at 215 *per* Bowen LJ. Some of the key judgments on the specific (non-renounceable) mortgagor's right to the return of the mortgaged asset upon discharge of the secured obligation are *Newcombe v Bonham* (1681) 22 ER 1063; *Spurgeon v Collier* (1758) 28 ER 605; *Vernon v Bethell* (1761) 28 ER 838; *Northampton v Pollock* (1890) 45 ChD 190; *Samuel v Jarrah* [1904] AC 323; *De Beers v British South Africa Company* [1912] AC 52; and *Fairclough v Swan Brewery* [1912] AC 565. With recourse by appropriation allowed by the Directive, instead, the collateral taker's proprietary right is no longer limited by the existence of the collateral giver's (residual) proprietary right to the return of the identical assets on the discharge of the collateralised obligation.

to give effect to the Directive's scope (i.e. the collateral taker must have the means of 'rapid and non-formalistic enforcement'). This reasoning allowed the Privy Council to conclude that for a valid appropriation it was not necessary for the collateral taker to become the absolute owner, the registered holder of the shares. In many cases, their Lordships argued, 'where the registrars of charged shares had no reason to make difficulties about registration, it would be easy (and no doubt convenient) for the collateral taker to become the registered owner either just before or soon after exercising its power of appropriation. But it is not necessary'[206] according to the correct interpretation of the Regulations. In other words, the Privy Council concluded that the idea that appropriation cannot take effect in equity and that the legal title must vest for appropriation to be effective is flawed. The notion of full ownership according to the Community meaning is capable of referring to full or absolute ownership of the beneficial interest. It easy to see the far-reaching relevance of this pattern of hybridisation for the evolution of English law. The new notion of appropriation, resulting from contributions of the Member States in the process of formation of the Directive, *de facto* obscures in its second step the need the traditional English distinction between legal and equitable mortgage to survive in certain commercial transactions (i.e. the ones covered by the scope of the Directive).[207]

2.4. *Conclusions*

Section 2 has emphasised the need for a harmonised framework of substantive law in order to address the uncertainties associated with domestic and cross border transfers of intermediated shares. It has pointed out in particular that, given the international diversification of securities portfolios and the volumes of cross-border trading, the only way to achieve modernisation and harmonisation of the substantive law in the area is by simultaneously promoting sound domestic rules and predictable outcomes where the laws of one or other legal system are applied to cross border settlement of securities. It was in that light that two major concurring law reform initiatives in the area were considered: the UNIDROIT project on intermediated securities and the EU Commission project on clearing and settlement. Particular attention was paid to the process of formation and on the relationship between the Geneva Securities Convention and the 2008 LCG Advice/Consultation Document.

The analysis carried out in the first part of the section was essential to properly introduce the discussion on the evolution of law. This was tackled by focusing on three

206 *Cukurova Finance International Limited v Alfa Telecom Turkey Ltd* [2009] 1 CLC 701 at 714.

207 On the issues discussed in *Cukurova*, see G Yeowart 'Privy Council Upholds Appropriation of Shares' (2009) 27 BJUB & FL 384; Id 'Remedy of Appropriation Upheld by Privy Council' (2009) 4 LFMR 339; and Lord Millett 'The Remedy of Appropriation Under a Share Mortgage' (2008) 4 LFMR 333. On the scope and implementation of the Financial Collateral Directive in England, see the critical comments put forward by L Chan Ho 'The Financial Collateral Directive's Practice in England' 26 (2011) JIBLR 151; and with specific reference to indirectly held securities, A Zacaroli 'Taking Security over Intermediated Securities: Chapter V of the Unidroit (Geneva) Convention on Intermediated Securities' in L Gullifer and J Payne (eds) *Intermediated Securities. Legal Problems and Practical Issues* (Hart Oxford 2009) 167.

issues of legal uncertainty raised by the FMLC report to see how they had been addressed in the Geneva Securities Convention and in the 2008 LCG Advice/Consultation Document. The specific normative inquiry showed that the pattern of formation of the international instrument and the way in which it will possibly be implemented is the outcome of a process of cultural interaction and hybridisation. In the course of the negotiations traceable in the history of the preparatory works contained in the Official Commentary to the Convention,[208] national models lost their peculiar national doctrinal meanings in the interaction with others. Delegations contributed at different levels and with different weight to the shaping of an optimal 'hybrid' model. As a consequence, the final product does not reproduce the same traits of the original ones nor is it a mere fusion of the various contributions. No express reference is for example made to trust law and to equitable interests. It is a new legal framework in its own right. Moreover, the hegemonic force of the (possible) implementation of the Geneva Securities Convention on the pre-existing national legal framework and its variable impact on domestic legal traditions suggested the existence of a pattern of reception that involves a second step of hybridisation.

A significant confirmation of the observed two-step process of hybridisation was found in relation to the formation of other supranational normative instruments including EU Directives. Specific reference was made to the notion of appropriation employed in the Directive 2002/47 on financial collateral arrangements as discussed in the reasoning of the Judicial Committee of the Privy Council in *Cukurova Finance International Limited v Alfa Telecom Turkey Ltd.*[209]

[208] H Kanda, C Mooney, L Thevenoz and S Beraud with the assistance of T Keijser on behalf of the UNIDROIT Secretariat *Official Commentary on the UNIDROIT Convention on Substantive Rules for Intermediated Securities* (OUP Oxford 2012) 3.

[209] [2009] 1 CLC 701.

Chapter 7

THE PROTECTION OF THE INNOCENT TRANSFEREE OF INTERMEDIATED SHARES

This final substantive chapter draws on the discussion on the general law reform developed in Chapter 6. It considers in greater depth the specific property law issue of whether the innocent purchaser for value of intermediated shares is adequately protected under English law. In line with the FMLC[1] and the Law Commission,[2] section 1 argues that this is not the case. Existing legal concepts do not adequately meet the practical needs of investors in intermediated shares and legislative intervention is highly desirable to keep up with changing financial practice.

Without dwelling on the possible defences against equitable personal claims,[3] section 1 contends, in particular, that there is a disparity in the degree of protection available along the chain of indirect holding, apparently without justification. Building on this inconsistency, section 2 confronts the situation with the Italian legal framework and UCC Article 8 in order to offer a critical comparative background for the discussion on legal change addressed in section 3. It is in that context that the law reform proposals are examined and how they reflect a process of hybridisation of national models is shown. This outcome is consistent with the general analysis presented in Chapter 6 and reiterates with greater emphasis and depth the arguments of this study on the significance of comparative law to understand the pattern of legal evolution in terms of a process of cultural interaction and hybridisation.

1 FMLC *Property Interests in Investment Securities – Issue 3* (5 July 2004) and available at <www.fmlc.org/papers/fmlc1_3_july04.pdf> (accessed 7 August 2013).

2 Law Commission *UNIDROIT Convention on Substantive Rules Regarding Intermediated Securities – Further Advice to HM Treasury* (May 2008) and available at <www.lawcom.gov.uk/docs/intermediated_securities_advice_May2008.pdf> (accessed 7 August 2013).

3 e.g. the possible defence against the action for knowing receipt where the innocent purchaser's liability is based on his knowledge that the assets were transferred in breach of trust (*El Ajou v Dollar Land Holdings plc* [1994] 2 ER 685) and on the fact that it would be 'unconscionable' for him to retain the benefit of the receipt (*BCCI v Akindele* [2001] Ch 437 *per* Nourse LJ at 455).

1. The English Legal Framework

As stated in Chapter 6, section 1, the conventional legal characterisation of indirectly held shares in England is based on the device of trust.[4] In the indirect holding system, account holders retain an equitable interest in the pool of shares held by the relevant intermediary. This is different from the pattern of direct holding where investors enjoy a direct relationship with the issuer and maintain an absolute right in the shares.

The distinguishing elements of holding and transfer directly held shares have been spelt out in Chapter 4. This section clarifies the significance for an account holder of having an equitable interest in shares rather than a legal title, and specifies how equitable interests circulate under English law (section 1.1). It is only against this background that the legal position of the innocent purchaser of directly held shares can be evaluated (section 1.2) and properly compared with the one available for the transferee of intermediated shares (section 1.3). Quite surprisingly, it will be seen, there is a disparity between the protection of the innocent purchaser, not only between the direct and indirect holding system, but also within the same indirect holding system along the chain of intermediation (section 1.4). This fragmentation of (economically) similar positions is unconvincing and has recently led to a call for statutory intervention. Different options for law reform are available (section 1.5). Their analysis sets the perimeter of the comparative investigation in section 2 and the basis for evaluating the provisions of the Geneva Securities Convention in section 3.

1.1. The Concept of Equitable Interest in Shares

In line with the structure just outlined, this section presents the cases where an equitable interest in shares may possibly arise (under 1.1.1), and a brief account of the constituent elements/nature of such interest (under 1.1.2 and 1.1.3) before dealing with the modes of circulation (under 1.1.4). This explanatory exercise primarily provides the doctrinal background for the subsequent discussion on the terms in which an innocent purchaser of intermediated shares is protected under English law (section 1.3), and compares it with the position of the innocent purchaser of directly held shares (sections 1.2 and 1.4).

1.1.1. Relevance

It is usually perceived that, apart from the case where a trust is voluntarily constituted,[5] the most common situation where equitable interests in a share arise is (by operation of

4 The possible objections on grounds of uncertainty of subject matter to a trust of part of a shareholding have been definitively settled in *Hunter v Moss* [1994] 1 WLR 452 (CA), as recently reiterated in *Re Lehman Brothers International (Europe), Pearson v Lehman Brothers Finance SA and Others* [2010] EWHC 2914 (Ch) *per* Briggs J.

5 And, of course, outside the possible existence of equitable security interests such as charges or equitable mortgages.

law) in the event of failure to transfer legal title because of some lack of formality.[6] In dealing with this, a distinction has to be drawn depending on whether a consideration has been given. The cases where consideration has been given are analysed first.

1.1.1.1. Sale

In a sale transaction, equity looks upon 'that as done what ought to be done',[7] and (unlike the common law where a contract operates *in personam* and only the remedy of damages are available)[8] by treating an agreement for value as if it had been performed at the time it should have been performed, with the same consequences as if it had then been fully performed, it causes a contract to have proprietary implications. This is established in the leading case of *Walsh v Lonsdale*[9] relating to leases but extends to personalty and to *choses* in action in particular.[10] The doctrine that follows from *Walsh v Lonsdale* (also known as the doctrine of conversion) gives effect to the agreement to transfer by enforcing a promise to assign a future *chose* in action,[11] imposing a constructive trust arising from the contract itself on the transferor for the benefit of the transferee.[12]

Although it has been strongly argued that the *ratio* for delivering equitable ownership by constructive trust applies only when the subject matter of the sale is appropriated to the beneficiary (i.e. the obligation is specifically enforceable),[13] there now seems to be

6 A peculiar case is when uncertificated shares are converted to the certificated form. This is a possible consequence of a time lag from the moment when the EUI sends an instruction to the issuer for it to enter the relevant number of shares as certificated on the issuer's register and the time of the actual entry pursuant to USR 2001 (SI 2001/3755) reg 31(1)(b). USR 2001 reg 31(2)(a) expressly establishes that, notwithstanding the deletion of the entry in the operator's register of securities, the transferor shall retain legal title until the transferee's name is entered on the issuer register. The transferee will be vested with an equitable interest to the shares during that period.

7 A well-known maxim established by the Court of Equity 'where an act is done by a trustee' – *Banks v Sutton* (1732) 2 P Wms 700 at 715, 24 ER 922 at 928. More recently, see *Banner Homes Group Plc v Luff Developments Ltd and Another* [2000] Ch 372 *per* Chadwick LJ at 397.

8 Similarly to the case of a promise to assign a *chose* in action.

9 (1882) LR 21 ChD 9 (CA) at 14 *per* Jessel MR.

10 *Tailby v The Official Receiver* (1888) 13 App Cas 523 (HL) and *Re Trytel* [1952] 2 TLR 32.

11 *Tailby v The Official Receiver* (1888) 13 App Cas 523 (HL) at 533. See S Gardner 'Equity, Estate Contracts and the Judicature Acts: *Walsh v Lonsdale Revisited*' (1987) 7 OJLS 60.

12 See *Shaw v Foster* (1872) LR 5 HL 321. With specific reference to shares, see *Oughtred v Inland Revenue Commissioners* [1960] AC 206 (HL) at 227–228 *per* Lord Radcliffe; *Neville v Wilson* [1997] Ch 144 at 157 *per* Nourse L; and *Mills v Sportdirect.com Retail Ltd* [2010] EWHC 1072 (Ch). See P Milne 'Oughtred Revisited' (1997) 113 LQR 213; and G Watt 'The Proprietary Effect of a Chattel Lease' (2003) Convenyancer and Property Lawyer 61 at 70.

13 *Lowther v Heaver* (1889) 41 ChD 248 (CA) at 264; *Manchester Brewery Co v Coombes* [1901] 2 Ch 608 (ChD) *per* Farwell J at 617; *R v Tower Hamlets LBC, ex p Von Goetz* [1999] QB 1019 (CA) at 1025; and K Gray and SF Gray *Elements of Land Law* (OUP Oxford 2009) at paras 4.2.8; 4.2.94 and 4.2.97. See also the interpretation of *Re Wait* [1927] 1 Ch 606 (CA) *Re Goldcorp Exchange Ltd* [1995] 1 AC 74 (PC) offered by S Worthington *Proprietary Interests in Commercial Transactions* (OUP Oxford 1996) 196; Id 'Sorting Out Ownership Interests in a Bulk: Gifts, Sales and Trusts' (1999) JBL1. A more flexible approach to the issue has been followed in *Mills v Sportdirect.com Retail Ltd* [2010] EWHC 1072 (Ch) *per* Lewison J at 74–76.

robust academic support[14] and clear authority[15] for the thesis that specific performance should not be regarded as a prerequisite of general application,[16] a requirement for an agreement to be enforceable in equity. In other words, in deciding whether or not to grant specific performance, a court considers the availability of the remedy, not the acquisition of an equitable interest.[17]

Following the reasoning of Lord Macnaghten in *Tailby v Official Receiver*,[18] Eden clarifies the issue on the specific performance requirement with regard to shares[19] and, in doing so, supports the argument that the doctrine of conversion applies to the equitable transfer of shares even when traded in secondary markets.[20] In particular, he argues that 'assignment and specific performance are discrete (albeit overlapping) and that a general rule requiring specific enforceability as an essential prerequisite for an equitable ownership interest to arise by operation of law whenever shares are sold would be over-restrictive and would operate as a quasi-technicality that might tend to frustrate a court when deciding what the justice of a particular case demanded unless the courts were prepared to extend greatly their discretion to order specific performance for fungibles'.[21]

1.1.1.2. Gift

When shares are transferred by way of a gift, it is much more difficult to rescue a transfer[22] because, in principle, equity does not assist a volunteer.[23] The basic principle as established in *Milroy v Lord*[24] is a harsh one. It requires that the settlor with the intention of creating

14 See S Gardner 'Equity, Estate Contracts and the Judicature Acts: *Walsh v Lonsdale* Revised' (1987) 7 OJLS 60; M Smith and N Leslie *The Law of Assignment* (OUP Oxford 2012) 321; and P Eden 'The Equitable Ownership of Shares' in E Cooke (ed) *Modern Studies in Property Law*, vol II (Hart Oxford 2003) 183.

15 *Tailby v The Official Receiver* (1888) 12 App Cas 523 (HL) at 545–548 *per* Lord Macnaghton.

16 See the declaration on the need to distinguish between equitable assignment and specific performance stated by Sargant LJ (dissenting) in *Re Wait* [1927] 1 Ch 606 (CA) at 647. Consider also the critical statements of Lord Westbury's *dictum* in *Holroyd v Marshall* (1862) 10 HCL 191 (i.e. the right to specific performance is a pre-requisite for an equitable assignment) made by Atkin LJ in *Re Wait* [1927] 1 Ch 606 (CA) at 634.

17 See B McFarlane *The Structure of Property Law* (Hart Oxford 2008) 246; and S Gardner 'Equity, Estate Contracts and the Judicature Acts: *Walsh v Lonsdale* Revised' (1987) 7 OJLS 60.

18 (1888) LR 13 App Cas 523 (HL) at 547 who closely considered the specific performance requirement as articulated by Lord Westbury in *Holroyd v Marshall* (1862) 10 HLC 191 at 209, 11 ER 999.

19 P Eden 'The Equitable Ownership of Shares' in E Cooke (ed) *Modern Studies in Property Law*, vol II (Hart Oxford 2003) 192–193.

20 And not specified in the contract. Support for this interpretation can be found in *Paine v Hutchinson* (1866) LR 3 Eq 257 (a case of specific performance for listed shares).

21 P Eden 'The Equitable Ownership of Shares' in E Cooke (ed) *Modern Studies in Property Law*, vol II (Hart Oxford 2003) 192–193.

22 See FW Maitland *Equity: A Course of Lectures* (CUP Cambridge 1936) 71–72.

23 i.e. person who has given no consideration. See *Jones v Lock* (1865) LR 1 Ch App Cas 25; *Richards v Delbridge* (1874) LR 18 Eq 11; and *Wale v Harris* [1956] 1 WLR 1346.

24 (1862) 4 De GF &G 264 at 274 *per* Turner LJ, later approved in *Re Fry* [1946] Ch 312 *per* Romer J at 317. See the *ratio* of both cases explained in *Mascall v Mascall* (1985) 50 P & CR 119.

a trust or completely divesting himself of the legal ownership must have done everything that, according to the nature of the property comprised in the settlement, 'was necessary to be done in order to transfer the property and render the settlement binding upon him'.[25] This principle has not always been enforced with full rigour by English courts.[26] It has been occasionally circumvented with respect to the principle of intention and sometimes tempered in its rigidities by utilising the device of the constructive trust.[27] In this latter respect, notwithstanding certain criticisms,[28] it has been argued for example that the rule in *Milroy v Lord* is fully consistent with cases where the gift was considered valid even if certain further activities were required to transfer the legal title.[29] A transfer in the form appropriate under the company's articles, coupled with delivery of the transfer and certificate to the transferee, therefore 'does suffice, as between the transferor and transferee, to constitute the transferee the beneficial owner of the shares, and the circumstance the transferee must do a further act in the form of applying for and obtaining registration in order to get in and a perfect his legal title, having been equipped by the transferor with all that is necessary to enable him to do so, does not prevent the transfer from operating, in accordance with its terms as between the transferor and transferee, and making the transferee the beneficial owner'.[30] The test followed by Arden LJ in *Pennington v Waine (No 1)*[31] should be considered a step forward.[32] There it was held that the formalities of the transfer can be dispensed with when the point had been reached where it would be unconscionable for the donor to recall the gift and for the donor's personal representatives to refuse to hand over the share transfer to the donee after the donor's death. The risk, of course, is that unconscionability is too permissive a judicial criterion and lacks precise boundaries.[33]

25 *Milroy v Lord* (1862) 4 De GF & G 264 at 274, 45 ER 1185 *per* Turner LJ. See also *Richards v Delbridge* (1874) LR 18 Eq 11 at 14 *per* Jessell MR.

26 However, with respect to shares, see *Curtis v Pulbrook* [2011] EWHC 167 (Ch) par 15–54 *per* Briggs J.

27 See, for example, the statements of Lord Browne-Wilkinson in *T Choithram International SA v Pagarani* [2001] 1 WLR 1 (PC) at 11 and of Sir R Evershed MR in *Re Rose, Rose v Inland Revenue Commissioners* [1952] Ch 499 at 510. Consider also J Morris 'Questions: When is an Invalid Gift a Valid Gift? When is an Incompletely Constituted Trust a Completely Constituted Trust? Answer: After the Decisions in *Choithram and Pennington*' (2003) PCB 393.

28 See Clarke LJ's analysis of *Re Rose, Rose v Inland Revenue Commissioners* in *Pennington v Waine (No 1)* [2002] 1 WLR 2075 (CA) at 2097, par 91.

29 Consider the ways Lord Evershed and Jenkins LJ were able to prove the consistency of the principle established in *Midland Bank Executor and Trustee Co v Rose* [1949] Ch 78 at 89 *per* Jenkins J with *Milroy v Lord* in *Re Rose, Rose v Inland Revenue Commissioners* [1952] Ch 499 (CA).

30 *Re Rose, Rose v Inland Revenue Commissioners* [1952] Ch 499 (CA) per Jenkins LJ at 518. The same *ratio*, but with opposite consequences for the donee given the factual differences, see *Giselle Zeital, Kim Zeital v David Noman Kaye and Others* [2010] EWCA Civ 159 *per* Rimer J paras 33–46.

31 [2002] 1 WLR 2075 (CA).

32 Under very similar circumstances to *re Rose*. In *Re Rose, Rose v Inland Revenue Commissioners* [1952] Ch 499 (CA) the share transfer form had been signed, but not delivered.

33 This circumstance is clear in the academic debate. See H Delany and D Ryan 'Unconscionability: a Unifying Theme in Equity' (2008) 5 Conveyancer and Property Lawyer 401; M Halliwell 'Perfecting Imperfect Gifts and Trusts: Have we Reached the End of the Chancellor's Foot?' [2003] 67 Conveyancer and Property Lawyer 192; and H Tjio and TM Yeo '*Re Rose* Revisited: the Shorn Lamb's Equity' [2003] LMCLQ 296.

1.1.2. The Constituent Elements of the Equitable Interest in Shares

As far as the inquiry into what equitable rights in shares amount to, it follows from the decisions in *Re Rose*[34] and *Re Rose*[35] that the transferee may obtain first of all the right to be registered as a member of the company in the transferor's place.[36] In more general terms, although technically he is not yet a member of the company, the transferee is entitled to be accounted by the transferor with any rights he receives as shareholder.[37]

1.1.3. The Legal Nature of Intermediated Shares

While it is relatively easy to identify the contents of equitable interests in a share, it is extremely difficult to assess their legal nature under English law. The issue is largely unsettled and is at the heart of a lively taxonomical debate in academia between different understandings of the very concept of property (as opposed to obligation) held on trust.[38] To add to this, there have been certain challenging recent views that describe the nature of equitable rights in terms of persistent rights (i.e. rights against specific rights held by a trustee).[39]

1.1.4. The Legal Nature of Successive Transfers of Equitable Interests in Shares

It has been clarified above that, outside the case of security interests, the creation of an equitable right in shares is always by way of trust. This can be voluntary or by operation of law. The same rule does not always apply to successive dealings. Sub-trust is, of course, a possible option. In this case, the explanation offered above under 1.1.1 based on the device of trust can be fully replicated. However, when the transfer of an equitable interest in a share is not by way of trust but it amounts to an outright transfer, a conceptual conundrum may arise.

Given that a share comprises a bundle of rights and obligations on the part of each member in relation to the company and every other member,[40] it is inaccurate to characterise the transfer of the equitable interest in a share in terms of assignment. This is because a well-settled principle of the law of assignment establishes that only rights

34 *Midland Bank Executor and Trustee Co Ltd v Rose* [1949] Ch 78.

35 *Rose v Inland Revenue Commissioners* [1952] Ch 499 (CA).

36 Ibid *per* Lord Evershed at 510 and *per* Jenkins LJ at 517.

37 e.g. dividends declared in the *interim* before the shares are registered in the transferee's name. See *Rose v Inland Revenue Commissioners* [1952] Ch 499 (CA) per Jenkins LJ at 518.

38 A Pretto-Sakmann *Boundaries of Personal Property* (Hart Oxford 2005) argues that shares (and sub-shares) are not property rights as they are not rights in relation to a specific object that can be located in physical space. The contrary position (with limited respect to intermediated shares) is put forward by J Benjamin *Interests in Securities* (OUP Oxford 2000). This debate has been recently enriched by comparative contributions. See, in particular, E Micheler 'The Legal Nature of Securities: Inspirations from Comparative Law' in L Gullifer and J Payne (eds) *Intermediated Securities – Legal Problems and Practical Issues* (Hart Oxford 2010) 131.

39 See B McFarlane *The Structure of Property Law* (Hart Oxford 2008) 23 and 73.

40 See the discussion on the nature of a share in Chapter 4 above.

and not burdens/obligations can be assigned.[41] The transfer of a burden ought generally to require the consent of the transferor, transferee and obligee/beneficiary.[42] This result can only be obtained by way of novation. Unlike the transfer of shares at common law, in the case of the transfer of successive equitable interests in a share, the technique of novation is also hardly available. This is because company law statutes always refer to rights vested in the holder of shares as legal. Section 126 of the Companies Act 2006[43] expressly provides that 'no notice of any trust, express, implied or constructive, shall be entered on the register, or be receivable by the registrar, in the case of companies registered in England and Wales'. This means that the statutory obligation of the company to account exclusively to the member as far as the payment of dividends or the right to vote remains unchanged even if the company has been expressly notified that there had been an equitable transfer of the shares or that these are held on trust.[44] Hence there is not a new contract that comes into being, an agreement between the company, the transferor and the transferee where the transferee substitutes the transferor as member of the company under the same terms and conditions.

That said, an important exception to the above general picture for the transfer of equitable interest in a share should be allowed. This is the case of the alienation of intermediated shares where the mechanics of transfer closely resemble those of the legal title in registered shares discussed in Chapter 4. The account of the intermediary in which intermediated shares are recorded is in fact comparable to the company's register.[45] Consistent with the *ratio* of the House of Lords in *R v Preddy*,[46] if the transfer takes place on the books of the intermediary (and even if no change is made to the records of the

41 See *Linden Gardens Trust Ltd v Lenesta Sludge Disposal Ltd* [1994] 1 AC 85 at 103 *per* Lord Browne-Wilkinson; and *Tolhurst v Associated Portland Cement Manufacturers* [1902] 2 KB 660 at 668 *per* Collins MR.

42 In addition to that, the statutory framework of section 126 of the Companies Act 2006 implicitly provides another argument against the characterisation of the transfer of an equitable interest in a share in terms of assignment. Even if the company had been expressly notified of an equitable assignment of the shares, the obligation of the company would still remain in respect of the member. This contrasts with the rule on assignment that establishes that when a debtor has notice of an assignment, he must account to the assignee, not the assignor. This is well settled in a long line of cases (see *Jones v Farrell* (1857) 1 De G&J 208, 44 ER 703; *Stock v Dobson* (1853) 4 De GM&G 11 at 16 and 17, 43 ER 411) and made clear by Brown LJ in *Deposit Protection Board v Dalia* [1994] 2 AC 367 (CA) 381, by stating that 'once notice of an equitable assignment is given to the debtor, he cannot thereafter deal inconsistently with the assigned interest, for instance by making payment to the assignor'.

43 The same wording was also used in section 360 of Companies Act 1985. Reference should also be made to a similar rule as to the non-recognition of trusts with regard to the operator of an electronic transfer system under USR 2001 (SI 2001/3755) reg 40(3).

44 In the words of Lord Hoffmann (*Village Cay Marina Ltd v Acland* [1998] 2 BCLC 327 (PC) 338), 'shareholders can hold their shares on trust for anyone they like; that is a matter between them and the beneficiaries. Company law is not concerned with trusts of shares'.

45 J Benjamin *Interests in Securities* (OUP Oxford 2000) 70.

46 [1996] AC 815 where it was held that debiting of a bank account and the corresponding crediting of another's bank account brought about by dishonest misrepresentation did not amount to the obtaining of property within section 15 of the Theft Act 1968. The credit does not involve an acquisition of the lender's *chose* in action. On the contrary the *chose* in action is extinguished or reduced *pro tanto* and a *chose* in action is brought into existence representing a debt in an equivalent sum owed to the lender.

issuer or the upper-tier intermediaries above the intermediary on whose book the transfer was made) the transfer as a disposition of an equitable interest still involves novation.

1.2. The Direct Holding System

On the basis of the above doctrinal analysis and of the analysis offered earlier in Chapters 4 and 5 for directly held shares, the distinction between the nature and the modes of transfer of legal title and equitable interests in shares should now be clear. Building on this understanding, this section looks specifically at the position of the innocent purchaser of directly held shares. The subsequent section will consider the position of the innocent purchaser of indirectly held shares. The scope of the discussion in the two sections is to show the disparity in the degree of protection available under the two scenarios (and also along the chain of indirect holding) as a background inquiry for the analysis on legal change that will be carried out in sections 2 and 3 below.

1.2.1. General

It was observed in Part II that, outside the case of negotiability where the acquisition of a negotiable instrument confers good title free of any prior defects or adverse claims upon a holder in due course[47] and certain common law[48] and statutory exceptions,[49] the default principle for the transfer of title at common law is *nemo dat quod non habet*.[50] The justification for the rule is fairly straightforward. A person cannot transfer what he has not got. Although there are exceptions, 'this intuitive idea is the reason why all such exceptions need to be justified in terms of fairness.'[51]

1.2.2. Dichotomy

In a direct holding system the *nemo dat* rule operates unevenly depending on the legal nature of shares.

The borrower did not obtain the lender's *chose* in action and, accordingly, did not obtain 'property belonging to another' within the meaning of section 15 of the Theft Act 1968.

47 Section 38 of the Bills of Exchange Act 1882.

48 e.g. the case of successive assignments of *choses* in action which is governed by *Dearle v Hall* (1828) 3 Russ 1 (an assignee without notice who notifies the debtor obtains priority over an earlier assignee who has given notice later in time). Inapplicable to the transfer of shares where no notice of any trust shall be entered in the register (section 126 of the Companies Act 2006).

49 A comprehensive account of the statutory exceptions can be found in M Bridge (ed) *Benjamin's Sale of Goods* (Sweet & Maxwell London 2010) Chapter 7; and Id *The Sale of Goods* (OUP Oxford 2009) Chapter 5.

50 A person cannot confer a better title than he himself has.

51 H Beale, M Bridge, L Gullifer and E Lomnicka *The Law of Security and Title-Based Financing* (OUP Oxford 2012) 13.01.

(i) *Registered Shares.* In the case of registered shares, it is irrelevant whether the innocent transferee acquired title to shares in good faith and for value. Apart from the binding PADI sent on behalf of a legal owner of uncertificated securities from its computerised link with CREST without his consent to an innocent purchaser[52] and the circumstance where the shareholder is estopped from asserting his title because of his representations to the buyer or his negligent failure to act in order to prevent the seller from appearing as the owner,[53] the (original) legal owner always prevails over the good faith purchaser of registered shares for value and can have the register rectified.

(ii) *Share Warrants to Bearer.* The maxim *nemo dat quod not habet* has no application in the case of share warrants to bearer. These instruments qualify as negotiable instruments. It follows from this characterisation that a good faith purchaser for value[54] of share warrants to bearer obtains good title notwithstanding defects in the title of his transferor of which he was unaware.[55]

1.3. *The Indirect Holding System*

This section deals with the protection available for the transferee when shares are held on trust. The picture is different from the one just considered.

1.3.1. General

In contrast to the limited common law exceptions to the *nemo dat rule*, equity has a general defence against the claims of a beneficial owner over trust assets in the hands of a third party. This is the well-established[56] defence which protects a good faith[57] purchasers of legal title[58] for value[59] without notice[60] of prior equitable rights.[61] In the words of Millett J in *Macmillan Inc v Bishopsgate Investment Trust plc (No 3)*, 'equity's

52 SI 2001/3755 reg 35(4). The protection for the innocent transferees in this case is wider that in the case of certificated securities as there is no requirement for value and only actual notice is necessary.

53 See above *sub* Chapter 4, section 1.5.

54 There is a presumption that the holder has given value for the instrument – see for example section 27(2) of the Bills of Exchange Act 1882.

55 For the analogous rules applying to other types of bearer instruments, see section 29(1) of the Bills of Exchange Act 1882 (negotiable bills of exchange) and *Garey v Dominion Manufacturers Ltd* [1925] 1 DLR 99 (bearer bonds). See above *sub* Chapter 5, section 1.5.

56 *Pilcher v Rawlins* (1872) LR 7 Ch App 259 at 268.

57 See the *dictum* of Lord Wilberforce in *Midland Bank Trust Co Ltd v Green* [1981] AC 513 at 528.

58 Better, legal interest. The rule applies to the purchaser of legal interest, not just legal title in the property. This extends its application to the case of creation of legal security interest on trust property. See H Beale, M Bridge, L Gullifer and E Lomnicka *The Law of Security and Title-Based Financing* (OUP Oxford 2012) Chapter 14.

59 In *Re Diplock* [1948] Ch 465.

60 On the definition of notice, see section 199 of the Law of Property Act 1925.

61 The defence is well established in the history of English law. See *Pilcher v Rawlins* (1872) LR Ch App 259 *per* James LJ at 268; *Joseph v Lyons* (1884) 15 QBD 280; and *Hallas v Robinson* (1885) 15 QBD 288 at 292.

darling' is a *bona fide* purchaser for value 'who obtains the legal estate at the time of his purchase without actual or constructive notice of prior equitable rights is entitled to priority in equity as well as at law [...] But he must have obtained the legal estate, and the question of notice is normally tested at the time he obtained it.'[62]

The most convincing explanation for this exception to the *nemo dat* rule has a very pragmatic rationale.[63] In creating a trust, the property, by the nature of the device, may present to the world a possibly misleading factual situation. The settlor who has privately established to create a trust is exposed to the risk that the trustee who will deal with it may be incompetent or a rogue.[64] The fact is that, in the case of equitable owners, there is a trust and a trustee cannot be simply ignored. In the words of Penner, since a settlor creates the risk, 'the results of things going wrong when the risk materializes should fall on the beneficiaries rather than on third parties who have acquired the trust property innocently and paid good value for it (i.e. the good faith purchasers).'[65]

1.3.2. Availability of the Defence for the Purchaser of Intermediated Shares

The *bona fide* purchaser defence is of limited help for the innocent purchaser of intermediated shares. In explaining this statement, a distinction should be drawn between different levels of intermediation.

(i) *Sale by a Trustee.* The most relevant case of application of the defence is the one affecting the good faith acquisition of a legal estate held in trust for an investor for value without notice.[66] Contrary to the terminology adopted by the Law Commission, this cannot be classified as an example of direct holding.[67] Outside the case of a security

62 [1995] 1 WLR 978 (ChD) at 1000. See also *Pilcher v Rawlins* (1872) LR 7 Ch App 259. A sophisticated analysis of the elements of *bona fide* purchase for value (with specific reference to money) is provided by D Fox *Property Rights in Money* (OUP Oxford 2008) 277–303.

63 Other rationales have been proposed in the past. The most often-invoked is the 'jurisdictional' one which maintains that, in the case of a *bona fide* purchaser of a legal estate, a court of equity has no jurisdiction to recognise that the purchaser is under a duty to the beneficiary of the trust. See *Pilcher v Rawlins* (1872) LR 7 Ch App 259 at 268 *per* James LJ; J Hackney *Understanding Equity and Trusts* (Fontana Press London 1987) Chapter 1, s 2(a); and W Swadling 'Restitution and Bona Fide Purchase' in Id (ed) *The Limits of Restitutionary Claims: A Comparative Analysis* (United Kingdom Comparative Law Series London 1997) 80. This jurisdictional explanation is fundamentally flawed if only reflecting upon the circumstance that the defence does not apply when the *bona fide* purchaser acquires a legal estate for free (i.e. even if the transferee has acquired a legal interest).

64 See L Smith 'Unjust Enrichment, Property and the Structure of Trusts' (2000) 116 LQR 412 at 431.

65 J Penner *The Law of Trusts* (OUP Oxford 2006) 33. See B McFarlane *The Structure of Property Law* (Hart Oxford 2008) 246.

66 Another possible circumstance where it may possibly apply is the good faith acquisition for value without notice of an equitable interest provided that the purchaser is in the position to demand the transfer of a legal estate from the relevant intermediary.

67 Law Commission *UNIDROIT Convention on Substantive Rules Regarding Intermediated Securities – Further Advice to HM Treasury* (May 2008) available at <www.lawcom.gov.uk/docs/intermediated_securities_advice_May2008.pdf> (accessed August 2013) 95.

interest,[68] the same nature of the defence necessarily presupposes a pattern of intermediation.

(ii) *Sale by a Sub-trustee*. In the majority of cases, however, the *bona fide* purchaser defence is not available in the context of intermediated shares. These are in fact located in a chain of trusts. Given that sub-trustees have merely beneficial interest in the shares held by the relevant intermediary, the innocent purchaser of intermediated shares from a sub-trustee does not acquire a legal estate, but merely an equitable interest in the shares. As between two equitable interests, the general rule, similar in substance to the *nemo dat principle*, is *qui prior est in tempore potior in iure*.[69]

1.3.3. Absence of Legal Alternatives to Assist an Innocent Purchaser of Intermediated Shares

When the *bona fide* purchaser defence is not available, there are no alternative methods to protect an innocent purchaser of intermediated shares under English law.[70]

The doctrine of the *tabula in naufragio* or 'quasi-tacking',[71] in particular, cannot be successfully invoked in this context. This doctrine is based on the struggle between competing equitable interests for the legal estate when the subordinated holder of equitable interest has a clear incentive in incurring the expense of acquiring the legal estate (and rank ahead of other existing equitable interests).[72] In essence, it allows the purchaser of an equitable interest to acquire a legal interest at a later date even if he was aware of the existence of a prior equitable interest at the time he purchased the legal estate.[73] As already suggested, however, given the existence of a long chain of sub-trusts, it will be difficult for the purchaser of an equitable interest in intermediated shares 'to obtain the legal estate without further action on the part of the upper tier intermediary that holds legal title'.[74]

The defence of 'change of position' is also not available. That defence only protects a defendant in a restitutionary claim whose position has so changed that it would be

68 e.g. unregistered equitable mortgages and charges. See L Gullifer 'Exceptions to the *nemo dat* rule in relation to goods and the Law Commission's proposals in the Consultative Report' in J de Lacy (ed) *The Reform of UK Personal Property Security Law* (Routledge London 2010) 195.

69 He who is first in time is better in law. The rule is explained by Lord Westbury LC in *Phillips v Phillips* (1861) 4 De GF&J 208 at 215, 45 ER 1164.

70 The Law Commission in its final report to HM Treasury explores without success other options. Law Commission *UNIDROIT Convention on Substantive Rules Regarding Intermediated Securities – Further Advice to HM Treasury* (May 2008) available at <www.lawcom.gov.uk/docs/intermediated_securities_advice_May2008.pdf> (accessed 7 August 2013) 103.

71 According to the terminology coined by Millett J in *Macmillan Inc v Bishopsgate Investment Trust plc (No 3)* [1995] 1 WLR 978 at 1002.

72 See AG Guest *Guest on the Law of Assignment* (OUP Oxford 2012) 219.

73 See *Bailey v Barnes* [1894] 1 Ch 25 CA; *Harpham v Shacklock* (1881) 19 Ch D 207 *per* Jessel MR at 214; and *Taylor v Russell* [1892] AC 244 HL.

74 Law Commission *UNIDROIT Convention on Substantive Rules Regarding Intermediated Securities – Further Advice to HM Treasury* (May 2008) available at <www.lawcom.gov.uk/docs/intermediated_securities_advice_May2008.pdf> (accessed 7 August 2013) 104.

inequitable to require him to make restitution.[75] In *Foskett v McKeown*,[76] Lord Millett clarified the issue pointing out that equitable proprietary claims are not concerned with unjust enrichment, but with the vindication of the claimant's property rights over assets or its traceable proceeds.

1.4. Comparison and Rationales

The analysis carried out in sections 1.2 and 1.3 above has set out, it is hoped, a composite picture for the protection of a purchaser in good faith of shares and intermediated shares. The general scenario can be described in a tripartite scheme, as follows.

(i) *Direct Holding System*. Apart from the limited exception concerning the acquisition of share warrants to bearer, the registered holder of (legal) title to shares is protected at common law from any third party interference. Against pre-existing legal property rights the *bona fide* purchaser defence is not available.

(ii) *Indirect Holding System* (shares transferred directly by the trustee in breach of trust). Where shares are held on trust, the beneficiary has an equitable interest over the shares. If the trustee acting beyond his powers transfers the shares to a third party who acquires them for value, in good faith, and without notice of the pre-existing equitable rights,[77] this same third party acquires legal title over the shares and takes priority over the investor's equitable interest. This is the effect of the *bona fide* purchaser defence.

(iii) *Indirect Holding System* (shares transferred by a sub-trustee in breach of trust). Where a sub-trustee acting beyond his powers disposes of his beneficial interest in the shares to a third party who acquires them for value, in good faith, and without notice of the pre-existing equitable rights, this same third party does not acquire legal title, but an equitable interest in intermediated shares. This does not take priority over pre-existing equitable interests. The rule *qui prior est in tempore potior in iure* applies.

A critical comparison between the protection of an innocent purchaser of shares is set out below. This is a helpful exercise ahead of the discussion on legal change addressed in sections 2 and 3. For an explanation of the current law, a separate investigation has to be carried out under the scenarios presented above depending not just on the different regime for direct and indirect holding (i), but also within the same pattern of intermediation (ii).

75 *Lipkin Gorman v Karpnale* [1991] 2 AC 548.

76 *Foskett v McKeown* [2001] 1 AC 102 *per* Lord Millett at 129.

77 In this case, given that the rights that vest in the legal holder of a share are in the eyes of the company his rights, it is unlikely the legal transferee will ever have notice of existing prior equitable interests. Reference should be made to the above discussion on the notice of trust as defined by section 126 of Companies Act 2006.

(i) *Direct/Indirect Holding.* The rationale for the distinction between the protection available for the innocent purchaser of directly and indirectly held shares following an unauthorised transfer is based on the historical divide between equity and common law and, in particular, on the requirement for registration (and publicity) at common law.[78] While in the case of directly held shares, it is in fact possible for the purchaser to verify the seller's title by looking at the company's register (or to obtain the possession of the certificate in the case of share warrants to bearer), in the case of indirectly held shares, the purchaser cannot have knowledge of existing equitable interests as section 126 of the Companies Act 2006 clearly suggests.

Under this scenario, it is appropriate that the owner of the equitable interest suffers the potential risk of an unauthorised transfer by the trustee. He is in fact the one who 'has some control and choice over the level of risk it bears in relation to the protection of its property rights'.[79]

(ii) *Indirect Holding.* The distinction in the protection available for the innocent transferee of intermediated securities depending on the position of the seller in the chain of intermediation is difficult to justify. This is because the factual scenario in the indirect holding system is always identical. The *bona fide* transferee acquires intermediated shares for value and without notice of the underlying beneficiary's interest held on trust.

However, when the transferee does not acquire a legal estate from the trustee, but merely an equitable interest from the sub-trustee, the protection of the *bona fide* purchaser defence is not available. This distinction does not seem to have a logic rationale and it is discriminatory among innocent purchasers. The historical explanation according to which in the case of acquisition of a legal estate the court of equity has no jurisdiction to recognise that a transferee is under a duty to the beneficiary[80] is difficult to defend. It creates inconsistencies in the property law system and, above all, may cause unwanted obstacles in the circulation of intermediated shares in financial markets.

1.5. The Way Forward

In the light of the issues presented and of concerns arising from the (soundness of the) existing English legal framework, this final section outlines the possible alternative approaches *de iure condendo* for the protection of the innocent purchaser of intermediated shares. The scope of the analysis is to present a toolbox of available normative options for law reform to be tested in the comparative inquiry (section 2) and, above all, in the discussion on the law reform initiatives and the process of legal change addressed below (section 3).

There are essentially three possible alternative approaches. These are outlined below.

78 It will be seen in section 2 below that the distinction between the protection available for the innocent purchaser of directly and indirectly held shares following an unauthorised transfer is not the default rule in all jurisdictions.

79 Law Commission *UNIDROIT Convention on Substantive Rules Regarding Intermediated Securities – Further Advice to HM Treasury* (May 2008) available at <www.lawcom.gov.uk/docs/intermediated_securities_advice_May2008.pdf> (accessed 7 August 2013) 112.

80 See *Pilcher v Rawlins* (1872) LR 7 Ch App 259 *per* James LJ at 268.

1.5.1. The Establishment of a General Defence

The first approach does not distinguish between shares and intermediated shares. The rule for the protection of innocent purchasers of shares should work without exceptions under all circumstances when a good faith transfer for value without notice occurs. Above all, it should never be compromised depending on its historical origin.

The rationale is straightforward. Although, as a general principle, a seller should not be able to confer on a purchaser a right which he himself does not possess (*nemo dat quod non habet*), the need to facilitate transactions in a fast-moving marketplace (liquidity) of *choses* requires the purchaser to be protected. In a dynamic and efficient commercial environment, 'security of transaction'[81] should always take priority over 'security of title'[82] (*favor commercii*).[83] If every purchaser had to investigate the seller's title and authority to sell free of any pre-existing interests, the circulation of movables would be greatly hampered.[84]

As observed in Chapter 5 this is already the case for the holder in due course of negotiable instruments. Notwithstanding all the differences in the nature and modes of transfer, the same rule should equally protect all innocent purchasers of registered (no matter whether they are certificated or uncertificated) and intermediated shares without allowing differences in priority between legal and equitable interests.[85]

1.5.2. The Reality of Modern Financial Transactions

The second approach follows a more pragmatic rationale. It argues that there is no need to have an *ad hoc* rule to protect an innocent purchaser of intermediated shares. Even without considering the operational difficulties of tracing intermediated shares when mechanisms of clearing and netting are in place, in financial markets 'security of transaction' is achieved by reliance on the stability and reputation of financial intermediaries under governmental supervision.[86] There is simply no need to invoke the notion of good faith purchase. As the scarcity of litigation in this area of law suggests, the idea that in the absence of a rule that protects the innocent purchasers, the acquisition of shares would not be secure and detrimental to the operation of financial markets is largely a myth.[87]

This is not a novelty. It has historically been true with regard to negotiability in general. Reference could be made, for example, to certain exceptions to the *nemo dat* rule such as the 'market overt' where any sale from the shops in the City of London was

81 i.e. protection of innocent purchaser and perfection of otherwise defective titles.

82 i.e. property rights survive disposition by non-owners.

83 See the comprehensive discussion on the political and economic conundrum in AJ Levitin 'Finding Nemo: Rediscovering the Virtues of Negotiability in the Wake of Enron' (2007) Colum Bus L Rev 86 at 99.

84 See G Gilmore 'The Commercial Doctrine of Good Faith Purchase' (1954) 63 Yale LJ 1057–68.

85 See J Benjamin *Interests in Securities* (OUP Oxford 2001) 329.

86 CW Mooney Jr 'Beyond Negotiability: A New Model for Transfer and Pledge of Interests in Securities Controlled by Intermediaries' 1990) 12 Cardozo L Rev 305.

87 JS Rogers 'Negotiability as a System of Title Recognition' (1987) 48 Ohio St L J 197.

regarded to be a sale in the open market, protecting therefore, the good faith purchaser from adverse claims. One commentator has convincingly argued that this rule was unlikely to be 'known beyond the commercial law trivia circles,' and, above all, that it did not cause 'any significant difference in market practices or pricing between the City of Westminster'.[88]

1.5.3. An *Ad Hoc* Amendment of the Existing Law

The third approach has a narrower scope. It considers the position under section 1.5.1 to be difficult to rationally accept in a common law jurisdiction where the unity of the codification is not present. It acknowledges the arguments under section 1.5.2, but it also maintains that 'the huge value of investment securities traded in securities settlement systems for investment or as collateral means that even a small chance of a purchaser or pledgee losing the priority to security can be sufficient to cause concern'.[89]

In the light of these critiques, this final approach finds it more sensible to change the current law simply by extending the protection available for the *bona fide* purchaser of intermediated shares when the acquired property rights are equitable. As observed in the sections above, there are no convincing legal or economic reasons why purchasers should be treated differently depending on whether the intermediary's unauthorised transfer results in the transfer of legal title or of an equitable interest.

1.6. Conclusions

Against the characterisation of the indirect holding system as a chain of trusts, section 1 considered first the meaning of having an equitable interest in shares. This investigation was done in order to properly establish the legal framework for the discussion on how innocent purchasers of shares and intermediated shares are protected against adverse claims under English law. Section 1.1, in particular, showed that apart from the case where a voluntary trust is created, the most common circumstance where equitable interests in a share arise is the failure to transfer legal title because of some want of formality. This may occur according to different rules depending on whether consideration has been given. Section 1.1 also briefly focused on the rights of the transferee of an equitable interest in shares. It suggested that they consist primarily of the right to be registered as member of the company in the transferor's place and to be accounted by the transferor with any rights he receives as shareholder. Finally, some words were used in clarifying the legal nature of successive transfers of equitable interest in shares arguing that, outside the case of the creation of sub-trusts, with respect to intermediated shares the model is based (as it was for registered shares) on novation.

88 JS Rogers 'Negotiability, Property and Identity' (1990) 12 Cardozo L Rev 482.

89 Law Commission *UNIDROIT Convention on Substantive Rules Regarding Intermediated Securities – Further Advice to HM Treasury* (May 2008) available at <www.lawcom.gov.uk/docs/intermediated_securities_advice_May2008.pdf> (accessed 7 August 2013) 114.

Building on that introductory picture, sections 1.2 and 1.3 looked at the position of the innocent purchaser of directly and indirectly held shares. Section 1.2, in particular, pointed out that with the exception of share warrants to bearer and certain cases based on estoppel, the innocent purchaser of shares from someone who is not the owner is never protected at common law. It is irrelevant whether the innocent transferee acquired title to shares in good faith and for value. The default rule for the transfer of title at common law is *nemo dat quod non habet*. Section 1.3 suggested that with respect to intermediated shares the scenario is different. Equity has in fact a general defence that protects a good faith purchaser of legal title for value without notice of prior equitable rights. However, the *bona fide* purchaser defence is not always available for the innocent purchaser of intermediated shares: unless intermediated shares are acquired directly from the trustee, purchasers of intermediated shares in financial markets obtain a beneficial interest in the shares held by the sub-trustee and not a legal estate. As between two equitable interests the general rule, similar in substance to the *nemo dat* rule is *qui prior est in tempore potior in iure*.

Section 1.4 evaluated the fragmented picture offered in sections 1.2 and 1.3 and searched for its rationale. It found that the distinction between the protection available to the innocent purchaser of directly and indirectly held shares carries a sensible explanation in the existing dichotomy between equity and common law. In the case of indirectly held shares, the purchaser cannot have knowledge of existing equitable interests as established by section 126 of the Companies Act 2006 and it is appropriate that the potential risk of an unauthorised transfer by the trustee is posed by the owner of the equitable interest who has some form of control over the trust he created. On the contrary, the distinction in the level of protection available for the innocent transferee of intermediated securities depending on the position of the seller in the scale of intermediation is difficult to justify. It lacks a logical rationale in allowing a different regime between categories of innocent purchasers of intermediated shares depending on their position in the chain of intermediation.

In the light of the observed inconsistencies in the English legal framework, section 1.5 outlined three possible alternative models for law reform. The first approach protects a purchaser of shares without exceptions whenever a good faith transfer for value without notice occurs. The second one supports an entirely different view. It argues that the discussion on the *bona fide* purchaser defence is fundamentally otiose. In the current system of settlement for intermediated shares where tracing is *de facto* impossible, 'security of transaction' is achieved by reliance on the stability and reputation of financial intermediaries under governmental supervision rather by presence of a rule that protects an innocent purchaser. The third model has a short-term claim for immediate reform. It finds it sensible to amend the current law by extending the protection available for the *bona fide* purchaser of intermediated shares when the acquired property rights are equitable.

Section 2 now examines these three approaches in a comparative inquiry in preparation for the discussion on the law reform initiatives and the process of hybridisation addressed in section 3 below.

2. A Comparative View

This section draws on the themes developed in section 1. It does not look at English law. It has a comparative agenda. More accurately, it reviews the methods of protection of the innocent purchaser of intermediated shares under Italian law (section 2.1) and under the Uniform Commercial Code (section 2.2). The scope of the analysis is to discuss the different possible approaches outlined in the penultimate paragraph of section 1 in the light of existing normative frameworks. This is primarily to provide a comparative background for the inquiry on the process of legal evolution and hybridisation that will be carried out in section 3 when dealing with the law reform initiatives.

2.1. The Italian Legal System

Contrary to the English fragmented scenario, Italian law has a general defence for the innocent purchaser of movables, which works by analogy for all types of shares (no matter whether they are dematerialised or not) as well as for intermediated shares.

Before dealing with the specific elements of the defence, a brief introductory outline on the nature and methods of circulation of Italian shares is presented below (section 2.1.1). This is intended to set up the legal context and to clarify the underlying themes of the ways in which innocent purchasers of intermediated shares are protected (section 2.1.2).

2.1.1. Nature and Modes of Transfer

2.1.1.1. Nature

Notwithstanding their type (or lack)[90] of representation, Italian shares (*azioni*) are, from a quantitative and formalistic perspective, the minimum fractions of the corporate capital.[91] They state the measure of the members' contractual rights[92] in a company limited by shares (*società per azioni*). In essence, shares are rights *in personam*. They represent members' intangible rights exigible against the company.[93]

90 The alternative (paper-based) share certificates/dematerialised shares is not the only available alternative. Although it is not customary (but not totally unusual in 'closed companies'), the company's entitlement not to issue share certificates is expressly provided under article 2346(1) of the Italian Civil Code (to be read together with Regio Decreto no 239 of 29 March 1942, article 5).

91 Article 2346(1) of the Italian Civil Code which refers to the shares as unit of corporate capital and article 2347 of the Italian Civil Code according to which 'shares are indivisible'. Extensive investigations focused on the notion of shares as units of shareholders' participation in the company have been carried out by P Spada *La Tipicità delle Società* (Cedam Padova 1974) 386; Id 'Dalla Nozione al Tipo della Società per Azioni' (1985) Riv dir civ 95.

92 More accurately, both contractual and statutory to be asserted against the company and other shareholders. This measure can be expressed either in terms of nominal value (see article 2346(2) of the Italian Civil Code) or as percentage of company's whole undertaking (article 2346(3) of the Italian Civil Code).

93 What distinguishes shareholders (as residual claimants) from other investors under Italian law is the formal nature of the contribution to the company as established in the memorandum of association and in compliance with certain specific mandatory provisions. See article 2342 of the Italian Civil Code.

When presented in the form of certificates, however, Italian shares (both bearer and registered) may enjoy a double nature. They lie in contract (i.e. *rights in personam*) as between the shareholder and the issuing company and they are also property (i.e. *rights in rem*) as against third parties.[94] This is because the document, qualified by analogy in terms of *titolo di credito*,[95] carries the value of the intangible rights which it evidences. As with negotiable instruments in England, historically the reification of shares into the document[96] served the commercial purpose of allowing the law to treat intangible rights as though they were corporeal chattels (tangibles). At the time of the enactment of the Italian Civil Code in 1942, the device provided a more efficient and secure mode of circulation to cope with the increased volumes of commercial transactions. More accurately, it enabled the circumvention of the burdensome Italian legal regime on assignment of claims[97] and, therefore, greatly enhanced transferability.

The characterisation of shares as documentary intangibles can be stretched to the ones that circulate under the (settlement) system of immobilisation,[98] but not to those that circulate under the regime of dematerialisation.[99] In the first case, share certificates, although deposited in a CSD (*società di gestione accentrata* in Italian), do still exist in their materiality and, therefore, the depositors' entitlement can still be asserted as proprietary as is the case with *titoli di credito*.[100] In the case of dematerialisation, as the law expressly states, the recourse to share certificates is dispensed with altogether and the paper document is substituted by an electronic record.[101] Accordingly, the only way to qualify the incorporeal significance of uncertificated shares is by direct reference to their nature of *rights in personam*.[102]

94 See G Ferri 'La Teoria Realista dei Titoli di Credito' (1972) Banca, Borsa e Titoli di Credito 41; G Oppo 'Titolo di Credito. I) In generale' (1994) in *Enc Giur Treccani*, vol XXXI Roma §7; and T Ascarelli 'La letteralità nei Titoli di Credito' (1932) in Riv Dir Comm 238.

95 Titolo V arts 1992–2027 of the Italian Civil Code. See F Martorano *Titoli di Credito* (Giuffrè Milano 2002) 5.

96 i.e. the transformation of an intangible contractual right into a corporeal *res*. See GL Pellizzi *Principi di Diritto Cartolare* (Zanichelli Bologna 1967) 21; and A Fiorentino 'Dei Titoli di Credito' in A Scialoja and G Branca (eds) *Commentario del Codice Civile* (Zanichelli Bologna-Roma 1974) *sub* 1992–2002.

97 An outline of the existing framework is provided by A Dolmetta 'Cessione dei Crediti' in *Digesto Discipline Privatistiche Sezione Civile* (Utet Torino 1988) 291. See also the analysis offered by L Buttaro 'Tullio Ascarelli e il Titolo di Credito' (1981) Banca Borsa e Titoli di Credito 424.

98 Legislative Decree no 58 of 24 February 1998, Consolidated law on financial intermediation pursuant to Articles 8 and 21 of Law no 52 of 6 February 1996 (hereinafter 'TUF') articles 79 *quarter* to 90, to be read together with the *Rules Governing Central Depositories, Settlement Services, Guarantee Systems and Related Management Companies* (adopted by the Bank of Italy and Consob on 22 February 2008 and amended on 24 December 2010, available at <www.consob.it/mainen/documenti/english/laws/bi_consob_post_trading_20080222.htm> (accessed 7 August 2013)).

99 Article 83 *bis* TUF.

100 See G Ferri 'La Immissione dei Valori Mobiliari nel Sistema di Gestione Accentrata e i Suoi Effetti Giuridici' (1988) Riv Dir Comm 252; and G Oppo 'Una Svolta nei Titoli di Massa (il Progetto Monte Titoli)' (1986) Riv Dir Civ 558.

101 Pursuant article 83 *bis* TUF, freely transferable shares traded or to be traded in the Italian capital market can no longer be represented and regulated as documentary intangibles (*titoli di credito*) in compliance with the provisions contained in the Italian Civil Code.

102 See G Guizzi *Il Titolo Azionario come Strumento di Legittimazione* (Giuffrè Milano 2000) 96.

2.1.1.2. Modes of Transfer

Following the differences in the juridical nature of shares outlined above, the transfer of Italian shares is characterised and fragmented according to different legal patterns.

When certificates are not issued[103] and the mandatory rules on dematerialisation do not apply,[104] shares circulate according to the provisions established for the transfer of contract pursuant to articles 1406 *et seq* of the Italian Civil Code.

When shares are embodied in *titoli di credito*, the methods of alienation (*circolazione cartolare*) vary depending on whether shares are bearer[105] or registered.[106] While in the first case they circulate by delivery,[107] registered shares are either transferred by transferor's endorsement in the name of the transferee (*girata*)[108] or by double inscription of the transferee's name in the document and in the issuer's register (*transfert*).[109] It is commonly perceived among Italian scholars that the registration formality in the case of registered shares is aimed at making the transfer (to a limited extent) effective as against the issuing company, but that title would pass on the basis of the agreement between the parties pursuant to article 1376 of the Italian Civil Code as the wording of article 2355(3) of the Italian Civil Code seems to suggest.[110]

Shares immobilised in a CSD are transferred upon depositors' specific instructions,[111] directly or via the (mandatory) sub-depositors by means of computer entries (*scritture di giro*) in the register kept by the CSD.[112]

103 As mentioned above, the company's right not to issue share certificates is expressly provided under article 2346(1) of the Italian Civil Code (to be read together with Regio Decreto no 239 of 29 March 1942, article 5).

104 i.e. shares are not freely transferable shares traded or to be traded in the Italian capital market. See article 83 *bis* TUF.

105 i.e. may be subsumed under the category of *titoli di credito al portatore* – bearer documentary intangibles. Bearer shares are admitted for only a limited number of companies and in any case outside the framework of the Italian Civil Code. e.g. preference shares pursuant to TUF article 145(3) (see M Notari 'Emissione delle Azioni' in PG Marchetti and LA Bianchi (eds) *La disciplina delle società quotate nel Testo Unico della Finanza. D Lgs. 24 febbraio 1998, n. 58 Commentario vol II (artt. 136–212)* (Giuffrè Milano 1998) 1532) and ordinary shares issued by SICAV (*società di investimento a capitale variabile*) pursuant to TUF article 45(4) (see R Lener 'Capitale e Azioni' in G Alpa and F Capriglione (eds) *Commentario al Testo Unico delle disposizioni in materia di intermediazione finanziaria* (Cedam Padova 1998) 466; and A Antonucci 'Le Società di Investimento a Capitale Variabile' in A Patroni Griffi, M Sandulli and V Santoro (eds) *Intermediari Finanziari, Mercati e Società Quotate* (Utet Torino 1999) 99).

106 i.e. *titoli nominativi* when the holder's name appears both on the body of the document and on the issuer's register.

107 Article 2355(2) of the Italian Civil Code.

108 Written in the body of the certificate and authenticated by a public notary. Article 2355(3) of the Italian Civil Code by reference to article 2023 of the Italian Civil Code. In such case the endorsee is entitled to obtain entry of the transfer in the issuer's register.

109 Articles 2355(4) and 2022 of the Italian Civil Code. See S Gatti *L'Iscrizione nel Libro Soci* (Giuffrè Milano 1969) 237.

110 In greater depth on this issue, see N De Luca *Circolazione delle Azioni e Legittimazione dei Soci* (Giappichelli Torino 2007).

111 Article 86(1) TUF.

112 See G Partesotti 'Profili Cartolari del Sistema Monte Titoli' (1987) Banca Borsa e Titoli di Credito 601.

Even the process of transfer of dematerialised shares involves the activity of a CSD where both issuers and intermediaries have opened accounts. This broadly entails two steps. First, upon the investors' specific instructions via the intermediaries, the CSD debits the 'general account' held by the seller's intermediary and credits the 'general account' held by purchaser's intermediary. Second, once the CSD notifies both the seller's and the purchaser's intermediaries about the completion of the transaction, the seller's intermediary debits the seller's shares account and the purchaser's intermediary credits the purchaser's shares account.[113] The process concludes with the entries in the shareholder's book pursuant to the intermediary's report to be sent to the issuer after completing the formalities of transfer.[114]

2.1.2. The Operation of the *Bona Fide* Purchaser Defence

As already suggested, Italian law has a general rule for the protection of an innocent purchaser of shares. This clearly mirrors the first scenario pictured under section 1.5.1. When the essential requirements are met, the rule applies without exceptions to the circulation of directly and indirectly held shares.

The paradigm is set out by article 1153(1) of the Italian Civil Code,[115] which presupposes in its sphere of application the well-known historical provision of the French Civil Code *en fait de meuble possession vaut titre*.[116] In particular, it establishes that a good faith purchaser for value will take good title even though the seller has none, provided that he retains possession over the acquired assets and the transfer has been lawfully executed. This is because article 1147 of the Italian Civil Code establishes the principle based on possession as a rebuttable presumption of ownership. In short, similar to the case of negotiable instruments under English law, the holder in due course is not subject to vindication (*rei vindicatio*).

An identical defence is established under Article 1994 of the Italian Civil Code for *titoli di credito*. Given that bearer and registered shares belong by analogy to the genus of *titoli di credito*, it follows that the same protection of the holder in due course for movables applies to directly held shares.

Finally, the general rule contained in the Civil Code has also been replicated (by legal fiction this time) in the legislation on immobilisation[117] and, recently, in the provisions dealing with uncertificated shares.[118] Given that under Italian law dematerialisation

113 Article 83 *quarter* TUF.

114 Article 29 of the Rules Governing Central Depositories, Settlement Services, Guarantee Systems and Related Management Companies (adopted by the Bank of Italy and Consob on 22 February 2008 and amended on 24 December 2010, available at <www.consob.it/mainen/documenti/english/laws/bi_consob_post_trading_20080222.htm#Article_26> (accessed 7 August 2013).

115 The provision was also contained in the 1865 Italian Civil Code (article 707). It represented at the time of the enactment of the code one of the most radical novelties with respect to the Roman law of vindication (*rei vindicatio – ubi rem meam invenio ibi vindico*).

116 Currently under article 2279 of the French Civil Code.

117 L 19 June 1986 no 289, art 4(2) (now repealed by art 86(2) TUF).

118 Article 83 *quinquies* TUF.

necessarily involves an intermediated settlement system,[119] it follows that the general *bona fide* purchaser defence applies to the transfer of intermediated shares.[120]

2.2. *UCC Article 8*

As outlined in Chapter 6, UCC Article 8 and the related provisions contained in UCC Article 9 offer the essential framework for the circulation of intermediated securities,[121] substantially in all states of the United States.[122]

The current version of UCC Article 8 was revised in 1994[123] following the United States Department of Treasury proposals, prompted by legal uncertainties evidenced in financial litigation.[124] By distinguishing between the direct and indirect holding system, the revision was, above all, 'one part of worldwide effort to assure that clearance and settlement system for securities trading'[125] operates in a way to preclude the occurrence of systemic risk. In the words of Rogers who served as rapporteur to the NCCULSL/ALI Drafting Committee to Revise UCC Article 8, the most significant element in the Revised Article 8 project 'was the realization that the system of securities holding through intermediaries was sufficiently different from the traditional system in which an investor's right to the underlying security was represented by a definitive paper certificate, or from a system of the sort contemplated by the 1978 revision, where the investor's interest would be recorded electronically on the issuer's shareholder registry, that it required a different set of commercial law concepts and rules'.[126]

It is against this very innovative perception that this section outlines the techniques of protection of the innocent purchaser of intermediated shares under UCC Article 8.[127]

119 Article 83 *quater* (1) TUF.

120 The possible sphere of application for the defence is limited. It primarily relates to the sale of dematerialised shares OTC (e.g. shares have been accounted from a sale and purchase agreement which has been later proved void or shares have been transferred, but not registered in the account before) or in the stock exchange (e.g. a sale from someone who is not the owner but has been erroneously entitled off-market to the shares or in the case of an erroneous or fraudulent sale by the custodian) to a good faith purchaser in the event of defect or want of title on the part of the seller. See GP La Sala '*L'acquisto A Non Domino di Strumenti Finanziari Dematerializzati*' (2004) II Banca, Borsa e Titoli di Credito 467.

121 Together with the relevant federal law on securities regulation (e.g. Securities Exchange Act of 1934, 15 USC §§78A *et seq*) and insolvency proceedings of intermediaries (e.g. Bankruptcy Code, Subchapter III (stockbroker liquidation), 11 USC §§741 *et seq* and Securities Investor Protection Act, 15 USC §§78 *et seq*).

122 As of June 1999, the revised version of Article 8 had been adopted by 48 states, the District of Columbia and Puerto Rico, as reported by FJ Facciolo 'Father Knows Best: Revised Article 8 and the Individual Investor' (2000) 27 Fla St U L Rev 616 footnote no 2.

123 See CW Mooney, S Rocks and RS Schwartz 'Article 8 and Review of Other Recent Developments with Investment Securities' 49 (1994) Bus Law 1891.

124 e.g. the Drexel Burnham Lambert Group bankruptcy case reported by CW Mooney Jr 'Beyond Negotiability: A New Model for Transfer and Pledge of Interests in Securities Controlled by Intermediaries' (1990) 12 Cardozo L Rev 315 footnote 13.

125 JS Rogers 'Policy Perspectives on Revised UCC Article 8' (1996) 43 UCLA L Review 1435.

126 JS Rogers 'An Essay on Horseless Carriage and Paperless Negotiable Instruments: Some Lessons from the Article 8 Revision' (1995) 31 Idaho L Rev 689 at 691.

127 For an overview to the development of negotiability of securities in the US, see G Gilmore 'The Commercial Doctrine of Good Faith Purchase' (1954) 63 Yale L J 1057.

Before dealing with the specific rules in the area (section 2.2.2) and discussing their rationale (section 2.2.3), a brief introduction to the peculiar elements of the indirect holding system under UCC Article 8 is provided below (section 2.2.1).

2.2.1. Overview

UCC Article 8 relates to investment securities in general and establishes a separate legal regime for directly (paper-based and uncertificated) and indirectly held securities. In this latter respect, it addresses primarily the problem of the discrepancy between the legal rules for physical delivery of shares certificates (replicated by legal fiction also in 1977 UCC Article 8) and the realities of netting and book entries circulation that are peculiar to the indirect holding system. Part 5 of UCC Article 8, in particular, considers the position of account holders and securities intermediaries. The cornerstone is the concept of securities entitlement as 'the rights and property interest of an entitlement holder with respect to a financial asset specified in Part 5'[128] against the intermediary. Part 5 also clarifies the duties of the intermediary towards entitlement holders.[129]

An investor becomes an entitlement holder (acquiring, therefore, a securities entitlement with respect to a securities account) by book entry, which shows that a financial asset has been credited to a securities account.[130] This mechanism, which closely mirrors the one already observed when discussing the novative nature of the transfer of intermediated shares under English law,[131] is different from the one under the direct holding system based on the rules of transfer for movables. In the indirect holding system, there is no real transfer of securities involved from an identifiable transferor. Settlement is achieved by availing of netting techniques. When an entitlement holder acquires a security entitlement, he simply acquires a new interest. The only reason 'that one would need to trace the path of an individual item of property through the settlement process is to enable one, by the technique made famous to Procustes, to squeeze the analysis into the same conceptual structure used for simple face to face deliveries of discrete identifiable physical objects'.[132]

2.2.2. The Legal Framework for the Protection of the Innocent Purchaser of Intermediated Shares

There is a general defence for the good faith purchaser for value and without notice of directly held shares under UCC Article 8.[133]

128 §8-102 (a)(17).

129 §8-504 to §8-508.

130 §8-501(b)(1).

131 See Chapter 7, section 1.1.4.

132 JS Rogers 'An Essay on Horseless Carriage and Paperless Negotiable Instruments: Some Lessons from the Article 8 Revision' (1995) 31 Idaho L Rev 694.

133 A protected purchaser who obtains control of the security according to the terminology provided under §8-303 (a) and (b).

For the reasons suggested under section 2.2.1, the scenario is different in Part 5 for the indirect holding system. The traditional rules based on the concept of negotiability involving the transfer of discrete chattels from person to person do not operate in modern settlement systems where tracing is *de facto* impossible. Under the legal framework for the indirect holding system provided by UCC Article 8, there is a fundamental rule that protects an innocent purchaser of intermediated shares against adverse claims (i) and two other ones, (ii) and (iii), that address peculiar (sometimes overlapping) factual situations concerning the protection of entitlement holders (or transferees from entitlement holders) against third party claims. Finally, a related provision protects intermediaries in their ordinary transfer activities, (iv). The four provisions operate as follows.

(i) *Protection of an Innocent Purchaser Against Entitlement Holder's Claims: §8–503 (e).* This rule protects innocent purchasers from claims specifically made by entitlement holders and has precedence over rules (ii) and (iii) below. It protects any purchaser of a financial asset or interest therein who gives value, obtains control, and does not act in collusion with the securities intermediary in violating the securities intermediary's obligations under §8–504.[134] Briefly, except under exceptional circumstances,[135] in the case of an unauthorised transfer by the intermediary, the entitlement holder will bring claims against the relevant intermediary and not against the innocent purchaser.[136]

(ii) *Protection of an Entitlement Holder Against Third Party Claims: §8–502.* This is a direct counterpart of the 'protected purchaser rule' mentioned above for the direct holding system.[137] It protects an entitlement holder (and its transferees) who acquires a securities entitlement by a credit to the entitlement holder' securities account from third party claims. It establishes that 'an action based on an adverse claim to a financial asset, whether framed in conversion, replevin, constructive trust, equitable lien, or other theory, may not be asserted against a person who acquires a security entitlement under section 8–501 for value and without notice of the adverse claim'.[138] Notice means 'actual knowledge'[139] or 'wilful blindness' (i.e. notice from a person who deliberately avoids information).[140] However, when the third party claimant is itself an entitlement holder, the rule under (i) applies.

134 i.e. the maintenance of sufficient financial assets.

135 §8–503 (d) and (e).

136 §8–503 (c).

137 §8–303.

138 §8–502.

139 §8–105 (a)(1).

140 §8–105 (a)(2). These novelties, which it is argued have been inserted to minimise confusion (JS Rogers 'Policy Perspectives on Revised UCC Article 8' (1996) 43 UCLA L Rev 1469–73), however, have posed severe concerns as case law suggests. In short, 'there is no legal consensus on the type of notice of adverse claims that is appropriate under Article 8 or on whether there is a difference between good faith and notice' – FJ Facciolo 'Father Knows Best: Revised Article 8 and the Individual Investor' (2000) 27 Fla St U L Rev 658.

(iii) *Protection of an Innocent Purchaser of a Security Entitlement (or an Interest Therein) from the Entitlement Holder: §8–510.* This third rule mirrors the one under (ii) but has a narrower scope. It provides protection for a person (not an entitlement holder) 'who purchases a security entitlement or any interest therein, from an entitlement holder' against adverse claims and if the purchaser 'gives value, does not have notice of the adverse claim, and obtains control'.[141] This usually means that a control agreement whereby the securities intermediary complies with the instructions given by the purchaser without further consent by the entitlement holder has been entered into.[142]

(iv) *Protection of an Innocent Purchaser in the Case of Effective Entitlement Order: §8–115.* Finally, a fourth rule, subject to certain exceptions,[143] protects an innocent purchaser of intermediated shares in case an intermediary transfers a financial asset in response to an effective entitlement order.[144] The scope is to foster the reliability and rapidity of the circulation of securities.

2.2.3. Rationale

The fundamental provision under (i) establishes that, apart from in exceptional circumstances, in the case of unauthorised transfer, the claims of the entitlement holder will be against the relevant intermediary and not against the innocent purchaser.[145] In this way, the transferee is treated as a defendant of last resort. The policy behind this choice is that normally an entitlement holder 'should look only to his or her securities intermediary for performance of the obligations that give content to a securities entitlement. After all, in contrast to the common law concepts underlying 1977 Article 8 that are based on claims to specific physical certificates, Revised Article 8 creates a new type of property interest that is not a claim to a specific identifiable thing; [rather] it is a package of rights and interests that a person has against the person's securities intermediary and the property held by the intermediary'.[146] By assuring that the interest of innocent purchasers is very rarely disputed and that the loss of an unauthorised transfer is usually placed on the intermediaries, it aims to achieve the goal of increasing liquidity in the financial market and settlement finality. In doing so, it clearly distinguishes from English and Italian law and broadly endorses the second approach *de iure condendo* outlined in section 1.5 above.

This interpretation is confirmed by observing, for example, that the traditional requirement of good faith has been deleted from the 1977 version and replaced by the

141 §8–510 (a).
142 §8–106 (d)(2).
143 §8–115 (1)(2)(3).
144 §8–102 (a)(8).
145 Once again, as the commentary to §8–503 describes it, 'the idea that discrete objects might be traced through the hands of different persons has no place in the Revised article rules for the indirect holding system'.
146 FJ Facciolo 'Father Knows Best: Revised Article 8 and the Individual Investor' (2000) 27 Fla St U L Rev 615 at 620.

'notice of adverse claim' (or 'wilful blindness) test ((ii) and (iii)) or, alternatively, by a standard of 'collusion' with the wrongdoer ((i) and (iv)). Although the case law following the 1994 revision of UCC Article 8 seems to suggest that the wilful blindness and collusion standards do not amount to a *de facto* rule of non-liability,[147] it is true that the changes have significant and far-reaching consequences. The introduction of the test of collusion under §8–503, in particular, by not imposing on acquirers of intermediated shares any duty to investigate whether the transferor had the authority to make the transfer, has essentially shifted the burden of proof from the purchaser to the entitlement holder rendering it, together with the mentioned complexities of tracing securities in modern settlement systems, more difficult to bring an action against the transferee.

2.3. *Conclusions*

Section 2 considered the modes of protection of the innocent purchaser of intermediated shares in Italy and under the UCC Article 8. The comparative analysis allowed for a reflection on the different approaches for law reform outlined in the penultimate paragraph of section 1 when dealing with inconsistencies of English law. The scope of the exercise was primarily to provide a wider normative background for the discussion on the process of legal evolution and hybridisation that is addressed in section 3 below.

As for the holder in due course of negotiable instruments under English law, section 2.1 found that Italian law has a general defence for the innocent purchaser of movables, which works by way of analogy for all types of shares (no matter whether they are dematerialised or not) as well as for intermediated shares. This is in line with the first approach for law reform outlined in the penultimate paragraph of section 1. The paradigm is set out by article 1153(1) of the Italian Civil Code. It establishes that a good faith purchaser for value will take good title even though the seller has none, provided that he retains possession over the acquired assets and the transfer has been lawfully executed. The same wording is repeated in article 1994 of the Italian Civil Code for *titoli di credito* and, recently, in the provisions dealing with uncertificated shares which circulate under a mandatory system of intermediation.

UCC Article 8 follows an entirely different route. Broadly in line with the second approach for law reform outlined in the penultimate paragraph of section 1, it argues that the traditional rules based on the concept of negotiability involving the transfer of discrete chattels from person to person cannot operate in modern settlement systems where tracing is virtually impossible. The picture is fragmented into a number of rules, but the fundamental one (§8–503) establishes that, apart from exceptional circumstances, in the case of unauthorised transfer, the claims of the entitlement holder will be against the relevant intermediary and not against the innocent purchaser. The rationale is

[147] *Decker v Yorkton Securities, Inc*, 106 Cal.App. 4th 1315, 131 Cal. Rptr.2d 645, 50 U.C.C. Rep.Serv.2d 271 (1st Dist. 2004); and *H&R Block Financial Advisors, Inc v Express Scripts, Inc*, 426 F.Supp. 2d 656 (E.D. Mich. 2006), later proceeding, 60 U.C.C. Rep. Serv. 2d 656 (E.D. Mich 2006).

straightforward. Security of transaction is achieved by reliance on the stability and reputation of financial intermediaries rather than by the existence of an *ad hoc* rule that protects an innocent purchaser.

3. The Process of Law Reform

It has been argued in section 1 above that the protection available for the innocent purchasers of intermediated shares against adverse claims is somewhat deficient under English law. The *bona fide* purchaser defence operates differently depending on the position of the seller in the chain of intermediation, depending on whether the innocent purchaser acquires legal title or an equitable interest. This disparity, it has been suggested, does not have a convincing legal rationale. Moreover, it may also have unwelcome economic effects as the level of risk for purchasers may reduce their willingness to invest. In a broader perspective, it may deprive the English securities market of the benefits of intermediation altogether and cause potential negative competitive consequences *vis-à-vis* other jurisdictions.

A vigorous debate on law reform in this area emerged in 2004 in England with the publication of the already mentioned FMLC report,[148] later reiterated in substance by the Law Commission in 2008.[149] This fact is *per se* quite surprising, as the issue cannot be regarded a novelty. The system of indirect holding has been dominant in financial markets at least since the 'paper crunch' in the 1970s. In the larger picture, the disparity in the protection of innocent purchasers of propriety from a trustee or from a sub-trustee dates back to the historical roots of the jurisdictional dichotomy between equity and common law. It has survived unchanged for centuries until today, apparently for no substantial reason.

Reflecting on these peculiar elements also in the light of the different scenarios resulting from the comparative investigation developed in section 2, this section critically deals with the current law reform process. For this purpose, it looks at the proposals made by the Law Commission (section 3.1) and it examines the specific provisions of the Geneva Securities Convention (section 3.2). The two projects take different views. However, it is questionable whether they are really alternatives. Now that the Convention has been finalised, it is unlikely that the recommendations of the Law Commission to change English law will be followed. The concrete possibility that the Convention will soon be ratified (or transposed in similar form in a European instrument) recommends that domestic legislation not be changed, but that it be amended immediately after. Under the force of this pragmatic argument, the inquiry on legal change below acknowledges the contribution made by the Law Commission in the area, but focuses primarily on the enacted provisions of the Geneva Securities Convention. In doing so, it

148 FMLC *Property Interests in Investment Securities – Issue 3* (5 July 2004) available at <www.fmlc.org/papers/fmlc1_3_july04.pdf> (accessed 7 August 2013).

149 Law Commission *UNIDROIT Convention on Substantive Rules Regarding Intermediated Securities – Further Advice to HM Treasury* (May 2008) available at <www.lawcom.gov.uk/docs/intermediated_securities_advice_May2008.pdf> (accessed 7 August 2013).

concludes that the regime of the Geneva Securities Convention represents the outcome of the first step of a process of hybridisation. It also shows that England (and, similarly, any other jurisdiction) will take one step of a process of hybridisation when implementing the Convention (section 3.3).

3.1. *The Recommendations of the Law Commission*

Consistent with the FMLC arguments for passing domestic legislation to rectify certain deficiencies of English law,[150] the Law Commission examined the level of protection currently available to innocent purchasers of intermediated securities against the adverse claims of third parties. At the end of the inquiry, it made recommendations for the creation of a legal defence. The proposal is sketched below in section 3.1.1 together with an explanation for the choice under section 3.1.2.

3.1.1. Amendments to the Existing Law

The remedy proposed by the Law Commission to address the disparity in the protection of innocent purchasers of intermediated shares does not clash with the fundamental principles of English property law. It amounts to an extension of the sphere of application of the *bona fide* purchaser rule to protect the innocent purchasers of equitable intermediated shares. More accurately,[151] the defence consists in an amendment of equitable priority rules such that the purchaser's equitable interest in intermediated shares is unaffected (albeit not superior) by earlier equities and equitable interests. The rationale is that 'of the two innocent parties, it is the claimant that permitted the fraud or in some way allowed the fraudster to represent itself as the unencumbered owner. Accordingly, the equitable interest of the good faith purchaser without notice should prevail.'[152]

In line with FMLC recommendations,[153] however, the sphere of application of the defence made by the Law Commission is limited when the transfer relates to a pooled account. In that case, the risk of unauthorised transfers by an intermediary who later becomes insolvent and is unable to make up the shortfall has to be shared between the original account holders and the innocent purchaser. There is in fact no justification for treating the original account holder and the purchaser differently. The underlying principle is that account holders that choose to hold securities through a pooled account accept the same custody risk. This means that the availability of the *bona fide*

150 FMLC *Property Interests in Investment Securities – Issue 3* (5 July 2004) available at <www.fmlc.org/papers/fmlcl_3_july04.pdf> (accessed 7 August 2013), Principle 7(e) at 25.

151 In line with fundamental jurisdictional issues on the essential nature of the defence. See DB O'Sullivan 'The Rule in *Phillips v Phillips*' (2002) 118 LQR 296 at 302.

152 Law Commission *UNIDROIT Convention on Substantive Rules Regarding Intermediated Securities – Further Advice to HM Treasury* (May 2008) available at <www.lawcom.gov.uk/docs/intermediated_securities_advice_May2008.pdf> (accessed 7 August 2013).

153 FMLC *Property Interests in Investment Securities – Issue 3* (5 July 2004) and available at <www.fmlc.org/papers/fmlcl_3_july04.pdf> (accessed 7 August 2013), Principle 7(e) at 25.

purchaser defence does not entirely nullify the original owner's own equitable interest in the pool.

In short, according to the Law Commission, the innocent purchaser's interest in the intermediated securities should be unaffected by prior equitable interests or equities of which it had no notice. However, when the transfer is unauthorised within a pooled account and the intermediary is unable to make up the shortfall, the purchaser does not have a superior equity to the original owner. The purchaser 'will instead share *pro rata* in any loss with the other account holders in the pool'.[154]

3.1.2. Other Possible Options

In endorsing this discrete approach to law reform, the Law Commission rejected the idea of creating a new conceptual model along the lines of Article 8 UCC or a new domestic proprietary framework for intermediated securities.[155] The proposed amendments were regarded to be of rapid implementation and in line with the mandate from the Treasury. The underlying assumption was also that it was uncertain whether a final agreement for the Convention could have been reached in the short term or whether the EU would have adopted the model proposed in the Convention.

As already suggested, with the completion of the diplomatic Conference in Geneva and the adoption of a final text for the UNIDROIT project, the scenario has changed and the proposals made by the Law Commission have lost part of their strength.

3.2. *The Geneva Securities Convention*

This second section presents the provisions of the Geneva Securities Convention relating to the protection of an innocent purchaser of intermediated securities under 3.2.1 together with some observations from the preparatory works under 3.2.2. The results are compared briefly with the findings of the parallel European project carried out by the LCG/Consultation Document under 3.2.3. Building on the analysis of English law set out in section 1 and on the comparative inquiry presented in section 2, the scope of this section is to assess in detail the formation of most relevant law reform initiative in the area for the benefit of the analysis of legal change and hybridisation addressed in section 3.3.

154 Law Commission *UNIDROIT Convention on Substantive Rules Regarding Intermediated Securities – Further Advice to HM Treasury* (May 2008) available at <www.lawcom.gov.uk/docs/intermediated_securities_advice_May2008.pdf> (accessed 7 August 2013) 123.

155 Ibid 118. The report is based on the findings of R Goode (now in L Gullifer *Goode on Legal Problems of Credit and Security* (Sweet & Maxwell London 2008) 239) on intermediated shares as bundles of personal and co-ownership rights separate from the underlying securities. See also the analysis proposed by M Khimji 'Intermediary Credit Risk – A Comparative Law Analysis of Property Rights in Indirectly Held Securities' (2005) JBL 287 at 316.

3.2.1. The Legal Framework

The cornerstone for the protection of the innocent purchasers of intermediates shares under the Geneva Securities Convention is Article 18.[156] This rule provides the 'minimum harmonisation' standard. According to the Official Commentary, it sets out a 'last in time' priority rule reflecting 'the general idea that once a person has acquired a right or interest over intermediated securities for value and unless the person has actual knowledge or ought to know of the relevant interest or fact, no adverse claim can be asserted against that person'.[157]

In the first paragraph, it protects an acquirer[158] against competing claims from third parties. More accurately, when a person has purchased at the 'relevant time'[159] for value and without notice (or constructive notice)[160] of third party's interest or rights an interest in intermediated shares by way of credit[161] or according to the other methods provided in the Convention,[162] three forms of protection are available. First, the acquirer's right or interest in intermediated securities is not subject to adverse claim.[163] Second, the acquirer is not liable to the adverse claimant (a general immunity from liability).[164] Third, the credit, designating entry or interest granted is not rendered invalid, ineffective against third parties or liable to be reversed based on an earlier credit, designating entry or interest granted in violation of the rights of the adverse claimant.[165]

156 An outline of the relevant issues in a comparative perspective is offered by CW Mooney and H Kanda 'Core Issues under the UNIDROIT (Geneva) Convention on Intermediated Securities: Views from the United States and Japan' in L Gullifer and J Payne (eds) *Intermediated Securities – Legal Problems and Practical Issues* (Hart Oxford 2010) 94; and L Thevenoz 'Transfer of Intermediated Securities' in P Conac, U Segna and L Thevenoz (eds) *Intermediated Securities – The Impact of the Geneva Securities Convention and the Future European Legislation* (CUP Cambridge 2013) 151.

157 H Kanda, C Mooney, L Thevenoz and S Beraud with the assistance of T Keijser on behalf of the UNIDROIT Secretariat *Official Commentary on the UNIDROIT Convention on Substantive Rules for Intermediated Securities* (OUP Oxford 2012) 113–114.

158 The definition of acquirer is provided under Article 17(a). He is any person who acquires an interest in intermediated securities by credit (Article 11) or by the granting of an interest according to the methods set out in Article 12 (grant to the relevant intermediary, designating entry or control agreement).

159 i.e. the time that the credit is made or the time specified under Article 19(3).

160 The sphere of application of the notion of constructive notice ('ought to know') is provided under Article 17(b). This element should be applied in the light of the peculiar circumstances applicable to intermediated shares (Article 17(b)(i)) and it does not impose on an acquirer a general duty of inquiry or investigation (Article 17(b)(ii)). Mere negligence is not enough.

161 Article 11.

162 Article 12.

163 Article 18(1)(a).

164 Article 18(1)(b).

165 Article 18(1)(c).

Article 18(2) protects a purchaser from the risks arising from 'earlier defective entries'.[166] It clarifies that a purchaser without notice (or constructive notice)[167] of an earlier defective entry acquires an interest in intermediated shares and is protected from entries' invalidity or reversal made by its relevant intermediary. Contrary to the case of the first paragraph, this one is subject to the provisions of the uniform rules of a securities system or an account agreement.[168] This means that if the relevant rule of the securities settlement system so provides,[169] in case of defective entry, the book entry is liable to be reversed.

Unless the acquirer's interest is a security interest,[170] an innocent acquirer by way of gift or otherwise gratuitously is not eligible for protection under paragraphs one and two.[171]

Failure to qualify for the innocent acquisition protection under the first two paragraphs of Article 18 does not necessarily mean that the defence is unavailable: it simply means that the framework of the Convention does not apply and the applicable (national) law will solve the issues on third party claims and reversibility of the book entries.[172] Symmetrically, the rules of the Convention operate even if the applicable (national) law does not provide any protection for the innocent purchaser of intermediated shares.

3.2.2. Genesis of Article 18 and the Debate in the Preparatory Works

The wording of Article 18 closely replicates the provision on the protection of innocent acquirers contained in the preliminary draft Convention adopted by the CGE at its fourth session.[173]

166 The definition of 'defective entry' is provided under Article 17(d). A defective entry is a credit or a designating entry that is invalid or liable to be reversed (or a conditional entry that is rendered invalid or liable to be reversed as a result of a condition that is not fulfilled) according to the non-Convention law and, in some circumstances, to the account agreement or the uniform rules of a securities settlement system (Article 16).

167 See the explanation provided above on the notion of constructive notice according to the Convention.

168 Article 18(5).

169 And unless one of the grounds of defence in Article 18(1) applies.

170 This exception finds its rationale in the need to extend the protection of Article 18 to security interests granted by one corporate affiliate to secure the obligations of another affiliate.

171 Article 18(3).

172 Article 18(4).

173 Article 14 of the UNIDROIT – CGE for the Preparation of Harmonised Substantive Rules regarding Intermediated Securities (fourth session) *Preliminary Draft Convention and Explanatory Notes to the Preliminary Draft Convention* (May 2007) Docs 94 and 95 (paras 159–166), part of Study LXVIII <www.unidroit.org/english/documents/2007/study78/s-78-094-e.pdf> and <www.unidroit.org/english/documents/2007/study78/s-78-095-e.pdf> (accessed 7 August 2013). The genesis of Article 14 can be traced by referring to earlier documents discussed by CGE for the Preparation of Harmonised Substantive Rules regarding Intermediated Securities in various sessions (e.g. Doc 24 – Articles 7.6 and 11; Doc 42 – Article 7; Doc 57 – Article 12 and Doc 74, available at <www.unidroit.org/english/conventions/2009intermediatedsecurities/study78-archive-e.htm#NR2> (accessed 7 August 2013).

The rule originated from the search for a uniform (functional) standard for protecting innocent acquirers capable of application at national level regardless of the local legal characterisation of intermediated securities and the methods of transfer. The drafting group of the CGE agreed on a final text which replaced the traditional concept of good faith acquisition valid for tangible property for a 'more neutral and fact-based language'[174] related to book-entries based on a test of 'knowledge or wilful blindness' before the end of the fourth session.

In the penultimate day of the plenary, however, the French delegation criticised the results of the negotiations as they could give rise to a substantial level of uncertainty[175] and suggested to amend the agreed provision by referring to domestic (non-Convention) law for establishing when a person has wrongful knowledge. Following an intense debate among the delegates of the CGE, it was concluded that there was not sufficient consensus on the appropriate test for innocent acquisition and a post-sessional working group (chaired by Spain) was formed to explore the possible normative options.[176] Two alternatives were examined, other than the residual possible opting in/out mechanisms available when signing the Convention. The first one was based on a direct *renvoi* to national law. This could have allowed signatories to preserve settled concepts of national legal tradition such as good faith (e.g. Italy and France), avoiding possible conflicts with uniform standards (e.g. constructive notice or wilful blindness) of uncertain application and often unknown to the jurisdiction. The second one considered a harmonised standard founded on the notion of knowledge of the adverse claim and the wilful blindness test. This could have promoted predictability among operators and it could have addressed certain conflict of laws concerns. Above all, it would have been more in line with international market practice as the traditional good faith clause more appropriately relate the circulation of movables based on possession rather to book-entry securities.

The responses of national delegations to a specific questionnaire prepared by the working group clearly supported the second option and argued for a harmonised Convention standard in line with the wilful blindness standard already considered by the CGE at its fourth session.[177] This view was reiterated in the final report of the working

174 See UNIDROIT – CGE for the Preparation of Harmonised Substantive Rules regarding Intermediated Securities (first session) *Preliminary Draft Convention and Explanatory Notes to the Preliminary Draft Convention* (May 2007) Doc 19, part of Study LXVIII <www.unidroit.org/english/documents/2004/study78/s-78–019-e.pdf> (accessed 7 August 2013).

175 UNIDROIT – CGE for the Preparation of Harmonised Substantive Rules regarding Intermediated Securities (fourth session) *Preliminary Draft Convention and Explanatory Notes to the Preliminary Draft Convention* (May 2007) Doc 95 – Appendix 4, part of Study LXVIII <www.unidroit.org/english/documents/2007/study78/s-78–095-e.pdf> (accessed 7 August 2013).

176 Ibid Doc 95 (para 248), part of Study LXVIII <www.unidroit.org/english/documents/2007/study78/s-78–095-e.pdf> (accessed 7 August 2013).

177 UNIDROIT – contributions to the working group on the *Preliminary Draft Convention and Explanatory Notes to the Preliminary Draft Convention* (May 2007) Docs 97–107, 109, 112 and 114, part of Study LXVIII <www.unidroit.org/english/conventions/2009intermediatedsecurities/study78-archive-e.htm#NR4> (accessed 7 August 2013).

group before the Diplomatic Conference in 2008[178] and, as seen above, has been finally endorsed in the first two paragraphs of Article 18.

3.2.3. The Advice of the LCG/Consultation Document

The 2008 recommendations of the LCG, which constitute the blueprint for the future EU legislation,[179] are consistent in substance with the wording of Article 18 of the Geneva Securities Convention. The underlying assumption is in fact similar.[180] The traditional version of the *bona fide* purchaser rule that protects the innocent acquirer for value without notice of adverse claims is problematic when employed in relation to the circulation of intermediated shares. In that context the idea of having a transfer of definite shares between identifiable parties is fictitious. What matters is rather that an account holder is able to rely on a credit in his account. Against this background, the LCG argues for a harmonised protection rule 'based on a purely functional provision without allusions to traditional legal concepts and employ neutral terminology in order to avoid misinterpretation'.[181]

This rule is now established in Recommendation 7. It relies on the concept that an account holder whose account is credited acquires good title to the book-entry securities unless he has knowledge (or constructive knowledge) that the account should not have been credited. The same applies to the acquirer of a security interest in the account. No reference is made to the protection against the risks arising from 'earlier defective entries'. The provision now contained in the second paragraph of Article 18 of the Geneva Securities Convention has probably been regarded superfluous as most of the cases of detective entries are already covered in the general provision that protects an innocent acquirer from competing claims from another person.

Similarly, under Principle 8 of the Consultation Document, the national law of Member States must 'ensure' that an account holder is protected against reversal of crediting and earmarking, unless such person knew or ought to have known that the relevant credit or earmarking should not have been made. While it has to be observed that the sphere of application of Principle 8 of the Consultation Document is narrower than Article 18 of the Geneva Securities Convention, as it deals, probably for the purpose of consultation, exclusively with the validity or irreversibility of book-entries,[182] the innocence test is substantially the same.

[178] UNIDROIT – *Diplomatic Conference to adopt a Convention on Substantive Rules regarding Intermediated Securities (first session)* (September 2008) Doc 8, part of Study LXVIII <www.unidroit.org/english/documents/2003/study78/s-78-008-e.pdf> (accessed 7 August 2013).

[179] P Paech and K Lober 'Post-trading of securities: shaping the European Response to Legal Barriers' (2009) 4 JIBFL 211.

[180] Second Advice of the Legal Certainty Group *Solutions to Barriers related to Post-Trading within the EU* (August 2008) available at <www.ec.europa.eu/internal_market/financial-markets/docs/certainty/2ndadvice_final_en.pdf> (accessed 7 August 2013).

[181] *Second Advice of the Legal Certainty Group Solutions to Barriers related to Post-Trading within the EU* (August 2008) 60, available at <www.ec.europa.eu/internal_market/financial-markets/docs/certainty/2ndadvice_final_en.pdf> (accessed 7 August 2013).

[182] i.e. not considering other types of claims resulting from the acquisition. See L Thevenoz 'Transfer of Intermediated Securities' in P Conac, U Segna and L Thevenoz (eds) *Intermediated Securities – The*

3.3. *Legal Change and Hybridisation*

The analysis above has outlined two very different normative ways to tackle the same issue of legal uncertainty. The model proposed by the Law Commission is in line with the first scenario pictured under section 1.5.1. It does not offer a general defence for the innocent purchasers of shares as has been observed for Italian law, but it extends the protection available for the *bona fide* purchaser of intermediated shares when the acquired property rights are equitable. Arguing that there are no convincing legal or economic reasons why purchasers should be treated differently depending on whether the intermediary's unauthorised transfer consists in the transfer of legal title or of an equitable interest, the proposal aims to amend a specific deficiency of English law.

The approach is different under the Geneva Securities Convention. This does not consist in an *ad hoc* amendment of the current law. It is also distinct from the procedural bar against adverse claims pictured in the scenario under section 1.5.2 and under UCC Article 8. Within a new comprehensive framework on the circulation of intermediated securities, it amounts to the creation of a defence entailing a minimum level of protection for innocent purchasers.

Notwithstanding the differences, the two models are not *per se* irreconcilable. Their relationship could be described as one of *genus ad speciem*. As the Law Commission submitted, incorporating the Convention into English law would adequately rectify the existing disparity 'by granting purchasers of intermediated securities a level of protection that closely matches that of purchasers of directly held securities'.[183] What is peculiar and distinctive in the projects is the pattern of legal change. While the Law Commission's proposal is the result of a unilateral national initiative to correct existing law, the Geneva Securities Convention is part of a supranational project for law reform aimed at 'establishing finality and repose in the financial markets'.[184] It is argued below that this latter pattern of legal evolution is reminiscent of the one observed in Part II where the phenomenon of assimilation and interaction between legal cultures was explained in terms of hybridisation. Similar arguments to the ones employed to understand the process of cross-cultural exchange between imported legal models and indigenous legal traditions can be used by analogy to explain the formation of an international legislative instrument. As borrowed legal paradigms become unsettled outside their original context and indigenous traditions do not survive their original identities when in contact with foreign models, national models lose their particular meanings in the interaction with others during the negotiations in the drafting of the Geneva Securities Convention. The final system for innocent acquisition of intermediated shares provided under

Impact of the Geneva Securities Convention and the Future European Legislation (CUP Cambridge 2013) 153.

183 Law Commission *UNIDROIT Convention on Substantive Rules Regarding Intermediated Securities – Further Advice to HM Treasury* (May 2008) available at < www.lawcom.gov.uk/docs/intermediated_securities_advice_May2008.pdf> (accessed 7 August 2013) 93.

184 CW Mooney and H Kanda 'Core Issues under the UNIDROIT (Geneva) Convention on Intermediated Securities: Views from the United States and Japan' in L Gullifer and J Payne (eds) *Intermediated Securities – Legal Problems and Practical Issues* (Hart Oxford 2010) 96.

Article 18 has unique doctrinal characteristics clearly distinguishable from the legal tradition of the various contributors. It is more than a functional compromise that mirrors the pre-existing legal frameworks. It is a new (hybrid) model in its own right. When implemented under its hegemonic force in the national legal system, this same model will vary considerably along different lines depending on the existing legal tradition and mechanisms of transposition.[185] In other words, this process of reception involves a second step of hybridisation. Similarly to the colonial context, neither colonial norms nor indigenous traditions survive, but both give way to an entirely new system of doing things and perceiving meanings, which is peculiar to each colonial situation. In short, a new legal tradition, a third space that is peculiar to the specific contact situation is created in each step of hybridisation.

In the light of the relevance of these arguments for the scope of this study, and considering that, as already suggested, it is questionable whether the two projects really are alternative, the following inquiry will specifically show that the provision of the Geneva Securities Convention on the protection of the innocent purchaser of intermediated securities is the result of a process of hybridisation. More accurately, it will consider the formation, under section 3.3.1, and the possible consequences of its implementation, under section 3.3.2, as evidence of two steps of the same process of hybridisation.

3.3.1. First Step

Article 18 of the Geneva Securities Convention is the final result of a complex *iter* of negotiations. This is clear when reflecting on the wording of the provision and when observing the history of the preparatory works. It does not mirror one single normative model, but it weights and takes into account elements of different legal traditions. While there has always been wide consensus between delegates on the necessity of providing an adequate level of protection to innocent acquirers, finding a solution consistent with the different national characterisations of the rights over intermediated securities (property/obligation/entitlement) and the modes of transfer proved to be challenging. The final compromise was achieved by keeping the wording of the provision as neutral and fact-based as possible in compliance with the functional approach.

Achieving the perfect equilibrium was however not always possible. Elements pertaining to various legal traditions can be clearly traced in the current text. The similarity with non-conventional laws, however, does not transform Article 18 into a mere blueprint of one or several legal traditions. This is also because, as observed with the pattern of borrowing and reception in Parts I and II, legal paradigms outside their original meanings become unsettled. They interact at different levels with other traditions not surviving in their original identities but creating an entirely new legal space peculiar to the specific contact situation.

185 See the analysis of H Kronke 'Remarks on the Geneva Securites Convention's Development and its Future' in L Gullifer and J Payne (eds) *Intermediated Securities – Legal Problems and Practical Issues* (Hart Oxford 2010) 248.

More accurately, Article 18 provides a harmonised defence for innocent purchasers of indirectly held shares. This approach is different from the one endorsed by UCC Article 8 for indirectly held securities where the requirement for the account holder to bring an action first against its own intermediary and only after certain factual criteria have been satisfied against an innocent purchaser *de facto* creates a procedural bar against claims[186] rather than a defence. The 'collusion test' under UCC Article 8, in particular, switches the burden of proof from the purchaser to the claimant (better, the entitlement holder) and imposes a standard of fault (wrongful conduct) considerably higher than the test of knowledge set out by the Convention.[187]

That said, the way the defence is structured does not replicate the existing paradigm under Italian law and under English law. It is not based on the general concept of good faith, but on the notion of purchaser's knowledge (or constructive knowledge) of an existing interest. This is consistent with the general test for notice of an adverse claim established for all investment securities (directly and indirectly held) under UCC Article 8.[188] The argument is that this scheme is a better adapted test for modern securities markets where the notion of constructive possession of traceable assets based on good faith is difficult to apply. It also make it possible to reduce the courts' discretion in considering the constituting elements of innocent acquisition. Even the level of knowledge required by the Convention distinguishes it from current English law with respect to transactions involving financial instruments,[189] and it closely mirrors the general pro-purchaser provision for investment securities under UCC Article 8.[190] Although it is questionable whether the test for constructive notice based on the possible existence of earlier rights established by the Court of Appeal in *Barclays Bank plc v O'Brien*[191] is of general application,[192] 'removing any obligation to investigate suspicious facts and attributing constructive notice only to purchasers that deliberately avoid information', as established by the Convention 'is probably a step beyond where the courts have reached',[193] in England. By considering the opposite view, it should however be clear that the employment of the knowledge test outside of the proprietary canon of

186 See UCC §8–503(d) and (e).

187 Article 18(1) and (2).

188 UCC §8–105(a)(2).

189 In commercial transaction, constructive notice has no role to play *Manchester Trust v Furness* [1895] 2 QB 539 at 545. In transactions involving land the general rule under section 199 of the Law of Property Act 1925 applies.

190 UCC §8–105(a)(2).

191 [1994] 1 AC 180 *per* Lord Browne-Wilinson at 196. See A Lawson 'O'Brien and its Legacy: Principle, Equity and Certainty?' (1995) 54 CLJ 280 at 283.

192 See *Macmillan Inc v Bishopsgate Trust (No 3)* [1995] 1 WLR 978 *per* Millett J at 1014.

193 Law Commission *UNIDROIT Convention on Substantive Rules Regarding Intermediated Securities – Further Advice to HM Treasury* (May 2008) available at <www.lawcom.gov.uk/docs/intermediated_securities_advice_May2008.pdf> (accessed 7 August 2013) 70; and UNIDROIT – CGE for the Preparation of Harmonised Substantive Rules regarding Intermediated Securities Informal Working Group on Article 14 of the Draft Convention (submitted by the delegation of the United Kingdom) Doc 106, part of Study LXVIII <www.unidroit.org/english/documents/2008/study78/s-78-106-e.pdf> (accessed 7 August 2013) 3.

'securities entitlement' and its context produces an entirely different result from the one promoted by UCC Article 8.

All in all, Article 18 contains elements from all the different models described in this chapter and takes into account the approaches described under section 1.5. The final outcome, however, is a normative model, a third space that is peculiar to the contact situations experienced during the negotiations of the Convention. It is the outcome of a process of hybridisation where fragments of national contributions remained 'almost the same, but not quite'[194] and which does not amount to the mere sum of features of identifiable legal traditions, but a new legal creation in its own right.

3.3.2. Second Step

The possible ratification and implementation into national law of the Convention represent the second step in the process of hybridisation. This is based on the supremacy of the international instrument over the national legal framework and reflects the notion of hegemony. In essence, as has been seen for the description of the dominance relationship between colonisers and colonised set out in Part I, the interaction of the Convention with the pre-existing legal tradition will be construed on the primacy of the international instrument and will produce different results through a process of hybridisation. The differences arise from the interaction of the scheme of protection of innocent purchasers in intermediated systems endorsed by the Convention with the existing legal framework. It is difficult to predict whether the transposition of the Convention will have a limited impact on English law or whether it will have more radical consequences (possibly drawing from *Cukurova* examined before), casting doubts on the maintenance of a distinction between legal and equitable title in modern financial markets. What is certain is that the outcome will vary from jurisdiction to jurisdiction, depending on the similarity of the existing legal framework to the model offered by the Convention. The case of the implementation of the Financial Collateral Directive[195] in European Member States provides a good example in this respect. Even if the transposition in the UK[196] was less radical than in other Member States reflecting a pre-existing business practice,[197] very significant concerns arose in relation to the impact of the notion of control (and the exemption from the requirement to register security) on floating charges[198] as in contrast with their essential characteristic based on the collateral

194 H Bhabha 'Of Mimicry and Men' in Id (ed) *The Location of Culture* (Routledge London 1994) 123.

195 Directive 2002/47/EC on financial collateral arrangements (Financial Collateral Directive) [2002] OJL168/43, as amended by Directive 2009/44/EC.

196 Financial Collateral Arrangements (No 2) Regulations 2003, as amended by the Financial Markets and Insolvency (Settlement Finality and Financial Collateral Arrangements) (Amendment) Regulations 2010.

197 This is the case of TTCA or outright collateral transfers according to the terminology used by J Benjamin before the enactment of the Financial Collateral Directive. See J Benjamin *Interests in Securities* (OUP Oxford 2000) 83 and Chapter 7.

198 Financial Collateral Arrangements (No 2) Regulations 2003, as amended by the Financial Markets and Insolvency (Settlement Finality and Financial Collateral Arrangements) (Amendment) Regulations 2010, reg 3(2). See J Perkins 'Registration of Charges over Intangibles' (2010) 4 LFMR 360 at 361.

giver freedom to deal with the charged assets.[199] As the case law demonstrated,[200] these concerns were peculiar to the implementation of the Directive in England and were not faced in other Member States, making the English regime an original hybrid model resulting from the interaction between the international normative instrument and the pre-existing legal framework.[201]

The effect of this process of hybridisation through implementation will be amplified by the wording of Article 18, which allows national law to provide protection for the innocent purchaser outside its direct sphere of application. The failure to qualify for Article 18 protection does not in fact cancel the availability of other defences for the innocent purchasers under the applicable law. Apart from the possible existence of particular national alternatives, it is possible that these defences may possibly unevenly allow for a wider sphere protection for the innocent acquirers. This is the case, for example, of purchasers of securities and depository instruments settled in CREST who do not need to show they had constructive notice[202] as required by the Convention.

3.4. *Conclusions*

This section discussed the law reform process relating to the protection of innocent purchasers of intermediated shares against adverse claims under English law. The proposals made by the Law Commission and the provisions of the Geneva Securities Convention were considered in the first two sections.

The Law Commission found unjustifiable the current distinction based on whether the innocent purchaser acquires legal title or an equitable interest to shares. It made *ad hoc* recommendations to rectify the legal framework so that the purchaser's equitable interest in intermediated shares is unaffected by earlier equities and equitable interests. In doing so, it rejected the idea of creating a new conceptual domestic proprietary framework for intermediated securities. The Geneva Securities Convention, on the other hand, established a 'minimum harmonisation' standard structured on a neutral and fact-based language related to book-entries and based on a test of knowledge. In essence, when a person acquires a right or interest over intermediated securities for value and without notice, no adverse claim can be asserted against that person. The scope is to protect an acquirer against competing claims from third parties and against the risks arising from earlier defective entries. Failure to qualify for the innocent acquisition

199 See *National Westminster Bank plc v Spectrum Plus Limited* [2005] UKHL 41; and *Re Cosslett (Contractors) Ltd* [1999] 1 BCLC 205 (CA) *per* Millet LJ 217. See J Benjamin *Financial Law* (OUP Oxford 2008) 478 and on the possible inclusion of the floating charges in the scope of the Geneva Securities Convention, see A Zacaroli 'Taking Security over Intermediated Securities: Chapter V of the UNIDROIT (Geneva) Convention on Intermediated Securities' in L Gullifer and J Payne (eds) *Intermediated Securities – Legal Problems and Practical Issues* (Hart Oxford 2010) 186.

200 *Gray v G-T-P Group Limited, Re F2G Realisations Limited (in liquidation)* [2010] EWHC 1772 (Ch) paragraphs 58–62 *per* Vos J.

201 See the critical analysis on the implementation of the Directive in general and on floating charges in particular offered by G Gretton 'Financial Collateral and the Fundamentals of Secured Transactions' (2006) 10 Edin LR 209 at 230.

202 USR 2001(SI 2001/3755) reg 35(5)(a).

protection under the Geneva Securities Convention does not imply *per se* that the defence is unavailable. It simply means that it will be for the applicable (national) law to solve the issues on third party claims and reversibility of the book entries.

The last section suggested that the two projects are not *per se* irreconcilable. Rather, their relationship should be described as one of *genus ad speciem*. What really distinguishes them is the pattern of legal change. While the Law Commission's proposal is the result of a unilateral national initiative, the Geneva Securities Convention is part of a larger supranational project for law reform involving long negotiations between national delegates at international *fora*. This latter pattern, it has been claimed, closely mirrors the one observed in Part II where the phenomenon of assimilation and interaction between legal cultures was described in term of hybridisation. The resulting instrument is a new legal creation in its own right and not the mere sum of features of identifiable legal backgrounds. It is also the starting point for understanding a (possible) second step of hybridisation based on the supremacy of the international instrument over the national legal framework and on the notion of hegemony. This consists in the implementation of the international instrument in the national legal framework. In essence, as was seen in Part I for describing the dominance relationship between colonisers and colonised, the interaction of the Convention with the pre-existing legal tradition will be construed on the primacy of the international instrument and it will produce different original national results through a process of hybridisation.

Summary

SUMMARY OF PART III

Part III looked at the process of legal change in the area of post-trading following the growth of intermediation in financial markets and considered the mechanism of circulation of (interests) in shares.

Chapter 6 was introductory. It clarified the meaning of the move from direct to indirect (book-entry) holdings, from the pattern of holding shares to the one of holding interests/entitlements in shares where investors purchase and sell and provide collateral to secured lenders on their holdings by means of book-entries made in the securities account kept with the intermediary. It then considered some of the most significant sources of legal risk arising from the evolution of financial practice, giving special attention to certain deficiencies and ambiguities in English law and arguing for law reform. The analysis was carried out by focusing on three examples of substantive English law raised by the FMLC and by sketching the major causes of ambiguity in the area of conflict of laws. Not addressing the uncertainties associated with domestic/cross-border transfers of intermediated shares and the legal risk arising from certain conceptual incompatibilities may leave investors in a weaker position than when they hold the securities directly from the issuer. This was regarded as an unwelcome scenario that might, in turn, undermine the attractiveness of the indirect holding system and, possibly, the efficiency of financial markets. Building on this picture, Chapter 6 assessed the responses to legal uncertainty provided by two of the most relevant existing normative projects with a view to creating an harmonised international regime on the transfer of indirectly held securities: the Geneva Securities Convention and the EU Commission project on clearing and settlement. The analysis was carried out by focusing on three issues of legal uncertainty raised by the FMLC report to see how they had been addressed in the Geneva Securities Convention and in the 2008 LCG Advice/Consultation Document. By considering the process of legal evolution that led to the final text of the Convention and estimating its possible implementation in England, the normative inquiry suggested that that pattern can be described in terms of hybridisation by way of analogy with postcolonial arguments addressed in Part I. In the course of the negotiations traceable in the history of the preparatory works contained in the Official Commentary to the Geneva Securities Convention,[1] national models lost their peculiar meanings in the interaction with others.

1 H Kanda, C Mooney, L Thevenoz and S Beraud with the assistance of T Keijser on behalf of the UNIDROIT Secretariat *Official Commentary on the UNIDROIT Convention on Substantive Rules for*

Delegations contributed at different levels and with different weight to the shaping of a final 'hybrid' model. As a consequence, the final product does not reproduce the same traits as the original ones nor is it a mere fusion of the various contributions. A confirmation of the observed two-step process of hybridisation was found in relation to the formation of other supranational normative instruments such as EU Directives. Specific reference was made to the notion of appropriation employed in Directive 2002/47 on financial collateral arrangements as discussed in the reasoning of the Judicial Committee of the Privy Council in *Cukurova Finance International Limited v Alfa Telecom Turkey Ltd.*[2]

Chapter 7 followed from the general discussion developed in Chapter 6 and considered the specific property law issue of whether the innocent purchaser for value of intermediated shares is adequately protected under English law. In line with the conclusions of the FMLC and the Law Commission, it argued that this was not the case. Existing legal concepts do not adequately meet the practical needs of investors in intermediated shares, and legislative intervention is highly desirable to keep up with changing financial practice. With the exception of share warrants to bearer and certain cases based on estoppel, the innocent purchaser of shares from someone who is not the owner is never protected at common law. It is irrelevant whether the innocent transferee acquired title to shares in good faith and for value. The default rule for the transfer of title at common law is *nemo dat quod non habet*. The scenario with respect to intermediated shares is not different. Although equity has a general defence that protects a good faith purchaser of legal title for value without notice of prior equitable rights, it is not always available for the innocent purchaser of intermediated share. This is because unless intermediated shares are acquired directly from the trustee, purchasers of intermediated shares in financial markets obtain a beneficial interest in the shares held by the sub-trustee and not a legal estate. As between two equitable interests the general rule, similar in substance to *nemo dat*, is *qui prior est in tempore potior in iure*. In other words, there is a disparity in the degree of protection available along the chain of indirect holding depending on whether the innocent purchaser acquires legal title or an equitable interest to shares, apparently without justification. It lacks a logical rationale in allowing a different regime between categories of innocent purchasers of intermediated shares depending on their position in the chain of intermediation.

In the light of this inconsistency and following a comparative analysis of the methods of protection of the innocent purchaser of intermediated shares under Italian law and under the Uniform Commercial Code, the last part of Chapter 7 discussed the law reform process relating to the protection of innocent purchasers of intermediated shares against adverse claims under English law. The proposals made by the Law Commission and the provisions of the Geneva Securities Convention were considered in some depth. It was found that they are not *per se* irreconcilable. What really distinguishes them is the pattern of legal change. While the Law Commission's proposal is the result of a unilateral national initiative, the Geneva Securities Convention is part of a larger supranational project of law reform involving long negotiations between national delegates at

Intermediated Securities (OUP Oxford 2012) 114.

2 [2009] 1 CLC 701.

international *fora*. This latter pattern, it was argued, closely mirrors the one observed in Part II where the phenomenon of assimilation and interaction between legal cultures was described in term of hybridisation. The resulting instrument is a new legal creation in its own right and not the mere sum of features of identifiable legal backgrounds. It is also the starting point for understanding a possible second step of hybridisation. This consists in the implementation of the international instrument in the national legal framework. It is based on the supremacy of the international instrument over the national legal framework based on the notion of hegemony. In essence, as was discussed in Part I when describing the dominance relationship between colonisers and colonised, the interaction of the Convention with the pre-existing legal tradition will be construed on the primacy of the international instrument and will produce different results depending on the existing legal tradition through a process of hybridisation.

CONCLUSIONS

These conclusions review the fundamental themes discussed in the preceding Parts and draws together the findings of the investigation.

Part I dealt with the conceptual framework of this study. It examined the comparative debate on the pattern, meaning and significance of the circulation of legal paradigms across national frontiers. The discussion centred on whether it was appropriate to describe the movement of law from one country to another by using the metaphor of a 'legal transplant'. Broadly, two approaches to this question were explored. The first one, relying on historical evidence, suggested that the evolution of law is largely autonomous from society, as it primarily consists of a function of rules being imported from another legal system driven by legal elites. The second approach was sceptical about the role of history and of comparative law as tools to detect the pattern and the drivers of legal change. It pointed out that the development of law does not take place through borrowing because law mirrors, and is responsive to, situated linguistic, cultural and moral national frameworks. The two approaches are irreconcilable with each other. And both views were found to be misleading, as they overlook the relationship between legal comparison and sociology of law and over-simplify the concepts of language and culture, respectively. To address these shortcomings an original interpretation of the pattern of legal change was offered.

The underlying theme put forward was that the practice of borrowing is not exclusively a legal phenomenon; it reflects a common trend of social life, a mechanism of culture diffusion. It applies to law because law is itself a form of culture. Building on this understanding, Part I proposed a new perspective for considering the significance of legal borrowing and for explaining legal evolution. The main argument was that the movement of legal paradigms from one country to another rarely consists of a mere transplantation of rules. Instead, it generally involves a complex and gradual process of interaction between legal and social consciousness, between imported models and indigenous traditions. From that perspective, specific attention was paid to recent studies on acculturation, colonialism and contact situations in general. The focus of the analysis was on the notion of 'hybridity'. This theme, fundamental in cultural and postcolonial debates, suggests that the claim for a hierarchical purity of cultures is untenable in colonial situations and that the copying of the colonisers' culture and values is not a simple reproduction of the same traits.

Cultural norms in colonial contexts are peculiar to each contact situation and they do not qualify as either colonial or indigenous 'in disguise'. In other words, hybrid culture is more than the result of the fusion of features of colonial and indigenous backgrounds. It is a new creation in its own right.

The possible conceptual pitfall inherent in the notion of cultural hybridity based on the presumption of the existence of once pure cultures was overcome by redefining it with the term 'hybridisation'. This gave a more appropriate representation of the process of interaction and negotiation between the social actors in the colonial situation and ensures there is no need for references to a reified concept of culture and culturally predetermined identities.

Part I further observed that the idea of hybridisation as the process of cultural mixture for colonial situations originally developed in postcolonial studies is not specifically modern and western. It goes beyond particular temporal and spatial contexts. While colonialism is an abstract concept, restricted to the dominance assumptions of European historical experience, 'pseudo-colonialism' does not coincide with the meaning and connotations of modern times where it has often been associated with the idea of political, military and economic domination by intrusive foreign groups over indigenous people. 'Pseudo-colonialism' embodies a much broader idea where asymmetric socio-economic relationships between the colonising groups and the inhabitants of the colonised region are initially in place. It refers primarily to the 'absence from home and being in a foreign country', a notion more akin to the Greek *apoikiai* than to the Latin equivalent *colonia*. From this perspective, the process of hybridisation can be regarded as a recurring feature of most contact situations (i.e. both 'non-hegemonic' and 'hegemonic'), including pre-modern ones. This view was supported by reference to cases of material culture taken from archaeology. Even in hegemonic contact situations (e.g. the Roman Empire), cultural evolution was never restricted to a one-way process. It involved a more complex phenomenon of interaction and negotiation between the traditions of the colonisers and of the indigenous people, which eventually led to the formation of a middle ground, of an original hybrid colonial culture.

Building on this conceptual scenario taken from postcolonial scholarship, this study found an interesting analogy between the dynamics at the basis of colonialism, 'pseudo-colonialism' and the movement of law from one country to another. It suggested that similar arguments to the ones posed in the postcolonial debate could be employed to explain the reception mechanism, the process of interaction between imported legal models and indigenous legal traditions. As with colonial norms and standards, legal paradigms borrowed outside their original meanings become unsettled. They interact at different levels with local traditions, with certain indigenous perceptions, and do not survive in their original identities. No matter whether this occurs by way of imposition or as a result of a voluntary process, a new legal tradition, a third space that is peculiar to the specific contact situation, is created each time. Borrowed legal paradigms in their new environment become almost the same as the original ones, but not quite.

The complexities of the inquiry in comparative jurisprudence were then explored by focusing on the specific case of the transfer of shares in England. In doing so, this study considered, in Part II, the circumstance where the shares are held directly by the owner (direct holding system) and, in Part III, the case of one or more persons standing in the chain of ownership (indirect holding system).

The choice of the jurisdiction was significant *per se*. England represents a very challenging case for examining the theory of legal transplants and for considering the pattern of legal evolution. British historians have in fact often claimed that the development of English law has consisted of an autochthonous national achievement, independent from continental law. This historical perception is largely a myth. England was never entirely isolated from continental culture. This study, among other things, contributes to supporting this position by looking at certain areas of the growth and patterns of foreseeable change of English commercial law.

Part II investigated the historical evolution of the modes of shares transfer. It suggested that contrary to the conventional interpretation, the original form of the joint stock company and its structural elements of association were not a spontaneous indigenous creation. They were borrowed from abroad and, starting from the sixteenth century with the growth of international trade, progressively integrated into the pre-existing English legal framework via a process of hybridisation.

The inquiry distinguished between the transfer of registered shares and share warrants to bearer. Although they both enjoy the same economic function of units of the corporate capital, they are different in terms of their legal nature, regulation and modes of circulation. The explanation for these differences is historical.

In the case of registered shares where legal title (is given and) passes by an entry of the transferee's name in the members' register according to a tripartite scheme of transfer akin to novation, strong links between the growth of the legal tradition and the present characterisation were evidenced. The analysis of the concept of incorporation suggested that the historical connections between the development of the partnership model and the evolution of the company form have been very strong, at least until the enactment of the Joint Stock Companies Act in 1844. The discussion of the mechanism of transfer of legal title to shares both for incorporated and unincorporated companies supported this view, evidencing among other things the similarities with the current legal characterisation based on novation. Nevertheless, it was also shown that reference to path dependence alone does not provide a comprehensive and satisfactory explanation for the pattern of legal change. While it is incontrovertible that the current legal characterisation of the circulation of registered shares, as crystallised in the Companies Act 2006, follows from the development of the principles of the joint stock company and partnership law, the historical analysis carried out in Chapter 4 suggested that the embryonic paradigm of business association was not of English origin. It was the model of maritime partnership (the *societas maris*), as refined in the scheme of a joint stock fund in Genoa that was most likely borrowed and employed for part-ownership in ships in England starting from the beginning of the sixteenth century. The reception was facilitated by the commercial interaction arising from the existence of Italian commercial settlements active in the wool trade in the south of England, from the cultural influence of the Italian mercantile community and from the widespread recourse in practice to certain Genoese/Venetian forms of business association. The web of connectivity (rather than the military or demographic expansion) was the object of colonisation. However, these elements did not lead to the univocal conclusion that the Genoese model adopted was in its original form. It was modelled in accordance with the indigenous legal tradition founded on the fellowship relations typical of the trading guilds. The role of the Court of Chancery in shaping the evolution of the law of partnership and trust later led to the unique evolution of the paradigm of the English joint stock company when incorporation was not easily available. It was clear from the historical inquiry into the circulation of registered shares that a hybrid paradigm progressively emerged from the interaction of the original Genoese model and the indigenous legal tradition. This analysis confirmed the arguments on postcolonial discourse set out in Part I.

With respect to share warrants to bearer, where possession, as opposed to registration, is the method of evidencing title to company shares and where title passes from one person to another by delivery, reference was made to the evolution of the law of negotiable instruments and to the concept of negotiability. It was found that negotiable instruments originated and developed in the thirteenth century from a variation of certain Italian notarial exchange contracts and the contract of *cambium* as effected under the machinery of the bill of exchange (*tratta*, to use the Italian terminology). In essence, the *tratta* consisted of an instrument specifically devised by sedentary merchants for long-distance trade to obviate the risk of the physical transport of money from one fair to another or from one country to another. The Italian *tratta* was received in English commercial practice when English merchants became the principal dealers in commodities (wool and cloth exports) in the fifteenth century. The process of reception and the advent of negotiability in England was, however, peculiar. This is because although they progressively converged, the class of negotiable instruments and the concept of negotiability have not always coincided. Historically, they developed at different stages in response to changing commercial needs, and following different legal patterns. Mercantile conditions changed over the centuries and it was only at the beginning of the nineteenth century that the commercial practice needed debt instruments capable of being transferred as a means of payment in accordance with the rules of negotiability. From this finding, it followed that the Italian *tratta* evolved in England in a distinct pattern from the original paradigm in accordance with the changing economic, legal and social circumstances. This pattern of legal change, once again, is consistent with the hypothesis about the process of cultural interaction and hybridisation made in Part I. Above all, it applies to the evolution of the mechanism of transfer of share warrants to bearer. This is because the scheme for promissory notes followed from the original model of the bill of exchange and, in the terms codified in the Bills of Exchange Act 1882, formed the basis of reference for the subsequent development of certain categories of negotiable instruments among which the scrip certificates, the legal ancestors of share warrants to bearer.

Part III of the inquiry focused on the second leg of the case study on comparative jurisprudence according to the programme outlined at the end of Part I. It examined the process of legal change in the area of post-trading following the growth of intermediation in financial markets and it considered the mechanism of circulation of (interests) in shares. In doing so, it looked at the limits of current practice of holding and disposition of shares through intermediaries and discussed the initiatives for modernising the existing legal framework. It was proposed that good use could be made of the concept of hybridisation outside the specific context of non-hegemonic contacts observed in Part II.

The initial analysis in Part III placed special attention on three examples of substantive English law raised by the FMLC and on the major causes of ambiguity in the area of conflict of laws. It was observed that not addressing the uncertainties associated with domestic/cross-border transfers of intermediated shares and the legal risk arising from certain conceptual incompatibilities may leave investors in a weaker position than when they hold the securities directly from the issuer. This was regarded as an unwelcome scenario that might, in turn, undermine the attractiveness of the indirectly holding system and possibly the efficiency of financial markets.

The international responses to legal uncertainty provided by the Geneva Securities Convention and the 2008 LCG Advice/Consultation Document were considered in detail. Special emphasis was given to discuss the three issues of legal uncertainty raised by the FMLC report. By examining the process of legal evolution that led to the drafting of the final text of the Convention and discussing its possible implementation in England, the normative inquiry suggested that that pattern could be described in terms of hybridisation. In the course of the negotiations traceable in the history of the preparatory works contained in the Official Commentary to the Convention, national models simply lost their peculiar meanings in the interaction with others. Delegations contributed at different levels and with different weight to the shaping of a final 'hybrid' model. As a consequence, the final product does not reproduce the same traits of the original ones nor it can be regarded as the mere fusion of the various contributions.

Building on this general discussion, Part III then considered the specific property law issue of whether the innocent purchaser for value of intermediated shares is adequately protected under English law. In line with the conclusions of the FMLC and of the Law Commission, it argued that this was not the case. Existing legal concepts are not adequate to meet the practical needs of investors in intermediated shares, and legislative intervention is highly desirable to keep up with changing financial practice. Outside certain limited exceptions, the innocent purchaser of shares from someone who is not the owner is never protected at common law (*nemo dat quod non habet*). This is also true in the case of the transfer of intermediated shares. Even if equity has a general defence that protects a good faith purchaser of legal title for value without notice of prior equitable rights, it is not always available for the innocent purchaser of intermediated shares. Unless intermediated shares are acquired directly from the trustee, purchasers of intermediated shares in financial markets obtain a beneficial interest in the shares held by the sub-trustee and not a legal estate. As between two equitable interests, the general rule, similar in substance to the *nemo dat*, is *qui prior est in tempore potior in iure*. Part III pointed out that the disparity in the degree of protection available along the chain of indirect holding depending on whether the innocent purchaser acquires legal title or an equitable interest to shares lacks a logical rationale.

In the light of this inconsistency, and following a comparative analysis on the methods of protection of the innocent purchaser of intermediated shares under Italian law and under the Uniform Commercial Code, Part III discussed the law reform process relating to the protection of innocent purchasers of intermediated shares against adverse claims under English law. The analysis of the proposals made by the Law Commission and the provisions of the Geneva Securities Convention suggested some conclusions on the pattern of legal change. While the Law Commission's proposal is the result of a unilateral national initiative, the Geneva Securities Convention is part of a larger supranational project for law reform involving long negotiations between national delegates at international *fora*. This latter pattern, it was argued, closely mirrors the one observed in Part II where the historical phenomenon of assimilation and interaction between legal cultures was described in term of hybridisation. The final instrument is a new legal creation in its own right and not the mere sum of features of identifiable legal backgrounds. This is also the starting point for understanding a possible second step of hybridisation that consists in the implementation of the international instrument in the national legal framework. In essence, it was argued that, as has been seen in Part I when describing the dominance relationship between colonisers and colonised, the interaction of the Convention with the pre-existing legal tradition will be construed on the primacy of the international instrument. This will inevitably produce different results depending on the existing legal tradition via a process of hybridisation.

From the analysis of the law of shares transfer in England, this study has shown that, contrary to the conventional view, the movement of legal paradigms from one country to another does not consist of a mere transplantation of rules, but involves a complex and gradual process of interaction between imported models and indigenous traditions. It is a process of culture contact, which is not peculiar to law. No matter whether the view is based on legal history or *de lege ferenda* or whether the pattern of borrowing is based on hegemonic or non-hegemonic contact situations, the conclusion is that the use, by way of analogy, of arguments on hybridisation posed in the postcolonial debate are helpful to explain the reception mechanism and the dynamics at the basis of the movement of law from one country to another.

In other words, even conceding that when the cultural background of the societies are different and the reception of law produces slightly different results in the development of law, if 'one society copies the rules, institutions, concepts and structures of another, then it is profoundly influenced by that society's law'.[1] Legal borrowing, however, *per se* provides an empty and possibly superficial explanation for legal evolution. In particular, it does not reflect on the sociological context, on the process of reception and the possible formation of original (hybrid) paradigms. An analogy attempted by Watson outside the rigidity of the orthodox view of legal transplant, is very helpful in clarifying this point:

> 'I am a tomato grower. I have plastic trays each with 24 small containers filled with a soil mix. Into each container, I place a tomato seed which I proceed to water and fertilize. When the plants are about six centimetres tall, I sell them. A buyer takes one, pinches it out of its container, and plants in his yard. The plant soon stretches out its roots into the surrounding, very different soil. The purchaser fertilizes it with his own, different from mine, fertilizer. The tomato plant is in a very different ethos on which its future depends. Even the sun strikes

1 A Watson 'Legal Transplants and European Private Law' (2000) Electronic Journal of Comparative Law VII, available at <www.ejcl.org/44/art44-2.html> (accessed 7 August 2013).

> differently. The tomato plant may flourish or even wither. Now, to put a question not considered by the Greek philosophers, is the tomato plant the same plant as it was under my care?'[2]

It is almost the same but not quite, should be the straightforward answer. Legal models are not just static entities that can be transplanted like a tomato seed. They are embedded in cultural, economic and social contexts that necessarily influence and shape their existence. Only an analysis of such contexts and of the process of reception can give meaning and substance to the peculiar growth and development of the borrowed model. This, as was observed throughout the case study in Parts II and III, is largely missing in Watson's analysis. It has been the task of this inquiry to unveil it in all its intricacies by employing postcolonial theory.

2 Ibid vii.

BIBLIOGRAPHY

Abel RL 'Law as Lag: Inertia as a Social Theory of Law' (1982) 80 Mich L Rev 785

Adamensteanu D 'Greeks and Natives in Basilicata' in JP Descoeudres (ed) *Greek Colonist and Native Populations* (OUP Oxford 1990)

Ainsworth JE 'Categories and Culture: On the "Rectification of Names in Comparative Law"' (1996) 82 Cornell L Rev 19)

Alborn TL *Conceiving Companies: Joint Stock Companies in Victorian England* (Routledge London 1998)

Anderson GM and Tollison RD 'The Myth of the Corporation as a Creation of the State' (1983) 3 International Review of Law and Economics 107

Anderson P *Lineages of the Absolutist State* (NBL London 1974)

Anderson RG *Assignation* (Edinburgh Legal Education Trust Edinburgh 2008)

Antonaccio C 'Hybridity and the Cultures Within Greek Culture' in C Dougherty and L Kurke (eds) *The Cultures Within Greek Culture: Contact, Conflict, Collaboration* (CUP Cambridge 2003)

Antoniadou S and Pace A (eds) *Mediterranean Crossroads* (Pierides Foundation Athens 2007)

Antonucci A 'Le Società di Investimento a Capitale Variabile' in A Patroni Griffi, M Sandulli and V Santoro (eds) *Intermediari Finanziari, Mercati e Società Quotate* (Utet Torino 1999)

Arangio-Ruiz V *La Società in Diritto Romano* (Jovene Napoli 1950)

Archibald ZH *The Odrysian Kingdom of Thrace: Orpheus Unmasked* (OUP Oxford 1998)

Argenti P *The Occupation of Chios by the Genoese and their administration of the island 1346–1566* (CUP Cambridge 1958)

Armour J 'Companies and Other Associations' in P Birks (ed) *English Private Law* (OUP Oxford 2007)

Aronstein MJ 'The Decline and Fall of the Stock Certificate in America' (1978) 1 J Comp L & Sec Reg 273

Aronstein MJ 'A Certificateless Article 8? We Can Have it Both Ways' (1976) 31 Bus Law 727

Arvind EE and Stirton L 'Explaining the Reception of the Code Napoleon in Germany: a Fuzzy-set Qualitative Comparative Analysis' (March 2010) 30 Legal Studies 1

Ascarelli T 'La Letteralità nei Titoli di Credito' (1932) Riv Dir Comm 238

Ashcroft B, Griffith G and Tiffin H *Key Concepts in Post-Colonial Studies* (Routledge London 1998)

Ashley WJ *An Introduction to English Economic History and Theory* (Longmans, Green and Co London 1906)

Astuti G 'Note sulla Collegantia Veneta' in G Diurni (ed) *Tradizione Romanistica e Civiltà Giuridica Europea: Raccolta di Scritti di Guido Astuti* (Edizioni Scientifiche Italiane Napoli 1984)
Astuti G *Origini e Svolgimento Storico della Commenda Fino al Secolo XIII* (Utet Torino 1933)
Aubet ME *The Phoenicians and the West: Politics, Colonies, and Trade* (CUP Cambridge 1993)
Bailey SJ 'Assignment of Debts in England from the Twelfth to the Twentieth Century' (1932) 48 LQR 547
Baker JH 'The Law Merchant and the Common Law Before 1700' (1978) 38 Cam L J 295
Baker JH *An Introduction to English Legal History* (Butterworths London 2002)
Baker JH *The Oxford History of the Laws of England vol VI 1483–1558* (OUP Oxford 2007)
Bakhtin MM *The Dialogic Imagination: Four Essays* (University of Texas Press Austin 1981)
Balen M *A Very English Deceit: The Secret History of the South Sea Bubble and the First Great Financial Scandal* (Harper Collins London 2003)
Barnham R 'CREST: the Phoenix from the Ashes of Taurus' (1993) JIBL 426
Barreca F *La Civiltà Fenicio-punica in Sardegna* (Delfino Sassari 1986)
Bartlett R 'Colonial Aristocracies of the High Middle Ages' in R Bartlett and A MacKay (eds) *Medieval Frontier Societies* (OUP Oxford 1989)
Barton G 'The Legal Nature of a Share' in N Palmer and E McKendrick (eds) *Interests in Goods* (LLP London 1998)
Baskin B and Miranti PJ *A History of Corporate Finance* (CUP Cambridge 1997)
Baxi U 'The Colonialist Heritage' in P Legrand and R Munday (ed) *Comparative Legal Studies: Traditions and Transitions* (CUP Cambridge 2003)
Bayley J *A Short Treatise on the Law of Bills of Exchange, Cash Bills, and Promissory Notes* (E Brooke London 1789)
Beale H 'Reform of the Law of Security – Another View' (2004) 4 JIBFL 117
Beale H 'The European Civil Code Movement and the European Union's Common Frame of Reference' (2006) Legal Information Management 11
Beale H 'The Future of the Common Frame of Reference' 3 (2007) ERCL 257
Beale H, Bridge M, Gullifer L and Lomnicka E *The Law of Security and Title-Based Financing* (OUP Oxford 2012)
Beardwood A *Alien Merchants in England, 1350–1377* (The Medieval Academy of America Cambridge Mass 1931)
Beaves AW 'Global Custody: A tentative Analysis of Property and Contract' in N Palmer and E McKendrick (eds) *Interests in Goods* (LLP London 1998)
Bebchuck LA and Roe M 'A Theory of Path Dependence in Corporate Ownership and Governance' (1999) 52 Stan L Rev 127
Bell AP *Modern Law of Personal Property in England and Ireland* (Butterworths London 1989)
Bellomo M *The Common Legal Past of Europe, 1000–1800* (Catholic University of America Press Washington 1995)
Benjamin J 'Cross-Border Proprietary Rights' (1997) 1 JIBFL 6
Benjamin J 'Determining the *situs* of Interests in Immobilised Securities' (1998) 47 Int Comp L Q 923
Benjamin J 'Negotiability and Computerisation' (1995) 10 JIBFL 253
Benjamin J *Interests in Securities* (OUP Oxford 2000)
Benjamin J 'Overview of Post-Trade Infrastructure. Part 1' (2003) JIBFL 127
Benjamin J 'Overview of Post-Trade Infrastructure. Part 2' (2003) JIBFL 171

Benjamin J 'Overview of Post-Trade Infrastructure. Part 3' (2003) JIBFL 223

Benjamin J and Maher F 'Lessons from Cukurova' (2008) 3 Capital Markets LJ 126

Benjamin J *Financial Law* (OUP Oxford 2008)

Berkovitz D, Pistor K and Richard J 'The Transplant Effect' (2003) 51 Am J Comp L 163

Berman H and Kaufman C 'The Law of International Commercial Transactions (*Lex Mercatoria*)' (1978) 19 Harv Int'l LJ 221

Berman H *The Formation of the Western Legal Tradition* (Harvard UP Cambridge Massachusetts 1983)

Berman N 'Aftershocks: Exoticization, Normalization, Normalization and the Hermeneutic Compulsion' (1997) 2 Utah L Rev 282

Bernasconi C, Potok R and Morton G 'General Introduction: Legal Nature of Interests in Indirectly Held Securities and Resulting Conflict of Laws Analysis' in R Potok (ed) *Cross Border Collateral: Legal Risk and the Conflict of Laws* (Butterworths London 2001)

Beutel FK 'The Development of Negotiable Instruments in Early English Law' (1938) 51 Harv L Rev 831

Bhabha H 'Of Mimicry and Men' in H Bhabha (eds) *The Location of Culture* (Routledge London 1994)

Bhabha H 'Signs Taken for Wonders: Questions of Ambivalence and Authority Under a Tree Outside Dehli, May 1817' in H Bhabha (eds) *The Location of Culture* (Routledge London 1994)

Bhabha H 'The Commitment to Theory' in H Bhabha (eds) *The Location of Culture* (Routledge London 1994)

Birks P *Unjust Enrichment* (OUP Oxford 2005)

Bjerre CS and Rocks SM *The ABC of the UCC: Article 8, Investment Securities* (American Bar Association Chicago 2004)

Blackburn C *A Treatise on the Effect of the Contract of Sale* (William Benning and Co London 1845)

Blakeway A 'Prolegomena to the Study of Greek Commerce with Italy, Sicily and France in the Eight and Seventh Centuries BC' (1932) 33 ABSA 170

Blomquist TW 'The Dawn of Banking in an Italian Commune: Thirteenth Century Lucca' in *The Dawn of Modern Banking* (Yale UP New Haven 1979)

Boardman J *The Greeks Overseas: Their Early Colonies and Trades* (Thames & Hudson London 1999)

Borkowski A and Du Plessis P *Texbook on Roman Law* (OUP Oxford 2005)

Braddick MJ *The Nerves of State: Taxation and the Financing of the English State, 1558–1714* (Manchester UP Manchester 1996)

Bratton WM and McCahery JA 'Comparative Corporate Governance and the Theory of the Firm: The Case Against Global Cross Reference' (1999) 38 Colum J Transnat' L 213

Bridge M 'How Far is Article 9 Exportable? The English Experience' (1996) 27 CBLJ 196

Bridge M *Personal Property Law* (OUP Oxford 2002)

Bridge M 'The Law Commission's Proposals for the Reform of Corporate Security Interests' in J Getzler and J Payne (eds) *Company Charges (Spectrum and Beyond)* (OUP Oxford 2006)

Bridge M *The Sale of Goods* (OUP Oxford 2012)

Brine EH *Genoese Shipping in the Twelfth and Thirteenth Centuries* (The Medieval Academy of America Cambridge Massachusetts 1930)

Buchinsky M and Polak B 'The Emergence of a National Capital Market in England 1710–1880 (1993) Journal of Economic History 1

Buchner G 'Early Orientalizing: Aspects of the Euboean Connection' in D Ridgway and F Ridgway (eds) *Italy before the Romans: The Iron Age, Orientalizing and Etruscan Periods* (Academic Press London 1979)

Buckland WW *A Textbook of Roman Law from August to Justinian* (CUP Cambridge 1950)

Burdick FM 'What is the Law Merchant' (1902) Colum L Rev 470

Burn EH and Cartwright J *Cheshire and Burn's Modern Law of Real Property* (OUP Oxford 2006)

Bussani M 'Integrative Comparative Law Enterprises and the Inner Stratification of Legal Systems' (2000) 8 Euro Rev Priv L 85

Bussani M and Mattei U 'The Common Core Approach to European Private Law' (1997) 3 Colum J Eur L 339

Bussani M and Mattei U (eds) *The Common Core of European Private Law* (Kluwer London 2002)

Buttaro L 'Tullio Ascarelli e il Titolo di Credito' (1981) Banca Borsa e Titoli di Credito 424

Byrne E 'Commercial Contracts of the Genoese in the Syrian Trade of the Twelfth Century' (1916–1917) 31 Quarterly Journal of Economics 129

Byrne E *Genoese Shipping in the Twelfth and Thirteenth Centuries* (The Medieval Academy of America Cambridge Massachusetts 1930)

Caenegem RC *The Birth of English Common Law* (CUP Cambridge 1988)

Cairns JW and Robinson OF *Critical Studies in Ancient Law, Comparative Law and Legal History* (Hart Oxford 2001)

Callender G and Hinsley FH *The Naval Side of British History 1458–1945* (Christophers London 1952)

Carlos AM and Nicholas S 'Agency Problems in Early Chartered Companies: The Case of the Hudson's Bay Company' (1990) 50 Journal of Economic History 853

Carswell J *The South Sea Bubble* (Sutton Publisher Limited University of California 1993)

Carruthers G *City of Capital: Politics and Markets in the English Financial Revolution* (Princeton UP Princeton 1996)

Caterina R 'Comparative Law and the Cognitive Revolution' (2004) 78 Tul L Rev 1501

Chalmers MD 'An Experiment in Codification' (1886) 3 LQR 125.

Chalmers MD *A Digest of the Law of the Law of Bills of Exchange, Promissory Notes and Cheques* (London 1878)

Chang R 'Comparison and Justification of Choice' (1998) 146 U Pa L Rev 1569

Chancellor E *Devil Take the Hindmost: A History of Financial Speculation* (Plume Books New York 1999)

Cheffins B *Corporate Ownership and Control* (OUP Oxford 2008)

Chen-Wishart M 'Legal Transplants and Undue Influence: Lost in Translation or a Working Misunderstanding?' (2013) 62 ICLQ 1

Chiaudano M *Studi e Documenti per la Storia del Diritto Commerciale Italiano* (Università di Torino Torino 1930)

Chiaudano M and Moresco M *Il Cartolare di Giovanni Scriba* (Istituto Storico Italiano per il Medio Evo Roma 1935)

Chippindale C 'Theory in Archaeology: A World Perspective' (20 October 1995) Times Literary Supplement 1

Chitty J *A Treatise on the Law of Bills of Exchange, Checks on Bankers, Promissory Notes, Bankers' Cash Notes, and Bank-Notes* (E&R Brooke London 1799)

Christie F and Dosanjh H 'The Practical Elements of Settlement and Custody' in F Oditah (ed) *The Future for the Global Securities Market – Legal and Regulatory Aspects* (OUP Oxford 1996)

Chun C *Cross-Border Transactions of Intermediated Securities* (Springer Heidelberg 2012)

Cipolla CM *European Society and Economy before the Industrial Revolution: 1000–1700* (Routledge London 1993)

Cizakca M *A Comparative Evolution of Business Partnerships: Islamic World and Europe, With Specific Reference to the Ottoman Archive* (Brill Leiden 1996)

Coffee JC 'The Future as History: The Prospects for Global Convergence in Corporate Governance and its Significance' (1999) 93 Northwest U L Rev 641

Cohn M 'Legal Transplants Chronicles: The Evolution of Unreasonableness and Proportionality Review of the Administration in the United Kingdom' (2010) 58 Am J Comp L 583

Collins H *The European Civil Code – The Way Forward* (CUP Cambridge 2008)

Coogan PF 'Security Interests in Investment Securities Under Revised Article 8 of the Uniform Commercial Code' (1979) 92 Harv L Rev 1013

Cook WW 'The Alienability of *Choses* in Action' (1916) 29 Harv L Rev 816

Cooke CA *Corporation, Trust and Company* (Manchester UP Manchester 1950)

Coquilette RE *The Civilian Writers of Doctors' Commons* (Duncker & Humblot Berlin 1988)

Cordes A 'The Search for a Medieval Lex mercatoria' in V Piergiovanni (ed) *From* Lex Mercatoria *to Commercial Law* (Dunker & Humblot Berlin 2005)

Cotterrell R 'Comparative Law and Legal Culture' in M Reinmann and R Zimmermann (eds) *The Oxford Handbook of Comparative Law* (OUP Oxford 2006)

Cotterrell R 'Is There a Logic of Legal Transplants?' in D Nelken and J Feest *Adapting Legal Cultures* (Hart Oxford 2001)

Cotterrell R *Law, Culture and Society* (Ashgate London 2006)

Cottrell PL *Industrial Finance 1830–1914* (Methuen London 1980)

Cowen DW and Gering L *Cowen's Law of Negotiable Instruments in South Africa* (Juta Cape Town 1985)

Cranston R 'Globalization: Its Historical Context' in S Worthington (ed) *Commercial Law and Commercial Practice* (Hart Oxford 2003)

Cunningham W *Alien Immigrants to England* (Cass London 1969)

Curran V 'Cultural Immersion, Difference and Categories in US Comparative Law' (1998) 46 Am J Comp L 43

D'Andria F 'Greek Influence in the Adriatic: Fifty Years after Beaumont' in JP Descoeudres (eds) *Greek Colonist and Native Populations* (OUP Oxford 1990)

Dahm G 'On the Reception of Roman and Italian Law in Germany' in G Strauss (ed) *Pre-Reformation Germany* (Macmillian London 1972)

Dailey DM 'The Early Development of the Note-Brokerage Business in Chicago' (1938) 46 J of Political Economy 202

Darwin C *Origin of the Species by Means of Natural Selection* (J Murray London 1859)

Davies KG 'Joint Stock Investment in the Later Seventeenth Century' (1952) 4 Economic History Review 283

Davis I 'Transferability and Sale of Goods' (1987) 7 LS 1

Davies PL and Worthington S *Gower and Davies' Principles of Modern Company Law* (Sweet & Maxwell London 2012)

Davis R *The Rise of the English Shipping Industry* (David & Charles Newton Abbot 1972)

Dawson JP *A History of Lay Judges* (Harvard UP Cambridge 1960)

De Angelis F 'Ancient Past, Imperial Present: the British Empire' in TJ Dunbabin's *The Western Greeks* (1998) 72 Antiquity 539

De Luca N *Circolazione delle Azioni e Legittimazione dei Soci* (Giappichelli Torino 2007)

De Roover R 'Discussion on NSB Gras' paper "Capitalism – Concepts and History"' (1942) 16 Bulletin of the Business Historical Society 37

De Roover R 'The Organization of Trade' in MM Postan and EE Rich (eds) *Cambridge Economic History of Europe* (CUP Cambridge 1963)

De Roover R 'The Story of the Alberti Company, 1302–1348, as revealed in its Account Books' (1958) 23 The Business History Review 14

De Roover R *L'Evolution de la Lettre de Change XIV-XVIII siécles* (Librairie Armand Colin Paris 1953)

De Roover R *Money, Banking and Credit in Medieval Bruges: Italian Merchant-Bankers, Lombards, and Money-Changers* (Medieval Academy of America Cambridge Mass 1948)

De Roover R *The Rise and Decline of the Medici Bank, 1397–1494* (Harvard UP Cambridge Mass 1963)

De Witte B 'The Convergence Debate' (1996) 3 Maast J Eur & Comp L 105.

Delany H and Ryan D 'Unconscionability: a Unifying Theme in Equity' (2008) 5 Conveyancer and Property Lawyer 401

Deschamps M 'The Geneva Securities Convention – Selected Issues Left to Law Outside the Convention' (2010) Uniform L Rev 703

Dickson PGM *The Financial Revolution in England: A Study in the Development of Public Credit 1688–1756* (Macmillian London 1967)

Dirks N 'Introduction: Colonialism and Culture' in Id (ed) *Colonialism and Culture* (University of Michigan Press Ann Arbour 1992)

Dolmetta A 'Cessione dei Crediti' in *Digesto Discipline Privatistiche Sezione Civile* (Utet Torino 1988)

Dominguez AJ 'Greeks in Iberia Colonialism without Colonization' in CL Lyons and JK Papadopulos (eds) *The Archaeology of Colonialism* (Getty Research Institute Los Angeles 2002)

Donahue C '*Ius Commune*, Canon Law and Common Law in England' (1991) 66 Tul L Rev 1748

Donahue C 'Medieval and Early Modern *Lex Mercatoria*. An Attempt at the *Probatio Diabolica*?' (2004) 5 Chicago J Int'l Law 21

Donald D 'The Rise and Effects of the Indirect Holding Systems – How Corporate America Ceded its Shareholders to Intermediaries', working paper, available at <www.papers.ssrn.com/sol3/papers.cfm?abstract_id=1017206> (accessed 7 August 2013)

Du Plessis J 'Comparative Law and the Study of Mixed Legal Systems' in M Reinmann and R Zimmermann (eds) *The Oxford Handbook of Comparative Law* (OUP Oxford 2006)

Dubois AB *The English Business Company After the Bubble Act 1720–1800* (Commonwealth Fund New York 1938)

Duff PW *Personality in Roman Private Law* (CUP Cambridge 1938)

Dunbabin TJ *The Western Greeks* (OUP Press Oxford 1948)

Eden P 'The Equitable Ownership of Shares' in E Cooke (ed) *Modern Studies in Property Law* (Hart Oxford 2003)

Eidenmuller H, Faust F, Grigoleit HC, Jansen N, Wagner G and Zimmermann R 'The Common Frame of Reference for European Private Law – Policy Choices and Codification Problems' (2008) 28 OJLS 659

Epstein M *The Early History of the Levant Company* (George Routledge & Sons Ltd London 1908)

Epstein SA *Genoa and the Genoese 958–1528* (University of North Carolina Press Chapel Hill 1996)

Ewald W 'Comparative Jurisprudence (I): What it was Like to Try a Rat?' (1995) 143 Penn L Rev 1189

Ewald W 'Comparative Jurisprudence (II): The Logic of Legal Transplants' 43 (1995) Am J Comp L 489

Ewart JS 'Negotiability and Estoppel' (1900) 16 LQR 135

Ewart JS *An Exposition of the Principles of Estoppel by Misrepresentation* (The Carswell Company Toronto 1900)

Ewart JS 'What is the Law Merchant?' 3 (1903) Colum L Rev 135

Facciolo FJ 'Father Knows Best: Revised Article 8 and the Individual Investor' (2000) 27 Fla St U L Rev 616

Feltham P, Hochberg D and Leech T *The Law Relating to Estoppel by Representation – the Original Text by George Spencer Bower* (LexisNexis London 2004)

Femia J 'Hegemony and Consciousness in the Thought of Antonio Gramsci' 23 (1975) Political Studies 30

Ferrarese MR *Le Istituzioni della Globalizzazione* (Il Mulino Bologna 2000)

Ferri G 'La Immissione dei Valori Mobiliari nel Sistema di Gestione Accentrata e i Suoi Effetti Giuridici' (1988) Riv Dir Comm 252

Ferri G 'La Teoria Realista dei Titoli di Credito' (1972) Banca, Borsa e Titoli di Credito 41

Fiorentino A 'Dei Titoli di Credito' in A Scialoja and G Branca (eds) *Commentario del Codice Civile* (Zanichelli Bologna-Roma 1974) 1992–2002

Foster A 'Sale by a Non-owner: Striking a Fair Balance Between the Rights of the True Owner and Buyer in Good Faith' (2004) 9 Cov LJ 1

Foster N 'Transmigration and Transferability of Commercial Law in a Globalized World' in AJ Hardin and E Orucu (eds) *Comparative Law in the 21st Century* (Kluwer Leiden 2002)

Fox D *Property Rights in Money* (OUP Oxford 2008)

Frank T *An Economic History of Rome* (Jonathan Cape London 1927)

Frankenberg G 'Critical Comparisons: Re-thinking Comparative Law' (1985) 26 Harv Int'l LJ 411

Frankenberg G 'Stranger than Paradise: Identity & Politics in Comparative Law' (1997) 2 Utah L Rev 259

Fratianni M 'Government Debt, Reputation and Creditors' Protection: The Tale of San Giorgio' (2006) 10 Review of Finance 492

Fratianni M 'The Evolutionary Chain of International Financial Centres', Mofir working paper, available at <www.dea2.univpm.it/quaderni/pdfmofir/Mofir006.pdf> (accessed 7 August 2013)

Fratianni M and Spinelli F 'Did Genoa and Venice Kick a Financial Revolution in the Quattrocento?', 2005 working paper (no 112), available at <www.oenb.at/en/img/wp112_tcm16-38081.pdf> (accessed 7 August 2013)

Freedman CE *Joint-Stock Enterprise in France 1807–1869: From Privileged Company to Modern Corporation* (University of North Carolina Press 1979)

Freeman EA *A History of Sicily from the Earliest Times* (OUP Oxford 1891)

Freeman M, Pearson R and Taylor J '"A Doe in the City": Women and Shareholders in the Eighteenth and Early Nineteenth Century Britain' (2006) 16 Accounting, Business & Financial History 265

Friedman J 'Global Crises, the Struggle for Cultural Identity and Intellectual Porkbarrelling: Cosmopolitans Versus Locals, Ethnics and Nationals in an Era of Dehegemonisation' in P Werbner and T Modood (eds) *Debating Cultural Hybridity: Multi-cultural Identities and the Politics of Anti-racism* (Zed Books London 1997)

Friedman J 'Global System, Globalization and the Parameters of Modernization' in M Featherstone, L Lash and R Robertson (eds) *Global Modernities* (Sage London 1995)

Friedman J 'The Hybridization of Roots and the Abhorrence of the Bush' in M Featherstone and S Lash (eds) *Spaces of Culture. City, Nation, World* (Sage London 1999)

Friedman L 'Borders on the Emerging Sociology of Transnational Law' (1996) 32 Stan J Int'l L 65

Friedman L 'Some Comments on Cotterrell and Legal Transplants' in D Nelken and J Fest (eds) *Adapting Legal Cultures* (Hart Oxford 2001)

Galgano F *Storia del Diritto Commerciale* (Il Mulino Bologna 1976)

Gardner S 'Equity, Estate Contracts and the Judicature Acts: Walsh v Lonsdale Revisited' (1987) 7 OJLS 60

Garber PM *Famous First Bubble: The Fundamentals of Early Manias* (MIT Press MIT 2001)

Garoupa N and Ogus A 'A Strategic Interpretation of Legal Transplants' (2003) CEPR Discussion Paper no 4123, available at <www.mle.economia.unibo.it/Papers%20MTM/Garoupa%20-%20Legal%20Transplants.pdf> (accessed 7 August 2013)

Gatti S *L'Iscrizione nel Libro Soci* (Giuffrè Milano 1969)

Gerber D *Global Competition: Law, Markets and Globalization* (OUP Oxford 2010)

Getzler J and Macnair M 'The Firm as an Entity before the Companies Act' in P Brand, K Costello and WN Osborough (eds) *Adventures of the Law. Proceedings of the Sixteenth British Legal History Conference – Dublin 2003* (Four Courts Press Dublin 2005)

Gillespie J 'Transplanted Company Law: an Ideological and Cultural Analysis of Market-Entry in Vietnam' (2002) Int & Comp L Q 641

Gilmore G 'The Commercial Doctrine of Good Faith Purchase' (1954) 63 Yale L J 1057–68

Gilmore G 'On the Difficulties of Codifying Commercial Law' (1948) 57 Yale L J 1341

Gilson RJ 'Globalizing Corporate Governance: Convergence of Form or Function' (2001) 43 Am J Comp L 329

Gioffrè D *Il Debito Pubblico Genovese: Inventario delle Compere Anteriori a San Giorgio o non Consolidate nel Banco* (Giuffrè Milano 1967)

Glenn G 'The Assignment of *Choses* in Action: Rights of *Bona Fide* Purchaser' (1934) 20 Virgina L Rev 621

Glenn HP 'Are Legal Traditions Incommensurable?' 49 (2001) Am J Comp L 133

Goode R 'Are intangible assets fungible?' in A Pretto and P Birks (eds) *Themes in Comparative Law* (OUP Oxford 2002)

Goode R 'Security Entitlements as Collateral and the Conflict of Laws' (1998) 9 JIBFL (special supplement) 22

Goode R 'Security in Cross-Border Transactions' (1998) 33 Texas Int'l L J 47

Goode R, Kanda H and Kreuzer K *Hague Securities Convention Explanatory Report* (HCCH Publications 2005)

Goode R 'The Case for the Abolition of the Floating Charge' in J Getzler and J Payne (eds) *Company Charges* (Spectrum and Beyond) (OUP Oxford 2006)

Goode R, Kronke H and McKendrick E *Transnational Commercial Law* (OUP Oxford 2007)

Gordley J 'Myths of the French Civil Code' (1994) 42 Am J Comp L 459

Gordley J 'Why Look Backward' (2002) 50 Am J Comp L 657

Gourvish TR 'A British Business Elite: The Chief Executive Managers of the Railway Industry, 1850–1922 (1973) 47 Business History 289

Gourvish TR *Railways and the British Economy 1830–1914* (Palgrave Macmillian Basingstoke 1980)

Gower LCB 'Some Contrasts Between British and American Corporation Law' (1956) 69 Harv L Rev 1371–72

Gower LCB *Gower's Principles of Modern Company Law* (Stevens & Sons London 1979)

Gramsci A *Opere di Antonio Gramsci. Il Risorgimento* vol IV (Einaudi Torino 1949)

Gras NS *Business and Capitalism, an Introduction to Economic History* (FS Crofts New York 1939)

Grayand WD and Scavone M 'A Primer on the Uniform Securities Transfer Act' (2004) Ontario Branch of the Canadian Bar Association 1, available at <www.mcmillan.ca/Upload/Publication/2A.pdf> (accessed 7 August 2013)

Graziadei M 'Changing Images of the Law in XIX Century English Legal Thought (The Continental Impulse)' in M Reinmann (ed) *The Reception of Continental Ideas in the Common Law World 1820–1920* (Duncker & Humlot Berlin 1993)

Graziadei M 'Legal Transplants and the Frontiers of Legal Knowledge' (2009) 10 Theoretical Inq L 723

Graziadei M 'The Functionalist Heritage' in P Legrand and R Munday (ed) *Comparative Legal Studies: Traditions and Transitions* (CUP Cambridge 2003)

Graziadei M 'Transplants and Receptions' in M Reinmann and R Zimmermann (eds) *The Oxford Handbook of Comparative Law* (OUP Oxford 2006)

Gretton G 'Financial Collateral and the Fundamentals of Secured Transactions' (2006) 10 Edin LR 209

Grisoli A *La Cambiale nel Diritto Inglese* (Cedam Padova 1957)

Gross C and Hall H (ed) *Selected Cases Concerning the Law Merchant, AD 1239–1633* (Bernard Quatrich London 1930) vol 46 SS

Gross C *The Gild Merchant: a Contribution to British Municipal History* (OUP Press Oxford 1890)

Großfeld B 'Comparatists and languages' in P Legrand and R Munday (eds) *Comparative Legal Studies: Traditions and Transitions* (CUP Cambridge 2003)

Gruppi L 'Il Concetto di Egemonia' (1967) 3 Prassi Rivoluzionaria e Storicismo in Gramsci, Critica Marxista 78

Guest AG (ed) *Benjamin's Sale of Goods* (Sweet & Maxwell London 2006)

Guizzi G *Il Titolo Azionario come Strumento di Legittimazione* (Giuffrè Milano 2000)

Gullifer L *Goode on Legal Problems of Credit and Security* (Sweet & Maxwell London 2008)

Gullifer L 'The Proprietary Protection of Investors in Intermediated Securities' in J Armour and J Payne (eds) *Rationality in Company Law – Essays in Honour of DD Prentice* (Hart Oxford 2009)

Gullifer L 'Exceptions to the *nemo dat* rule in relation to goods and the Law Commission's proposals in the Consultative Report' in J de Lacy (ed) *The Reform of UK Personal Property Security Law* (Routledge London 2010)

Guynn RD and Marchand RJ 'Transfer of Pledge of Securities held through Depositories' in H Van Houtte (ed) *The Law of Cross-Border Securities Transactions* (Sweet & Maxwell London 1999)

Halliwell M 'Perfecting Imperfect Gifts and Trusts: Have we Reached the End of the Chancellor's Foot?' (2003) 67 Conveyancer and Property Lawyer 192

Hansmann H, Kraakman R and Squire R 'Law and the Rise of the Firm' (2006) 119 Harv L Rev 1383

Harris M *Culture, Man, and Nature. An Introduction to General Anthropology* (Crowell New York 1971)

Harris R 'The Institutional Dynamics of Early Modern Eurasian Trade: The *Commenda* and the Corporation' 16–17, working paper, available at <www.papers.ssrn.com/sol3/papers.cfm?abstract_id=1294095> (accessed 7 August 2013)

Harris R *Industrializing English Law* (CUP Cambridge 2000)

Hasebroek J *Trade and Politics in Ancient Greece* (Biblio and Tannen New York 1965)

Hayton D 'Uncertainty of Subject Matter of Trusts' (1994) 110 LQR 335

Helmholz RE 'Continental Law and Common Law: Historical Strangers or Companions?' (1990) 6 Duke L J 1208

Helmholz RE 'Magna Carta and the *Ius commune*' (1996) 66 U Chi L Rev 297

Helmholz RE *Canon Law and the Law of England* (Hambledon London 1987)

Herres J 'Les Genois en Angleterre: La Crise de 1458–1466' in *Studi in Onore di Armado Sapori* (Istituto Editoriale Cisalpino Milano 1957)

Heydebrand W 'From Globalization of Law to Law under Globalization' in D Nelken and J Fest (eds) *Adapting Legal Cultures* (Hart Oxford 2001)

Hill J 'Comparative Law, Law Reform and Legal Theory' (1989) 9 OJLS 101

Hingley R *Roman Officers and English Gentlemen: the Imperial Origins of Roman Archaeology* (Routledge London 2000)

Holden JM *The History of Negotiable Instruments in English Law* (The Athlone Press London 1955)

Holdsworth WS *A History of English Law* (Metheuen & Co London 1925) vol VIII

Holdsworth WS 'Origins and History of Negotiable Instruments' (1915) 31 LQR 12

Holdsworth WS 'The History of the Treatment of *Choses* in Action by the Common Law' (1920) 33 Harv L Rev 997

Hoppit J *Risk and Failure in English Business 1700–1800* (Manchester UP Manchester 1987)

Hoppit J 'The Myth of the South Sea Bubble' (2002) Transactions of the Royal History Society 141

Horvath R 'A Definition of Colonialism' (1972) 13 Current Anthropology 45

Hunt BC *The Development of the Business Corporation in England 1800–1867* (Harvard UP Cambridge Massachusetts 1936)

Hunt ES and Murray JM *A History of Business in Medieval Europe 1200–1550* (CUP Cambridge1999)

Hurst JW *The Legitimacy of the Business Corporation in the Law of the United States* (University Press of Virginia Charlottesville 1970)

Ireland P 'Company Law and the Myth of Shareholder Ownership' (1999) 62 MLR 32

Ireland P 'Limited Liability, Rights of Control and the Problem of Corporate Irresponsibility' (2010) 34 Camb J Econ 837

Ireland P 'The Rise of the Limited Liability Company' (1984) 12 Int J of the Soc L 240

Ireland P 'The Triumph of the Company Legal Form, 1856–1914' in J Adams (ed) *Essays for Clive Schmitthoff* (Professional Books Limited Abingdon 1983)

Ireland P, Grigg-Spall I and Kelly D 'The Conceptual Foundations of Modern Company Law' (1987) 14 Journal of Law and Society 150

Jackson BS 'Evolution and Foreign Influence in Ancient Law' (1968) 16 Am J Comp L 372

James J *Richardson's Guide to Negotiable Instruments* (Butterworths London 1991)

Jefferys JB *Business Organisation in Great Britain, 1856–1914* (Arno Press New York 1977)

Jenkinson H and Formoy B (eds) *Select Pleas in the Court of Admiralty* (Selden Society London 1894)

Jenks E 'The Early History of Negotiable Instruments' (1893) LQR 70

Johansson E *Property Rights in Investment Securities and the Doctrine of Specificity* (Springer Berlin Heidelberg 2009)

Johnson C 'An Italian Finance House in the 14th Century' (1903) 1 Transactions of St Albans and Hertfordshire Architectural and Archaeological Society 320

Jones S *The Archaeology of Ethnicity. Constructing Identities in the Past and Present* (Routledge London 1997)

Kadens E 'Order within Law, Variety within Customs. The Character of Medieval Merchant Law' (2004) 5 Chicago J of Int'l Law 39

Kaeuper RW *Bankers to the Crown. The Riccardi of Lucca and Edward I* (Princeton UP Princeton 1973)

Kahn-Freund O 'On Uses and Misuses of Comparative Law' 37 (1974) MLR 6

Kahn-Freund O 'Common Law and Civil Law-Imaginary and Real Obstacles to Assimilation' in M Cappelletti (ed) *New Perspectives for a Common Law Europe* (LeMonnier Firenze 1978)

Kanda H and Milhaupt CJ 'Re-examining Legal Transplants: The Director's Fiduciary Duty in Japanese Corporate Law' (2003) Columbia Law School – The Centre for Law and Economic Studies, working paper no 219, available at <www.law.columbia.edu/center_program/law_economics/wp_listing_1/wp_listing/211-220#6990> (accessed 7 August 2013)

Kanda H, Mooney C, Thevenoz L and Beraud S with the assistance of Keijser T on behalf of the Unidroit Secretariat *Official Commentary on the Unidroit Convention on Substantive Rules for Intermediated Securities* (OUP Oxford 2012)

Keay S and Terrenato N *Italy and the West. Comparative Issues in Romanization* (Oxbow Oxford 2001)

Kelly DP 'Civil Science in the Renaissance: Jurisprudence Italian Style' (1979) 22 The Historical Journal 777

Kennedy D 'New Approaches to Comparative Law: Comparativism and International Governance' (1997) 2 Utah L Rev 544

Kessler AD *A Revolution in Commerce. The Parisian Merchant Court and the Rise of Commercial Society in Eighteenth-Century France* (New Haven Yale 2007)

Kettering K 'Repledge Deconstructed' (1999) 61 U Pitt L Rev 45

Khimji M 'Intermediary Credit Risk – A Comparative Law Analysis of Property Rights in Indirectly Held Securities' (2005) JBL 287

Kim K *Aliens in Medieval Law* (CUP Cambridge 2000)

Kirby J 'Assignment and Transfers of Contractual Duties: Integrating Theory and Practice' (2000) 31 VUWL Rev 319

Knott R and Mills A 'Modelling Risk in Central Counterparty Clearing Houses: a Review' (2002) Bank of England Financial Stability Review 162

Kostal RW *Law and English Railway Capitalism 1825–1875* (OUP Press Oxford 1994)

Kraakman R, Armour J, Davies P, Enriques L, Hansmann H, Hertig G, Hopt K, Kanda H and Rock E *The Anatomy of Corporate Law* (OUP Oxford 2009)

Kronke H 'Remarks on the Geneva Securites Conention's Development and its Future' in L Gullifer and J Payne (eds) *Intermediated Securities – Legal Problems and Practical Issues* (Hart Oxford 2010)

Kronke H The Draft Unidroit Convention on Intermediated Securities: Transactional Certainty and Market Stability (2006) IMF Seminar on Current Development in Monetary and Financial Law, available at <www.imf.org/external/np/seminars/eng/2006/mfl/hk.pdf> (accessed 7 August 2013)

Kurtz D 'Hegemony and Anthropology. Gramsci, Exegeses, Reinterpretations' (1996) 16 Critique of Anthropology 103

Kyd S *A Treatise on the Law of the Bills of Exchange and Promissory Notes* (Thomas, Andrew and Penniman Albany 1800)

La Sala GP '*L'acquisto* A Non Domino *di Strumenti Finanziari Dematerializzati*' II (2004) Banca, Borsa e Titoli di Credito 467

Lambert LM *Two Thousand Years of Gild Life* (Brown Hull 1891)

Lando O 'The Structure and Legal Values of the Common Frame of Reference (CFR)' (2007) 3 ERCL 245

Larouche P and De Chirico F (eds) *Economic Analysis of the DCFR* (Sellier Munich 2010)

Lawson A 'O'Brien and its Legacy: Principle, Equity and Certainty?' (1995) 54 CLJ 280

Lawson FH and Rudden B *The Law of Property* (OUP Oxford 2002)

Lawson WJ *The History of Banking* (Richard Bentley London 1855)

Ledrut E and Upper C 'The US Paper Crunch' (2007) BIS Quarterly Review

Lee TV 'Risky Business: Courts Culture, and the Market Place' (1993) 47 U Miami L Rev 1335

Legrand P 'European Legal Systems are not Converging' (1996) 45 ICLQ 52

Legrand P 'Against a European Civil Code' (1997) 60 MLR 44

Legrand P 'The Impossibility of "Legal Transplants"' (1997) 4 Maast J Eur & Comp L 111

Legrand P 'What "Legal Transplants"?' in D Nelken and J Fest (eds) *Adapting Legal Cultures* (Hart Oxford 2001)

Legrand P 'The Same and the Different' in P Legrand and R Munday (eds) *Comparative Legal Studies Traditons and Transitions* (CUP Cambridge 2003)

Legrand P 'Word/World (of Primordial Issues for Comparative Legal Studies)' in H Petersen, AL Kjaer, H Krunke and M R Madsen (eds) *Paradoxes of European Legal Integration* (Ashgate Aldeshot 2008)

Lener R 'Capitale e Azioni' in G Alpa and F Capriglione (eds) *Commentario al Testo Unico delle disposizioni in materia di intermediazione finanziaria* (Cedam Padova 1998)

Levitin AJ 'Finding Nemo: Rediscovering the Virtues of Negotiability in the Wake of Enron' (2007) Colum Bus L Rev 86

Levy AB *Private Corporations and Their Control* (Routledge London 1950)

Lewin HG *The Railway Mania and its Aftermath 1845–1852* (David & Charles Newton Abott 1968)

Lieber AE 'Eastern Business Practices and Medieval European Commerce' (2) 21 Economic History Review 230

Lindley WB *Law of Companies* (Sweet & Maxwell London 1902)

Lindley WB *A Treatise on the Law of Partnership* (Sweet & Maxwell London 1924)

Lloyd TH *The English Wool Trade in the Middle Ages* (CUP Cambridge 1977)

Lloyd TH *Alien Merchants in England in the High Middle Ages* (The Harvester Press Limited Brighton 1982)

Lobban M 'Commercial Law' in Cornish, Anderson, Cock, Lobban, Polden and Smith (eds) *The Oxford History of the Laws of England Volume XII 1820–1914 – Private Law* (OUP Oxford 2010)

Lopez RS *The Commercial Revolution of the Middle Ages: 950–1350* (CUP Cambridge 1976)

Lyons CL 'Sikel Burials at Morgantina: Defining Social and Ethnic Identities' in R Leighton (eds) *Early Societies in Sicily: New Developments in Archaeological Research* (Accordia Research Centre, University of London London 1996)

Lyons CL and Papadopulos JK 'Archaeology of Colonialism' in CL Lyons and JK Papadopulos (eds) *The Archaeology of Colonialism* (Getty Research Institute Los Angeles 2002)

Mackie JD *The Earlier Tudors 1485–1558* (OUP Press Oxford 1952)

Maitland FW 'The Unincorporated Body' and 'Trust and Corporation' in Id (ed) *Selected Essays* (CUP Cambridge 1936)

Maitland FW 'Why the History of English Law is not Written' in HAL Fisher (eds) *The Collected Papers of Frederic William Maitland* (CUP Cambridge 1911)

Maitland FW *Equity: A Course of Lectures* (CUP Cambridge 1936)

Malkin I 'A Colonial Middle Ground: Greek, Etruscan, and Local Elites in the Bay of Naples' in CL Lyons and JK Papadopulos (eds) *The Archaeology of Colonialism* (Getty Research Institute Los Angeles 2002)

Manchester AH *Modern Legal History of England and Wales 1750–1950* (Butterworths London 1980)

Marengo E, Manfroni C and Pessagno G *Il Banco di San Giorgio* (A Donath Editore Genova 1911)

Markesinis BS *The Gradual Convergence: Foreign Ideas, Foreign Influences, and English Law on the Eve of the 21st Century* (OUP Oxford 1994)

Marshall J and Herrod N 'Lehman Brothers Insolvency – Client Assets' (2009) 3 LFMR 145

Marshall OR *The Assignment of Choses in Action* (Pitman & Sons Ltd London 1950)

Martin J 'Certainty of Subject Matter: a Defence of *Hunter v Moss*' (1996) Conv 223

Martorano F *Titoli di Credito* (Giuffrè Milano 2002)

Massa-Pairault FH *Iconologia e Politica nell'Italia Antica: Roma, Lazio ed Etruria dal VII al I secolo AC* (Longanesi Milano 1992)

Mattei U 'Comparative Law and Critical Legal Studies' in M Reinmann and R Zimmermann (eds) *The Oxford Handbook of Comparative Law* (OUP Oxford 2006)

Mattei U 'Efficiency in Legal Transplants: An Essay in Comparative Law and Economics' (1994) 14 International Review of Law and Economics 3

Mattei U and Monti A 'Comparative Law and Economics: Borrowing and Resistance' (2001) 2 Global Jurist Frontiers 5

Mattei U and Di Robilant A 'The Art and Science of Critical Scholarship: Postmodernism and International Style in the Legal Architecture of Europe' (2001) 75 Tul L Rev 1054

Mattei U *Comparative Law and Economics* (University of Michigan Press Ann Arbor 1997)

McCormick R *Legal Risk in the Financial Markets* (OUP Oxford 2010)

McFarlane B and Stevens R 'Interest in Securities – Practical Problems and Conceptual Solutions' in L Gullifer and J Payne (eds) *Intermediated Securities – Legal Problems and Practical Issues* (Hart Oxford 2010)

McFarlane B *The Structure of Property Law* (Hart Oxford 2008)

McKendrick E *Goode on Commercial Law* (Penguin London 2010)

McQueen R *A Social History of Company Law* (Ashgate Farham 2009)

Merrett L 'The importance of delivery and possession in the passing of title' (2008) 67 Cambridge LJ 376

Micheler E 'English and German Securities Law: A Thesis in Doctrinal Path Dependence' (2007) LQR 251

Micheler E 'Modernising securities settlement in the UK' (2002) 23 Company Lawyer 9

Micheler E *Property in Securities. A Comparative Study* (CUP Cambridge 2007)

Michie M *The London Stock Exchange: A History* (OUP Oxford 1999)

Micklethwait J and Wooldridge A *The Company, A Short History of a Revolutionary Idea* (Phoenix Paperbacks London 2005)

Milgrom PR, North DC and Weingast BR 'The Role of Institutions on the Revival of Trade, Part I: The Medieval Law Merchant' (1990) 2 Economics and Politics 1

Millett M *The Romanization of Britain: an Essay in Archaeological Interpretation* (CUP Cambridge 1990)

Millett P 'Equity's Place in the Law of Commerce' (1998) 114 LQR 214

Milne P 'Oughtred Revisited' (1997) 113 LQR 213

Mirowski P 'The Rise (and Retreat) of a Market: English Joint Stock Shares in the Eighteenth Century' (1981) 41 Journal of Economic History 559

Mitchell W *An Essay on the Early History of the Law Merchant* (CUP Cambridge 1904)

Mokyr J 'Editor's Introduction: The New Economic History and the Industrial Revolution' in Id (ed) *The British Industrial Revolution: An Economic Perspective* (Westview Press Oxford 1999)

Montesquieu CS *De l'Esprit des Lois* (Gallimard Paris 1970) reprint JP Mayer and AP Kerr (eds)

Mooney C 'The (Unidroit) Geneva Securities Convention on Intermediated Securities' (2009) 10 JIBFL 596

Mooney CW 'Beyond Negotiability: A New Model for Transfer and Pledge of Interests in Securities Controlled by Intermediaries' (1990) 12 Cardozo L Rev 305

Mooney CW 'Law and System for Intermediated Securities and the Relationship of Private Property Law to Securities Clearance and Settlement: United States, Japan and the Unidroit Draft Convention' Discussion Paper no 2008-E-7, IMES Bank of Japan, available at <www.ideas.repec.org/p/ime/imedps/08-e-07.html> (accessed 7 August 2013)

Mooney CW and Kanda H 'Core Issues under the UNIDROIT (Geneva) Convention on Intermediated Securities: Views from the United States and Japan' in L Gullifer and J Payne (eds) *Intermediated Securities – Legal Problems and Practical Issues* (Hart Oxford 2010)

Mooney CW, Rocks S and Schwartz RS 'Article 8 and Review of Other Recent Developments with Investment Securites' (1994) 49 Bus Law 1891

Morris J 'Questions: When is an Invalid Gift a Valid Gift? When is an Incompletely Constituted Trust a Completely Constituted Trust? Answer: After the Decisions in *Choithram and Pennington*' (2003) PCB 393

Moss G 'Intermediated Securities: Issues Arising from Insolvency' in L Gullifer and J Payne (eds) *Intermediated Securities – Legal Problems and Practical Issues* (Hart Oxford 2010)

Motani H 'The Proposed EU Legislation on Securities Holding' in P Conac, U Segna and L Thevenoz (eds) *Intermediated Securities – The Impact of the Geneva Securities Convention and the Future European Legislation* (CUP Cambridge 2013)

Munzi M *L'Epica del Ritorno* ('L'Erma di Bretshneider' Roma 2001)

Neal L *The Rise of Financial Capitalism* (CUP Cambridge 1990)

Nederveen Pieterse J 'Globalization as Hybridization' in M Featherstone, L Lash and R Robertson (eds) *Global Modernities* (Sage London 1995)

Neederveen Pieterse J 'Hybrity, So What? The Anti-hybridity Backlash and the Riddles of Recognition' (2001) 18 Theory, Culture & Society 219

Nelken D 'Beyond the Metaphor of Legal Transplants? Consequences of Autopoietic Theory for the Study of Cross-Cultural Legal Adaptation' in J Priban and D Nelken (eds) *Law's New Boundaries: The Consequences of Autopoiesis* (Aldershot Dartmouth 2001)

Nelken D 'Comparatists and Transferability' in P Legrand and R Munday (eds) *Comparative Legal Studies: Traditions and Transitions* (CUP Cambridge 2003)

Nelken D 'Legal Transplants and Beyond: of Disciplines and Metaphors' in A Harding and E Orucu (eds) *Comparative Law in the 21st Century* (Kluwer London 2002)

Nelli HO 'The Early Insurance Contract. A New Discovery' (1972) 39 Journal of Risk and Insurance 215

Nicholson P *Borrowing Court Systems: The Socialist Experience of Vietnam* (Brill Academic Publishers Leiden 2007)

Nicholson P and Gillespie G 'Interpreting Legal Transfers: The Implications for Law and Development' in P Nicholson and J Gillespie (eds) *Law and Development and the Global Discourses of Legal Transfers* (CUP Cambridge 2012)

Nishimura S *The Decline of Inland Bills of Exchange in the London Money Market, 1855–1913* (CUP Cambridge 1971)

Noonan J *The Scholastic Analysis of Usury* (Harvard UP Cambridge Massachusetts 1957)

Notari M 'Emissione delle Azioni' in PG Marchetti and LA Bianchi (eds) *La disciplina delle società quotate nel Testo Unico della Finanza. D Lgs. 24 febbraio 1998, n. 58 Commentario vol II (artt. 136–212)* (Giuffrè Milano 1998) 1532

Ogus A 'Competition between National Legal Systems: A Contribution of Economic Analysis to Comparative Law' (1999) 48 ICLQ 415

Ogus A 'The Economic Base of Legal Culture: Networks and Monopolization' (2002) 22 OJLS 419

Ogus A *Costs and Cautionary Tales: Economic Insights for the Law* (Hart Oxford 2006)

Ooi MS *Shares in the Conflict of Laws* (OUP Oxford 2003)

Oppo G 'Una Svolta nei Titoli di Massa (il Progetto Monte Titoli)' (1986) Riv Dir Civ 558

Oppo G 'Titolo di Credito. I) In generale' (1994) in *Enc Giur Treccani*, vol XXXI Roma

Orucu E 'A Synthetic and Hyphenated Legal System: The Turkish Experience' (2006) 1 J Comp L 27

Orucu E 'Law as Transposition' (2002) 51 ICLQ 206

Orucu E 'The Impact of European Law on the Ottoman Empire and Turkey' in WJ Mommsen and A de Moor (eds) *European Expansion and Law: The Encounter of European and Indigenous Law in 19th and 20th Century Africa and Asia* (Berg Oxford 1992)

Orucu E 'Turkey: Change Under Pressure' in E Orucu, E Attwooll and S Coyle (eds) *Studies in Legal Systems: Mixed and Mixing* (Kluwer London 1996)

Orucu E *Critical Comparative Law: Considering Paradoxes for Legal Systems in Transition* (Kluwer Deventer 1999)

Osborne R 'Early Greek Colonization? The nature of Greek settlement in the West' in N Fisher and H van Wees (eds) *Archaic Greece: New Approaches and New Evidence* (Duckworth London 1998)

Owen S 'Analogy, Archaeology & Archaic Greek Colonization' in H Hurst and S Owen (eds) *Ancient Colonization (Analogy, Similarity & Difference)* (Duckworth London 2005)

Paech P 'Harmonising Substantive Rules of the Securities Held with Intermediaries as Collateral' (2002) Uniform Law Review/Revue de droit uniforme 1154

Paech P and Lober K 'Interconnecting Law of Securities Holding and Transfer – a chance for seamless international improvements' (2007) 1 JIBFL 9

Paech P and Lober K 'Post-trading of Securities: Shaping the European Response to Legal Barriers' (2009) 4 JIBFL 211

Paech P 'Market Needs as Paradigm – breaking-up the thinking on EU securities law' in P Conac, U Segna and L Thevenoz (eds) *Intermediated Securities – The Impact of the Geneva Securities Convention and the Future European Legislation* (CUP Cambridge 2013)

Papaspyrou N 'Immobilisation of Securities: Part 1 Proprietary Rights of Indirect Holders' (1996) 10 JIBL 430

Papaspyrou N 'Immobilisation of Securities: Part 2 Personal Rights of Indirect Holders' (1996) JIBL 459

Papastergiadis N 'Tracing Hybridity in Theory' in T Werbner and T Modood (eds) *Debating Cultural Hybridity: Multi-cultural Identities and the Politics of Anti-racism* (Zed Books London 1997)

Parry B 'Problems in Current Discourse Theory' (1987) 9 Oxford Literary Review 27

Partesotti G 'Profili Cartolari del Sistema Monte Titoli' (1987) Banca Borsa e Titoli di Credito 601

Patterson M and Reiffen D 'The Effect of the Bubble Act on the Market for Joint Stock Shares' (1990) 50 J Econ Hist 163

Pearson R 'Shareholder Democracies? English Stock Companies and the Politics of Corporate Governance During the Industrial Revolution' (2002) 117 English Historical Review 840

Pearson R *Insuring the Industrial Revolution: Fire Insurance in Great Britain, 1700–1850* (Aldershot Ashgate 2004)

Peernboom R 'What Have We Learned About Law and Development? Describing, Predicting and Assessing Legal Reforms in China' (2006) 27 Mich J Int'l L 823

Peernboom R 'Towards a Methodology for Successful Legal Transplants' (2013) The Chinese Journal of Comparative Law 4

Pellizzi GL *Principi di Diritto Cartolare* (Zanichelli Bologna 1967) 21

Penner J *The Law of Trusts* (OUP Oxford 2006)

Pennington R 'Can Shares in Companies Be Defined?' (1989) 10 Company Lawyer 140

Perkins J 'Registration of Charges over Intangibles' (2010) 4 LFMR 360

Peters A and Schwenke H 'Comparative Law Beyond Postmodernism' (2000) 49 ICLQ 800

Pettegree A *Foreign Protestant Communities in Sixteenth-Century London* (OUP Press Oxford 1986)

Phillips M *A History of Banks, Bankers and Banking* (Effingham Wilson & Co 1894)

Pistor K and Xu C 'Transplanting the Concept of "Fiduciary Duty" Evidence from Transition Economies' in CJ Milhaupt (ed) *Global Markets, Domestic Institutions: Corporate Law and Governance in a New Era of Cross-Border Deals* (Columbia UP New York 2003)

Plucknett TFT *A Concise History of the Common Law* (The Lawyers Co-Operative Publishing Company Rochester NY 1929)

Pollins H *Britain's Railways: An Industrial History* (David & Charles Newton Abbot 1971)

Pollock F and Maitland FW *The History of English Law* (CUP Cambridge 1968)

Postan MM 'Partnership in English Medieval Commerce' in *Studi in Onore di Armado Sapori* (Istituto Editoriale Cisalpino Milano 1957)
Postan MM 'Italians and the Economic Development of England in the Middle Ages' in Id (ed) *Medieval Trade and Finance* (CUP Cambridge 1973)
Postan MM 'Private Financial Instruments in Medieval England' in Id (ed) *Medieval Trade and Finance* (CUP Cambridge 1973)
Postan MM 'The Medieval Wool Trade' in Id (ed) *Medieval Trade and Finance* (CUP Cambridge 1973)
Potok R 'Legal Certainty for Securities Held as Collateral' (1999) 18 IFL Rev 12
Pound R *Contemporary Juristic Theory* (Claremont College Claremont 1940)
Power E *The Wool Trade in English Medieval History* (OUP Oxford 1941)
Powicke M *The Thirteenth Century 1216–1307* (OUP Press Oxford 1953)
Prabhu A *Hybridity: Limits, Transformations, Prospects* (State University of New York Press Albany 2007)
Pressnell LS *Country Banking in the Industrial Revolution* (OUP Press Oxford 1956)
Prestwich M 'Italian Merchants in the Late Thirteenth and Early Fourteenth Century England' in *The Dawn of Modern Banking* (Yale UP New Haven 1979)
Pretto-Sakmann A *Boundaries of Personal Property* (Hart Oxford 2005)
Pryor JH 'Origins of the Commenda Contract' (1977) 52 Speculum 33
Purcell N 'Colonization and Mediterranean History' in H Hurst and S Owen (eds) *Ancient Colonizations (Analogy, Similarity and Difference)* (Duckworth London 2005)
Raymond IW and Lopez RS (eds) *Medieval Trade in the Mediterranean World* (Columbia UP New York 2001)
Reed MC 'Railways and the Growth of the Capital Market' in MC Reed (ed) *Railways in the Victorian Economy* (David & Charles, Newton Abbot 1969)
Reed MC *Investment in Railways in Britain: 1820–1844 – A Study in the Development of the Capital Market* (OUP Oxford 1975)
Reiffen D 'The Effect of the Bubble Act on the Market for Joint Stock Shares' (1990) 51 Journal of Economic History 163
Reingold N and Rothenberg M 'Introduction' in N Reingold and M Rothenberg (eds) *Scientific Colonialism: A Cross Cultural Comparison* (Smithsonian Institute Press Washington 1987)
Reynolds RL 'Origins of Modern Business Enterprise: Medieval Italy' 12 (1952) Journal of Economic History 350
Rhodes WE 'The Italian Bankers in England and their Loans to Edward I and Edward II' in TF Toot and J Tait (eds) *Historical Essays by Members of the Owens College, Manchester* (London 1902)
Ridgway D 'La Presenza Etrusca nella Campania Meridionale' in P Gastaldi and G Maetzke (eds) *La Presenza Etrusca nella Campania Meridionale: Atti delle Giornate di Studio, Salerno-Pontecagnano 16–28 novembre 1990* (Olschki Firenze 1994)
Rogers C 'Gulliver's Troubled Travels, or the Conundrum of Comparative Law' (1998) 67 Geo Wash L Rev 149
Rogers JS 'Negotiability as a System of Title Recognition' (1987) 48 Ohio St L J 197
Rogers JS 'The Myth of Negotiability' (1990) 31 BCL Rev 265
Rogers JS 'Negotiability, Property and Identity' (1990) 21 Cardozo L Rev 471

Rogers JS 'An Essay on Horseless Carriage and Paperless Negotiable Instruments: Some Lessons from the Article 8 Revision' (1995) 31 Idaho L Rev 691

Rogers JS *The Early History of the Bills and Notes* (CUP Cambridge 1995)

Rogers JS 'Policy Perspectives on Revised UCC Article 8' (1996) 43 UCLA L Rev 1431

Rogers JS 'Of Normalcy and Anomaly: Thoughts on Choice of Law for Indirect Holding System' (1998) 9 JIBFL (special supplement)

Rogers JS 'Conflict of Laws for Transactions in Securities Held Through Intermediaries' (2005) Boston College Law School Faculty Research Paper 108

Rogers JS 'The Revision of Canadian Law on Securities Holdings Through Intermediaries: Who What, When, How and Why?' (2007) 45 CBLJ 49

Rogers JS *The End of Negotiable Instruments* (OUP Oxford 2012)

Roseveare H *The Financial Revolution: 1660–1760* (Longman London 1991)

Ruddock AA *Italian Merchants and Shipping in Southampton 1270–1600* (University College Southampton 1951)

Sacco R 'Legal Formants: a Dynamic Approach to Comparative Law' (Instalment II) (1991) 39 Am J Comp L 343

Said EW *Culture and Imperialism* (Knopf New York 1994)

Said EW *Orientalism* (Penguin London 1985)

Samuel G *Epistemology and Method in Law* (Aldershot Ashgate 2003)

Sanborn FR *Origins of the Early English Maritime and Commercial Law* (The Century Co London 1930)

Santarelli U *Mercanti e Società fra Mercanti* (Giappichelli Torino 1992)

Santarelli U *Per la Storia del Fallimento nelle Legislazioni Italiane dell'età intermedia* (Cedam Padova 1964)

Sapori A 'La famiglia e la compagnia degli Alberti del Giudice' in *Studi in Onore di Armado Sapori* (Istituto Editoriale Cisalpino Milano 1957)

Sapori A *La Compagnia dei Frescobadi in Inghilterra* (Oschki Florence 1926)

Sapori A *La Crisi delle Compagnie Mercantili dei Bardi e dei Peruzzi* (Oschki Florence 1926)

Sapori A *Una Compagnia di Calimala ai Primi del Trecento* (Olschki Editore Firenze 1932)

Sapori A *The Italian Merchant in the Middle Ages* (Norton & Company New York 1970)

Schlesinger RB *Formation of Contracts: A Study of the Common Core of Legal Systems* (Oceana New York 1968)

Schroeder JL 'Is Article 8 Finally Ready This Time? The Radical Reform of Secured Lending on Wall Street' (1994) 3 Columbia Bus L Rev 291

Schulz F *Classical Roman Law* (OUP Press Oxford 1951)

Schulze R *Common Frame of Reference and Existing EC Contract Law* (Sellier Munich 2008)

Schwarcz SL 'Intermediary Risk in a Global Economy' (2001) 50 Duke LJ 1541

Schwarcz SL 'Systemic Risk' (2008) 97 Geo LJ 194

Schwartz S and Benjamin J 'Intermediary Risk in the Indirect Holding System for Securities' (2002) 12 Duke J Comp Comp & Int'l L 312

Scott WR *The Constitution and Finance of English, Scottish and Irish Joint-Stock Companies to 1720* (CUP Cambridge 1912)

Scrutton TE *The Elements of Mercantile Law* (William Clowes and Sons London 1891)

Shannon HA 'The Coming of General Limited Liability' (1931) 2 Economic History 267

Shepherd G 'The Pride of Most Colonials: Burial and Religion in the Sicilian Colonies' (1995) 6 Acta Hypeborea 51

Siems M *Convergence in Shareholder Law* (CUP Cambridge 2007)

Sigman H and Bernasconi C 'Myths about the Hague Convention Debunked' (2005) 24 IFLR 31

Simpson 'The Rise and Fall of the Legal Treatise. Legal Principles and Forms of Legal Literature' (1981) 48 U Chi L Rev 632

Smethurst J and Benjamin J 'Restatement of the Law Relating to Client Securities' (2009) 4 Capital Markets LJ 311

Smith JW *A compendium of Mercantile Law* (Sweet & Maxwell London 1843)

Smith L 'Unjust Enrichment, Property and the Structure of Trusts' (2000) 116 LQR 412

Smith L *The Law of Tracing* (OUP Oxford 1997)

Smith M and Leslie N *The Law of Assignment* (OUP Oxford 2012)

Smith RB 'A Piece of Paper Revisited' (1971) 25 Bus Law 1769

Smith T *The Original Ordinances of more than one hundred Early English Gilds* (Early Eng Text Society London 1870)

Snodgrass A '"Lesser Breeds": The History of a False Analogy' in H Hurst and S Owen (eds) *Ancient Colonizations (analogy, similarity and difference)* (Duckworth London 2005)

Solimano S *'Il Letto di Procuste': Diritto e Politica nella Formazione del Codice Civile Unitario. I Progetti Cassinis (1860–1861)* (Giuffrè Milano 2003)

Spada P 'Dalla Nozione al Tipo della Società per Azioni' (1985) Riv dir civ 95

Spada P *La Tipicità delle Società* (Cedam Padova 1974) 386

Stein E 'Uses, Misuses – and Nonuses of Comparative Law' (1977) 72 NW U L Rev 198

Stein G 'Colonies without Colonialism: A Trade Diaspora Model of Fourth Millennium B.C. Mesopotamian Enclaves in Anatolia' in CL Lyons and JK Papadopulos (eds) *The Archaeology of Colonialism* (Getty Research Institute Los Angeles 2002)

Stein P *Legal Evolution: The Story of an Idea* (CUP Cambridge 1980)

Stein P *Roman Law in European History* (CUP Cambridge 1999)

Strauss G *Law, Resistance and the State: The Opposition to Roman Law in Reformation Germany* (Princeton UP Princeton 1986)

Swadling W 'Restitution and *Bona Fide* Purchase' in W Swadling (ed) *The Limits of Restitutionary Claims: A Comparative Analysis* (United Kingdom Comparative Law Series London 1997)

Taylor J *Creating Capitalism: Joint Stock Enterprise in British Politics and Culture, 1800–1870* (Royal Historical Society London 2006)

Terrenato N 'The Deceptive Archetype: Roman Colonialism in Italy and Postcolonial Thought' in H Hurst and S Owen (eds) *Ancient Colonizations (analogy, similarity and difference)* (Duckworth London 2005)

Teubner G 'Legal Irritants: Good Faith in British Law or How Unifying Law Ends Up in New Divergences' (1998) 61 MLR 10

Teubner G *Law as a Autopoietic System* (Blackwell Oxford 1993)

Thevenoz L 'Intermediated Securities, Legal Risk, and the International Harmonization of Commercial Law' (2007) 13 Standford Journal of Law, Business and Finance 384

Thevenoz L 'The Geneva Securities Convention: Objectives, History and Guiding Principles' in P Conac, U Segna and L Thevenoz (eds) *Intermediated Securities – The Impact of the Geneva Securities Convention and the Future European Legislation* (CUP Cambridge 2013)

Thomas A 'Cultural Hegemony: the Exportation of Anglo-Saxon Corporate Governance Ideologies to Germany' (1998) 73 Tul L Rev 69

Thomas AH *Calendar of Early Mayor's Court Rolls Preserved among the Archives of the Corporation of the City of London at the Guildhall, AD 1298–1307* (CUP Cambridge 1934)

Thomas N *Colonialism's Culture: Anthropology, Travel and Government* (Polity Cambridge 1994)

Thomas WA *The Provincial Stock Exchanges* (Frank Cass London 1973)

Thorne P 'Goodbye Geneva '48, Hello Cape Town '01' (2006) 10 JIBFL 439

Thornely JWA 'Thives, Rogues, Innocent Purchasers and Legislatives Tangles' (1988) 47 Cam LJ 15

Tillyard F *Banking and Negotiable Instruments* (Adam & Charles Black London 1908)

Tjio H and Yeo TM '*Re Rose* Revisited: the Shorn Lamb's Equity' [2003] LMCLQ 296

Tolhurst G *The Assignment of Contractual Rights* (Hart Oxford 2006)

Torelli M 'The Encounter with the Etruscans' in G Pugliese Caratelli (eds) *The Greek World: Art and Civilization in Magna Grecia and Sicily* (Rizzoli New York 1996)

Trakman LE *The Law Merchant. The Evolution of Commercial Law* (Colorado Legal Publishing Littleton 1983)

Trebilcock C *Phoenix Assurance and the Development of British Insurance, vol I 1782–1870* (CUP Cambridge 1985)

Treitel G *The Law of Contract* (Sweet & Maxwell London 2003)

Turing D and Meinertz C 'The Securities Law Directive: Implications for Account Provisions, Custody and Collateral Arrangements' (2011) 4 JIBFL 198

Turing D *Clearing and Settlement in Europe* (Bloomsbury Professional Haywards 2012)

Twining W 'Surface Law' in H Petersen, AL Kjaer, H Krunke and M R Madsen (eds) *Paradoxes of European Legal Integration* (Ashgate Aldeshot 2008)

Udovitch AL 'At the Origins of the Western Commenda. Islam, Israel, Byzantium' (1962) 37 Speculum 198

Udovitch AL *Partnership and Profit in Medieval Islam* (Princeton UP New Jersey 1970)

Usher AP *The Early History of Deposit Banking in Mediterranean Europe* (Harvard UP Cambridge Massachusetts 1943)

Van Dommelen P 'Ambiguous Matters: Colonialism and Local Identities in Punic Sardinia' in CL Lyons and JK Papadopulos (eds) *The Archaeology of Colonialism* (Getty Research Institute Los Angeles 2002)

Visser D 'Cultural Forces in the Making of Mixed Legal Systems' (2003) 41 Tul L Rev 44

Von Bar C and Clive E *Principles Definitions and Model Rules of European Private Law – Draft Common Frame of Reference* (OUP Oxford 2010)

Waley D *The Italian City-Republics* (Longman London 1988)

Watson A *Legal Transplants: An Approach to Comparative Law* (Scottish Academic Press Edinburgh 1974)

Watson A 'Legal Transplants and Law Reform' (1976) 92 LQR 79

Watson A *Society and Legal Change* (Scottish Academic Press Edinburgh 1977)

Watson A *The Nature of Law* (Edinburgh UP Edinburgh 1977)

Watson A 'Comparative Law and Legal Change' (1978) 37 CLJ 313

Watson A *Making of the Civil Law* (Harvard UP Cambridge 1981)

Watson A 'Legal Change: Sources of Law and Legal Culture' (1983) 131 U Pa L Rev 112

Watson A *The Evolution of Law* (John Hopkins UP Baltimore 1985)

Watson A 'The Impact of Justinian's Institutes on Academic Treaties: Blackstone's Commentaries' in Id (ed) *Roman Law and Comparative Law* (University of Georgia Press Georgia 1991)
Watson A *Legal Origins and Legal Change* (Hambledon London 1991)
Watson A *Roman Law and Comparative Law* (University of Georgia Press Athens Ge 1991)
Watson A *Law Out of Context* (University of Georgia Press Athens GA 2000)
Watson A *The Evolution of Western Private Law* (John Hopkins UP Baltimore 2001)
Watt G 'The Proprietary Effect of a Chattel Lease' (2003) Convenyancer and Property Lawyer 61
Watt HM 'Globalization and Comparative Law' in M Reinmann and R Zimmermann R (eds) *The Oxford Handbook of Comparative Law* (OUP Oxford 2006)
Weber M *The History of Commercial Partnerships in the Middle Ages* (Rowman & Littlefield Publishers Lanham 2003)
Webster J 'Roman Imperialism and the Post-Imperial Age' in J Webster & N Cooper (eds) *Roman Imperialism: Post-Colonial Perspectives* (University of Leicester Leicester 1996)
Weir T 'Taking for Granted – the Ramifications of the *Nemo Dat*' (1996) 49 CLP 325
Westbrook DA 'Theorizing the Diffusion of Law: Conceptual Difficulties, Unstable Imaginations, and the Effort to Think Gracefully Nonetheless' (2006) 58 Harv Int'l LJ 493
White R *The Middle Ground: Indians, Empires, and Republics in the Great Lakes Region, 1650–1815* (CUP Cambridge 1991)
Whitt Sciente L *Colonialism and Indigenous People: the Cultural Policy of Law and Culture* (CUP Cambridge 2009)
Wieacker F *A History of Private Law in Europe* (OUP Oxford 1995)
Wijffels A 'Business Relations Between Merchants in Sixteenth-Century Belgian Practice-Oriented Civil Law Literature' in V Piergiovanni (ed) *From* Lex Mercatoria *to Commercial Law* (Duncker und Humblot Berlin 2004)
Wilkinson S 'The collapse of TAURUS' (1993) Int'l Company & Com L Rev 207
Willan TS *The Early History of the Russia Company 1553–1603* (Manchester UP Manchester 1956)
Willis W *The Law of Negotiable Instruments (six lectures delivered at the request of the Council of Legal Education* (Stevens & Haynes London 1896)
Wilson J *British Business History 1720–1994* (Manchester UP Manchester 1995)
Wilson JP 'The Nature of Greek Overseas Settlements in the Archaic Period: *Emporion* or *Apoikia*?' L Mitchell and PJ Rhodes (eds) *The Development of the Polis in Archaic Greece* (Routledge London 1997)
Wise EM 'The Transplant of Legal Patterns' (1990) 38 Am J Comp L 1
Wood AC *A History of the Levant Company* (Frank Cass & Co London 1964)
Wool J 'Economic Analysis and Harmonized Privatisation of Private Law' (2003) 8 Uniform Law Review 389
Wool J 'Rethinking the Notion of Uniformity in the Drafting of International Commercial Law: A Preliminary Proposal for the Development of a Policy-based Unification Model' (1997) 2 Uniform Law Review 45
Woolcock S 'Competition Among Rules in the Single European Market' in W Bratton, J McCahery, S Picciotto and C Scott (eds) *International Regulatory Competition and Coordination: Perspectives on Economic Regulation in Europe and the United States* (OUP Oxford 1996)
Woolf G 'Beyond Romans and Natives' (1997) 3 World Archaeology 339
Worthington S 'Shares and Shareholders: Property, Power and Entitlement. Part 1' (2001) 22 Company Lawyer 260

Worthington S 'Sorting out Ownership Interests in a Bulk: Gifts, Sales and Trusts' (1999) JBL 1
Worthington S *Equity* (OUP Oxford 2006)
Worthington S *Personal Property Law: Text and Materials* (OUP Oxford 2000)
Worthington S *Proprietary Interests in Commercial Transactions* (OUP Oxford 1996)
Yates M 'UK Settlement' in M Blair and G Walker (ed) *Financial Markets and Exchanges Law* (OUP Oxford 2012)
Yates M and Montagu G *The Law of Global Custody* (Tottel London 2013)
Yeowart G 'Privy Council Upholds Appropriation of Shares' (2009) 27 BJUB & FL 384
Yeowart G 'Remedy of Appropriation Upheld by Privy Council' (2009) 4 LFMR 339
Young R *White Mythologies. Writing History and the West* (Routledge London 1990)
Young R *Colonial Desire. Hybridity in Theory, Culture and Race* (Routledge London 1995)
Young R *Postcolonialism. A Very Short Introduction* (OUP Oxford 2003)
Zacaroli A 'Taking Security over Intermediated Securities: Chapter V of the UNIDROIT (Geneva) Convention on Intermediated Securities' in L Gullifer and J Payne (eds) *Intermediated Securities – Legal Problems and Practical Issues* (Hart Oxford 2010)
Zeno R *Documenti per la Storia del Diritto Marittimo nel secoli XIII e XIV* (Lattes Editori Torino 1936)
Zimmermann R 'A Change in Perspective' in Id (ed) *Roman Law, Contemporary Law, European Law* (OUP Oxford 2001)
Zimmermann R 'Roman Law and European Legal Unity' in A Hartkamp, M Hesselink, E Hondius, C Joustra and E du Perron (eds) *Towards a European Civil Code* (Kluwer The Hague 1998)
Zweigert K and Kotz H *Introduction to Comparative Law* (OUP Oxford 1998)
Zywicki TJ 'The Rise and Fall of Efficiency in the Common Law: A Supply-Side Analysis' (2003) 97 NW U L Rev 1551

IUS COMMUNE EUROPAEUM

A peer-reviewed book series in which the common foundations of the legal systems of the Member States of the European Union are the central focus.

The *Ius Commune Europaeum* series includes horizontal comparative legal studies as well as studies on the effect of treaties within the national legal systems. All the classic fields of law are covered. The books are published in various European languages under the auspices of METRO, the Institute for Transnational Legal Research at Maastricht University.

Recently published:
Volume 117: *European Union Property Law. From Fragments to a System*, E. Ramaekers
Volume 118: *Comparing Ecological Damage. Comparative and Economic Observations*, J. Liu
Volume 119: *Parliamentary Immunity. A Comprehensive Study of the Systems of Parliamentary Immunity of the United Kingdom, France, and the Netherlands in a European Context*, S. Hardt
Volume 120: *The Effects of Judicial Decisions in Time*, P. Popelier, S. Verstraelen, D. Vanheule and B. Vanlerberghe (eds.)
Volume 121: *The Position of Small and Medium-Sized Enterprises in European Contract Law*, I. Samoy and M.B.M. Loos (eds.)
Volume 122: *Property Law Perspectives II*, B. Akkermans, E. Marais and E. Ramaekers (eds.)
Volume 123: *The Treaty on European Union 1993-2013 Reflections from Maastricht*, M. de Visser and A.P. van der Mei (eds.)
Volume 124: *Inside Police Custody. Training Framework on the Provisions of Suspects' Rights*, T. Spronken, J. Blackstock, E. Lloyd-Cape, J. Hodgson, A. Ogorodova, M. Vanderhallen
Volume 125: *Coordinating Ombudsmen and the Judiciary. A comparative view on the relations between ombudsmen and the judiciary in the Netherlands, England and the European Union*, M. Remac